Lecture Notes in Artificial Intelligence   3371

Edited by J. G. Carbonell and J. Siekmann

Subseries of Lecture Notes in Computer Science

Michael Wayne Barley   Nik Kasabov (Eds.)

Intelligent Agents and Multi-Agent Systems

7th Pacific Rim International Workshop
on Multi-Agents, PRIMA 2004
Auckland, New Zealand, August 8-13, 2004
Revised Selected Papers

 Springer

Series Editors

Jaime G. Carbonell, Carnegie Mellon University, Pittsburgh, PA, USA
Jörg Siekmann, University of Saarland, Saarbrücken, Germany

Volume Editors

Michael Wayne Barley
University of Auckland
Department of Computer Science
Private Bag 92019, Auckland, New Zealand
E-mail: barley@cs.auckland.ac.nz

Nik Kasabov
Auckland University of Technology
School of Computer and Information Sciences
Knowledge Engineering and Discovery Research Institute (KEDRI)
Private Bag 92006, Auckland, New Zealand
E-mail: nkasabov@aut.ac.nz

Library of Congress Control Number: 2005922102

CR Subject Classification (1998): I.2.11, I.2, C.2.4, D.2, F.3

ISSN 0302-9743
ISBN 3-540-25340-8 Springer Berlin Heidelberg New York

Springer is a part of Springer Science+Business Media

springeronline.com

© Springer-Verlag Berlin Heidelberg 2005
Printed in Germany

Typesetting: Camera-ready by author, data conversion by Olgun Computergrafik
Printed on acid-free paper   SPIN: 11407997   06/3142   5 4 3 2 1 0

Preface

Autonomous agents and multi-agent systems are computational systems in which several (semi-)autonomous agents interact with each other or work together to perform some set of tasks or satisfy some set of goals. These systems may involve computational agents that are homogeneous or heterogeneous, they may involve activities on the part of agents having common or distinct goals, and they may involve participation on the part of humans and intelligent agents.

This volume contains selected papers from PRIMA 2004, the 7th Pacific Rim International Workshop on Multi-agents, held in Auckland, New Zealand, during August 8–13, 2004 in conjunction with the 8th Pacific Rim International Conference on Artificial Intelligence (PRICAI 2004). PRIMA is a series of workshops on autonomous agents and multi-agents that focusses on the research activities in the Asian and Pacific Rim countries. PRIMA 2004 was built upon the great successes of its predecessors.

Fifty-two papers were submitted to the workshop, each paper was reviewed by three internationally renowned program committee members. After careful review, 24 papers were selected for this volume. We would like to thank all the authors who submitted papers to the workshop. We would also like to thank all the program committee members for their diligent work in reviewing the papers. We would like to thank our invited speakers, Sandip Sen and Toru Ishida. Additionally, we thank the editorial staff of Springer for publishing this volume in the series Lecture Notes in Artificial Intelligence. Lastly, we want to thank our sponsors, the Auckland University of Technology's Knowledge Engineering and Discovery Research Institute (KEDRI), and the University of Auckland's Department of Computer Science, for the financial support provided.

December 2004

Mike Barley
Nik Kasabov

PRIMA 2004 Organization

General Chair

Nik Kasabov
KEDRI, Auckland University of Technology
New Zealand
nkasabov@aut.ac.nz

Program Chair

Mike Barley
Department of Computer Science
University of New Zealand
barley@cs.auckland.ac.nz

Local Organizing Committee

Gary Cleveland   (University of Auckland)
Stephen Cranefield   (University of Otago)
Hans Guesgen   (University of Auckland)
Ute Loerch   (University of Auckland)
Cameron Skinner   (University of Auckland)
Ian Watson   (University of Auckland)

Program Committee

Cristiano Castelfranchi (Italy)
Brahim Chaib-draa (Canada)
Joongmin Choi (Korea)
John Debenham (Australia)
Klaus Fisher (Germany)
Chun-Nan Hsu (Taiwan)
Michael Huhns (USA)
Toru Ishida (Japan)
Ilkon Kim (Korea)
Incheol Kim (Korea)
Minkoo Kim (Korea)
David Kinney (Australia)
Yasuhiko Kitamura (Japan)
Kazuhiro Kuwabara (Japan)
Jaeho Lee (Korea)
Jimmy H.M. Lee (China)
Ho-fung Leung (China)
Chao-Lin Liu (Taiwan)
Jyi-shane Liu (Taiwan)
Rey-long Liu (Taiwan)

Jian Lu (China)
Xudong Luo (UK)
John Jules Meyer (The Netherlands)
Joerg Mueller (Germany)
Hideyuki Nakashima (Japan)
Ichiro Osawa (Japan)
Sascha Ossowski (Spain)
Young-Tack Park (Korea)
Anita Raja (USA)
Zhongzhi Shi (China)
Liz Sonenberg (Australia)
Von-Wun Soo (Taiwan)
Toshiharu Sugawara (Japan)
Ron Sun (USA)
Qijia Tian (China)
Jung-Jin Yang (Korea)
Makoto Yokoo (Japan)
Soe-Tsyr Yuan (Taiwan)
Zili Zhang (Australia)

Additional Reviewers

Jamal Bentahar
Emiliano Lorini

Ris Falcone
Fabio Paglieri

Jonathan Teutenberg

Table of Contents

A Combined System
for Update Logic and Belief Revision

Guillaume Aucher

Department of Computer Science,
University of Otago,
PO Box 56 Dunedin 9015,
New Zealand
aucher@atlas.otago.ac.nz

Abstract. In this paper we propose a logical system combining the
update logic of A. Baltag, L. Moss and S. Solecki (to which we will refer
to by the generic term BMS, [BMS04]) with the belief revision theory as
conceived by C. Alchourròn, P. Gärdenfors and D. Mackinson (that we
will call the AGM theory, [GardRott95]) viewed from the point of view
of W. Spohn ([Spohn90,Spohn88]). We also give a proof system and a
comparison with the AGM postulates.

Introduction and Motivation: Update logic is a modal logic trying to model
epistemic situations involving several agents, and changes that can occur in
these situations due to incoming information or more generally incoming action.
Belief revision theory typically deals with changes (revisions) that a database
representing a belief state of a unique agent must undergo after adding conflicting
information to the database. Roughly speaking, these two theories thus deal
with the same kind of phenomenon. However, there are some dissimilarities. On
the one hand, belief revision theory is not a logic and it deals with a single
agent, unlike update logic. On the other hand, belief revision theory deals with
revision (and expansion) of information unlike update logic which deals only
with expansion of information. Far from being in contradiction, it seems then
that these theories have a lot to give each other. So it makes sense to look for a
way in which they can be merged.

In Sect. 1, we will set out the BMS theory and the AGM theory viewed from
the point of view of W. Spohn. In Sect. 2 we will propose a system combining
these two theories. In Sect. 3, we will give an axiomatization of it with a soundness and completeness proof. In Sect. 4, we will show that it fulfills the 8 AGM
postulates.

1 Update Logic and Belief Revision Theory

1.1 Update Logic

In this section we set out the core of update logic as viewed by BMS. We split this
account into three parts: 1. static part, 2. dynamic part ('dynamic' because we

M.W. Barley and N. Kasabov (Eds.): PRIMA 2004, LNAI 3371, pp. 1–18, 2005.

deal with actions) and 3. update mechanism. Throughout this exposition and this paper we follow a simple example called the 'coin' example taken from [BMS04]. This is the following:

"A and B enter a large room containing a remote-control mechanical coin flipper. One presses the button, and the coin spins through the air, landing in a small box on a table. The box closes. The two people are much too far to see the coin. The coin actually heads up."

1. Static Part. We classically represent the above (static) situation s by the 'epistemic model' depicted in Fig. 1.

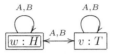

Fig. 1. BMS model for the 'coin' example.

The tokens w and v represent *possible worlds*. The double border around w means that it is the *actual world*. In this world, the coin is heads up. This last point is rendered formally by assigning the propositional letter H to w, which stands for 'the coin is Heads up'. Similarly, in the possible world v the coin is tails up. this is rendered formally by assigning the propositional letter T to v, which stands for 'the coin is Tails up'. This assignment of propositional letters to worlds is rendered formally by what we call a *valuation*: see definition below.

The *accessibility relation* $w \to_A v$ intuitively means that while A is in world w where the coin is heads up, he still considers possible that he is in world v where the coin is tails up (because he does not know whether the coin is heads or tails up). More generally, we set an accessibility relation $w \to_j v$ when 'on the basis of agent j's information in world w, the world v is a possible world'.

This epistemic representation of a particular situation is caught by the following general definition:

Definition: We call epistemic model M a tuple $M = (W, \to_j, V, w_0)$ where W is a set of possible worlds, $\to_j$ are finitely many accessibility relations indexed by the agents j, V is a valuation function which assigns a set of possible worlds to each propositional letter, and w_0 is the actual world. $\diamond$

We can then 'say things' about specific epistemic models (modeling specific situations) by introducing a language whose one of the components is a knowledge operator K_j defined like that:

$$M, w \models K_j\phi \text{ iff for all } v \text{ such that } w \to_j v, M, v \models \phi.$$

Intuitively $M, w \models K_j\phi$ means 'in world w, j Knows that ϕ' . We can then check with this definition that in our example, the epistemic model of Fig. 1 captures what we want (e.g. the sentence 'in the actual world, A does not know whether the coin is Heads or Tails up' is rendered by the formula $M, w \models \neg K_A H \wedge \neg K_A T)$.

See [FHMV95] for an extensive account of what is just outlined here.

2. Dynamic Part. Now we consider the following epistemic action a: 'A cheats and learns that the coin is Heads up, B suspecting anything about it'. We use the term "epistemic" (in "epistemic action") in the sense that the action doesn't change facts in the world. We represent how this action is perceived by the agents (just as we represented above how a situation is perceived by the agents) by the action model depicted in Fig. 2.

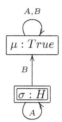

Fig. 2. BMS action model for the action 'A cheats'.

The token σ represents the *simple action* 'A looks at the coin and observes that the coin is heads up'. A double border around σ means that it is the *actual action*. For this action to be carried out in a particular possible world, the coin needs to be Heads up in this possible world. That's the intuitive meaning of the *precondition* H in the action model. The token τ represents the simple action 'nothing happens'. This action can be carried out in any possible world, hence its precondition is the tautology $True$, which is true in any possible world.

The *accessibility relation* $\sigma \rightarrow_B \tau$ intuitively means that 'while A looks at the coin and observes that it is heads up (σ), *for B* nothing actually happens (τ)'. More generally, we set an accessibility relation $\sigma \rightarrow_j \tau$ when the following condition is fulfilled: 'if σ occurs then in j's view τ is one of the action that might have happened'.

This epistemic representation of a particular action is caught by the following general definition:

Definition: We call an action model Σ a tuple $\Sigma = (\Sigma, \rightarrow_j, Pre, \sigma_0)$ where Σ is a set of simple action tokens, $\rightarrow_j$ are finitely many accessibility relations indexed by the agents j, Pre is a function which assigns preconditions to each action token, and σ_0 is the actual action. $\diamond$

3. Update Mechanism. Now, in reality the agents update their beliefs according to these two pieces of information: action a and situation s. This gives rise to a new situation $s \times a$. This actual update is rendered formally by the following mathematical update product:

Definition: Let $M = (W, \rightarrow_j, V, w_0)$ be an epistemic model and $\Sigma = (\Sigma, \rightarrow_j, V, \sigma_0)$ an action structure. We define their update product to be the epistemic model $M \otimes \Sigma = (W \otimes \Sigma, \rightarrow'_j, V', w'_0)$ where

1. $W \otimes \Sigma = \{(w, \sigma) \in W \times \Sigma; w \in V(Pre(\sigma))\}$.
2. $(w, \sigma) \rightarrow'_j (v, \tau)$ iff $w \rightarrow_j v$ and $\sigma \rightarrow_j \tau$.
3. $V'(p) = \{(w, \sigma) \in W \otimes \Sigma; w \in V(p)\}$.
4. $w'_0 = (w_0, \sigma_0)$. $\diamond$

Intuitive Interpretation: 1. The possible worlds that we consider after the update are all the ones resulting from the performance of one of the actions in one of the worlds, under the assumption that the action can 'possibly' take place in the corresponding world (assumption expressed by the function Pre).

2. The components of our action model are 'simple' actions (in the sense of BMS, see [BMS04] for more precision). It allows us to state that the accessibility (or uncertainty) relations for the epistemic model and the epistemic action model are independent from one another. This independence allows us to 'multiply' these uncertainties to compute the new accessibility (or uncertainty) relation.

3. The definition of the valuation exemplifies the fact that our actions do not change facts. (That is why we call them *epistemic* actions, as already said above.)

4. Finally, we naturally assume that the actual action can 'possibly' take place in the actual world.

Let us get back to our 'coin' example. The update product of Fig. 1 and Fig. 2 yields the model depicted in Fig. 3. This model presents some flaws and will be discussed in the rest of the paper.

We have set out the core of update logic as viewed by BMS. Yet, bear in mind that in [BMS04] a genuine logical system is built out of it, that we do not expound here.

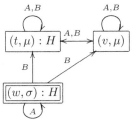

Fig. 3. BMS model corresponding to the situation after the action 'A cheats'.

1.2   Belief Revision Theory: W.Spohn's Approach

In this section, we set out a simplified account of W.Spohn's approach to belief revision theory as conceived by AGM (see [GardRott95]).

Generally speaking, belief revision theory deals with changes that must undergo a database representing a belief state of an agent after adding to the database information. (Note that it deals only with the notion of belief and not with the one of knowledge like in update logic.)

The format of the database can take two main different forms: syntactic and semantic. The former consists of a belief set K that consists of *propositional* formulas (also called sentences, representing the facts accepted in the belief state) and that is closed under logical consequences. The latter consists of a set W of possible worlds (representing the narrowest set of possible worlds in which the individual believes that the actual world is located). It can be shown that these two representations are actually equivalent.

The type of change for a state of belief which interests us most is *revision* (the other classical ones are *expansion* and *contraction*). It consists of adding to the belief set K a new sentence ϕ that is typically inconsistent with K. In order that the resulting belief set $K * \phi$ be consistent, some of the old sentences in ϕ are deleted. Now two basic questions come up to mind:

1. What general conditions this revised belief set $K * \phi$ must fulfill in order that the revision process be the closest possible to one performed by rational agents? This is the concern of the 8 AGM postulates that can be found in [GardRott95].

2. What sentences should be actually deleted from the belief set in order to form the new belief set $K * \phi$? In the literature, there are several explicit procedures that compute the new belief set $K * \phi$ after a revision. We focus on the one proposed by W.Spohn based on a possible world semantics ([Spohn90,Spohn88]). His approach satisfies moreover the 8 AGM postulates.

Definition: An ordinal conditional function is a function κ from a given set W of possible worlds into the class of ordinals such that some possible worlds are assigned the smallest ordinal 0. ◇

Intuitively, κ represents a plausibility grading of the possible worlds: the worlds that are assigned the smallest ordinals are the most plausible, according to the beliefs of the individual. Then,

Definition: We define $\kappa(\phi)$ as $\kappa(\phi) := min\{\kappa(w); w \in \phi\}$.

We say that a formula ϕ is *believed* (with degree of firmness α) when $\kappa^{-1}(0) \subseteq \{w; w \in \phi\}$ (resp. and $\kappa(\neg\phi) = \alpha$).

The belief set K *associated with* the ordinal conditional function κ is the set of all propositions believed in κ. ◇

Now assume the sentence ϕ is announced and the agent believes it with a degree of firmness α. We can then define the resulting ordinal conditional function $\kappa * (\phi, \alpha)$ representing the new state of belief:

Definition: Let ϕ be a proposition such that $\{w; w \in \phi\} \neq \emptyset$. We define the ordinal conditional function $\kappa * (\phi, \alpha)$ by:

$$\kappa * (\phi, \alpha)(w) = \begin{cases} \kappa(w) - \kappa(\phi) & \text{if } w \in \phi \\ \alpha + \kappa(w) - \kappa(\phi^c) & \text{if } w \in \phi^c. \end{cases} ◇$$

Note that in this new belief state, ϕ is believed with firmness α. Finally,

Proposition: If we define $K * \phi$ as the belief set associated with $\kappa * (\phi, \alpha)$, the revision function * thus defined satisfies the 8 AGM postulates. ⋄

So we have set out update logic and belief revision theory as viewed by W. Spohn. Now we are going to propose a system combining these two theories and see what insights it provides us regarding information change. As in the BMS exposition, we split our account in three parts: 1. Static part 2. Dynamic part 3. Update mechanism (inspired from W. Spohn's theory).

2   A Combined System

2.1   The Static Part

Definition. Just as in the BMS system, we want to represent how a static situation is perceived by the agents from the point of view of their beliefs *and* knowledge. That is to say, we want to represent what the agents know and believe about the actual world and also about what the other agents know and believe in general. We do that thanks to what we call a belief epistemic model.

From now on and in the rest of the paper, *Max* is an arbitrary fixed natural number different from 0.

Definition 1. *A belief epistemic model (be-model)* $M = (W, \{\sim_j; j \in G\}, \{\kappa_j; j \in G\}, V, w_0)$ *is a tuple where:*

1. *W is a set of possible worlds.*
2. *w_0 is the possible world corresponding to the actual world.*
3. *$\sim_j$ is an equivalence relation defined on W for each agent j.*
4. *κ_j is an operator, ranging from 0 to Max, defined on the set of possible worlds.*
5. *V is a valuation.*
6. *G is a set of agents.*

Intuitive Interpretation. Points 1,2,5,6 are clear (see Sect. 1.1). It remains to give intuitive interpretations for points 3 and 4.

3. The equivalence relation $\sim_j$ intuitively models the notion of knowledge. Its intuitive interpretation is:

$$w \sim_j v \text{ iff agent } j\text{'s knowledge in } w \text{ and } v \text{ is the same.}$$

Note that this implies that j cannot distinguish world w from v (otherwise she would not have the same knowledge in w and v) and that her information is the same in w and v. This also implies that $\sim_j$ is an equivalence relation, as mentioned in the definition.

4. The plausibility assignment κ_j intuitively models the notion of belief. Among the worlds j cannot distinguish (the worlds where her knowledge is the same), there are worlds that j might consider more plausible than others. This is expressed by the plausibility grading κ_j: the more plausible a world is for the agent

j, the closer its plausibility value is to 0 (this is of course completely similar to W. Spohn's approach set out in Sect. 1.2). A maximal degree of plausibility Max (originally needed for technical reasons: see Sect. 3.1) is introduced and we assume that beyond a certain degree of plausibility (Max), the agent can not distinguish two different worlds of different plausibility.

Remark 1. Note that one could argue that this plausibility assignment should be dependent on the world w in which the agent dwells. This is wrong. Indeed, in a particular world w, j bases her plausibility assignment only on information she has in w. Yet this information is the same in any world indistinguishable from w, as noted in point **3**. So the assignment will be the same for any world indistinguishable from w: that is why we consider a 'global' plausibility assignment.

Static Language and Example. We can easily define a language $\mathcal{L}_{St}$ for be-models (St for Static).

Definition 2. *The syntax of the language $\mathcal{L}_{St}$ is defined by,*

$$\phi := p \mid \neg\phi \mid \phi \wedge \psi \mid K_j\phi \mid B_j^n\phi \text{ where } n \in \mathbb{N}$$

Its semantics is defined by,

$$M, w \models K_j\phi \text{ iff for all } v \text{ st } w \sim_j v, M, v \models \phi.$$
$$M, w \models B_j^n\phi \text{ iff for all } v \text{ st } w \sim_j v \text{ and } \kappa_j(v) \leq n, M, v \models \phi.$$

The intuitive meaning of $M, w \models B_j^n\phi$ is that 'in world w, j believes with plausibility (a degree of) at most n that ϕ is true'. The definition of B_j^n is taken from [vDL03]. K_j is the usual knowledge operator (see [FHMV95] or Sect. 1.1).

Example 1. Let us get back to the 'coin' example introduced in Sect. 1.1. We model the initial situation in our system by the be-model depicted in Fig. 4. The same situation is modeled in the BMS system by the model depicted in Fig. 1.

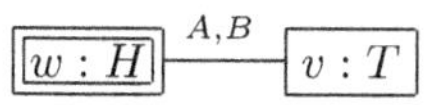

$$\kappa_A(x) = \kappa_B(x) = 0 \text{ for all } x.$$

Fig. 4. be-model for the 'coin' example.

The belief epistemic model depicted in Fig. 5 corresponds to the situation resulting from the action 'A cheats and learns that the coin is heads up' occurring in the initial situation. We assume *moreover* that in this action 'B suspects that A cheats', unlike the BMS framework . The labeling of the worlds will become clear in Sect. 2.3; for the time being, just ignore it. Relations in the model are equivalence relations; again, H is for 'Heads', T is for 'Tails' and the double bordered world corresponds to the actual world.

In this model and in the actual world (w, σ), A *knows* that the coin is heads up (formally: $K_A H$) and B *believes* that A doesn't know whether the coin is Heads or Tails (formally: $B_B^0(\neg K_A H \wedge \neg K_A T)$).

The corresponding model of BMS is depicted in Fig. 6 (or Fig. 3.). In this model, The nuance of concepts (belief B and knowledge K) is not displayed because we use the same crude accessibility relation $\rightarrow_j$ for both the notions of knowledge and belief. So, when we read what is true in the actual world (w, σ), we have *personally* to introduce this nuance of concept (belief B and knowledge K) because it is not displayed in the formalism itself. This is of course a flaw of the BMS system.

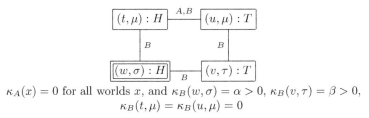

$\kappa_A(x) = 0$ for all worlds x, and $\kappa_B(w, \sigma) = \alpha > 0$, $\kappa_B(v, \tau) = \beta > 0$,
$$\kappa_B(t, \mu) = \kappa_B(u, \mu) = 0$$

Fig. 5. be-model corresponding to the situation after the action 'A cheats'.

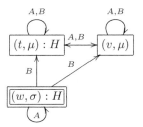

Fig. 6. BMS model corresponding to the situation after the action 'A cheats'.

2.2   The Dynamic Part

Again, just as in BMS, we want to represent how an action is perceived by several agents from the point of view of their beliefs and knowledge. That is to say, we want to do the same thing as in the last section, but with an action instead of a static situation. We do that thanks to what we call a belief epistemic action model.

Definition 3. *A belief epistemic action model (be-action-model) Σ is a tuple $(\Sigma, \{\sim_j; j \in G\}, \{\kappa_j^*; j \in G\}, Pre, \sigma_0)$ such that:*

1. *Σ is a set of possible actions.*
2. *σ_0 is the possible action corresponding to the actual action.*
3. *$\sim_j$ is an equivalence relation on Σ indexed by the set of agents.*
4. *κ_j^* is an operator indexed by the set of agents, ranging from 0 to Max.*
5. *Pre is a function from the set of simple actions to the formulas of $\mathcal{L}_{St}$.*
6. *G is a set of agents.*

The intuitive interpretation is very similar to the one spelled out for the notion of a belief epistemic model. So we refer the reader to the previous section for a correct interpretation of the definition: the term 'world' just has to be replaced by the term 'action'. The only differences concern the absence of a valuation and the introduction of the function Pre. Intuitively, $Pre(\sigma)$ is a necessary condition for the action σ to be performed in a particular world (see Sect. 1.1).

Here again, $\sim_j$ and κ_j, modeling respectively the notions of knowledge and belief, are refinements of the crude epistemic relation $\rightarrow_j$ of BMS.

Example 2. We reconsider the example of cheating (see Sect. 1.1): 'A cheats and learns that the coin is heads up, B suspecting that A cheats'. We propose the belief epistemic action model depicted in Fig. 7 for this action (where the double border corresponds to the actual action and relations are equivalence relations). In this be-action-model, while 'A looks at the coin and observes H' (action σ), B *believes* 'nothing happens' (action μ) but nevertheless considers plausible (with plausibility α and β) that A looked at the coin (actions σ and τ respectively), because she suspects that A has cheated.

The corresponding action model of BMS is depicted in Fig. 8 (or Fig. 2). Contrary to this one, we add one other possible action, that B may consider possible: 'A looks at the coin and observes tail' (depicted as τ). Indeed, in our framework, B suspects A of having cheated but doesn't know whether in that case A has observed Heads or Tails. Hence we have to consider two possible actions for cheating: 'A looks at the coin and observes H' (action σ) and 'A looks at the coin and observes T' (action τ). The third action μ represents the action where 'nothing happens'.

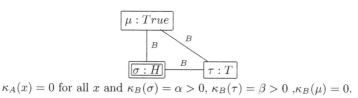

$\kappa_A(x) = 0$ for all x and $\kappa_B(\sigma) = \alpha > 0$, $\kappa_B(\tau) = \beta > 0$,$\kappa_B(\mu) = 0$.

Fig. 7. be-action-model for the action 'A cheats'.

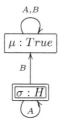

Fig. 8. BMS action model for the action 'A cheats'.

Example 3. We consider the action consisting of the public announcement 'A knows whether the coin is Heads or Tails' (formally: $K_A H \vee K_A T$). There is no essential difference between our model (depicted in Fig. 9) and the BMS model (depicted in Fig. 10) but we need their introduction for the purpose of the following section.

$$\frac{\boxed{\rho : K_A H \vee K_A T}}{\kappa_A(\rho) = \kappa_B(\rho) = 0.}$$

Fig. 9. be-action-model for the action 'public announcement that A knows whether the coin is Heads or Tails'.

A,B

$$\boxed{\rho : K_A H \vee K_A T}$$

Fig. 10. BMS action model for the action 'public announcement that A knows whether the coin is Head or Tail'.

2.3   The Update Mechanism

We now define the mathematical update product. It is supposed to render the actual update performed by the agents which follows their apprehension of the action. The apprehension (or perception) of the action corresponds to what we modeled in the last section by a be-action-model. Note that this process (apprehension + update) may be done simultaneously in reality, but in our formalism we clearly separate it.

Definition 4. *Given a belief epistemic model $M = (W, \sim_j, \kappa_j, V, w_0)$ and a belief epistemic action model $\Sigma = (\Sigma, \sim_j, \kappa_j^*, Pre, \sigma_0)$ we define their update product to be the belief epistemic model $M \otimes \Sigma = (W \otimes \Sigma, \sim_j', \kappa_j', V', w_0')$, where:*

1. $W \otimes \Sigma = \{(w, \sigma) \in W \times \Sigma; w \in V(Pre(\sigma))\}$.
2. $(w, \sigma) \sim_j' (v, \tau)$ *iff* $w \sim_j v$ *and* $\sigma \sim_j \tau$
3. $\kappa_j'(w, \sigma) = Cut_{Max}(\kappa_j^*(\sigma) + \kappa_j(w) - \kappa_j^w(\phi))$ *where* $\phi = Pre(\sigma)$, $\kappa_j^w(\phi) = \min\{\kappa_j(v); v \in V(\phi) \text{ and } v \sim_j w\}$ *and*

$$Cut_{Max}(x) = \begin{cases} x & \text{if } 0 \leqslant x \leqslant Max. \\ Max & \text{if } x > Max \end{cases}$$

4. $V'(p) = \{(w, \sigma) \in W \times \Sigma; w \in V(p)\}$
5. $w_0' = (w_0, \sigma_0)$.

Intuitive Interpretation. Points 1,2,4,5 have exactly the same interpretation as in BMS (see Sect. 1.1). It remains to motivate the key point concerning the update of plausibility, which is inspired from W. Spohn's ordinal conditional function $\kappa * (\phi, \alpha)$ (see Sect. 1.2). We will give two justifications. The first one is 'intuitive' and the second one is related to probability theory.

First of all, $\kappa_j^*(\sigma) + \kappa_j(w) - \kappa_j^w(\phi)$ is the core of the update. Cut_{Max} is just a minor technical device so that the new plausibility assignment fits into the set $\{0, .., Max\}$. However it has also an intuitive import if we refer to the assumption motivating the introduction of Max in Sect. 1.1.

1. Now the first justification. We are interested in an update performing a genuine belief revision. So, our rational intuition should guide us in order to determine the correct plausibility update. In that respect, it seems intuitively clear that,

'If you believe an action has taken place, then after the update you should believe what is *then* (after the update) true in the worlds where the action has taken place.'

Or more generally and precisely,

'In a current world w, if you believe with plausibility $\kappa_j^*(\sigma)$ that an action σ has taken place, then after the update you should believe with plausibility $\kappa_j^*(\sigma)$ what is *then* true in the worlds where the action has taken place and that you cannot distinguish from your current world w.'

So we would be tempted to assign roughly to the worlds accessible from w where the action σ has taken place the plausibility $\kappa_j^*(\sigma)$. Yet doing so, we would lose part of the overtones and information present in the former model amongst the worlds where the action σ has taken place (and that are accessible from w). So we add $\kappa_j(w) - \kappa_j^w(\phi)$ to $\kappa_j^*(\sigma)$ in order to keep track of and incorporate this former information (glance at the definition of $\kappa_j^w(\phi)$).

2. Now another justification. W. Spohn showed in [Spohn90] that we can draw a precise and rigorous parallel between probability theory and his plausibility theory. More precisely, he showed that sum, multiplication, and division of probabilities can be replaced respectively by the minimum, addition, and subtraction of plausibilities. This will be of interest for us: we will jump from plausibility to probability, then use probability results to get what we want and finally jump back to plausibility by translating our probabilistic outcome.

For our purpose, note that we can perfectly replace in this justification plausibility of worlds $\kappa_j(w)$ (and actions $\kappa_j(\sigma)$) by probability of worlds $P_j(w)$ (and actions $P_j(\sigma)$ respectively). Now, we want to determine $\kappa_j(w, \sigma)$. That is to say, in a probabilistic setting, we want to determine $P_j(w, \sigma) = P_j(W \cap A)$ where W stands for 'we were in world w' and A for 'action σ occurred in w'. Probability theory tells us that

$$P_j(W \cap A) = P_j(A).P_j(W|A).$$

Clearly,

$$P_j(A) = P_j(\sigma).$$

So it remains to determine $P_j(W|A)$, that is to say the probability that we were in world w *given* the extra assumption that action σ occurred in this world. We reasonably claim

$$P_j(W|A) = \frac{P_j(w)}{\sum\{P_j(v); w \sim_j v \text{ and } v \in V(Pre(\sigma))\}}.$$

That is to say, we *conditionalize* the probability of w for j ($P_j(w)$) to the worlds where the action σ has taken place and that may correspond for j to the actual world w ($\{v; w \sim_j v \text{ and } v \in V(Pre(\sigma))\}$). That is how it would be done in classical probability theory. The intuition behind it is that we now possess the extra piece of information that σ occurred in w, so the worlds indistinguishable from w where the action σ did *not* occur do not play a role anymore for the determination of the probability of w: we can then get rid of them and conditionalize on the relevant worlds.

Finally we get:

$$P_j(w, \sigma) = \frac{P_j(\sigma).P_j(w)}{\sum\{P_j(v); w \sim_j v \text{ and } v \in V(Pre(\sigma))\}}.$$

Now with the translation from probability to plausibility proved in [Spohn90] ('sum $\rightarrow$ minimum', 'multiplication $\rightarrow$ addition', 'division $\rightarrow$ subtraction'), we get the expected outcome:

$$\kappa'_j(w, \sigma) = \kappa^*_j(\sigma) + \kappa_j(w) - \kappa^w_j(\phi)$$

Remark 2. The first justification of the plausibility assignment stresses the priority of the plausibility assignment of the be-action-model upon the plausibility assignment of the be-model. So in a sense, it stresses also the priority of new information upon former information, just as in belief revision theory. We think this is how the plausibility assignment of action should be interpreted.

Remark 3. We have implicitly assumed in these two justifications that the plausibility of the actions are independent from the worlds in which they are performed. However, this is wrong for some cases. Indeed, for example consider a vague announcement of a formula ϕ that the agent j cannot distinguish from ϕ' because she is not sure whether she heard it correctly. In a $\sim_j$-equivalence class where the agent j knows more formulas that logically imply ϕ than ϕ', j will find the announcement ϕ more plausible than ϕ' because she will have more actual evidence at her disposal to think so. However, in another $\sim_j$-equivalence class of the same model where the agent j knows more formulas that logically imply ϕ' than ϕ, j will find the announcement of ϕ less plausible than ϕ' because she will have less actual evidence that would prompt her to think so.

Example 4. In this example, we are going to see the added value of a combined system.

Yet, first, let us briefly give an example of update. If we update the be-model depicted in Fig. 4 by the be-action-model depicted in Fig. 7, we get the be-model depicted in Fig. 5. That is what we want. (Note that correlatively, in the BMS system, the update of the model depicted in Fig. 1 by the action model depicted in Fig. 8 (or Fig. 2) would yield the model depicted in Fig. 6 (or Fig. 3).)

Now in the actual world of the model depicted in Fig. 5 (respectively Fig. 6 for the BMS system), B *believes* that A doesn't know whether the coin is Heads or Tails. Yet, A actually knows whether the coin is Heads or Tails. B's belief is consequently wrong. So, what happens if we update these models by a public announcement that 'A knows whether the coin is Heads or Tails'? Indeed this public announcement would contradict B's beliefs and then B would have to *revise* her beliefs.

This public announcement is depicted in Fig. 9 (respectively Fig. 10 for the BMS system). This update yields the be-model depicted in Fig. 11 (respectively

Fig. 12 for the BMS system). In this be-model (Fig. 11), B now believes that A knows whether the coin is Heads or Tails, so B did revise her beliefs. On the other hand, in the BMS model (Fig. 12) B now believes everything. In a sense we could say that the announcement drives her 'crazy' because it contradicts her beliefs.

So, we see in this example that the BMS system does not perform belief revision, unlike our system. This is of course a flaw of the BMS system.

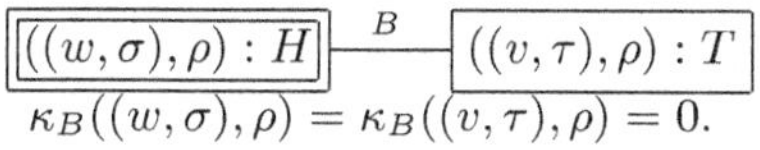

$$\boxed{((w,\sigma),\rho):H} \ \overline{}^{B}\ \boxed{((v,\tau),\rho):T}$$
$$\kappa_B((w,\sigma),\rho) = \kappa_B((v,\tau),\rho) = 0.$$

Fig. 11. be-model corresponding to the situation after the announcement 'A knows whether the coin is Head or Tail'.

$$A$$
$$\boxed{\boxed{((w,\sigma),\rho):H}}$$

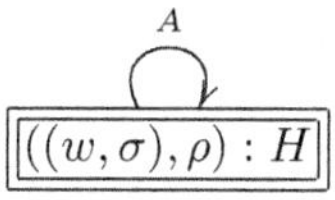

Fig. 12. BMS model corresponding to the situation after A has cheated and after the announcement 'A knows whether the coin is Head or Tail'.

Generally speaking, it seems that a system allowing for misperception (like cheating) *has* to incorporate a revision of belief feature.

2.4   The Full Language $\mathcal{L}(\Sigma_{sg})$

We extend the static language defined in Sect. 2.1. in order to incorporate the dynamic feature. This dynamic feature will be displayed in the full language by the programs and the modality $[\pi]$.

Let $\Sigma_{sg} = (\Sigma, \sim_j, \kappa_j^*)$ be a fixed action signature (see [BMS04]).

Definition 5. *The syntax of the language $\mathcal{L}(\Sigma_{sg})$ is defined by,*

- *Sentences $\phi := True \mid p \mid \neg\phi \mid \phi \wedge \psi \mid K_j\phi \mid B_j^n\phi \mid [\pi]\phi$ where $n \in \mathbb{N}$*
- *Programs $\pi := \sigma\psi \mid \pi + \rho \mid \pi.\rho$ (see [BMS04])*

Its semantics is completely similar to the BMS one (see [BMS04]), except for the operator B_j^n (see Sect. 2.1).

Intuitively, $M, w \models [\pi]\phi$ says that 'in world w, after the action corresponding to the program π has been performed, ϕ will hold'.

Our system is a semantically driven logical system. So naturally, we can try to find an axiomatization and a completeness proof for it. That is the concern of the next section.

3   Logic of Combined Update and Revision

3.1   The Full Proof System

We set out in this section the core of the proof system AX w.r.t. the semantics of $\mathcal{L}(\Sigma_{sg})$. The core of the sub-proof system AX' w.r.t. the semantics of $\mathcal{L}_{St}$ (see Sect. 2.1) is labeled with *. (For a full version of the proof system, see the web-site http://www.illc.uva.nl/Publications/reportlist.php?Series=MoL.)

1. $\vdash [\sigma_i\psi]p \leftrightarrow (\psi_i \to p)$
2. $\vdash [\sigma_i\psi]\neg\chi \leftrightarrow (\psi_i \to \neg[\sigma_i\psi]\chi)$
3. $\vdash [\sigma_i\psi]\phi \wedge \chi \leftrightarrow ([\sigma_i\psi]\phi \wedge [\sigma_i\psi]\chi)$
4. $\vdash [\sigma_i\psi]K_j\phi \leftrightarrow \{\psi_i \to \bigwedge\{K_j[\sigma_k\psi]\phi; \sigma_k \sim_j \sigma_i\}\}$
5. $\vdash [\sigma_i\psi]B_j^n\phi \leftrightarrow (\psi_i \to \bigwedge\{B_j^{p-1}\neg\psi_k \wedge \neg B_j^p\neg\psi_k \to B_j^{n+p-\kappa_j^*(Pre(\sigma_k))}[\sigma_k\psi]\phi;$
$\sigma_k \sim_j \sigma_i$ and $p \in \{0..Max\}\})$ where $n < Max$.
6. $\vdash [\pi.\rho]\phi \leftrightarrow [\pi][\rho]\phi$
7. $\vdash [\pi + \rho]\phi \leftrightarrow [\pi] \wedge [\rho]\phi$
8. *$\vdash K_j\phi \to \phi$
9. *$\vdash B_j^n\phi \to K_jB_j^n\phi$ for all $n \in \mathbb{N}$
10. *$\vdash \neg B_j^n\phi \to K_j\neg B_j^n\phi$ for all $n \in \mathbb{N}$
11. *$\vdash B_j^n\phi \to B_j^{n'}\phi$ for all $n \geq n'$
12. *$\vdash K_j\phi \leftrightarrow B_j^n\phi$ for all $n \geq Max$.

Axiom 12 is somewhat problematic. Indeed, we 'jump' from the notion of belief with highest plausibility to the notion of knowledge: this is somewhat mysterious! Note that we could avoid that by allowing an infinite number of degrees of belief (and then get rid of Max), but then in axiom 5 we would get an infinite conjunction in the second term.

Moreover, it seems unfortunately impossible to give an intuitive import to axiom 5.

3.2   Completeness and Soundness Proofs

An exhaustive completeness and soundness proof can be found on the web-site http://www.illc.uva.nl/Publications/reportlist.php?Series=MoL . We only provide a sketch of the proof here.

Soundness Proof. We only give the soundness proof of axiom 5. The soundness of the other axioms can be easily checked or are spelled out in [BMS04].

First, note that in any be-model M,

Fact: $\kappa_j^w(\phi) = l \Leftrightarrow M, w \models B_j^{l-1}\neg\phi \wedge \neg B_j^l\neg\phi.$

Now, if we spell out the definition of $M, w \models [\sigma_i\psi]B_j^n\phi$, we get at a certain point to the expression $Cut_{Max}(\kappa_j^*(\sigma_j) + \kappa_j(v) - \kappa_j^w(\psi_j)) \leq n$. Yet, $n < Max$, so this expression is equivalent to $\kappa_j^*(\sigma_j) + \kappa_j(v) - \kappa_j^w(\psi_j) \leq n$ which is again equivalent to $\kappa_j(v) \leq n + \kappa_j^w(\psi_j) - \kappa_j^*(\sigma_j)$. That is how the positions of $[\sigma_i\psi]$ and B_j are swapped in axiom 5. Finally the value of $\kappa_j^w(\psi_j)$ is determined by the Fact.

Completeness Proof. First we show:

Theorem 1. *AX' is a sound and strongly complete axiomatization with respect to the semantics of $\mathcal{L}_{St}$.*

Proof. We use the following canonical model:

> $M^c = (W^c, \sim_j, \kappa_j, V)$ where,
> - $W^c = \{w_W;$ W maximal AX'-consistent set$\}$.
> - $\sim_j = \{(w_V, w_W); V/_{K_j} \subseteq W\}$ where $V/_{K_j} = \{\phi; K_j\phi \in V\}$.
> - $\kappa_j(w_W) = min\{n; W/_{B_j^n} \subseteq W\}$.
> - $w_W \in V(p)$ iff $p \in W$.

Lemma 1. *For all $\phi \in \mathcal{L}(\Sigma_{sg})$, there is $\phi_{St} \in \mathcal{L}_{St}$ such that $\vdash \phi \leftrightarrow \phi_{St}$*

Proof. We prove it by successive inductions (see the web-site mentioned above). We use in great extent the 'reduction' axioms 1 to 5: they all 'push through' the epistemic operators and connectives, except for the basic case 1 where $[\sigma_i\psi]$ disappears.

Theorem 2. *AX is strongly complete with respect to the semantics of $\mathcal{L}(\Sigma_{sg})$.*

Proof. Thanks to lemma 1 and the soundness of our logic, the completeness proof with respect to the semantics of the full language boils down to the completeness proof with respect to the static language. This last point has been shown in theorem 1, so we have the expected result.

4   Comparison with the AGM Postulates

To check whether the AGM postulates are fulfilled, we first need to define, relatively to a world w and for an agent j, the belief set, the expanded belief set and the revised belief set. We will deal with propositional language as in the AGM theory (see Sect. 1.2). The type of be-action-model we naturally consider for the update is a public announcement of a propositional formula ϕ, depicted in Fig. 13.

$$\boxed{\sigma : \phi}$$
$$\kappa_j(\sigma) = 0 \text{ for all } j.$$

Fig. 13. be-action-model for the action 'public announcement of the propositional formula ϕ'.

Definition 6. *For each world w, we define*

- *the belief set $K^w = \{\phi \in \mathcal{L}; M, w \models B_j^0\phi\}$,*
- *the revision of the belief set K^w by ϕ, $K^w * \phi = \{\psi \in \mathcal{L}; M, w \models [\sigma, \phi]B_j^0\psi\}$,*
- *the expansion of the belief set K^w by ϕ, $K^w + \phi = \{\psi \in \mathcal{L}; M, w \models B_j^0[\sigma, \phi](\phi \to \psi)\}$,*

where $\mathcal{L}$ is the propositional language.

Theorem 3. *(If $M, w \models \neg K_j \neg \phi$ then) * defined by $K^w * \phi$ satisfies the 8 AGM postulates.*

Proof. The proof is standard and can be found on the web-site http://www.illc.uva.nl/Publications/reportlist.php?Series=MoL.

Note 1. In the theorem, the assumption within brackets is a natural one.

Remark 4. If we consider the epistemic language (i.e. with knowledge) instead of the propositional language $\mathcal{L}$ for the formation of belief sets, then some AGM postulates are not fulfilled. This failure is due to the fact that the epistemic formulas satisfiable in any world may change after an update with a public announcement (phenomenon called 'persistence'). Yet, assume we slightly change the be-action-model depicted in Fig. 13 and replace it with the one depicted in Fig. 14.

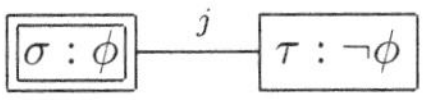

$$\boxed{\sigma : \phi} \xrightarrow{\quad j \quad} \boxed{\tau : \neg\phi}$$

$\kappa_j^*(\sigma) = 0$ and $\kappa_j^*(\tau) = \alpha_j$ for all agents j.

Fig. 14.

Then the 8 AGM postulates are satisfied for the epistemic language. (For a proof see the web-site mentioned above.) Indeed, the epistemic formulas satisfiable in any world are the same after an update with this type of be-action-model.

Moreover, after the update, ϕ is believed by all the agents j with *firmness* α_j in world w (see Sect. 1.2 for a definition of the notion of firmness).

General Conclusion: We have set out a logical system merging update logic and belief revision theory. This system satisfies the AGM postulates. However, extending the BMS framework with an accessibility relation for the notion of belief and updating it by 'multiplication' does not perform a *revision* of belief but rather an *expansion* of beliefs.

Nevertheless, our system presents some limitations. First, as mentioned in remark 3, we assume that the plausibility of an action does not depend on the world in which it is performed. Unfortunately, we cannot make small variations to our current system in order to avoid this assumption. This then shrinks the set of actions we can consider in our system. Second, the relationship between the notions of knowledge and belief is not properly rendered as it is suggested in axiom 12, and the theorem $\neg K_j \phi \rightarrow K_j \neg K_j \phi$ is inadmissible in many types of situations (although not in our example).

Concerning the second point, we believe one can tackle epistemic issues and describe (actual) epistemic situations accurately only with an epistemic formalism which renders properly all the nuances and overtones within and between these notions. This paper is a first step towards it: we enriched and refined our epistemic formalism by introducing the notion of belief explicitly. Further and better refinement is the concern of ongoing research.

Acknowledgement

I thank my master's thesis supervisors Johan van Benthem and Hans van Ditmarsch for their support during the process of my master's thesis. I also want to thank Andreas Herzig, Gary Cleveland and three anonymous referees for their comments about this paper.

References

[BMS04] A. Baltag, L.S. Moss,and S. Solecki. Logic for epistemic program. In *Synthese* Volume 139, Issue, March 2004. Pages: 165 - 224.

[FHMV95] R. Fagin, J.Y. Halpern, Y. Moses, and M.Y. Vardi. *Reasoning about knowledge*. MIT Press, Cambridge MA, 1995.

[GardRott95] P. Gardenfors and H. Rott, 1995, 'Belief Revision', in D. M. Gabbay, C. J. Hogger and J. A. Robinson, eds., *Handbook of Logic in Artificial Intelligence and Logic Programming* 4, Oxford University Press, Oxford 1995.

[Spohn90] W. Spohn. A general non-probability theory of inductive reasoning. In R. D. Schachter, T. S. Levitt, L. N. Kanal, and J. F. Lemmer, editors, *Uncertainty in artificial intelligence 4*, pages149-15. Norht-Holland, Amsterdam, 1990.

[Spohn88] W. Spohn. Ordinal conditional functions: A dynamic theory of epistemic states. In W. L. Harper and B. Skyrms,editors, *Causation in Decision, Belief Change, and Statistics*, vol.2, pages 105-134. reidel, Dordrecht, 1988.

[vDL03] H.P. van Ditmarsch and W.A. Labuschagne. *A multimodal language for revising defeasible beliefs*. In E. Álvarez and R. Bosch and L. Villamil, editors, *Proceedings of the 12th International Congress of Logic, Methodology, and Philosophy of Science (LMPS)*, pages 140-141, Oviedo University Press, 2003.

Using Messaging Structure
to Evolve Agents Roles in Electronic Markets

Ghassan Beydoun[1], John Debenham[1], and Achim Hoffmann[2]

[1] E-markets group, University of Technology of Sydney, Australia
{ghassan,debenham}@it.uts.edu.au
[2] AI group, University of New South Wales, Australia
achim@cse.unsw.edu.au

Abstract. Exogenous dynamics play a central role in survival and evolution of institutions. In this paper, we develop an approach to automate part of this evolution process for electronic market places which bring together many online buyers and suppliers. In particular, for a given market place, we focus on other market places doing similar business, as a form of exogenous evolutionary factor. Automatically tracking and analyzing how other market places do their business has a number of difficulties; for example, different electronic markets- with similar purpose- might use different names for similar agent roles and tasks. In this paper, we argue that low level analysis of sequences of messages exchanged between agents within e-markets is an effective mechanism in integrating similar roles specifications, independent of what names these roles – or even the messages themselves – may take. We focus on the structure of messages (message schemas), sequences of message schemas, sets of sequences of message schemas to compare and integrate roles. Using statistical analysis over such structures we bypass the difficult problem of identifying semantics of roles and exchanged messages through their human readable names (syntactic forms). To allow such low level analysis, different e-market specifications are expressed using the same language. Our language of choice is a recently developed multi agent systems specification language, Islander 2.0. We illustrate our approach with example specifications and institutions simulation traces.

1 Introduction

The world is a changing place and evolution is central to survival of any institution. Continuously, institutions dynamically evolve, it is their very structure which changes [8] throughout their lifetime. They evolve due to internal interactions within (endogenous) or exogenous interactions without [1]. Examples of endogenous interactions for a retailing institution are satisfaction surveys provided as buyers leave a store, management consulting intervention. An important example of exogenous variables interactions is observing how other stores might process their sales. In this paper, we focus on this second type of evolution due to interactions with external variables. We present a framework to automate part of such evolution processes for electronic markets (e-markets) which are multi-agent systems (MAS) places which bring together many online buyers and suppliers. For a given market place, we focus on how it can learn and evolve by considering how other similar market places do business. In other words, 'other market places' is the exogenous evolutionary factor of our interest.

M.W. Barley and N. Kasabov (Eds.): PRIMA 2004, LNAI 3371, pp. 18–28, 2005.

Much existing e-commerce ontology integration research work attempt to integrate products description catalogs e.g. [2, 9]. However, our work is distinct, in that we want to integrate the actual business processes. In other words, it is specifications of business processes which we want integrate for the purpose of improving the actual performance of an electronic e-market. Descriptions of behavior of different agents from different market places are ontological units in our framework.

Automatically tracking and analyzing how other market places do their business has a number of difficulties; for example, different electronic markets- with similar purpose- might use different names for similar agent roles and tasks. Syntactic analysis and comparison of agent roles is not sufficient. In this paper, we argue that low level analysis of sequences of messages exchanged between agents within e-markets is an effective mechanism in integrating similar roles specifications, independent of what names these roles -or even the messages themselves- may take. We focus on the structure of messages (message schemas), sequences of message schemas, sets of sequences of messages schema to compare and integrate roles. Using statistical analysis over such structures we bypass the difficult problem of identifying semantics of roles and exchanged messages through their human readable names (syntactic forms). To allow such low level analysis, different e-market specifications are expressed using the same language. Our language of choice is a recently developed multi agent systems specification language, Islander 2.0 [6, 7]. We illustrate our approach with example specifications of e-markets.

This paper is organized as follows: Sections 2 motivates and describes our e-market evolution approach in the context of ontology integration and the specific features of our work in that context. Section 3 presents technical details our approach, it introduces steps involved in evolving e-markets and illustrates our approach with example e-market specifications expressed in Islander 2.0. Section 4 analyses the steps involved theoretically and points to their statistical limits. Section 5 concludes with a discussion, summary and future work.

2   Evolving e-Markets by Integrating Their Specifications

In this section, we overview the motivation of evolving e-markets using their specifications. We foreshadow some of the problems and our approach to resolve these problems, in particular, we highlight those problems associated with ontology integration efforts in general.

Electronic institutions specification describes the high level aspect of the infrastructure of a multi agent system which implements the behavior and interactions between different agents within the system. In the case of e-market, agents would play the role of online sellers, online buyers, online auctioneers, .. Such high level or societal [10] aspects of the MAS systems can then be used as an input to development tools (e.g. JADE [3]) that automatically implements synchronization and low level generic aspects of the MAS and its agents. Thence nowadays implementing an e-market is largely a specification task. Against this background of automatic code generation and electronic distributed interactions, it is becomes more important to model and implement e-market automatic evolution mechanisms and tools. Without such mechanisms and tools, continuous manual tinkering of e-market agent systems would eventually dissipate gains and benefits of the automatic present development frameworks which are already in use. Further, opportunity for automatic learning from other e-markets (from the net) would be lost.

Electronic Institutions (and e-markets) are specified as a set of roles (and rules governing multiple agents and their behavior. Roles are recurring patterns of behavior of agents. Agents are assigned *roles* as agents enter an e-market. Roles dictate what messages can be received or sent by an agent. Roles can overlap between agents within institutions, and more importantly for our evolutionary goal, they might overlap between agents from different institutions which might be similar in purpose or culture. Agents in different institutions might behave in different ways to solve similar tasks: *better ways for solving similar tasks,* or agents in different institutions with similar intended roles might solve different tasks: *there might be scope for broadening agents' roles within their institutions.* For example, two mortgage brokers A and B from different lending firms could be achieving similar lending goals, but with broker A going through a more effective procedure; or borrower B might be doing more steps which enhance the overall function of the bank, e.g. he might be doing some the legal checking normally undertaken by the solicitor. In either case, host institutions would benefit by examining each other's lending brokers behavior.

We define institutional evolutionary learning as operations on agent roles within an institution (e.g. e-market). The purpose of these operations is to maximize using/serving/managing their internal and external agents. These operations include: extending, restricting or deleting an existing role, adding a new role, or merging two roles.

Agents in electronic markets with similar tasks might have different names to describe their roles and tasks. This is the problem of *synonymous terms* which is inherent in any ontology integration task [4, 9, 11, 12]. On the other hand, two roles in two different e-markets might not be always the same, but they might overlap under some conditions. Again, this is a form of the classical *overlapping information* problem in ontology integration. In our approach detailed in the rest of this paper, we use extensional definitions of roles, as a set of sequences of message schemas (that is a message template). Such level analysis of sequences of messages exchanged between agents within e-markets bypasses the aforementioned problems.

In our integration approach, we follow a *hybrid ontology integration* approach as described in [12]: our e-market specifications are integrated by taking a single specification at a time, however, a common ontology for low level role descriptions is assumed. Our chosen common language (ontology) is a recently developed multi agent systems specification language, Islander 2.0 [7]. This is overviewed in the next section; where we give a high level description of our integration approach.

3   e-Markets Learning from Each Other

In this section, we first give an overview of the common specification language we use, Islander 2.0. We then detail our assumptions in integrating two e-market specification. We give a high level description of the steps involved in the evolution, from detecting a possibility for learning from another e-market on the net, to integrating roles description from the discovered candidate e-market.

3.1 Islander 2.0

To enable low-level analysis of different e-markets agent roles, we assume a common language which describes them. We chose the language Islander 2.0 [6, 7]. Using Islander, an institution is described as a formal specification consisting of three components: The dialogical framework which describes the set of roles and the format of messages exchanged (i.e. the communication language between agents within the institution); the set of scenes which describe sequences of actions within different activities taken by groups agents; the performative structure which establishes how different activities relate in broader context of the institution [6, 7]. A high level specification of an e-market *negotiation_space* looks as follows in Islander:

```
(define-institution negotiation_space as
                dialogic-framework = negotiation_space_df
                performative-structure = negotiation_scenes
                norms = () )
```

Intra-scene activities are conditioned by messages exchanged and 'constraints' which can apply to the whole set of messages exchanged within a scene. Inter-scene activities are conditioned by inter scene obligations generated as a result of activities (communication) within a scene. Such obligations constitute a set of institutional 'norms'. Using Islander assumptions, the activities taken by agents are receiving and sending messages. Indeed, the lowest level description of all activities generated within an institution can be expressed as a sequence of messages. The list of permitted messages for our e-market *negotiation_space* is shown in Figure 3.2 (Top left). Figure 3.1 shows part of specification for the e-market *negotiation_space*, which models mediated negotiation between two generic negotiators (that usually are buyers and sellers). The figure shows specification of a scene and the list of agent roles within the market.

The specification in Islander is a description of messages exchanged between agents and constraints on which agent sends which message and when, according to the role of the agent and their state in the e-market. In the next section, based on this view, we describe our evolution framework which uses sets of messages as the basis of integration.

3.2 e-Market Evolution Framework

We assume that there is a population of e-markets and the structure of each of these e-markets is available to individual markets within this population. The first question to an e-market looking out for an exogenous evolutionary source, is which e-markets in this population it should consider learning from. Secondly, how is this learning implemented. As earlier mentioned, e-market evolution is a special case of institution evolution which is considered a dynamic evolution [8]. The structure of the e-market changes as a result.

To identify which individual e-markets may be useful for an evolving market, we examine the structure of the messages exchanged within. If a high degree of low-level similarity exists with an external market, then this external market is a candidate for use as an external evolutionary factor. Our heuristic is based on the idea that a high degree of similarity at the low level description of market interactions within, may

```
    define-scene negotiation as
        roles = (mediator negotiator)
        scene-dialogic-framework = generic_negotiation
        states = (Negotiator_act Initial_State Mediator_act Exit)
        initial-state = Initial_State
        final-states = (Exit)
        acces-states = ((mediator (Initial_State)) (negotiator (Initial_State)) )
        exit-states = ((mediator (Exit)) (negotiator (Exit)) )
        agents-per-role = (
            (1 <= mediator <= 1)
            (negotiator <= 2))
        connections = (
        ( ....
        (Mediator_act Exit (inform (!x mediator) (?y negotiator) offer(!good !neg_id
        !price) ) (= !price !price(Mediator_act, Negotiator_act) ) )
        (Mediator_act Negotiator_act (inform (!x mediator) (?y negotiator) offer(!good
        !neg_id ?price) ) (notin ?y !y(Negotiator_act, Mediator_act)
        != ?neg_id !neg_id(Negotiator_act, Mediator_act)
        != ?price !price(Mediator_act, Negotiator_act) ) )
        )
    )
    (define-dialogic-framework generic_negotiation as
        ontology = negotiation
        illocutionary-particles = (inform request failure )
        external-roles = (negotiator )
        internal-roles = (mediator )
        social-structure = (
            (negotiator ssd mediator))
)
```

Fig. 3.1. Part of Islander specification for mediated e-market *negotiation_space*. The first part is the specification of a scene, and the second part (below) is the set of roles within the dialogical framework.

imply a level of similarity at the high level between markets. This constitutes a first step 'DNA test' before high level checks and integration steps are carried through.

Once a candidate external evolutionary e-market is chosen, the second step is to examine structural similarity of messages used by individual roles between the evolved market and the external found market. This prepares candidate sets of roles for evolutionary operators between different e-markets

As earlier discussed, we define e-market evolution as evolving agent roles. Thus institutional evolutionary learning can be implemented as operations on agent roles within an institution (e.g. e-market). An e-market agent role may be extended so that the agent can send/receive a larger set of messages, it can be restricted to decrease that set, or finally a new role can be created as a result of examining an external e-market.

We define a role as a set message schema sequences. We say schema because our focus is on the structure of messages exchanged within the market rather than their content. This way we by-pass problems associated with naming within messages.

Defining a role as a set of sequence of message structures, bypasses integration problems associated with the naming conflict of roles between different markets. This also allows to do merge operations, and even when part of role definition is only available.

Let R_1 be a role in institution I_1 and R_2 a role in institution I_2 (I_1 and I_2 are identified according to step 1, R_1 and R_2 are identified according to step 2) then a new role $R_m = R_1 \circ R_2$ is the role resulting from the merging of the two roles. A most general evolutionary operator $\circ$ would be the set union of tasks of both roles. Applying role merge operators to 'promising roles' (as identified by step 2), is the third step of our evolutionary framework.

The more accurate the set representation of roles of R_1 and R_2, the more rewarding the merge operation and the more effective role R_m would be. Relation between actual R_m and the theoretical maximum merge possible between roles will be formalized in section 4. This will be the basis of evaluating the result of the merge and is the fourth step in our evolution framework.

Only those promising merges are filtered through to the final step. This is to interpret the new sets developed into the broad specification of the evolved e-market. There are a number of ways to change the specification e.g. adding a new state into scene (i.e. changing a scene specification), adding a new scene and using this in the performative structure, or adding a new scene instance within the performative structure. Note that it is the performative structure which gets used as the design of the e-market multi agent system.

In summary, given an e-market I_1 (formulated using Islander 2.0) to evolve, the evolution framework is as follows:

1. Using set of possible message structures, identify a candidate e-market as I_e an external evolutionary factor
2. Using corresponding subset of possible message structures for each role, identify subset of roles S_e in I_e which can be used for merging with a corresponding subset of roles S_1 in I_1
3. Merge corresponding roles:
   i. For each agent role in S_1 and S_e generate an extension using the performative structure of I_1 and I_e respectively.
   ii. Apply merge operators between corresponding role extensions
4. Evaluate result of merging and filter good 'merges' only
5. Map 'good' merges back to specification in expressed in Islander 2.0.

In Section 3.3, we show details of steps 1 and 2 from above using required parts from example Islander e-market specifications. In Section 4, we introduce theoretical framework to develop steps 4 and 5. Ideas to develop step 6 will be discussed in Section 5.

3.3   e-Markets Integration Algorithm

Role merging operations are executed using inputs from roles descriptions from other institutions similar to the current institution. In our framework, the first step is to identify candidate institutions where similar agent roles may be encountered. The next step is to identify which roles within the chosen institutions are worthy of examining for triggering our roles operations. These two preliminary steps are illustrated with examples in this section.

Our starting point in this example is the relevant parts of five Islander specifications[1] for five e-markets: *negotiation_space* (offering a generic space for mediated negotiation between two agents, potentially a buyer and a seller), *lottery, supplychain, auctionhouse and electricity market.* The relevant parts for this step 1 of the market specifications is the one, which specifies the set of types of messages exchanged between agents (called 'ontologies' in Islander 2.0) shown in figure 3.2. A comparison matrix is generated between the set of structure of messages exchanged in each e-market and is shown in table 3.1. It should be noted that the actual structure of the message is only compared.

At this first step, we are only pursuing 'potential' external evolutionary e-market factors. This comparison is a heuristic based on the idea that the low level similarities in messaging structure is essential in most high level similarity between different e-markets. In itself, it is not a guarantee to identify external evolutionary potential. In our preliminary example, the *auctionhouse* can be used as an external evolutionary factor for the *negotiation_space* e-market.

Fig. 3.2. The set of e-markets specifications.

---

[1] The last four specifications were downloaded from the website *www.iiia.csic.es*

The next step is to identify roles within the found evolutionary factor (e.g. *auctionhouse*' e-market) which can be used to evolve roles with the evolving e-market (e.g. *'negotiation_space*' e-market). That is, if the e-market *negotiation_space* is to use the *auctionhouse* as an external evolutionary source, in our framework we identify agent roles within *auctionhouse* which can be potentially used to evolve or merge with specific roles within *negotiation_space* e-market. This information is available dispersed in the scene specifications in Islander 2.0. We develop a comparison matrix with the promising evolutionary factor, where the comparison is between roles in each of the two e-markets. For example, in the *negotiation_space* there are two roles: *negotiator* and *mediator*; and in the most promising external e-market evolutionary factor *auctionhouse* there are five agent roles: *buyer, seller, guest, auctioneer, roommanager* and *staff*. The comparison matrix between these roles is shown in table 3.2.

Our similarity measure $S(R_1, R_2)$ between two roles, R_1 and R_2, is defined as follows:

$$S(R_1, R_2) = \sum_{w \in N} \Psi(w, L) + \sum_{x \in O} \Psi(x, M) +$$
$$\sum_{y \in L} \Psi(y, N) + \sum_{z \in M} \Psi(z, O)$$

Where, L is the set of message schemas received by R_1, M is the set of message schemas sent by R_1, N is the set of message schemas received by R_2, O is the set of message schemas sent by R_2. $\Psi(m, M)$ is a function which accepts a message structure m and calculates a degree of membership of the structure in a set M. It returns 1 if the exact structure of m exists in M, it returns 0.5 if the structure of m is subsumed by the structure of some message structure in M and it returns 0.25 if the structure m of subsumes a structure of some message in M.

Table 3.1. Comparison matrix of the five e-markets messages. 0.5 point is allocated to the measure when the message type of the evolved e-market is a super type of external e-market, it is 1 point when it is the same (regardless of the ordering of components).

	Negotiation_space	Lottery	Supply Chain	AuctionHouse	Electricity_market
Negotiation_Space	1	0	2.5/6	4.5/6	0
Lottery	0	1	3.5/5	2/5	5/5
SupplyChain	2.5	3/9	1	5.5	6.5
Auction-House	5/16	3/16	3/16	1	3.5/16
Electricity_Market	0	2.5/12	6.5/12	3.5/12	1

Our similarity function S is non-commutative (hence the matrix is asymmetric). Moreover, we compare messages sent by R_1 to those sent by R_2, and those received by R_1 to those received by R_2. The roles similarities matrix between the e-markets *negotiation_space* and *auction_house* is shown in table 3.2.

According to our heuristic results in table 3.2, the mediator in *negotiation_space* e-market might have something to learn from the auctioneer in the *auctionhouse*. The negotiator might have something to learn from the staff role in the *auctionhouse*. The room manager in the auction house seems to be of little use to the evolution of *negotiation_space*.

Table 3.2. Comparison matrix between roles in the negotiation space e-market (vertical), and roles in the auction house e-market (horizontal).

	Buyer	Seller	Guest	Auctioneer	Staff	Room manager
Negotiator	3	3.5	1.5	2.5	4.75	0
Mediator	1.5	2	0.75	3.0	2.5	0

In the next section, we examine the question of how many instances of messages is required in the extension of roles so that a merge operation can be meaningful.

4 Theoretical Analysis of Role Merging

A role in an e-market restricts messages sent and received by an agent. A role is defined as a set of sequences of messages. In an e-market, a log of agent performances can be easily kept and used to generate set extensions for roles. How accurate these sets represent the intended roles by the e-market designers, depends on the number of tasks (sequences of messages) which have been performed and logged by agents with those roles. Simulation of e-markets might produce such logs artificially. In this section, we assume extensional definition of roles (from log of tasks or artificially generated) to evaluate the effectiveness of merge between two candidate roles. The critical issue of how many examples are required to implement the actual evolution is considered.

Given a role R_1 in institution I_1 and a role R_2 in institution I_2 *(which are mergeable according to the heuristics shown in the previous section)*, then let $R_m=R_1 \circ R_2$ be the role resulting from the merging of the two roles using the merge operator $\circ$. A most general merge operator $\circ$ would be the set union of tasks of both roles. However, it is not always possible to represent the complete extension of a role. How much R_m reflects the merging of intended roles clearly depends on the extensional representation of R_1 and R_2, which is an important issue. Clearly, the more examples of the intended roles R_1 and R_2 are available, the more accurate can R_m be expected to match the target role R_t. The target R_t does not need to be precisely specified. It is only indicated by the message schemas being used, i.e. some examplaes of its full extension are provided. We assume some arbitrary, fixed but unknown probability distribution P on the possible set of tasks T. Then we say that a role R deviates from a target role R_t by ε, if the probability of randomly selecting a task t according to P such that t is either part of role R and not part of role S or vice versa is ε.

Theorem 4.1. Let R_1 be a role in institution I_1 and R_2 a role in institution I_2. Let $R_m=R_1 \circ R_2$ be the role resulting from the merging of the two roles. If $(R_m \setminus (R_1 \cup R_2)) = \varnothing$ then, the extension of R_m deviates from the target role R_t by at most ε more than either of R_1 or R_2 with probability of at least $1-\delta$, where the following inequality holds: $\delta < (1-\varepsilon)^{1/k}$ where k is the number of randomly generated tasks to test R_m.

Proof. The condition $(R_m \setminus (R_1 \cup R_2)) = \varnothing$ means all tasks generated by R_m have also been generated by either R_1 or R_2. If R_m deviates from the target role by more than ε than either R_1 or R_2, then the probability executing a task randomly chosen (according to P) falling into $(R_1 \cup R_2) \setminus R_m$ is greater than ε. If that is the case, then the probability of not executing a task falling into $(R_1 \cup R_2) \setminus R_m$ among k randomly generated tasks is greater or equal to $(1-\varepsilon)^k$. Since the task record (database) containing k tasks does not contain a task in $(R_m \setminus (R_1 \cup R_2))$, we obtain $\delta < (1-\varepsilon)^{1/k}$.   **QED**

Theorem 4.1 allows to automatically merge two role descriptions: For a required degree of accuracy ε it bounds the probability that a merged role definition will deviate from the target role by more than ε over the maximum deviation by any of the two merged specifications. I.e. it allows to perform merge operations automatically, if the probability of an inaccurate result is acceptable. If the chance of obtaining an inaccurate merged role is unacceptably large, a human expert can be requested to approve a proposed role merge operation.

5 Discussion and Conclusion

Evolution in response to a changing business environment is central to survival of institutions in general, and e-markets in particular. They dynamically must evolve continuously throughout their lifetime. In this paper, we focused on e-markets evolution due to interactions with other e-markets. We presented a framework to automate part of such evolution processes. For a given market place, we focus on how it can learn and evolve by considering how other similar market places do business. The result of the evolution is integration between agents 'roles from different e-markets.

Our integration framework relies on similarity in structures of messages exchanged between agents. Content of messages is ignored. The idea of this paper is that similarity in communication structure beyond a certain degree implies similarity in content and purpose on a higher level. Our current comparison of structures relies on examining the type of the messages. In the near future, we will consider the possibility of introducing higher-level intermediate structures, e.g. *type sets*. These are used in some functional languages, e.g. in Haskell, types *int* and *float* could belong to the same type set *Num*. Use of types sets would overcome any differences in messages due to the e-market specification being too domain specific. Currently, names of messages (available in Islander specification) are not used. Use of names dictionaries could also assist in detecting similarities which might not be captured by looking at the structure of the messages.

To complete our role integration framework, we need to map set theoretic merge of roles- in the form of sets of messages, to Islander specification. In particular the mapping required is to the *performative structure*. This is the component of Islander specification used to generate Java code implementing the MAS.

Updating the performative structure could take a direct form: adding a new instance of a scene to the performative structure or adding new transitions between scenes. Alternatively, it could take an indirect form: changing a scene specification used within the performative structure. This can be achieved by adding a new state, or a new state transition to the finite state description of the scene.

From past experience, changes at the higher level of the knowledge representation are more specific and easier to introduce than changes at the lower level of the specification, which might have some unforeseen side effect (e.g. inconsistencies) [5]. The decision between the levels of impact of the change might require human intervention. The exact details of this step in updating Islander specifications are currently work in progress.

References

1. Apesteguia, J.J. Institutions and Institutional Evolution. in Workshop In Political Theory and Policy Analysis. 1998. Indiana: Indiana University.
2. Baron, J., M. Shaw, and A. Bailey, Web-based E-catalog Systems in B2B Procurement. Communications of the ACM, 2000. **43**(5): p. 93-100.
3. Bellifemine, F., A. Poggi, and G. Rimassa, Developing multi agent systems with a FIPA-compliant agent framework, in Software Practice and Experience. 2001, John Wiley and Sons. p. 103-128.
4. Beydoun, G., J.T.F. Breis, et al. Statistical Monitoring of Ontology Integration for Corporate Memory. in Pacific Rim Knowledge Acquisition Conference (PKAW20002). 2002. Japan.
5. Beydoun, G. and A. Hoffmann, Theoretical Basis of Hierarchical Incremental Acquisition. International Journal of Human Computer Interactions, Academic Press, 2001. **54**(3): p. 407-452.
6. Esteva, M., Electronic Institutions: From Specification To Development, in Artificial Intelligence Research Insitute. 2003, UAB - Universitat Autonma de Barcelona: Barcelona.
7. Esteva, M., D.d.l. Cruz, and C. Sierra. ISLANDER: an electronic institutions editor. in International Conference on Autonomous Agents & Multiagent Systems (AAMAS02). 2002. Italy: ACM.
8. Hurwick, L., Toward Analyzing Institutions and Institutional Change, in Markets and Democracy, S. Bowles, H. Gintis, and B. Gustafsson, Editors. 1993, Cambridge University Press: New York. p. 51-67.
9. Omelayenko, B. Syntactic-Level Ontology Integration Rules for E-commerce. in 14th FLAIRS Conference. 2001. Florida, USA: AAAI Press.
10. Rodriguez, J.A., On The Design and Construction of Agent-Mediated Electronic Institutions, in Artificial Intelligence Research Insitute. 2003, UAB - Universitat Autonma de Barcelona: Barcelona.
11. Vargas-Vera, M., E. Motta, et al. MnM: Ontology Driven Semi-automatic and Automatic Support for Semantic Markup. in Knowledge Engineering and Knowledge Management. 2002. Spain: Springer.
12. Wache, H., T. Vogele, et al. Ontology-Based Integration of Information - A Survey of Existing Approaches in IJCAI Workshop on Ontologies and Information Sharing. 2001. Seattle.

Specifying DIMA Multi-agents Models Using Maude

Noura Boudiaf[1], Farid Mokhati[1], Mourad Badri[2], and Linda Badri[2]

[1] Département d'Informatique, Université d'Oum El-Bouaghi, Algérie
Boudiafn@yahoo.com, Mokhati@yahoo.fr
[2] Département de Mathématiques et d'Informatique
Université du Québec à Trois-Rivières, Canada, G9A 5H7
{Mourad_Badri,Linda_Badri}@uqtr.ca

Abstract. The lack of formalism and rigor in existing multi-agents models often leads to ambiguities and different interpretations. Those weaknesses combined with the inherent complexity of multi-agents systems generate many problems in their development process. Using formal notations to specify multi-agents systems' behavior makes it possible to produce precise description. This also offers a better support to their verification and validation process. The Maude language, based on rewriting logic, presents a rich notation supporting formal specification and implementation of concurrent systems. In this paper, we demonstrate the feasibility and the interest of formalizing the behavior of DIMA model's agents with the Maude language. The elaborated formal approach captures the inherent aspects of a DIMA model. The generated Maude descriptions have been validated using the platform supporting this language. Moreover, the proposed approach is generic and extensible. It offers, in particular, the advantage of being applicable to all multi-agents systems based on DIMA architecture and presents interesting extension possibilities.

1 Introduction

Research on Multi-Agents Systems (MAS) always gives an important place to the study of individual and collective behavior of agents [2]. It is, in fact, difficult to specify MAS' behavior without highlighting the behavior of their composing agents. In the field of agent's behavior specification, three major approaches emerge in the literature: state-charts based approaches [22, 20], Petri Nets (PN) based approaches [7, 3] and, finally, approaches representing adaptations of object-oriented specification methods [18, 19]. However, these methods offer only semi-formal specifications. This weakness, combined with the inherent problems of MAS' specification, often generates several difficulties and problems in their development process. The numerous underlying concepts of multi-agents models, as well as their complexity, require a powerful formal model in terms of description. Furthermore, this model must be able to support the description of diverse important aspects related to MAS' behavior, such as interactions between agents, and their concurrence at different levels. The presence of a tool supporting the model, for simulation and verification objectives, is in our opinion essential.

   DIMA model's architecture, thanks to its modularity features, helps to decompose the complex behavior of an agent within a set of specialized behaviors. Those diverse behaviors can eventually be leaded by a meta-behavior [12]. Aside from being con-

M.W. Barley and N. Kasabov (Eds.): PRIMA 2004, LNAI 3371, pp. 29–42, 2005.
© Springer-Verlag Berlin Heidelberg 2005

sidered as an open system, DIMA allows implementing agents having diverse granularities (size, internal behavior, knowledge). Moreover, heterogeneity is an important characteristic of MAS. The major existing systems do not grant the possibility to implement heterogeneous agents. Unlike others, DIMA supports three types of heterogeneity: multiplicity of execution platforms, multiplicity of knowledge representation formalisms and multiplicity of agent's models.

Knowing the richness and the complexity of the DIMA model, we retained in our approach the formal and object-oriented language Maude [13, 16]. The constructs offered by this language seem interesting and rich enough to capture the multiple aspects of the DIMA multi-agents model. Maude is, in fact, a formal language based on a sound and complete logic called the rewriting logic [16]. On certain aspects, it is close to the language Troll [21], also having a sound semantics. However, the absence of concurrence within objects in Troll makes Maude more advantages. The G-ECATNets [6], also represent another interesting and very expressive candidate. They present a sound integration of ECATNets [4] and of the object paradigm. The ECAT-Nets are also high-level Petri Nets. They integrate abstract algebraic types and Petri Nets formalism. The G-ECATNets have, in fact, a representation in the Maude language, making them a particular case of Maude. Furthermore, the G-ECATNets do not dispose of a tool independent of Maude. An execution of a description in G-ECATNets is exactly like executing their representation in Maude. In this paper, we demonstrate the feasibility as well as the interest of formalizing agent's behavior (individual and social) in DIMA model using the Maude language. The elaborated formal approach allows capturing the inherent aspects of the DIMA model. The Maude descriptions generated in the framework of our approach have been validated using the platform supporting this language. Our approach is generic and extensible. It has the advantage of being applicable to all MAS based on DIMA architecture and presents interesting extension possibilities.

The remainder of this paper is organized as follows: In section 2, we give a general outline on the major related works. We briefly present, in section 3, the DIMA multi-agents model. In Section 4, we introduce briefly the rewriting logic as well as the Maude language. Section 5 presents the process we propose to formalize the DIMA model using Maude. In order to validate the generated descriptions and the adopted approach, the simulation we realized is illustrated in section 6. In section 7, we give some conclusions and future work directions.

2   Related Works

Many researches based on previously quoted approaches have been conducted during the last decade. Tranvouez and al. proposed a formalism supporting the RCA roles protocol's descriptions [22]. This formalism, based on state diagrams, is used to represent agent's behaviors. Cost and al. [7] proposed an approach that allows representing the conversations between agents using Colored Petri Nets. Furthermore, Odell and al. proposed AUML [18] as an extension of UML, allowing modeling agent's behavior using artifacts such as activity diagrams, state diagrams and sequence diagrams. However, AUML remains, like UML, a semi-formal notation. Our approach is similar, in terms of objectives, to previously quoted approaches. Essentially, it consists of supporting the important step of MAS' specification. However, we adopted a more formal way in our approach because of the different advantages it procures. It is based on the formal and object-oriented language Maude [13, 14, 16].

3 DIMA Multi-agents Model

The first steps of MAS development process are very important and must be supported adequately. During those steps, several major and strategic decisions are taken, often starting from informal requirements. Those are often incomplete, ambiguous, contradictory and, in numerous cases, in continuous evolution [1]. Formalizing these requirements offers several advantages. It allows developers having a formal basis in the system's development process. In fact, formal specification greatly contributes to the production of high quality systems, in particular, in the case of complex systems such as MAS. Such an approach leads to precise and rigorous descriptions of MAS' properties, supporting as a consequence their verification and validation process. MAS' design, as mentioned by many authors, is still anticipated. One of the major reasons is related to the fact that no standard exists nowadays for an agent's definition nor for its internal architecture [9]. Throughout our approach, we opted for the DIMA agent's model proposed by Guessoum in [10]. This model is illustrated in figure 1. Contrary to different hybrid models (Touring Machines [8], InterRRap [17] and the Bussmann and Demazeau model [5]) that do not offer static planning of the different modules, the agent in the DIMA model has a supervision module that allows dynamically adapting its behavior to the changes it detects in its environment [11]. The major advantage of the DIMA model resides in its architecture model that allows producing modular agents. It also can be considered as an open model [12]. In this paper, we consider three types of modules: the perception module, the reasoning module (knowledge based behavior) and, finally, the communication module (procedural behavior).

3.1 Informal Description of the DIMA Multi-agents Model

Each agent is composed of three modules (perception, reasoning and communication) representing its behaviors and a supervision module representing its meta-behavior [11]:

- The *perception* module manages the interactions between the agent and its environment. The major role of this module is to initialize and update a set of data where are stored the external variables accessible by captors.
- The *reasoning* module represents the different abilities of the agent. It defines the adapted response, whether to the request received by the communication module, or by the evolution of the environment perceived through the perception module.
- The *communication* module has a mailbox and performs two functions: 1) Reception of messages from other agents and 2) Sending of messages for communicating with the agent's acquaintances or for acting on the environment.
- The *supervision* module is based on state and transition notions. Those states and transitions define and ATN (*Augmented Transition Network*) that is a synthetic and deterministic representation of the agent's behavior.

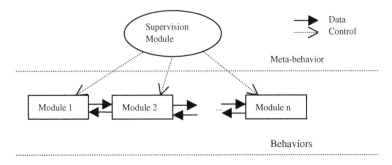

Fig. 1. DIMA.agents' model

Each of those modules can be found in an active or suspended state. The supervisor's state that represents an agent's state at a given moment is expressed in function of the states of different modules.

3.2 Control Mechanism

The control is on two levels: internal to each agent and inter-agents.

Internal Control. The internal control is managed on three levels:

– Supervision module: an ATN grants the possibility to specify an agent's behavior according to its internal states.
– Reasoning module: a meta-level architecture grants the possibility to specify in a declarative way the reasoning strategies of the agent.
– Internal parallelism: The management process associated to the asynchronous different modules of the agent grants the possibility to specify the allocation of available resources [10].

Inter-agents Control. The control of complex dynamic systems needs the collaboration of several agents. Agents reason according to their abilities on parts of the global task to realize. They must coordinate their actions to avoid inconsistencies. The use of messages as sole communication process does not solve certain problems related to the sharing of data or resources. Two mechanisms are used: a dependency mechanism and an anti-interference mechanism. Those two mechanisms are discussed in what follows.

Dependency Mechanism. The dependency mechanism can be defined on two different aspects:

– We associate to each agent a dependency graph giving the list of the other agents using it for each shared resource.
– The dependency graph is used by the agent to inform other agents about the modification, the creation or the suppression of a shared resource. It is updated progressively when the production rules using the shared resources are started.

Anti-interference Mechanism. The production rules are written without considering the interference with other rules. Knowing that they can be started on different locations and in a concurrent manner, interferences between executions can lead to an incoherent global execution on several base rules. The principle of the anti-interference mechanism is defined on four aspects:

- Each agent must have a *used-resources* list giving the list of shared resources presently used by the agent itself.
- Each agent must have a collection of *used-resources* list of the shared resources currently used by the other agents.
- Before starting a rule, the agent consults its collection of *used-resources* to verify that the shared resources used by this rule are available. In that case, it adds the shared resources used by this rule to its own *used-resources* list.
- At the end of the release, the agent removes from its *used-resources* list, the shared resources used by the started rule.

This mechanism allows avoiding all the inconsistencies that can provoke the concurrent execution of several interfering rules.

4 Rewriting Logic and Maude Language

4.1 Rewriting Logic

The rewriting logic, having a sound and complete semantics, was introduced by Meseguer [16]. It allows describing concurrent systems. This logic unifies most of the formal models describing concurrency [15]. In rewriting logic, the formulas are called rewriting rules. They have the following form: *R: [t] → [t'] if C*. Rule *R* indicates that term *t* becomes (is transformed into) *t'* if a certain condition *C* if verified. Term *t* represents a partial state of a global state *S* of the described system. The modification of the global state *S* of the system to another state *S'* is realized by the parallel rewriting of one or more terms expressing partial states.

The distributed state of a concurrent system is represented as a term which subterms represent the different component's states of the composite state. The concurrent state's structure can have a variety of equivalent representations because it satisfies certain structural laws (equivalence class). For example, in an object-oriented system, the concurrent state that is usually called configuration has the structure of a multi-set of objects and messages. Therefore, we can see the constructed configurations by a binary operator applied to binary sets:

```
1. sort Configuration .
2. sort Object .
3. sort Msg .
4. subsort Object < Configuration .
5. subsort Msg < Configuration .
6. op null : -> Configuration .
7. op ___ : Configuration Configuration -> Configuration [assoc comm
   id : null] .
```

The previous portion of program gives a definition of three types: *Configuration Object* and *Msg*. *Object* and *Msg* are sub-types of *Configuration*. Objects and messages are, in fact, multi-set configuration singletons. More complex configurations are generated from the application of the union on these multi-set singletons (objects and messages). In the case where there is neither floating messages nor live objects, we have an empty configuration (line 6). The construction of a new configuration in terms of other configurations is done with the operation given in line 7. We can see that this operation has no name and the two under-lines indicate the positions of the two parameters of configuration type. This operation, which is the multi-set union, satisfies the structural laws of association and of commutation. It also possesses a neutral element *null*. For example, if we have a message *M1* that represents a configuration, and an object *<O : C|atts >* (please note that *O* an object's identifier, *C* the class to which it belongs and *atts* is the list of its attributes) that represents in itself another configuration, then we can construct another configuration in terms of those two configurations: *M1 < O : C | atts >*. This one is equivalent to the configuration *< O : C | atts > M1* because the __ operation is commutative.

4.2 Maude

Maude is a specification and programming language based on the rewriting logic [13, 16]. Three types of modules are defined in Maude. The *functional* modules allow defining data types and their functions through equations theory. The *system* modules allow defining the dynamic behavior of a system. This type of module augments the functional modules by the introduction of rewriting rules. A maximal degree of concurrency is offered by this type of module. Finally, there are the *object-oriented* modules that can be reduced to system modules. The object-oriented modules explicitly offer the advantages related to the object paradigm. In relation to the system modules, the object-oriented modules offer a more appropriate syntax to describe the basic entities of the object paradigm, like messages or configuration, for example. Only one rewriting rule allows expressing the consumption of certain floating messages, the sending of new messages, the destruction of objects, the creation of new objects, state change of certain objects, etc.

5 Modeling of the DIMA Model Using Maude

In the context of the adopted method for the formalization of the DIMA model, we developed several modules (figure 2). Some are functional and others are object-oriented. Because of space limitation reasons, we only give a brief survey of certain parts of our modeling. They are elaborated enough to illustrate our approach. The functional modules developed are numerous; therefore we only illustrate some of them in what follows.

Module *RESSOURCE-LIST* allows describing the abstract algebraic type 'list of resources'. We also define another list, containing identifiers of agents. Module *DEP-MECLIST* contains a list's description (dependency mechanism) in which the elements are couples. The first element of the couple represents a resource and the second is a list of agents having the access right to this resource. Module *RESSOURCE-USE* also contains a list of couple's description. A couple of this list contains the identifier of an agent followed by a list of resources used by this agent at a given moment. In what follows, we discuss the object-oriented modules that capture the inherent aspects of the DIMA model. We use an object-oriented model *AGENT* to encapsulate all the components of an agent. This module contains both the structure and the internal behavior of the agent.

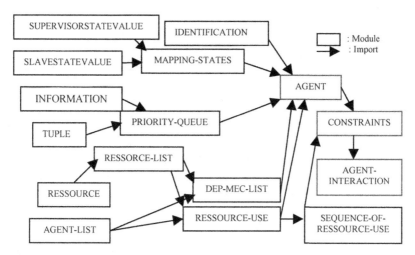

Fig. 2. Module Browser of the application

5.1 Formalizing the Internal Behavior of an Agent

For a formal description of an agent, we propose a class for each 'agent's component' module. In this case, we have four classes modeling the four modules of an agent: *Supervisor*, *Perception*, *Reasoning* and *Communication*. We add another class *AgentMec* to model the inter-agents controls mechanisms. All those classes are defined within the same *AGENT* model. Class Supervisor's definition possesses attributes *idSA*, *idSP*, *idSR* and *idSC* to contain, in order, the identifiers of its agents, of the perception, of the reasoning and of communication:

```
class Supervisor | idSA : Aoid, idSP : Poid, idSR : Roid, idSC : Coid,
StateS : SupervisorStateValues.
```

Types *Aoid*, *Poid* and *Coid* describe the identification mechanism of *agent*, *perception*, *reasoning* and *communication* objects. Attribute *StateS* contains the supervisor's state. Now, let's consider class *AgentMec* :

```
class AgentMec | DepMecListAtt : DepMecList, RessourceListAtt : Ressour-
ceList, RessourceUseListAtt : RessourceUseList .
```

It contains three attributes. Attribute *DepMecListAtt* defines the access's rights of the agents to the resources. This attribute is a list of couples, composed of a resource and a list of agents having the right to use this resource. Attribute *RessourceListAtt* contains the resources in progress of utilization by the agent. Finally, the attribute *RessourceUseListAtt* is a list of couples composed of an agent's identifier and of a list of resources in progress of utilization by that agent. To illustrate the definition of messages in Maude, we take as an example the definition of message *CatchP* that serves to import information to perception from the external environment:

```
msg CatchP : Poid Information -> Msg .
```

The dynamic behavior of an agent is expressed using rewriting rules. The interaction between different components of an agent belongs to this behavior. The quoted rule below describes how a perception object consumes an external message:

```
crl [PReceiveMsg]: CatchP(P, IP) Check(EmptyMsg, MR, MC)
< P : Perception | idPR : R, InfP : EmptyInformation, StateP : Activated
> < R : Reasoning | idRP : P, idRC : C, InfR : IR, StateR : SVR >
< C : Communication | idCR : R, InfC : IC, StateC : SVC >
< S : Supervisor | idSA : A, idSP : P, idSR : R, idSC : C, StateS : SVS
> => Check(CheckP(S, P, Activated) , MR, MC)
< P : Perception | idPR : R, InfP : IP, StateP : Suspended >
< R : Reasoning | idRP : P, idRC : C, InfR : IR, StateR : SVR >
< C : Communication | idCR : R, InfC : IC, StateC : SVC >
< S : Supervisor | idSA : A, idSP : P, idSR : R, idSC : C, StateS :
MappingState(Suspended, SVR, SVC) > if (IP =/= EmptyInformation) .
```

In the initial state (left part of the rule), we have the message's arrival *CatchP(P, IP)*, the empty attribute *infP* (Information) and the activated perception's state. After rewriting this rule (message consumption), the perception's state becomes *Suspended*, therefore the state of *S* must be recalculated using function *MappingState* and perception sends a message *CheckP(S, P, Activated)* (within message *Check*) to prevent supervisor *S* for activating it after. The received information *IP* by the perception must not be empty after the *if-statement*. We propose a message *Check* having three parameters. Each of those parameters contains an asked activation coming from the perception, from the reasoning and from the communication. This solution allows the supervisor to compare the requests and to activate the most urgent one. We can also choose the solution that consists of activating simultaneously all the modules sending their requests in parallel. In the following, we have an activation request coming from perception and another coming from reasoning:

```
Check(CheckP(S, P, Activated),  CheckR(S, R, Activated), EmptyMsg)
=> Check(EmptyMsg,  EmptyMsg, EmptyMsg)  CheckP(S, P, Activated)
CheckR(S, R, Activated) .
```

The following rule shows a perfect synchronization between a perception and reasoning during sending information from the first to the second:

```
crl [PsendToR]: Check(MP, EmptyMsg, MC)   < P : Perception | idPR : R,
InfP : IP, StateP : Activated >
< R : Reasoning | idRP : P, idRC : C, InfR : EmptyInformation, StateR :
Activated > < C : Communication | idCR : R, InfC : IC, StateC : SVC >
< S : Supervisor | idSA : A, idSP : P, idSR : R, idSC : C, StateS : SVS
> => < P : Perception | idPR : R, InfP : EmptyInformation, StateP :
Activated >
< R : Reasoning | idRP : P, idRC : C, InfR : IP, StateR : Suspended >
< C : Communication | idCR : R, InfC : IC, StateC : SVC >
< S : Supervisor | idSA : A, idSP : P, idSR : R, idSC : C, StateS :
MappingState(Activated, Suspended, SVC) >
Check(MP, CheckR(S, R, Activated), MC) if (IP =/= EmptyInformation)   .
```

The initial information *IP* of *InfP* is put in *InfR* after applying this rule. In this same rule, *InfP* became empty. This rule requires that the perception and the reasoning are both activated. The reasoning suspends itself when the rule ends and the supervisor state is recalculated to be adapted to the change of reasoning's state. A condition denotes that *IP* must not be empty.

5.2   Formalizing an Inter-agents Control Mechanism Using Maude

Interactions between agents are described in the module *AGENT-INTERACTION*. Especially, the description concerns the synchronization between agents in terms of resources sharing. If an agent *A1* requests the use of resources saved in list *L*, it confirms that those resources are free. Then, it sends this information to all other agents within its own *RessourceUseListAtt*. Agent *A1* cannot be totally synchronized with all the other agents within a sole rule. Such synchronization is not possible because the number of agents is not defined beforehand.

We go through the list *RessourceUseListAtt* of *A1*. We take each time the next agent, named *A2*, which is in this list. We add the list of resources *L* requested by *A1* in *RessourceUseListAtt*. Several agents can ask to use the resources in parallel. For this reason, the next scenario is possible: suppose that we have *A1,..., An* agents in our system. Take agent *A1* that wants to reserve resources *L*, it just informed a certain number of agents but it did not yet informed *Ai*. Suppose that *Ai*, in turn, wants to use resources that are in *L*. It starts informing the other agents. We can have a situation in which *Ai* has contacted agent *Ar*, which was not yet contacted by *Ai*. This one cannot transmit the reservation information of resources to *Ar*. In this case, *A1* blocks itself and waits for *Ai* to finish using the resources, and vice-versa. We are confronted with a deadlock situation. A simple solution to this problem consists of using another object called Synchronization. This object has *RessourceRequest* attribute containing the agent's requests during its communication with the other agents to inform them that it is in progress of utilization of certain resources. In the first contact of agent *A1* with the agent at the head of list *RessourceUseListAtt*, *A1* and the requested resources are placed in *RessourceRequest*. The agent removes its request when it finishes informing all the other agents. The previous scenario cannot take place: when another agent *Ai* wants to use the same resources as *A1*, it is forced to go through Synchronization object or it must find other resources already requested by another. Also note that agent *A1* puts the list *L1* (*ConcatRessourceList(L, L1)*), which it requests in its own list of currently used resources attribute *L*:

```
crl [AgentAskUseResources] : UsingRessource(A1, L)
< A1 : AgenMec | DepMecListAtt : DM1, RessourceListAtt : L1, RessourceU-
seListAtt : RU1 > < Y : Synchronisation | RessourceRequest : RQ > < A2
: AgentMec | DepMecListAtt : DM2, RessourceListAtt : L2, RessourceU-
seListAtt : RU2 >
=> UsingRessource(A1, L) Order(2) < A1 : AgentMec | DepMecListAtt : DM1,
RessourceListAtt : ConcatRessourceList(L, L1), RessourceUseListAtt : RU1
> < Y : Synchronisation | RessourceRequest : (A1 ;; L) :: RQ > < A2 :
AgentMec | DepMecListAtt : DM2, RessourceListAtt : L2, RessourceU-
seListAtt : AddAgentInRessourceUseList((A1 ;; L), RU2) >
if (RessourceListInDepMecList(L, DM1) == true) and
(A2 == 1stAgentElement(ReturnInOrder(RU1, 1))) and (DisjRessourceList-
WithRessourceUseList(L, RU1) == true) and (FindInRessourceUseList((A1
;; L), RQ) == false) and (DisjRessourceListWithRessourceUseList(L, RQ)
== true) and (RU1 =/= EmptyRessourceUseList) .
```

This rule generates a message *Order(2)* to converse with the next agent in the list. The following rules works recursively with the other agents in its list:

```
crl [AgentAskUseResources] : UsingRessource(A1, L) Order(N)
< A1 : AgentMec | DepMecListAtt : DM1, RessourceListAtt : L1, Ressour-
ceUseListAtt : RU1 >
< Y : Synchronisation | RessourceRequest : RQ >
< A2 : AgentMec | DepMecListAtt : DM2, RessourceListAtt : L2, Ressour-
ceUseListAtt : RU2 >
=> UsingRessource(A1, L) Order(N + 1)
< A1 : AgentMec | DepMecListAtt : DM1, RessourceListAtt : L1, Ressour-
ceUseListAtt : RU1 >
```

```
< Y : Synchronisation | RessourceRequest : RQ >
< A2 : AgentMec | DepMecListAtt : DM2, RessourceListAtt : L2, Ressour-
ceUseListAtt : AddAgentInRessourceUseList((A1 ;; L), RU2) >
if (A2 == 1stAgentElement(ReturnInOrder(DL, N)))   and (DisjRessource-
ListWithRessourceUseList(L,  RU2)  ==  true)   and  (FindInRessourceU-
seList((A1 ;; L), RQ) == true)   and  (DisjRessourceListWithRessourceU-
seList(L, RQ) == true)   and (RU1 =/= EmptyRessourceUseList)   and (N <
LengthRessourceUseList(RU1))   .
```

When an agent *A1* finishes communicating with all the other agents of its list, *(N >
LengthRessourceList(RU1))*, it makes disappear messages *UsingRessource(A1, L)* and
Order(N) to stop the communication process as following :

```
crl [AgentAskUseRessources] : UsingRessource(A1, L) Order(N)
< A1 : AgentMec | DepMecListAtt : DM1, RessourceListAtt : L1, Ressour-
ceUseListAtt : RU1 > < Y : Synchronisation | RessourceRequest : RQ > =>
< A1 : AgentMec | DepMecListAtt : DM1, RessourceListAtt : L1, Ressour-
ceUseListAtt : RU1 > < Y : Synchronisation | RessourceRequest :
EliminateRessourceUseElement((A1 ;; L), RQ) >
if (N > LengthRessourceUseList(RU1)) .
```

An agent must remove resources from all *RessourceUseListAtt* of the other agents
to get such resources free. We define rewriting rules to describe this operation. A first
rule specifying the liberation process of resources by the agent is as following :

```
crl [AgentLetRessources] : LetRessource(A1, L)
< A1 : AgentMec | DepMecListAtt : DM1, RessourceListAtt : L1, Ressour-
ceUseListAtt : RU1 > < A2 : AgentMec | DepMecListAtt : DM2, Ressource-
ListAtt : L2, RessourceUseListAtt : RU2 >
=> LetRessource(A1, L) Order(2)
< A1 : AgentMec | DepMecListAtt : DM1, RessourceListAtt : L1, Ressour-
ceUseListAtt : RU1 >
< A2 : AgentMec | DepMecListAtt : DM2, RessourceListAtt : L2, Ressour-
ceUseListAtt : EliminateRessourceListFromRUList ((A1 ;; L), RU2) > if
(A2 == 1stAgentElement(ReturnInOrder(RU1, 1))) and (RU1 =/= EmptyRes-
sourceUseList) .
```

A second rule describes the contact of this agent with the others by removing the
free resources from *RessourceUseListAtt* of each agent. A third rule ends the liberation process between the concerned agent and the others. We only explain the first.
When agent *A1* finishes using the resources in list *L*, it generates message *LetRes-
source(A1, L)*. Agent *A1* contacts the agent at the head of its *RessourceUseListAtt* list
and it removes itself from the list of this agent (*EliminateRessourceUseElement((A1;
L), RU2)*).

5.3 Integrity Constraints

To control the system's state, we introduced a part of Maude's code that insures the
respect of certain constraints. We introduced a control on the initial state relative to
the internal structure of a system and another on the configuration of the agent's
community when they interact. The constraints related to this last case are devised in
three points that can lead to an inconsistent state of the system. The first point guarantees that all resource lists currently being used by all agents are disjoined two by two
in any system's state. In the second, we verify that the lists used by the anti-
interference mechanism are identical. In the last, we verify that each list of resources
currently used by the agents do not contain duplicates. We propose function *Coher-*

entStateVerification having as parameter a configuration and returning a configuration. This function verifies that the initial configuration is perfectly coherent. Function *CoherentStateVerification* returns the configuration itself if it is coherent; otherwise it returns an error message configuration *Incoherent-System-State*.

```
eq CoherentStateVetification(C) =
if (CoherentRessourceList(C)  == true)  and (CoherentRessourceUseList(C)
== true) and (DisjointResssourceList(C)  == true) then C  else Incoher-
ent-System-State  fi .
```

This function calls three other functions, each one has as parameter a configuration and returns a boolean. Function *DisjointRessourceList(C)* extracts the currently used resources by the agents and verifies that they are completely disjoint. Function *CoherentRessourceUseList(C)* verifies that the lists used by the anti-interference mechanism are identical. Finally, the function *CoherentRessourceList* returns a positive response if each one of the resources lists currently used by an agent does not contain duplicates.

6 Simulation and Validation of a Multi-agents Model Using Maude

The rewriting logic offers a great flexibility in terms of simulation of a specification, in particular, concerning the choice of the initial configuration. Using all the system's description, we can validate a part of the system without involving the rest. We put forward the difference between the simulation of the internal behavior of an agent and the one related to the behavior of a group of agents in terms of information exchange and sharing of resources. The results of the first simulation do not affect the results of the second one. Because of space limitation reasons, we present only the validation of the internal behavior of an agent. For a validation of the internal behavior of an agent, we choose an initial configuration that contains solely the models related to this agent. In this case, the executed rules are only those relevant to the internal behavior of the agent. The same method is adopted when validating the relational behavior between agents.

6.1 Simulation and Validation of the Internal Behavior of an Agent

We worked on the simulation of several aspects related to the dynamic behavior of the agents. We also consider: (1) the behavior that begins by capturing a message by the perception module and ends by its sending away (environment or another agent) by the communication module and, (2) the behavior that is related to the reception of a message by the communication module and its sending by the reasoning module. We also can have the two cases together. We take an example of the first case with a given initial configuration:

```
CatchP(P, ExampleInformation) Check(EmptyMsg, EmptyMsg, EmptyMsg)
< P : Perception | idPR : R, InfP : EmptyInformation, StateP : Activated
> < R : Reasoning | idRP : P, idRC : C, InfR : EmptyInformation, StateR
: Suspended > < C : Communication | idCR : R, InfC : IC, StateC : Sus-
pended > < S : Supervisor | idSA : A, idSP : P, idSR : R, idSC : C,
StateS : State3 >
```

The infinite rewriting process (without indicating the number of rewriting steps) of this configuration gives the following result:

```
< P : Perception | idPR : R, InfP : EmptyInformation, StateP : Activated
> < R : Reasoning | idRP : P, idRC : C, InfR : EmptyInformation, StateR
: Suspended > < C : Communication | idCR : R, InfC : InsertInOrderQ((A ;
A1 ; ExampleInformation ; PR), IC), StateC : Activated >  < S : Supervi-
sor | idSA : A, idSP : P, idSR : R, idSC : C, StateS : State2 >
Check(EmptyMsg, EmptyMsg, EmptyMsg)
```

The perception receives information from the environment and transmits it to the reasoning. This last entity starts its own internal rules and constructs a message destined to agent $A1$ ($A1 \neq A$) with a priority flag of PR. The reasoning module sends a message to the communication module. Communication integrates the message in its sending queue, organized by priority. The rewriting of our initial configuration stops at this level because it contains the internal description of an agent A, not $A1$'s. This gives us the advantage of validating separately the parts of the specification. The rewriting of a configuration can also be limited by the number of rewriting steps, which allows us controling the intermediary steps. The rewriting of the previous initial configuration in 10 steps gives the following result:

```
< P : Perception | idPR : R, InfP : EmptyInformation, StateP : Activated
> < R : Reasoning | idRP : P, idRC : C, InfR : ExampleInformation,
StateR : Suspended > < C : Communication | idCR : R, InfC : IC, StateC :
Suspended >  < S : Supervisor | idSA : A, idSP : P, idSR : R, idSC : C,
StateS : State3 > CheckR(S, R, Activated) Check(EmptyMsg, EmptyMsg,
EmptyMsg)
```

We can rewrite the resulting configuration with a certain number of steps. Also, note that the initial state proposed is incoherent (for example, the value of the supervisor's state is not *state3* but *state0*, which does not correspond to *Activated, Suspended, Suspended* respectively for perception, reasoning and communication), we have in this case an error message.

6.2 Implementation

Figure 3 illustrates a part of the programming code we developed. It visualizes both the rewriting rule describing an agent's behavior when it captures an external event from its environment and the rewriting process limited to a certain number of steps

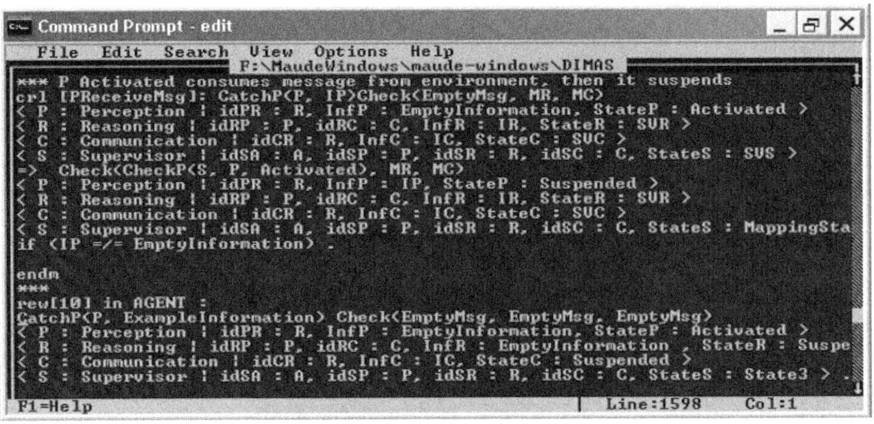

Fig. 3. Part of the developed code

(here 10 steps) of an initial configuration. The result of the rewriting process on the previous initial configuration after 10 steps is indicated in figure 4.

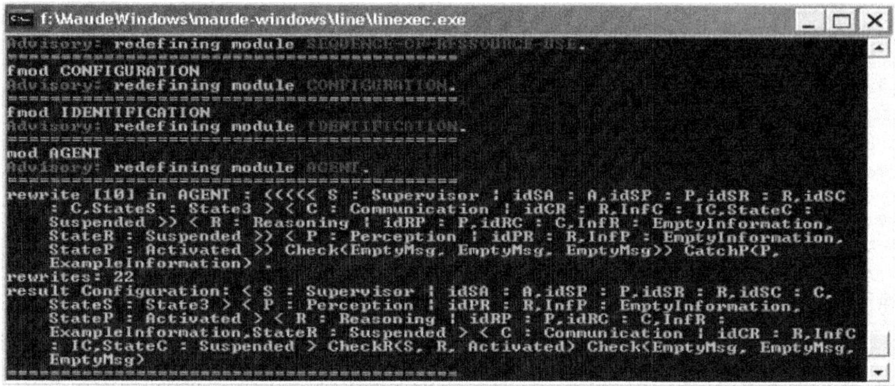

Fig. 4. Intermediary result (after 10 steps) of the rewriting process of the initial configuration

7 Conclusions and Future Work

In this paper, we proposed an approach based on the formal and object-oriented language Maude to formalize the behavior of agents of the DIMA model. Throughout the paper, we demonstrated the ability of this language to describe this type of system. The DIMA model presents an architectural model allowing to produce modular agents. It can also be seen as an open model. This model uses both the internal concurrency of an agent (between the different components of an agent) and the inter-agents concurrence. Using the Maude language we captured all these aspects, including concurrence.

The Maude language is supported by a tool. Aside from modeling, this allowed us performing a validation (based on a simulation) of our method. Our model is reusable and extendable. This reusability is expressed by the decomposition we performed. The validation of the internal behavior of the agents does not affect the collective behavior, and vice-versa. This is possible because of the high abstraction level of this language as well as its characteristic of being executable. The application of this approach on a real project is in progress.

References

1. Amyot, D., Logrippo, L., Burh, R.J.A.: Spécification et Conception de Systèmes Communicants: une Approche Rigoureuse Basée sur des Scénarios d'Usage. In: G. Leduc (Ed.), *CFIP 97, Ingénierie des protocoles*, Liège, Belgium, Hermès, (1997) 159-174
2. Andriamasinoro, F., Courdier, R.: Un Modèle Dynamique de Comportement Agent à Base de Besoins. In Journées Francophones sur l'IAD et les SMAs (JFIADSMA'01), Montréal, Québec, Canada (2001)

3. Bakam, I., Kordon, F., Le Page, C., Bousquet, F.: Formalization of a Spatialized Multi-agent Model Using Coloured Petri Nets for the Study of a Hunting Management System. First International Workshop, FAABS 2000, Greenbelt, MD, USA, April 2000. FAABS (2000)

4. Bettaz, M., Maouche, M.: How to specify Non Determinism and True Concurrency with Algebraic Term Nets. LNCS, N 655, Spring Verlag, Berlin, (1992) 11-30

5. Bussmann, S., Demazeau, Y.: An agent model combining reactive and cognitive capabilities. Proc of IEEE International conference on intelligent Robots and Systems - IROS'S 94, Munchen (1994)

6. Chaoui, A., Bouzenada, M.: G-ECATNets: An Object Petri Net-Based Framework for the Modular Design of Complex Information Systems. ISIICT'2001 (2001)

7. Cost, R., and al.: Modeling Agent Conversations with colored Petri Nets. Working Notes of the Workshop on Specifing and Implementing Conversation Policies, Autonomous Agents'99, Seattle, Washington (1999)

8. Ferguson, I. A.: On supporting rational behavior in real time multi-agent domains. Proc. Of AAAI Full Symposium on Rational Agency: concepts, theories, models and applications, Cambridge, MA, November, (1995) 61-65

9. Franchesquin, N., Espinasse, B.: Analyse multi-agents de la gestion hydraulique de la camangue: considérations méthodologiques. Communication soumise à JFIADSMA'2000, 2-4 oct 2000 Saint Etienne (2000)

10. Guessoum, Z.: Un Environnement Opérationnel de Conception et de Réalisation de Systèmes Multi-agents. Thèse de l'Université Paris 6, LAFORIA (1996)

11. Guessoum, Z., Briot, J-P., Dojat M.: Des objets concurrents aux agents autonomes. JFIADSMA' 97, J. Quinqueton, M.C. Thomas et B. Trousse (eds.), Hermès, (1997) 93-106

12. Guessoum, Z.: Modèles et Architéctures d'Agents et de Systèmes Multi-Agents Adaptatifs. Dossier d'habilitation à diriger des recherches de l'Université Pierre et Marie Curie, (2003)

13. Clavel, M. and al.: Maude: Specification and Programming in Rewriting Logic. Internal report, SRI International (1999)

14. McCombs, T.: Maude 2.0 Primer, Version 1.0. Internal report, SRI International (2003)

15. Meseguer, J.: Rewriting as a unified model of concurrency. In Proceedings of the Concur'90 Conference, Amsterdam, Springer LNCS Vol. 458 (1990) 384-400

16. Meseguer, J.: A Logical Theory of Concurrent Objects and its Realization in the Maude Language. In G. Agha, P. Wegner, and A. Yonezawa, Editors, Research Directions in Object-Based Concurrency. MIT Press (1992)

17. Muller, J-P., Pischel, M.: Modeling reactive behavior in vertically layered agents architectures. Proc of ECAI'94, Amsterdam, (NL) (1994) 709-713

18. Odell, J., Parunak, H. V. D., Bauer, B.: Representing agent Interaction protocol In UML. Conférence AAAI Agents 2000, Barcelone (2000)

19. Odell, J., Parunak, H. V. D., Bauer, B.: Representing agent Interaction protocol In UML. Agent Oriented Software Enginering, Paolo Ciancarini and Michael Wooldridge (eds.), Springer-Verlag, Berlin, (2001) 121-140

20. Paurobally, S., Cunningham, J.: Achieving Common Interaction Protocols in Open Agent Environments. 2nd international workshop on Challenges in Open Agent Environments, AAMAS 2003, Melbourne, Australia (2003)

21. G. Saake, T. Hartman, R. Junglaus, H-D. Ehrich: Object-Oriented Design of Information Systems: Troll language Features. In Procedings CISM School Udine'93, LNCS, Springer Verlag, (1993)

22. Tranvouez, E., Espinasse, B.: Protocoles de coopération pour le réordonnancement d'atelier. in actes des journées francophones d'IAD et SMAs (JFIADSMA'99) à Saint-Gilles, île de la Réunion, novembre 1999, Gleizes J.-P., Marcenac P., Ed. Hermès (1999)

picoPlangent: An Intelligent Mobile Agent System for Ubiquitous Computing

Kenta Cho[1], Hisashi Hayashi[1], Masanori Hattori[1],
Akihiko Ohsuga[1], and Shinichi Honiden[2]

[1] TOSHIBA Corporation,
1 Komukai-Toshiba-cho, Saiwai-ku, Kawasaki-shi, 212-8582, Japan
{kenta.cho,hisashi3.hayashi,masanori.hattori,akihiko.ohsuga}
@toshiba.co.jp
[2] National Institute of Informatics,
Graduate School of Information Science and Technology, University of Tokyo

Abstract. This paper describes an intelligent mobile agent named picoPlangent that we developed for use with portable devices. picoPlangent is designed with a component-based architecture. The agent functions are implemented by a set of small components, and the arrangement of these components can be easily changed within the limits of the available resources of each portable device. Agent actions are described into the goal tree that realizes the flexible actions of the agent on portable devices. The picoPlangent architecture is simple and easy to implement on various devices. We implemented picoPlangent using J2SE on PCs, GCC on PDAs (Palm devices) and J2ME on cellular phones (iAppli/ezPlus).

1 Introduction

In a ubiquitous computing environment, portable devices play an important role. PDAs and cellular phones enable mobile users to handle information wherever they are. However, since these devices have very small displays and limited storage, users cannot deal with large amounts of information at the same time. To support information handling with portable devices, systems that cooperate with portable devices need to summarize information in a form that users can handle easily on small displays. This information should be presented at the exact moment the user needs the information.

An intelligent mobile agent on a portable device can offer such a service. An agent on a portable device observes the user's action to learn the user's interests, and presents the appropriate information at the appropriate time. An agent moves to any device that the user uses so an agent can receive user's requests anytime, anywhere, and gather the knowledge required to infer the user's interests from the user's actions. The mobile agent can work in a stand-alone mode on the portable device and communicates with the server only when it needs the data or services on the server, and so the mobile agent can improve the response time and reduce the communication cost.

M.W. Barley and N. Kasabov (Eds.): PRIMA 2004, LNAI 3371, pp. 43–56, 2005.

Since portable devices have very limited resources, an agent on a portable device has to be very small. Even if an agent is small, it has to be intelligent enough to offer appropriate information to a user in a timely fashion.

This paper gives an account of picoPlangent, our intelligent mobile agent system. The picoPlangent agent can work with limited resources and perform flexible actions on portable devices. picoPlangent provides a planner that makes plans using a Prolog-like procedure. If the environment around the agent is dynamically changed, the agent uses the planner to create new plans adapted to the new environment.

In Section 2 we discuss the background to the problem and our approach. Section 3 presents the software architecture of picoPlangent. Details of an implementation are discussed in Section 4. Section 5 describes related work. Section 6 presents the discussion and indicates future work. Conclusions are presented in Section 7.

2 Background

In a ubiquitous computing environment, there are various types of devices, including cellular phones, PDAs, internet appliances, telematics equipment, sensing devices and PCs. Many of these devices have very restricted resources. To integrate information provided by these devices, mobile system middleware and a distributed system with mobility support for wide ranging devices are required in order to realize 'anytime anywhere' connectivity.

Our approach is to use an intelligent mobile agent to realize flexible software architecture for an open network environment. Intelligent agent technology provides autonomy, adaptability and flexibility for the system and mobile agent technology provides mobility.

We developed Plangent[1] an intelligent mobile agent system implemented in Java Standard Edition, which operates with PCs. Plangent provides a programming model based on knowledge definition and dynamic re-production of a plan(replanning).

We tried to develop an intelligent mobile agent that capable of operating with small devices, particularly with a cellular phone. Recently, Java enabled highly functional cellular phones have entered widespread use and so have Java-enabled sensor devices such as GPS for location awareness, RFID for authentication and camera for image recognition.

However, implementation of such agents is beset by several problems.

Limited Resources
  The traditional intelligent mobile agent is too large to work with a cellular phone. Program size should be less than 10Kbytes on the J2ME platform with tight memory constraints.

Vendor Dependency
  Each cellular phone vendor uses a different virtual machine. All VMs are based on Java Micro Edition, but class libraries, application lifecycles and extensions differ according to the vendor. Since the agent should respond to differences between VMs.

It is necessary for an agent to satisfy various requirements in order to work with a cellular phone.

Small Footprint
The agent should be designed for limited resources.
Vendor Neutral and Generality
The agent platform should support various vendors so that the developer of the agent does not have to pay strict attention to dependency issues.
Adaptability and Flexibility
Even in an environment with limited resources, the agent should still be adaptable and flexible.

For the implementation of out picoPlangent agent system, we adopted the approach described below.

Small Agent
The agent functions are divided into small components. These components are distributed to portable devices, and the agent works by using these components. So a minimum set of the agent system can be very small and agents can operate with the cellular phone despite rigid limitations.
Simple Goal-Based Architecture
Agents have a goal that describes the user's requirements. The lifecycle of the agent is managed by the plans consisting of sub-goals. As the plans are vendor neutral, the agent can move around the platform on various types of cellular phones, PDAs and PCs.
Planning Capabilities
To adapt to a dynamic environment, Prolog-like procedures are used to make inferences before performing actions. Plans are computed in a resource rich environment, and the agent uses these plans to migrate to a platform with limited resources.

3   Software Architecture

Here, we describe the details of the architecture of picoPlangent. The way to realize an agent's mobility is described in Section 4, The size of an agent system is evaluated in Section 6.

3.1   Agent and Agent's Goal

A picoPlangent agent has the goal that describes the user's requirements. The goals given to the agent can be general in nature such as 'get the information concerning ubiquitous computing' specific such as 'display this message'. These goals are described by Prolog terms (e.g., 'searchAbout('ubiquitous computing')', 'putMessage(['node1', 'node2'], 'hello')'), and decomposed into agent's actions. Each action is resolved by a picoPlangent component, a software component with an interface for communication with the agent.

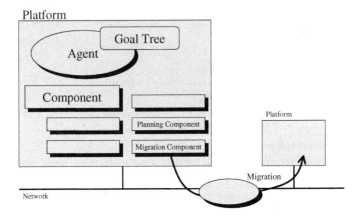

Fig. 1. Software Architecture.

Decomposed goals and actions are called sub-goals and the list of sub-goals is called a plan. picoPlangent provides a data structure called a goal tree that manages plans and a planner to decompose goals according to the rules.

The agent uses the picoPlangent component to solve the goal. The component receives the goal from the agent and executes the tasks to solve the goal. Components are registered on the platform, and the platform searches for the proper component to solve the goal. (Fig. 1) This process is performed as follows:

1. The agent sends the goal to the platform.
2. The platform asks each component whether it can solve this goal.
3. The platform gets a list of components that can solve the goal, and sends it to the agent.
4. The agent selects a component from the list and asks the component to solve the goal.
5. If the goal is specific, the component can solve the goal directly. But if it is general and there is no component that can solve the goal, the agent uses the planning component to decompose the goal.

There are many ways to know whether a component can solve the goal or not. A simple implementation is that of checking the predicate of the goal and if the predicate matches the keyword in the component, the component is considered to be able to resolve the goal.

3.2   Goal Tree

When the agent receives the goal, the agent divides the goal into plans. The plans are composed of sequences of sub-goals. The agent can hold several plans corresponding to one goal. These plans are composed of one main plan and several alternative plans. The structure to control the several plans is called the 'Goal Tree'. (Fig. 2)

The agent resolves the user's goal by solving the sub-goals in sequence. To accomplish the goal, the agent works as follows:

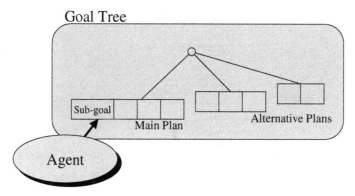

Fig. 2. Goal Tree.

1. Read the first sub-goal in the main plan.
2. Solve the first sub-goal.
3. If the agent succeeds in solving the sub-goal, this sub-goal is removed from the main plan. If the alternative plans have the same sub-goal as the first sub-goal, these sub-goals are also removed.
4. If the agent fails to solve the sub-goal, the main plan is removed from the goal tree and the next alternative plan becomes the main plan.
5. These actions are performed until all sub-goals in the main plan are solved or all plans are removed.
6. If all sub-goals are solved, the agent has carried out its task. If not, the agent has failed to end the task.

When the agent has to execute the action to solve the goal, the side effects of the action must be considered. The picoPlangent agent can handle knowledge about canceling actions in a plan that prevents execution of another plan. Due to space constraints, it isn't described here. Reference [10] shows details of action execution and side effects.

3.3   Planning Component

The goal tree is created according to the rules that represent the way to decompose a goal to sub-goals. This mechanism is performed by the planning component. (Fig. 3) The decomposition from a goal to sub-goals is done by the literal decomposition of Prolog. A plan in the goal tree corresponds to a total-order plan described by a list of literals[10]. We also developed an agent that can handle partial-order plans[11]. A partial-order plan can describe the actions that can be performed concurrently and avoid redoing unnecessary actions. Reference [12] shows our planning agent system is also useful for speculative computation in multi-agent systems.

Fig. 4 is an example of planning rules. The action represents the sub-goal that can be solved by the component. There are two actions in this example. A 'print' action means that an agent displays the message described in the

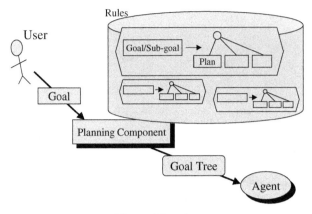

Fig. 3. Planning.

```
action(print(Msg)).
action(goto(_)).
axiom(message([],_),[]).
axiom(message([Node|Rest],Msg),
    [goto(Node),print(Msg),
     message(Rest,Msg)]).
```

Fig. 4. Planning Rules Example.

argument. A 'goto' action means that an agent migrates to the platform of that name is described in the argument. The axiom represents the rule to decompose the goal into sub-goals. Following the rules in Fig. 4 it is possible to create the plan that the agent moves around the platforms described in the first argument of the 'message' goal, and shows the message on each platform.

The developer can change the agent's behavior by writing the proper rules. The types of rules frequently used are listed below.

Reduction Rules

If the goal is too general to be solved by a single component, the reduction rules decompose the goal into more specific sub-goals. For example, the goal 'get the information concerning this keyword' is divided into 'send the keyword to a search engine', 'parse the result page', 'make the list of URLs' and 'get these pages'.

Replacement Rules

Replacement rules can make an alias of the goal by changing the goal to another goal. picoPlangent uses the 'goto' goal to move the agent to another device, but the components for the agent migration are prepared for each communication protocol. So the replacement rules change the 'goto' goal into 'gotoRmi' goal, 'gotoSoap' goal, etc. according to a schema of a destination URL.

Forwarding Rules

If the proper component for the goal exists at a remote device, forwarding rules are applied to send the agent to the device temporarily. The forwarding rule works as the directory service of the components and inserts a proper 'goto' goal in the plan.

Exception Handler Rules

A goal tree can handle the alternative plans executed when the agent fails to carry out a main plan. Exception handler rules add the alternative plans to the goal tree. For example, if the agent fails to execute the plan on the cellular phone, the agent goes back to the server and records the error log according to the alternative plan.

If the agent tries all plans in the goal tree and fails, the agent can try replanning. The agent uses the planner again to create new plans. If the environment around the agent changes (e.g., the agent moved from the platform where the agent created the first plan, and the planner on each platform has different rules), the planner may create another plan and that plan will be adapted to the new environment.

4 Implementation Details

In this section we shall discuss the way to implement the picoPlangent agent system on several devices.

The implementation of the agent, the component and the platform varies due to the distinctive features of the various devices. On a PC, it has a large amount of memory and computing power, and so the components can be fully functional. On a cellular phone, resources are very limited, and so some features of the component are omitted.

However, the agent has to move between these platforms seamlessly and answer user's requests on any platform continuously in order to accomplish the goal on the various devices that the user uses. To realize this seamless migration, the agent, component and platform should provide these functions:

- The agent should carry the goal tree and should handle the goal tree on any device. The goal tree represents what the agent should do next to complete the user's request.
- The component should know which goal can be solved by this component and have the interface to receive the goal from the agent.
- The platform should have an interface to register the component on the platform and should be able to ask these registered components whether or not a goal can be solved. In addition, the platform should have an interface to create the agent on the platform.

If these functions are realized on a device, the picoPlangent system can be implemented with any language on any device and the agent can be sent by any protocol. Language differences are absorbed by the goal tree and protocol differences are absorbed by the migration component.

Let us, for the moment, consider the practical implementation on PC, PDA (Palm) and a cellular phone (iAppli/ezPlus).

4.1   Implementation on PCs

On PCs, we implemented the system with J2SE. Java was used because it has an OS-independent VM and many cellular phones have recently included a Java VM.

The agent on PCs is implemented by the Agent class. The developer can customize the agent lifecycle and the data that the agent carries by extending the Agent class. The goal consists of the predicate represented by String class and arguments that can hold any Java objects.

The platform should implement the Platform interface. The basic platform implementation is offered by the DefaultPlatform class that provides the basic function to find the proper components to solve the goal.

The component should implement the Component interface. The Component interface has two methods. One is for asking if this component can solve the goal passed from the agent. The other is called when the agent asks the component to solve the goal.

To transport the agent between devices, the agent uses the migration component. The agent is serialized in the component and is sent to the remote device. There are several migration components corresponding to the communication protocols (RmiMigration, HotsyncMigration and SOAPMigration) to send the agent.

An RmiMigration component enables the migration of the agent by the Java RMI. The agent is serialized by the Java object serialization mechanism, and resumed at the remote platform. The agent's lifecycle is managed by the goal tree, and so the agent can realize the strong migration.

To move the agent from a PC behind a firewall to a servlet, we provide a SOAPMigration component. The agent is serialized by the SOAP serialization and sent to the remote Web server.

4.2   Implementation on Palm Devices

On Palm devices, the picoPlangent system is implemented by GCC. Although there is a Java VM, KVM that works on Palm devices, we didn't use it in view of its poor performance.

We implemented the platform and the component as native applications of PalmOS. To move the agent from a PC to a Palm device, we used Hotsync. Hotsync is a function to synchronize data between a PC and a Palm device.

When Hotsync starts, the picoPlangent conduit (conduit is the PalmOS framework for adding new functions to Hotsync) sends the agent data serialized by the HotsyncMigration component.

Agents moved to Palm devices are serialized by the HotsyncMigration component. The goal tree is converted into byte data that can be handled by the PalmOS. (Fig. 5)

The platform is composed of an OS-dependent part and an OS-independent part. If the developer wants to port the platform to another OS, the developer implements an OS-dependent part.

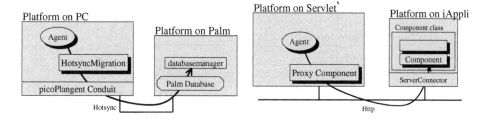

Fig. 5. HotsyncMigration Component.   **Fig. 6.** Proxy Component.

An OS-independent part consists of two modules, an agent manager and a goal tree manager. The agent manager module handles the agent's lifecycle that checks the first goal in the main plan and calls a suitable component. The goal tree module manages the goal tree. It offers functions to add/delete goals/plans.

An OS-dependent part of PalmOS consists of two modules, a PalmOS bootstrap and component caller and a database manager. PalmOS's bootstrap (Pilot-Main) and the function to call a component are defined in the PalmOS bootstrap and component caller module. The database manager provides the functions to pack/unpack the agent data from/to the PalmOS database. The agent data sent by Hotsync is stored in the PalmOS database.

4.3   Implementation on the Cellular Phone(iAppli/ezPlus)

iAppli[9] is the Java VM for NTT Docomo cellular phones. iAppli is based on J2ME, but the program size has a strict limit. In the most restricted environment, class files of the application cannot exceed 10 kilobytes in JAR (Java Archive) form.

To overcome this limit, the platform on iAppli uses a proxy component that works on the servlet. Since the proxy component has the same interface as the component on the PC, so the agent can deal it with the same way. Since the request from the agent is passed the component on iAppli by the proxy component via HTTP. (Fig. 6) The platform on iAppli handles the direct requests to the component only and the major part of the agent lifecycle is managed on the servlet, the platform on iAppli can be very simple and small.

The platform on iAppli consists of two classes:

ServerConnecter
>   The ServerConnector opens the connection to the servlet and receives the request from the proxy component. The request and the reply between the ServerConnector and the proxy component are performed by the protocol described in Fig. 7. This protocol is very simple, and has been designed with the objective of decreasing the amount of communications.

Component Class
>   On PCs, we implemented each component with a separate class. But on iAppli, all components on the platform are implemented in one class to reduce the size of the JAR file.

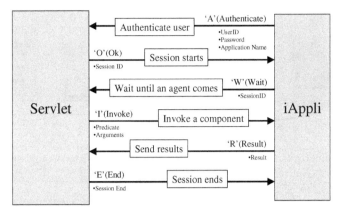

Fig. 7. Communication Protcol on iAppli.

We provide a utility to make templates of component classes on iAppli. The developer should write the component property file that represents which goal the component can solve. The utility converts the component property file (Fig. 8) into the template. The component property files are also referred to by the servlet to register the appropriate proxy components.

We also implemented the platform that can handle the whole agent lifecycle on a cellular phone. This platform can retrieve a goal from the goal tree, and executes a goal with the component. If the component failed to solve the goal or the agent couldn't find the proper component, the agent switches to the next plan in the goal tree. So if the planner on the server creates enough plans that can deal with many accidents on the cellular phone and these plans are packed into the goal tree, the agent can cope with many eventualities without communication with the server.

Since this platform inevitably increases the total size, the target device should have more memory resources than iAppli. We use cellular phones from au(KDDI) that have Java VMs based on J2ME (ezPlus) and the limit on the program size is 50 Kb.

The agent is serialized at the server and sent to the cellular phone by HTTP. Since ezPlus doesn't support Java RMI, we implemented the serialization mechanism for the basic Java objects and the goal tree.

We have to care about security issues of an agent that works on cellular phones. Java VMs on cellular phones have a sandbox model to restrict the access of Java applications, but there are still some possibilities that the harmful agent does inappropriate actions on a cellular phone. There are some ways to solve this problem 1) use authorized components or 2) limit the number of times an agent performs actions on a cellular phone. Due to space constraints, it isn't described here and we leave it to the future work.

5   Related Work

There are several mobile agent systems and ORBs for PDAs and cellular phones. In the SCARAB project[2], PDAProxy is used to implement an ORB on Palm

```
<?xml version=''1.0''?>
<pico-app
 name=''RadioP'' id=''radiop''
 version=''1.0''>
<agent-class>
 picoplangent.agent.radiop.RadioPAgent
</agent-class>
<iappli>
 <iappli-component>
   <predicate>putCnt</predicate>
   <argument>
    <type>int</type>
    <type>String</type>
   </argument>
</iappli>
<server>
 <server-component>
   <predicate>getGoogleQuery</predicate>
   <component-class>
    picoplangent.component.GoogleQueryMaker
   </component-class>
 </server-component>
</server>
</pico-app>
```

Fig. 8. Component Property File Example.

devices. The PDAProxy works like a proxy component of the picoPlangent system, but the communication between the PDAProxy and the Palm device is done by SMS (Short Message Service), and so the PDAProxy can't send complicated messages. The component that receives the message from the PDAProxy is called PDAGUI, which handles the GUI on Palm devices.

Ubiquitous Devices United[3] also has a feature to send notifications to cellular phones via SMS. CUES[4] realizes the remote control UI of embedded systems on cellular phones by WML (Wireless Markup Language) pages. These two systems apply mobile code techniques, but do not concern themselves with code migration to cellular phones.

The LEAP project[5] has implemented the FIPA platform on Java-enabled portable devices. On the LEAP platform, the agent can send an ACL message to another agent. The LEAP platform can be implemented with J2ME, but these target devices have much richer resources than the target devices of picoPlangent. The LEAP platform's implementations depend heavily on Java, but the picoPlangent platform can be implemented in other languages.

MobiAgent[6] is a mobile agent system implemented using J2ME. It uses an Agent Gateway to access the Voyager agent on the server. Agent Gateways do not have a function to move the agent from the server to the J2ME device.

MIA[7] is a mobile agent system using agent technology based on logic programming. The picoPlangent agent also uses the logic program at the planning component to create the agent's plan. The MIA agent mainly uses the logic program to provide information access at any time. The mobile agent on the portable device uses KQML to retrieve the information from the static agent on the server. The picoPlangent agent uses the planning component to create the plan to solve the user goal.

Jumon[8] is a mobile agent that works on ezPlus. This system emphasizes the ORB functions provided by Voyager. On the other hand, picoPlangent provides the goal tree to realize the flexible behavior of the agent.

6   Discussion and Future Work

picoPlangent helps realize an intelligent mobile agent system that works on devices with very limited resources. There are several Java VM implementations based on J2ME, but iAppli has an extremely severe memory limit. A JAR file downloaded to a cellular phone cannot be larger than 10K bytes.

The picoPlangent platform can be very small because its agent has a very simple lifecycle and the functions of the agent are separated from the platform as the components. On iAppli, the picoPlangent platform is about 4.6 Kb. On Palm devices, the picoPlangent platform written with GCC is about 6 Kb.

A simple agent's lifecycle also helps to port the system to other systems. The agent can be serialized in a suitable form according to the protocol that sends the agent between devices. The picoPlangent agent can be sent via RMI, SOAP, Hotsync, and the original protocol via HTTP.

Agent lifecycles implemented by the goal tree are very simple but are able to realize flexible action on portable devices. The main purpose of the goal tree is to use the planner's faculty on devices that do not have sufficient resources to use the planning component. The goal tree can manage the main plan and the alternative plans generated in the planning component. These plans are carried to the portable device with the agent. Even if the main plan fails, the agent can continue the process without the planner by using the alternative plan.

With the implementation on the iAppli platform, the proxy component on the server helps to reduce the platform size. However it also increases the frequency of communication between the server and the cellular phone because whenever the agent solves a goal, the proxy component communicates with a component in the cellular phone.

To reduce the amount of communication, the platform on cellular phones should implement functions to handle the agent's lifecycle. Fig. 9 represents the size of each subsystem on iAppli and the servlet. Since we assumed that class files are compressed to half the size by JAR, the developer can use 15.4 Kb for components.

On iAppli, the agent's lifecycle handler is placed on the servlet, and so a cellular phone and a server have to communicate each time an agent solves a goal. Each communication (receiving an invocation message and sending a result message) costs two packets(about 256bytes).

On ezPlus, the agent's lifecycle manager is placed on the cellular phone. The agent is created by the create message. This message includes the whole goal tree

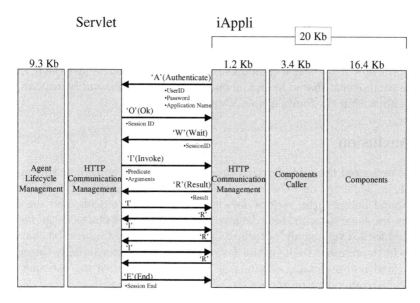

Fig. 9. Architecture on iAppli.

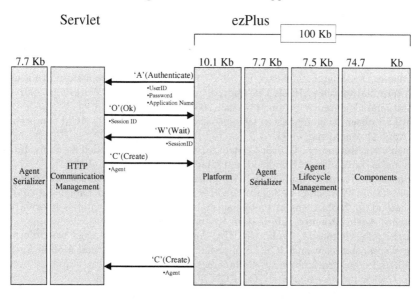

Fig. 10. Architecture on ezPlus.

structure, and the goal tree is handled by the agent's lifecycle manager. When the agent solves the migration goal, the agent is returned to the server. (Fig. 10)

Because the program size of components on cellular phones is limited, the developer should select the proper components to be placed on the cellular phone. Some components may be placed on the server, and the agent goes back to the server temporarily to use these components. The decision as to which components should be placed on the cellular phone affects the amount of communication and the response time. We plan to add a component rearrangement function to the agent. Agents with a rearrangement function will have a profiler that records how frequently a component is used. The agent decides the priority in which components should be placed on the cellular phone, and rearranges the components within the limits of the resources.

7   Conclusion

We have presented the architecture of picoPlangent and shown how this architecture is implemented on PCs, Palm devices and cellular phones. The agent can move around between the various devices with various protocols, and the user can share the same data on these devices. The picoPlangent platform can be implemented with a very small footprint, and the implementation can be changed easily to fit the resource limits of the device. The goal tree can simplify the agent lifecycle, and realize flexible action on a portable device with the assistance of the planning component on the server.

References

1. Ohsuga, A., Nagai, Y., Irie, Y., Hattori, M., and Honiden, S. :PLANGENT: An Approach to Making Mobile Agents Intelligent, IEEE Internet Computing, Vol. 1, No. 4, pp. 50–57, 1997. http://computer.org/internet/ic1997/w4050abs.htm
2. Ciminiera, L., Maggi, P., Sisto, R.: SCRAB: innovative services supporting user and terminal mobility, IEEE Distributed Computing System Workshop, 2001 International Conference on, pp. 487–493, 2001.
3. Kjetil Jacobsen, Dag Johansen: Ubiquitous devices united, 1999 ACM symposium on Applied computing, 1999.
4. Kangas, K., Roning, J.: CUES: Control for Ubiquitous Embedded Systems, International Symposium on Handheld and Ubiquitous Computing, 1999.
5. Bergenti, F., Poggi,A.: LEAP: A FIPA platform for handheld and mobile devices, International Workshop on Agent Theories, Architectures, and Languages, 2001.
6. Mahmoud,Q.: MobiAgent: A mobile agent-based approach to wireless information systems, Agent-Oriented Information Systems, pp. 87–90, 2001.
7. Beuster, G., Thomas,B., Wolff, C.: MIA: An ubiquitous multi-agent web information system, International ICSC Symposium on Multi-Agents and Mobile Agents in Virtual Organizations and E-Commerce, 2000.
8. http://www.jumon-agent.com/ OMRON SOFTWARE: Jumon.
9. http://www.nttdocomo.co.jp/english/p_s/i/java/ NTT DoCoMo: Java for i-mode.
10. H. Hayashi, K. Cho, A. Ohsuga: Mobile Agents and Logic Programming, IEEE International Conference on Mobile Agents, pp. 32–46, 2002.
11. H. Hayashi, K. Cho, A. Ohsuga: A New HTN Planning Framework for Agents in Dynamic Environments, International Workshop on Computational Logic and Multi-Agent Systems, 2004.
12. H. Hayashi, K. Cho, and A. Ohsuga: Speculative Computation and Action Execution in Multi-Agent Systems, ICLP Workshop on Computational Logic in Multi-Agent Systems, Electronic Notes in Theoretical Computer Science 70(5), 2002.

An Approach to Safe Continuous Planning

Gary Cleveland and Mike Barley

University of Auckland, New Zealand

Abstract. In this paper we discuss the "safe to act" problem, a problem associated with the safe interleaving of acting and planning. We also discuss previous research that is relevant to this problem. We then propose a specific search strategy for a general hierarchical plan-space planner that pushes portions of the emerging plan to become "execution ready" as quickly as possible. Finally, we discuss a property, critical serialisability, that is sufficient for a domain to possess in order for these portions to be "safely" executed.

1 Introduction

In this paper we discuss a problem associated with interleaving acting and planning, the "safe to act" problem. We also discuss previous research that is relevant to this problem. We then propose a specific search strategy for a general hierarchical plan-space planner that pushes portions of the emerging plan to become "execution ready" as quickly as possible. We also discuss a property, critical serialisability, that is sufficient for a domain to possess in order for these portions to be "safely" executed.

1.1 The "Safe to Act" Problem

Deliberative agents face a problem of knowing when to stop planning and when to start executing the plan. Often, it is neither desirable nor possible for the agent to defer acting until the entire plan has been created – there may not be enough information, or enough time, or the environment might be too volatile. So the agent must interleave its plan execution with its plan creation activities. However, the agent cannot just arbitrarily start executing its current partial plan. To do so is to risk the agent jeopardising its being able to achieve the rest of its goals – the so-called "painting oneself into a corner" effect where a partial solution can not be monotonically extended into an overall solution. We call this the "safe to act" problem: how should a deliberative agent interleave its plan execution and plan creation activities so that its actions do not jeopardise achieving the rest of its goals? Are there any formal criteria for when it is guaranteed to be safe for an agent to begin executing part of its plan?

One way to view the problem would be as a balance between deliberation and reaction. To be able to make the needed guarantees, the agent must plan at least some minimum amount. In many cases, the agent will otherwise wish to be as reactive as possible and execute the "next action" as soon as that action

M.W. Barley and N. Kasabov (Eds.): PRIMA 2004, LNAI 3371, pp. 57–66, 2005.

is determined and it is known that that action will not cause conflicts with later goals. Given an agent with this capability to execute planned steps as early as possible, one has a better handle on soft real-time issues. Similarly, greater planning efficiency may follow as a result of backtrack points being eliminated as actions are executed. Finally, this type of reassurance allows for a greater ability to guarantee the safety of the agent, the agent's goals, and the world at large. These three points – safety, efficiency, and real-time abilities – are the motivations behind this work.

One approach currently seen is that of hierarchical continuous planners, like Aspen [4]. However, there are currently no guarantees that their actions will not jeopardise their ability to solve the entire problem, e.g., that they won't paint themselves into a corner. At present, they rely solely upon the experience of the experts who represent the domain models through different levels of abstraction. Our research is interested in formulating the properties (sufficient for safe partial plan execution) that must be possessed by these abstraction levels, domain descriptions, and problem-solvers.

2   Related Research

As stated above, the problem being addressed is that of identifying points in the search where backtracking can be eliminated without affecting the solvability of the problem. This problem has been explored many times in the past. The core idea has been identifying planning islands which, in effect, decompose the goal into a sequence of simpler subgoals which can be achieved with no mutual threats. There has been two lines of attack. One line has been to employ levels of abstraction where the planner attempts to find a complete plan at a given level of abstraction before moving down to the next less abstract level. This is often called hierarchical planning. In hierarchical planning the abstraction levels recursively identify the planning islands. The other line of attack has been to find a sequence of subgoals which can be completely achieved in sequence and remain achieved without affecting the achievability of the remaining subgoals. This line of attack was called finding serialisable subgoals and was primarily pursued using totally ordered plan planners. Both lines are relevant to our own approach. We will first look at the research on serialisable subgoals and then at hierarchical planning and levels of abstraction.

2.1   Subgoal Independence and Serializability

Subgoal independence is defined by Korf [11] for subgoals having a set of operators partitioned into subsets such that each subset is relevant to only one subgoal. Clearly, one may solve each subgoal separately and, after creating a plan for one subgoal, the planner need never backtrack across it. Korf defines *subgoal serializability* for subgoals that can be ordered such that their plans do not threaten the preceding subgoals. Subgoal serializability can be thought of as a weak form of subgoal independence where subgoals can be solved sequentially, in smaller search spaces. Korf also found a weaker form of serialisability, called *block serializability*, where macro-operators are allowed to negate a preceding subgoal but then re-establish it before moving on to the next subgoal.

Ernst et al [8] described the concept of invariants and found ways of discovering them mechanically. Invariants provides the same forward motion through the problem space that serializability does. After achieving a subgoal, it is not necessary to consider backtracking to states that negate it.

The Remote Agent planner [2] is a recent example of a complex planner that used serialisable subgoals drastically reduce the size of its search space. According to Russell and Norvig [15] (page 407): "Taking advantage of the serialized ordering of goals, the Remote Agent planner was able to eliminate most of the search. This meant that it was fast enough to control the spacecraft in real time, something previously considered impossible."

2.2   Hierarchical Planning

Hierarchical planning lays out a search space through an abstraction hierarchy and attempts to solve a problem at a given level and only then advances to the next level of the hierarchy. Some hierarchical planners limit backtracking to within the current level and thus reducing search. Numerous systems have employed this approach in order to guide the search (and avoiding backtracking as much as possible). GPS [13], ABTWEAK [17], PRODIGY [9] have all used the technique successfully. A small number have also automatically generated those abstraction hierarchies to match the domains ([16,5]) or even the individual problems [9]. All of these systems that automatically generate the hierarchies, do so by drawing out the hierarchy through the preconditions of the domain's operators. Fink and Yang [7] describe a way to include the effects into the construction of the hierarchy in order to arrive at a finer-grained abstraction hierarchies.

2.3   Downward Refinability

Bacchus and Yang [3] defined the Downward Refinement Property (DRP) for abstraction hierarchies. The definition states that for abstraction hierarchies with this property, every abstract plan can be refined into a detailed plan. An important feature for our purposes is that these refinements can be found without backtracking across levels of the hierarchy – i.e., without needing to replan any of the established abstract plan. Bacchus and Yang show that planning problems can be more efficiently solved if their abstraction hierarchies have this property.

Knoblock, Tenenberg, and Yang [6] defined what consitutes a "good" abstraction. In this work, they defined the Monotonicity and Ordered Monotonicity Properties rather similarly to the DRP and with the same intent – to prune the search space and elliminate backtracking.

2.4   Other Related Research

There has also been work concerning *landmarks* [14] which resemble Melis' notion of island planning [12] in that they specifically work towards avoiding backtracking by identifying strong points in the search space. *Strong points* are important intermediate goal states that must be visited in most valid plans. Accordingly, landmark states provide important information regarding the reasonable goal orderings. They do not, however, work towards completely eliminating backtracking. In this case, one may not be able to completely avoid backtracking but should be able to greatly reduce it.

Knoblock's work of SAGE [10] delves into the world of tightly coupled planning and execution but with no real assurances that the plan being either constructed or acted upon does not carry negative consequences. This work takes a different tack of trying to spot and correct problems before they get too far out of hand.

3   Our Approach

Our objective is to push portions of the plan as quickly as possible towards being executable without jeopardising achieving the rest of the goals. In the next section, we will briefly describe what we think are components of a property that will guarantee the safeness of executing those portions of the partial plan. In the sections after that, we will describe our planner's architecture and how it pushes a portion of the plan quickly towards being executable.

3.1   Guaranteeing "Safeness to Act": Critical Serialisability

Serialisable subgoals allow us to plan for the first subgoal in the sequence, then execute that plan and still be guaranteed that we have not caused the rest of the subgoals to become unachievable. While there are important domains where experts know how to generate and serialise subgoals for certain problems, we suspect serialisability is too strong a property for general use. We do not believe that planners will usually be able to quickly and automatically generate useful serialisable subgoals for problems without looking at how those subgoals interact with each other.

In particular, serialisability says we can totally ignore how we are going to achieve the rest of the subgoals while we are working on how to achieve the current subgoal. This seems too strong an assumption. Instead, what we believe is more reasonable is that the planner should be able to make critical commitments about how we will achieve some of those other subgoals before we have totally committed to how we achieve the current subgoal. These commitments should then constrain how we achieve our current subgoal. This sounds similar to hierarchical planning.

We use an ABSTRIPS-style of abstraction and the definitions used in [3]. In this venue, hierarchical planning is about focusing on the different levels of critical decisions (commitments) in turn. Commitments are made concerning the current level of criticality before starting to consider what commitments to make about less critical decisions. These commitments then constrain what commitments can be made at lower levels. The Downward Refinement Property (DRP) states when the planner is guaranteed never to need to backtrack across levels of criticality in order to find a concrete solution. DRP is similar to the property we are seeking in that it eliminates backtracking across criticality levels. However, DRP only guarantees this when we move the entire plan down to lower criticality levels. Unfortunately, this would not allow us to execute any part of the plan until we have finished the entire plan.

We are in the process of formally defining a property, which we call *critical serialisability*, that is a synthesis of DRP and subgoal serialisability and which guarantees the safeness of executing the appropriate initial portion of the plan. Critical serialisability states that once a complete and correct plan is found at a given level of criticality, a step can be found in that plan which can be executed before any of the other steps, that we can then pursue making that step executable independently of the rest of the plan, and that this property holds recursively across the levels of criticality. We believe critical serialisability is weaker than serialisability but stronger than downward refinability.

Our planner will follow this procedure of finding a complete and correct plan at the highest criticality level, then finding a step that can be first to be executed, then focussing on making that step executable. To make the step executable, the agent will normally need to plan for steps that establish that step's preconditions, etc. This procedure will be recursively followed until we hit the least critical level and can start scheduling steps to be executed. When we select a step to be first made executable, there will be some causal links (as described in [15] p. 389) from the initial state to later steps. We must not introduce threats to these causal links while trying to make that step executable. The goals involved in these causal links, we will call *maintenance goals*. The goals involved in the causal links created at this level will be called *achievement goals*.

We will now try to make this planning process a little more concrete.

Figure 1 shows the situation after we have created a complete and correct plan at the highest criticality level. The figure shows I, the current initial state, G, the problem's goal, and two steps, *op1* and *op2*. The figure shows the causal links between the steps. We assume there are no additional ordering constraints.

Figure 2 shows the plan after we have expanded *op1* down to the next lower criticality level. The solid lines represent causal links created for the achievement goals at that criticality level. These are revokable at this level. The dashed lines represent the maintenance goals inherited from the higher criticality levels, threats to these cannot be introduced at this level. Assuming that this is the lowest criticality level then *op3* will executed followed by *op1* being executed.

Figure 3 shows the plan after the two steps have been executed and the current initial state has been updated to I'. Now *op2* is the next step to be made executable. The figure shows the expansion of that step to the next lower criticality level and the complete and correct plan created at that level.

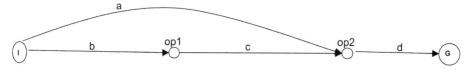

Fig. 1. Initial Abstract Plan.

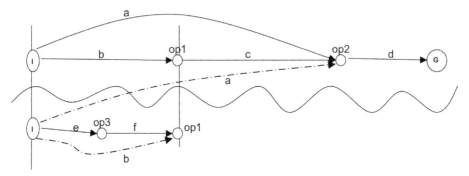

Fig. 2. 1st Detailed Subproblem Plan.

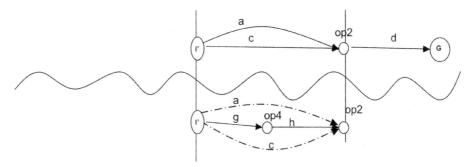

Fig. 3. 2nd Detailed Subproblem Plan.

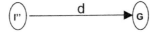

Fig. 4. Final Plan.

Figure 4 shows the plan after *op4* and *op2* have been executed and the current initial state has been updated to *I"*. We would now expand *G* down to the next lower criticality level (*G* might have goals at that next lower level which would need to be achieved). Assuming that there are no new goals at the lower levels and that the lower level is lowest level, then *I"* satisfies the preconditions of *G* and the planner is done.

3.2   Plans

Our planning algorithm uses pretty much the standard plan-space plan components. The planner has a current (partial) plan and an agenda. The plan has a "current state" pseudo-step which represents what the agent currently believes to be true about the world and a "goal" pseudo-step which represents what the agent desires to eventually be true . Plans are represented as a set of steps with ordering and (non)co-designation constraints and with causal links. One difference is that plans may also have one or more steps that are labelled as executable. An executable step must have all of its preconditions satisfied by the current state. When a step is executed its postconditions update the current state description and the step is removed from the plan.

The agenda describes what needs to be done in order to make the goal pseudo-step "executable" in the current state, i.e., to cause the current state to satisfy the problem's goal description. The agenda contains the following types of items:

- Achieve goal.
- Resolve threat.
- Expand step.
- Execute step.

Goals are simply preconditions of steps and have criticality levels associated with them. These criticality levels can be assumed to be the same as found in standard hierarchical planners. Specifically, criticality levels are assigned to partially instantiated goals, which we call critical goal patterns. If a goal unifies with more than one critical goal pattern, that goal assumes the criticality level of the most critical goal pattern it unifies with. A goal is *achieved* by creating a causal link from a step which has a postcondition that matches the goal to the step with that goal as a precondition.

Threats are to causal links and are steps which have either preconditions or effects that are inconsistent with the goal involved in that causal link. Threats are either necessary or possible. Necessary threats mean that the causal link is destroyed by that step. Possible threats are ones that might be resolved without necessarily destroying the causal link. The standard resolutions are to add either ordering or non-codesignation constraints.

Preconditions of a step are achieved in the order of their criticality. When the preconditions of a step have all been achieved at a certain criticality level, we can then start trying to achieve its next lower level of critical preconditions. We call this *expanding* the step and indicate that this should be done by adding an expand step item to the agenda.

When the planner determines both that a step can be executed in the current state and that it is safe to execute that step, then an execute step item is added to the agenda.

3.3   Determining Which Step Should Be Made Executable First: Distance to Execution

The notion of serialisable subgoals was developed during the classical period of totally-ordered plan planners, when planning order determined execution order. This meant that it was difficult, if not impossible, for a planner to dynamically determine which step should be first to be executed. Thus, the sequence of serialisable subgoals was normally given with the problem specification. However, the emergence of partially-ordered plan planners separated planning order from execution order. In partially-ordered plan planners, the planner can dynamically determine which step should be executed first. Our conjecture is that, for domain criticality levels which satisfy the critical serialisability criterion, the normal partially-ordered plan operations will identify those steps that, at the next lower level of criticality, can be planned for first and then executed without preventing the planner from being able to achieve the remaining goals.

Given a standard partially-ordered plan with its steps, causal links, order and (non-) co-designation constraints, there may be a number of steps which do not have any steps that necessarily precede them. How should the planner select which one to try to make executable first? Since our objective is to make some part of the plan executable as quickly as possible, we would like some estimate of the earliest we would be likely to be able to execute them. We call this estimated time, the *distance to execution* (DE). The DE of a step is best viewed as a guess of how many steps will be needed to make that step executable and is an extension of the idea of using a heuristic evaluation function to estimate how many steps will be need to be added to the current plan for it to solve the problem. However, here we are estimating for a given step how many steps will be needed to transform the initial state into one where that given step can be executed. So instead of estimating how many more steps need to be added to the plan so that it achieves all of the problem's goals, DE estimates how many more steps need to be added to the plan so that the current candidate first-to-execute step can be executed. Since the current plan may have causal links from the initial state to later steps, the DE is with respect to achieving the preconditions of the candidate step while not clobbering any of those existing causal links. The candidate with the lowest estimate is the one chosen to focus on making executable.

3.4   Simulating Hierarchical Planning via Agenda Selection

Unlike standard hierarchical planners, we do not have different plans at the different levels of abstraction. There is only one plan. Each agenda item is associated with a particular criticality level. The planner simulates hierarchical planning by only selecting agenda items from the current criticality level. For the moment, a depth-first strategy is employed where the planner selects only those agenda items with the current criticality level and whose DE measure is minimal. This strategy keeps the planner focused on the steps it believes can be expanded and safely executed the soonest.

4   Conclusions and Future Research

In this paper, we discussed the "safe to act" problem where an agent has to balance how much planning to do before it is safe to start executing any part of its current plan. We reviewed research relevant to this problem. In particular, we discussed the research that has been done on serialisable subgoals and on the downward refinement property for hierarchical planners. We then described a new approach to this problem that combines both of these lines of research. This approach involves a new planning strategy, which pushes portions of the plan to being executed before the rest of the problem has been completely solved.

We informally defined a property, critical serialisability, that specifies the type of abstraction hierarchy for which it is guaranteed that the planning strategy's early execution of actions will not cause the agent to become unable to achieve the rest of the problem's goals.

We are still in the very early stages of this research. Our next step is to implement a prototype hierarchical planner that uses our strategy to interleave its execution and planning activities on a simple domain. Our eventual target domain is the more complex RoboCup Rescue Simulation domain (url: http://www.rescuesystem.org/robocuprescue/).

Our early explorations have shown us that we will need to extend the least-commitment approach to planning to include the use of abstract actions. We have started work on this but have not incorporated it yet into our strategy. We expect this will be one of our first extensions to our prototype. An example of the need for this type of extension was shown to arise in the computation of the hierarchical distance to execution when the literal on(a,b) from the lowest level proved to be both a precondition for the goal step and also a hindrance to necessary operations at higher levels. This gives the metaplanning agent the choice among several ways to handle the conflict. As Knoblock treated the condition, we can graduate the level of the literal up to the higher level. This often has the effect of collapsing the hierarchy. The metaplanning agent may also choose to view the low level goal as "established" and treat it as a maintenance goal which brings forth a need for a form of "block serializability" and macro-operations. Another choice is to leave the low level goal as an agenda item (on the "To Do" list) and finally establish it with one of the last operations in the plan. This last choice is currently the one we favor but truly all of the solutions mentioned have serious faults and a comparison of various strategies needs to be made.

References

1. Robocup-rescue official web page. http://www.rescuesystem.org/robocuprescue/.
2. Nicola Muscettola Kanna Rajan Ari Jonsson, Paul Morris and Ben Smith. Planning in interplanetary space: Theory and practice. In *Proceedings of the 5th AIPS*, Breckenridge, CO, 2000.
3. Fahiem Bacchus and Qiang Yang. The downward refinement property. In *Proceedings of the Twelfth International Joint Conference on Artificial Intelligence*, pages 286–292, Sydney, Australia, 1991. IJCAI.
4. S. Chien, G. Rabideau, R. Knight, R. Sherwood, B. Engelhardt, D. Muts, T. Estlin, B. Smith, F. Fisher, T. Barrett, G. Stebbins, and D. Tran. Aspen – automating space mission operations using automated planning and scheduling, operations. In *International Conference on Space Operations (SpaceOps 2000)*, Toulouse, France, June 2000. European Space Agency.
5. Jens Christensen. *Automatic Abstraction in Planning*. PhD thesis, Department of Computer Science, Stanford University, 1991.
6. Josh D. Tenenberg Craig A. Knoblock and Qiang Yang. Characterizing abstraction hierarchies for planning. In *Proceedings of the Ninth International Conference on Artificial Intelligence*, pages 692–697, Anaheim, CA, 1991. AAAI.

7. Eugene Fink and Qiang Yang. Automatically abstracting the effects of operators. In J. Hendler, editor, *Artificial Intelligence Planning Systems: Proceedings of the First International Conference (AIPS92)*, pages 243–251, San Mateo, CA, 1992. AIPS, Morgan Kaufmann.

8. Raymond J. Hookway Richard A. Oyen George W. Ernst, Ranan B. Banerji and Donald E. Shaffer. Mechanical discovery of certain heuristics. Technical Report 1136-A, Case Western Reserve University, Cleveland, OH, January 1974.

9. Craig A. Knoblock. *Automatically Generating Abstractions for Problem Solving*. PhD thesis, School of Computer Science, Carnegie Mellon University, Pittsburgh, PA, 1991.

10. Craig A. Knoblock. Why plan generation and plan execution are inseparable. In *Proceedings of the AAAI Fall Symposium on Plan Execution*, Cambridge, MA, 1996.

11. Richard E. Korf. Planning as search: A quantitative approach. *Artificial Intelligence*, 33:65–88, 1987.

12. E. Melis and J.H. Siekmann. Knowledge-based proof planning. *Articial Intelligence*, 115(1), 1999.

13. Allen Newell and Herbert A. Simon. *Human Problem Solving*. Prentice-Hall, Englewood Cliffs, NJ, 1972.

14. J. Porteous and L. Sebastia. Extracting landmarks and ordering them for planning. In H. R. Arabnia, editor, *Proceedings of the International Conference on Artificial Intelligence*, Las Vegas, NV, 2001. ICAI.

15. Stuart Russell and Peter Norvig. *Artificial Intelligence: A Modern Approach*. Prentice Hall, 2nd edition, 2003.

16. Earl D. Sacerdoti. Planning in a hierarchy of abstraction spaces. 5(2):115–135, 1974.

17. Qiang Yang and Josh D. Tenenberg. Abtweak: Abstracting a nonlinear, least commitment planner. In *Proceedings of the Eighth National Conference on Artificial Intelligence*, pages 204–209, Boston MA, 1990. AAAI.

Modeling e-Procurement as Co-adaptive Matchmaking with Mutual Relevance Feedback

Reiko Hishiyama* and Toru Ishida

Department of Social Informatics, Kyoto University,
Yoshida honmachi, Sakyo-ku, Kyoto 606-8501, Japan
hishiyama@kuis.kyoto-u.ac.jp, ishida@i.kyoto-u.ac.jp

Abstract. This paper proposes a new e-procurement model for a large number of buyers and sellers interacting via the Internet. The goal of e-procurement is to create a satisfactory match between buyers' demand and sellers' supply. From our real-world experience, we view e-procurement as a process of negotiation to increase the matching quality of two corresponding specifications: one for buyers' demand and another for sellers' supply. To model scalable e-procurement, we propose a co-adaptive matchmaking mechanism using mutual relevance feedback. In order to understand the nature of the mechanism, we have developed two types of software agents, called e-buyers and e-sellers, to simulate human buyers and sellers. Multiagent simulation results show that the matching quality is incrementally improved if agents adaptively change their specifications. A realistic example is also provided to discuss how to extend our simulation to real-world e-procurement infrastructure.

1 Introduction

In the procurement process, buyers and sellers incrementally develop their mutual knowledge through making a deal between specifications of buyers' demand and sellers' supply. This paper proposes a computational model of an e-procurement process with a large number of buyers and sellers using the Internet. The motivation behind this research is as follows. There is a need for e-procurement infrastructure conducive to supporting complex dealings while taking into account a process for adjusting specifications. Procurement activities between buyers and sellers require negotiation to find ideal matching between demand and supply specifications, and there is a strong demand from industries to make procurement activities more open so that buyers have access to more sellers. This enables buyers to explore purchasing possibilities and to increase the transparency of their transactions. To develop e-procurement infrastructure, however, we need an e-procurement simulation model to help understand market performance when the market is scaled up.

According to literature on management science, in procurement, buyers and sellers share their purchasing and selling intentions through the exchange of information, expectations and perceptions. Their *creative collaboration* [20] leads to a successful deal. Landerous *et al.* [14] propose a buyer-seller partnership model that consists of five

---

* Reiko Hishiyama has been working in the procurement section of Japan Telecom Co., Ltd.

M.W. Barley and N. Kasabov (Eds.): PRIMA 2004, LNAI 3371, pp. 67–80, 2005.

stages: buyer's expectations, seller's perceptions, mutual understanding, performance activities, and collective actions. This model explains how the buyer-seller partnership mitigates troubles in the activity stage and increases long-term stability. Though several procurement models exist, no large-scale e-procurement model, which requires computational formalization, has been studied intensively in the field of management science.

In the multiagent research community, enormous effort has been spent on studying e-auction and e-negotiation mechanisms. In particular, theoretical mechanisms and computational models of multi-attribute negotiation [7] and multi-attribute auction [5, 3, 6] have been studied. This paper focuses on the "n:n" mutual selection process, unlike the multi-attribute negotiation, which generally focuses on the "1:1" negotiation process. In addition, the multi-attribute auction has been dealt with as a winner determination problem based on the optimization of utility functions from the view of economics. In contrast, we deal with matchmaking problems, where buyers and suppliers have heterogeneous utilities.

In real-world procurement, it is relatively common that the buyer shortlists suppliers through multilateral negotiation before auction, or negotiates with multiple suppliers to build a prototype of a new product after short-listing via auction [16].The overall procurement process is designed by combining auction and other selection methods. In the planning phase of procurement, the buyer does not have sufficient knowledge or information about the goods and services to give an announcement prepared for auction. Therefore, to make up for this lack, the buyers try to gather information and knowledge with making contact with the suppliers. These activities provide "clear focus and possibly a shortlist of qualified suppliers" [13]. On the other hand, the suppliers present several alternative proposals and look for the buyer's reaction, then conduct marketing activities to assess whether or not the buyer will be a profitable customer in the foreseeable future.

The goal of our research is to create a multiagent model for large-scale e-procurement, where buyers/sellers improve their demand/supply specifications interactively, while keeping their intentions (needs for the buyer and seeds for the supplier). To model a scalable e-procurement, we propose a *co-adaptive matchmaking mechanism* using *mutual relevance feedback*. To understand the nature of this mechanism, we have developed two types of software agents, called *e-buyers* and *e-sellers*, to simulate human buyers and sellers. Both agents present multiple attribute specifications to the market, and adjust their specifications to maximize their satisfaction. Simulation results show that the matching quality is incrementally improved if agents adaptively change their relevance feedback threshold. We have also applied this model to a procurement example in the real world, and clarified its performance and effectiveness in a practical domain.

2   Co-adaptive Matchmaking

When a buyer is willing to deal with sellers, he/she prescribes an RFI (Request for Information) and offers it to the market. However, it may not completely represent the buyer's purchasing intention. There are two reasons for this. First, the buyer does not know all products in the market. Sometimes, it is difficult for such a buyer to create RFIs to effectively distinguish a target product from others. Second, sellers may easily produce a new catalog if requested. There is also a chance that the buyer's RFI triggers sellers to create a new catalog, which may generate feedback to the original RFI. Thus, we view the buyer's and seller's demand/supply specifications as tentative representations of their intention. An interactive feedback process is necessary for both buyers and sellers to improve their specifications.

Fig. 1. Co-adaptive matchmaking.

In our model, each buyer delegates the desired specification to his/her *e-buyer*. The e-buyer retrieves sellers' specifications and supports the buyer to refine his/her specification incrementally. Similarly, each seller delegates the desired specification to his/her *e-seller*. The e-seller retrieves buyers' specifications and supports the seller to refine his/her specification. Figure 1 represents the e-procurement process model, which we call *co-adaptive matchmaking*.

The four elements of this model are listed in Table 1. *Demand intention* represents the buyer's intention to purchase, and *demand specification* is a description that expresses that demand intention to the market. Similarly, *supply intention* is the seller's intention to sell, and *supply specification* is a description that expresses that supply intention to the market. In short, we denote the buyer's and seller's intention as *retrieval intention* or *query*, and the buyer's and seller's specification as *retrieval specification* or *data*. We also denote a buyer and a seller as a *searcher*. Retrieval intention shows an abstract idea of goods/services that searchers want to find through negotiation, and is explicitly represented as retrieval specification. Searchers use their retrieval specification to search corresponding counterpart specifications, and the specifications that searchers find are called *retrieved specification*.

Table 1. Four elements in e-procurement.

element		definition
Buyer-side	Demand intention	Buyer's intention to purchase.
	Demand specification	Description that expresses demand intention to the market.
Seller-side	Supply intention	Sellers' intention to sell.
	Supply specification	Description that expresses supply intention to the market.

3   Mutual Relevance Feedback

3.1   Background

In this section, we implement co-adaptive matchmaking by using mutual relevance feedback. Relevance feedback [15] is one of the most popular query reformulation strategies, which automatically changes the set of query terms as well as the weights associated with those terms.

In term-weighting retrieval, a weight w_{ik} is associated with the index term t_k ($k = 1, \ldots, l$) of a document d_i ($i = 1, \ldots, n$), thus the subject of document i can be represented by l dimensional vectors $(w_{i1}, w_{i2}, \cdots, w_{il})^T$. The weight of an index term is, for instance, the product of its term frequency (TF), an occurrence frequency of the index term in a particular document, and its inverse document frequency (IDF), a factor which enhances the terms which appear in fewer documents. The query vector q_j is also represented by l dimensional vectors $(w_{j1}, w_{j2}, \cdots, w_{jl})^T$. This is called the *vector space model* [1]. The similarity between query q_j and document d_i is calculated by the cosine function of the query term-weight vector $(w_{j1}, w_{j2}, \cdots, w_{jl})^T$ and the document term-weight vector $(w_{i1}, w_{i2}, \cdots, w_{il})^T$, i.e.,

$$Similarity(q_j, d_i) = \frac{\sum_{k=1}^{l} w_{ik} w_{jk}}{\sqrt{\sum_{k=1}^{l} w_{ik}^2} \sqrt{\sum_{k=1}^{l} w_{jk}^2}} \tag{1}$$

When retrieving documents, this similarity value is compared to the pre-defined threshold: if the value exceeds the threshold, the document is retrieved.

In relevance feedback using the vector space model, the retrieved documents are further classified into relevant and irrelevant documents. Let D^+ be a set of relevant documents, where $d_1^+, \cdots, d_{|D^+|}^+$ are members of D^+, and let D^- be a set of irrelevance documents, where $d_1^-, \cdots, d_{|D^-|}^-$ are members of D^-. This classification is performed by humans. Then, the result of the classification leads to an improvement in the query term-weight vector: adjust the query term-weight vector toward the document term-weight vectors of relevant documents D^+ and away from the document term-weight vectors of irrelevant documents D^-. The adjusted query term-weight vector is given by,

$$\alpha \cdot q_j + \frac{\beta}{|D^+|} \sum_{i=1}^{|D^+|} d_i^+ - \frac{\gamma}{|D^-|} \sum_{i=1}^{|D^-|} d_i^- \qquad (2)$$

where α, β, and γ are appropriate constants. Generally, the relevant documents provide more important information than the irrelevant ones. Thus, the constant γ is usually smaller than the constant β.

3.2 Mechanism

In this paper, we apply relevance feedback to both buyers' and sellers' specifications. Figure 2 shows the matchmaking process among buyers and sellers. The intentions are explicitly written into specifications, which are to be enhanced through mutual relevance feedback. In the matchmaking process, the buyer's and seller's specifications are used as queries. At the same time, they are also data to be retrieved. In this paper, we assume that buyers' and sellers' intentions do not change in the course of procurement. This is because we are focusing on a short-term problem solving process in procurement; a long-term learning process will be discussed in later different paper. Rather, we assume these intentions are not clearly recognized by buyers or sellers at the beginning of procurement. Let $i(i = 1, \cdots, m)$ be buyers and $j(j = 1, \cdots, n)$ be sellers. Let $\hat{b}_i$ be buyer i's demand intention, and b_i be buyer i's demand specification, $\hat{s}_j$ be seller j's supply intention, and s_j be seller j's supply specification. $\hat{b}_i$, b_i, $\hat{s}_j$ and s_j represent the attribute value of goods or services in the range of [0, 1]. We define co-adaptive matchmaking as a mutual selection process in which demand specifications are selected by buyers, while supply specifications are selected by sellers. As discussed in Section 3.1, let w_{ik} be the weight associated with attribute t_k $(k = 1, \ldots, l)$ of the specification d_i $(i = 1, \ldots, n)$. Then, each specification is represented by a l dimensional attribute-weight vector $(w_{i1}, w_{i2}, \cdots, w_{il})^T$. Next, let us consider the case of a human buyer delegating demand specification b_i to his/her e-buyer. The delegation is carried out based on his/her demand intention. The e-buyer openly expresses the demand specification, and retrieves the set of supply specifications S from the market. Let S_{b_i} be the result of the retrieval, that is, $S_{b_i} = \{s | Similarity(b_i, s) > \theta, s \in S\}$, where θ is

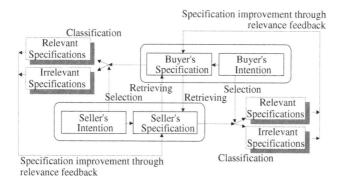

Fig. 2. Co-adaptive matchmaking process using mutual relevance feedback.

a selection threshold of similarity in specification retrieval. In the same way, a human seller delegates supply specification s_j to his/her e-seller. The delegation is carried out based on his/her supply intention. The e-seller subsequently openly expresses the supply specification, and retrieves the set of demand specifications B from the market. Let B_{s_j} be the result of the retrieval, that is, $B_{s_j} = \{b | Similarity(s_j, b) > \theta, b \in B\}$.

A set of the retrieved supply specifications, compiled by the e-buyer, is examined by the human buyer, and classified into relevant specifications $S_{b_i}^+$ and irrelevant specifications $S_{b_i}^-$. The e-buyer then computes the relevance feedback using $S_{b_i}^+$ and $S_{b_i}^-$ to refine the original demand specification. Similarly, a set of retrieved demand specifications, compiled by the e-seller, is examined by the human seller, and classified into relevant specifications $B_{s_j}^+$ and irrelevant specifications $B_{s_j}^-$. Then the e-seller computes relevance feedback using $B_{s_j}^+$ and $B_{s_j}^-$ to refine the original supply specification.

Mutual relevance feedback is very different to traditional information retrieval. In information retrieval, query term-weight vectors can be expanded but document term-weight vectors are always fixed. In this model, however, both buyers' and sellers' attribute-weight vectors can change. Relevance feedback is applied at both sides, though to the best of our knowledge, no studies have been conducted where relevance feedback is mutually applied. The performance of mutual relevance feedback can be evaluated by comparing retrieval intentions and specifications, but it is necessary to conduct simulations to determine how this co-adaptive process works in various situations.

4   Multiagent Simulation

4.1   Setting

In order to examine the behavior of co-adaptive matchmaking, we have implemented a multiagent simulator. To simulate human buyers and suppliers, we extend e-buyers and e-sellers so that they can distinguish relevant and irrelevant specifications. Figure 3 illustrates the relevance feedback cycle of e-buyers. We assume that demand intentions, which are usually determined by purchasing planners, can also be represented by attribute-weight vectors. Demand specifications, on the other hand, are often provided by operational buyers. As in Figure 3, the e-buyer comprises two main components: a *search and selection module* and a *relevance feedback module*. Note that the relevance feedback module is for simulating the behavior of human buyers. The search and selection module retrieves supply specifications based on the selection threshold θ, while the relevance feedback module classifies the selected specifications into relevant and irrelevant specifications based on the feedback threshold φ. That is, a set of relevant supplier specifications is represented by $S_{b_i}^+ = \{s | Similarity(\hat{b}_i, s) > \varphi, s \in S_{b_i}\}$, where φ is a feedback threshold of similarity. The same computational process is applied to e-sellers. (In the case of e-seller, a set of relevant demand specifications is represented by $B_{s_j}^+ = \{b | Similarity(\hat{s}_j, b) > \varphi, b \in B_{s_j}\}$.) The threshold θ represents the performance of information retrieval. We use a fixed value for θ (0.5 in this simulation), while the threshold φ represents the procurement allowance. We implement two types of agents with φ as follows:

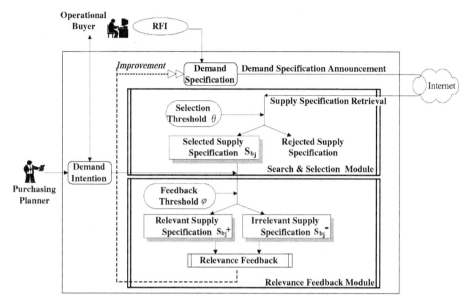

Fig. 3. Relevance feedback cycle of e-buyers.

Fixed Agent. The allowance φ is fixed (0.5 in this simulation). If the similarity exceeds the threshold, the specification is relevant, and if not, it is classified into irrelevant specifications.

Adaptive Agent. The allowance φ adaptively changes according to the market status. The threshold is set to the average similarity between the retrieval specification and all the selected specifications. The threshold φ for the buyer's classification is computed as follows.

$$\varphi = \frac{\sum\limits_{s \in S_{b_i}} Similarity(\hat{b}_i, s)}{|S_{b_i}|} \tag{3}$$

If the similarity exceeds φ, the specification is relevant, and if not, it is classified into irrelevant specifications.

The simulation settings are as follows. The number of buyers is 10 and the number of sellers is 100. The intention of each buyer and seller is initially represented by a five-dimensional binary random vector, which means there are five attributes for each item (i.e. good/service). Each initial value of the buyer's and seller's specifications is also defined by a five-dimensional binary random vector.

4.2   Result

The simulation results are shown in Figures 4, 5 and 6[1]. Figure 4 shows a comparison of the average similarity between retrieval intention and retrieval specification. The results

---

[1] Some agents remain at zero similarity, simply because the binary-vector dimension is small (five in this case).

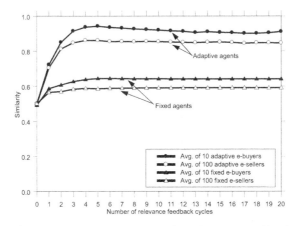

Fig. 4. Time-series similarity between intentions and specifications.

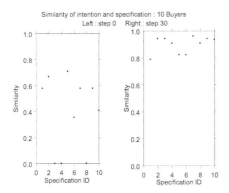 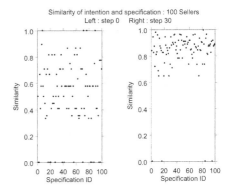

Fig. 5. Similarity distribution between intentions and specifications (10 buyers).

Fig. 6. Similarity distribution between intentions and specifications (100 sellers).

were obtained by averaging over 50 runs. The x-axis represents the number of relevance feedback cycles illustrated in Fig. 3, while the y-axis represents the average similarity between retrieval intentions and corresponding retrieval specifications. In the case of fixed agents, the similarity between intentions and specifications is not sufficient for successful matchmaking because the retrieval specifications cannot appropriately reflect buyers' or sellers' intentions. Conversely, in the case of adaptive agents, the result is satisfactory. The similarity between intentions and specifications is greatly improved in comparison to the case of fixed agents. Interestingly, in both cases, the average similarity among buyers is much higher than that among sellers, which means that a large population of counterparts provides a greater chance of retrieving a better specification. This shows that co-adaptive matchmaking is scalable: a large, open market can provide a better solution to agents.

Figures 5 and 6 display a similarity distribution between intentions and specifications. Figure 5 shows the similarity distribution of 10 buyers, and Fig. 6 shows the case

Criteria	Importance Weight		Vendor Proposal			Scoring		
Technical specifications			Vendor A	Vendor B	Vendor C	Vendor A	Vendor B	Vendor C
First copy time : sec.	10		3.2	3.3	3.4	10.00	5.00	0.00
Copying speed : PPM	10		81.0	85.0	90.0	0.00	4.44	10.00
Full dimensions : W	5		1,401	1,463	1,202	1.19	0.00	5.00
Full dimensions : D	5		777	865	858	5.00	0.00	0.37
Other conditions								
On-site service delivery	20		3H	7H	3H	20.00	0.00	20.00
Cost estimation			33,554	38,714	33,002	49.88	0.00	50.00
Delivery charge	50		35,000	0	45,000			
Performance charge			20,772	28,980	21,276			
Designated leasing company	No		Yes	Group businesses	No			
						86.07	9.44	85.37

Fig. 7. Example of vendor proposal analysis in real business world.

Table 2. Improvement in specification #4[2].

Feedback Cycle	$w1$	$w2$	$w3$	$w4$	$w5$	Similarity
Intention	0.333	0.333	0.667	0	1	$--$
0	0.8	0.8	0.0	0.0	0.0	0.3652
1	0.831	1	0.315	0	0.611	0.7538
2	0.657	0.874	0.67	0	1	0.9322
3	0.479	0.645	0.648	0	1	0.9738
4	0.378	0.616	0.661	0	1	0.9806
5	0.255	0.563	0.572	0	1	0.9800
6	0.547	0.489	0.502	0	1	0.9727

of 100 sellers. Each figure presents the initial state (left) and the final state after 30 relevance feedback cycles (right), clearly showing that mutual relevance feedback largely increases similarities in both cases. The specification is improved with respect to the humans' intention, which is not clearly recognized at the beginning of procurement.

5   Realistic Experiment

5.1   Setting

We applied co-adaptive matchmaking to a real-world procurement example. We consider a weighted point method to evaluate the specifications, and to ensure transparency (i.e. fairness) and objectivity in the selection process, the evaluation method weights the specifications in order of importance. This widely-used method is known as a *seller rating process*. In previous work, Forker and Lanson [8] and Thompson [19] also used weighted point models. In many cases, quantitative and qualitative information is mixed in the sellers' specifications; to rate each specification, all information is required to be

---

[2] Vector attributes are standardized.

Table 3. Best matching candidates for intention #4.

Ranking	Spec No.($\hat{s}_i$)	$w1$	$w2$	$w3$	$w4$	$w5$	Sim.($\hat{b}_4 \cdot \hat{s}_i$)
1	20	0.2	0.4	0.6	0.2	0.8	0.974
2	29	0.2	0.4	0.8	0.4	1.0	0.949
3	81	0.8	0.4	0.6	0.0	1.0	0.948
4	62	0.6	0.2	0.8	0.2	0.8	0.945
5	8	0.6	0.6	1.0	0.4	1.0	0.943
6	33	0.6	0.2	0.4	0.2	0.8	0.927
7	99	0.6	0.6	0.4	0.0	0.8	0.921
8	10	0.0	0.4	0.4	0.2	0.6	0.913
9	31	0.8	0.6	0.6	0.0	0.8	0.913
10	96	0.8	0.8	0.8	0.0	0.8	0.904

quantified. Figure 7 shows a typical example of purchasing decision employing the weighted point method in a real business process. When mapping a real world problem, such as is shown in Figure 7, onto the simulation, the following points should be considered: 1) Not only for achieving the match of demand specification and supply specification, we should calculate its utility. Goods/services are originally represented with a pair of an attribute and its value, for example, (Copying speed, 81.0ppm), (Designated leasing company, No), and buyers/suppliers have heterogeneous utilities. In section 4, we presented the value in the range of [0,1]. However, the similarity calculation is not better using the discrete data such as designated leasing company. In case of procurement of the copying speed, the speed does not need to be just 81.0ppm; it is better to have faster copying speed. Therefore, to calculate the coincidence level between the demand specification and the supply specification is not sufficient for this type of mapping; the degree of buyer's/supplier's satisfaction should be calculated from the (attribute) value of the demand specification and the supply specification. For example, when a buyer evaluates a supplier's specification, the degree of satisfaction for the (attribute) value that composes the supply specification is evaluated by utility. 2) The satisfaction is important for some attributes. However, for other some attributes, it may be less important. It is necessary to define the degree of importance from the both the buyer's and the supplier's viewpoints. The overall utility is calculated by adding up each utility of attribute value that is multiplied by the degree of importance.

Formula (1), which is the similarity calculation used for the relevance feedback, can be replaced by this overall utility calculation. To justify the formulation of the relevance feedback, the utility function should be a monotone increasing or decreasing function.

In the experiment we conduct, the settings are as follows. Each e-buyer and e-seller takes a five-dimensional vector for its intention and specification, and each of these vectors contains significance attribute value such as (First copy time, Copying speed, Wide, Depth, Cost estimation), encoded into an integer value from 0 to 1. If the demand intention is (0.8, 0.6, 0.6, 0.2, 0.2), and the selected supply specification is (0.4, 0.6, 0.2, 0.2, 0.2), then the similarity between the intention and specification is 0.917, which is very high. On the contrary, if the demand intention is (0.6, 0.2, 0.4, 1.0, 0.2), and the selected supply specification is (0.4, 0.8, 0.6, 0.2, 1.0), the similarity is 0.554, which is very low. The buyer's goal in matchmaking is to retrieve supply specifications as similar as possible to the demand intention.

Table 4. Time-series similarity between a buyer's intention and selected sellers' specifications[3].

Ranking	Number of relevance feedback cycles 1 Spec. Sim. (a)		2 Spec. Sim.		3 Spec. Sim.		4 Spec. Sim.		5 Spce. Sim.		6 Spec. Sim. (b)		Similarity 1 Sim. (a)	6 Sim. (b)	Improve-ment
1	100	0.924	88	0.963	*20	0.953	*81	0.979	*62	0.998	*62	0.953	0.924	0.953	3.146
2	49	0.915	66	0.957	51	0.950	*20	0.965	84	0.985	1	0.950	0.915	0.950	3.831
3	91	0.915	15	0.943	88	0.945	13	0.963	48	0.977	*81	0.941	0.915	0.941	2.840
4	45	0.906	32	0.939	*62	0.926	*62	0.961	*20	0.948	35	0.939	0.906	0.939	3.727
5	57	0.893	100	0.937	1	0.920	51	0.951	13	0.946	13	0.918	0.893	0.918	2.832
6	19	0.885	89	0.924	6	0.914	1	0.947	51	0.944	*20	0.917	0.885	0.917	3.602
7	23	0.877	6	0.911	32	0.914	*99	0.920	1	0.937	*96	0.911	0.877	0.911	3.967
8	41	0.873	91	0.895	5	0.912	84	0.916	*99	0.930	51	0.910	0.873	0.910	4.243
9	59	0.854	45	0.889	22	0.905	94	0.909	94	0.926	*99	0.909	0.854	0.909	6.498
10	18	0.852	2	0.885	15	0.897	*10	0.882	95	0.902	*31	0.905	0.852	0.905	6.178
11	*20	0.835	19	0.884	14	0.891	66	0.871	35	0.898	84	0.878	0.835	0.878	5.130
12	51	0.829	41	0.883	64	0.878	76	0.866	*8	0.893	*8	0.873	0.829	0.873	5.371
13	92	0.808	57	0.882	67	0.867	73	0.865	73	0.884	*10	0.872	0.808	0.872	7.885
14	97	0.807	74	0.872	*99	0.866	17	0.859	*10	0.875	52	0.872	0.807	0.872	7.974
15	*62	0.807	49	0.868	28	0.863	5	0.846	*96	0.862	*33	0.871	0.807	0.871	7.911
Number of satisfying specifications	2		0		3		5		6		9				

5.2   Result

Table 2 analyzes the negotiation process of buyer No. 4 (demand intention $\hat{b}_4$ =(0.2, 0.2, 0.4, 0.0, 0.6) and demand specification b_4 =(0.8, 0.8, 0.0, 0.0, 0.0)) in which the similarity between intention $\hat{b}_i$ and specification b_i is lower than other matching candidates at the beginning of procurement. In this example, attribute weight $w5$ is considered important, whereas $w4$ is not. The iterations show how the e-buyer's demand specification has been improved. The similarity between the demand intention and selected supply specifications increases step by step, and eventually arrives at a satisfactory close.

Table 3 shows best matching candidates for the demand intention of buyer No. 4, i.e., the table lists a similarity ranking of supply intentions for the demand intention of buyer No. 4. Table 4 shows a similarity ranking of the top 15 supply specifications for the demand intention of buyer No. 4, clearly indicating that the similarity increases at each cycle. The precise ranking changes at every cycle because of the change in market status. However, specifications with high similarity scores always stay in the list. The three rightmost columns of Table 4 show similarities before and after the repeated relevance feedback. Note that the lower the ranking, the greater the improvement. After six cycles of mutual relevance feedback, Table 4 includes nine out of ten best-matching candidates (seller's supply intentions) in Table 3. This fact supports the applicability of co-adaptive matchmaking in a procurement domain. Figure 8 displays similarities between buyer No. 4's intention and selected supply specifications. The average similarity

---

[3] The selected seller's specification marked with an asterisk (*) indicates that the specification is one of the best matching candidates; the corresponding seller's supply intention appears in Table 3.

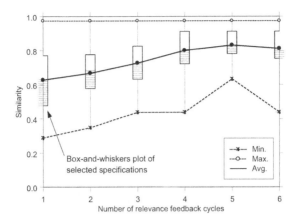

Fig. 8. Similarity between the buyer's intention and selected sellers' specifications.

of all the selected supply specifications increases; in practice, however, a few specifications with low similarity are still selected. To exclude low similarity specifications, it is reasonable to recommend the top five or so specifications. The human buyer, then, selects a few from the recommended list based on his/her purchasing knowledge. Thus, a combination of the human knowledge and co-adaptive matchmaking can offer a better way of enhancing the quality of e-procurement.

6   Related Work

A number of research projects have focused on autonomous agent technology for B2B e-commerce applications [11]. Our research was inspired by agent-mediated e-commerce systems with brokering, matchmaking, and bilateral negotiation. For example, MARI [18] was proposed as an agent-based intermediary architecture capable of supporting multiple sellers and buyers within a multiple product domain. MARI builds upon multi-attribute utility theory formulation, as introduced in Tete-a-Tete [9].

This paper also relates to matchmaking among profiles, which are mostly referred to as agent service descriptions. Kuokka and Harada [12] presented two matchmaking systems: COINS and SHADE. The former is based on free text matchmaking using TF-IDF. The latter uses a subset of KIF and a structured logic text representation called MAX. A more recent service broker-based information system is InfoSleuth [2]. They adopt *constrains matching*, which satisfies a user query with data constraints. Sycara *et al.* developed LARKS [17] for advertising, requesting, and matchmaking. LARKS performs both syntactic and semantic matchings. Veit *et al.* developed GRAPPA [21], whose matchmaking hosts an extensive collection of predefined profile schemas and distance functions based on a cosine similarity measure. We inherit the basic ideas of matchmaking from previous work to create a new co-adaptive matchmaking model.

In the context of e-auctions, we confirm that our system links to a special form of auction in which there are many kinds of goods to sell, and in which bidders can bid on combinations of items. Several multiple-attribute algorithms and protocols have been developed [4, 11].

He *et al.* [10] surveyed various e-commerce research projects, and pointed out that more advanced services (e.g. collaboration with other brokers) should emerge in order to provide more support to buyers and sellers involved in transactions. We think co-adaptive matchmaking will be the first step towards emerging long-term collaboration with other brokers through repeated negotiation.

7   Conclusions

In this paper, we proposed a multiagent model for a large-scale e-procurement: *co-adaptive matchmaking using mutual relevance feedback*. Our contribution is three-fold.

First, we studied cases of procurement in the real business world and proposed a co-adaptive matchmaking process in a simulation model of e-procurement using the Internet. Mutual relevance feedback is applied for modeling the negotiations between buyers and sellers to improve their demand/supply specifications. Second, to simulate human buyers and sellers, we implemented a simulation for e-buyers and e-sellers to analyze the behavior of this model. The simulation result showed that the matching quality is incrementally improved if both buyers' and sellers' adaptively change their relevance feedback threshold. Finally, we conducted realistic experiments in the context of real-world procurement activities, and confirm that co-adaptive agents are able to find desired specifications through repeated negotiation.The e-buyers/e-suppliers showed superior performance in handling transactions, monitoring the main features of products that are widely needed in the market, and screening the specifications to find the best.

This paper shows the effectiveness of co-adaptive matchmaking for *model* a large-scale e-procurement on the Internet. However, we still require an effective and efficient procurement infrastructure that actually *plays* a practical role in human users affording a diversity of reasoning. In order to handle transactions for goods/services with a large number of attributes from several hundred traders, we need software agents that act on behalf of human buyers or sellers. To extend our simulation model to real-world e-procurement infrastructure, software agents should be capable of estimating human intentions. The next step in this research, entails a plan to embed co-adaptive agents in actual e-procurement processes so as to enhance collaboration between human buyers and sellers.

References

1. Baeza-Yates, R. and Ribeiro-Neto, B.: Modern Information Retrieval, Addison Wesley (1999).
2. Bayardo, R., et al.: Infosleuth: Agent-based Semantic Integration of Information in Open and Dynamic Environments. In *ACM SIGMOD Conf. on Management of Data* , pp. 195–206 (1997).
3. Bichler, M., Kalagnanam, J.: Bidding Languages and Winner Determination in Multi-Attribute Auctions. *IBM Research Report*, RC22478, W0206-018 (2002).
4. Bichler, M. : An Experimental Analysis of Multi-attribute Auctions, *Decision Support Systems*, Vol. 29, No. 3, pp. 249–268 (2000).
5. Che, Y.K.: Design Competition Through Multidimensional Auctions, *RAND Journal of Economics* , Vol. 24, No. 4, pp. 668–680 (1993).

6. David, E., Azoulay-Schwartz, R. and Kraus, S.: Protocols and strategies for automated multi-attribute auctions, *Proceedings of the first international joint conference on Autonomous agents and multiagent systems (AAMAS-2002)* , pp. 77–85 (2002).

7. Faratin, P., Sierra, C. and Jennings, N.R.: Using Similarity Criteria to Make Issue Trade-offs in Automated Negotiations, *Artificial Intelligence* , Vol. 142, No. 2, pp. 205–237 (2002).

8. Forker, L.B. and Janson, R.L.: Ethical Practices in Purchasing, *Journal of Purchasing and Materials Management* , Vol. 26, No. 1, pp. 19–26 (1990).

9. Guttman, R.H. and Maes, P.: Agent-Mediated Integrative Negotiation for Retail Electronic Commerce, *Proceedings of the Workshop on Agent Mediated Electronic Trading* (1998).

10. He, M., Jennings, N.R. and Leung, H.F.: On Agent-Mediated Electronic Commerce, *IEEE Transactions on knowledge and data engineering*, Vol. 15, No. 4, pp. 985–1003 (2003)

11. Jennings, N.R., Norman, T.J., Faratin, P., O'Brian, P. and Odgers, B.: Autonomous agents for business process management, *Journal of Applied Artificial Intelligence* , Vol. 14, No. 2, pp. 145–189 (2000).

12. Kuokka, D. and Harada, L.: Supporting Information Retrieval via Matchmaking. Working Notes 1995 AAAI Spring Symposium on Information Gathering in Heterogeneous, Distributed Environments, Technical Report SS-95-08, AAAI Press (1995).

13. Laseter, T.: Balanced Sourcing :Cooperation and Competition in Supplier Relationships, Jossey-Bass Pulishers (1995).

14. Landeros, R., Reck, R. and Plank, E.: Maintaining Buyer-Supplier Partnership, *International Journal of Purchasing and Materials Management* , Vol. 31, No. 3, pp. 3–11 (1995).

15. Salton, G.: The SMART Retrieval System – Experiments in Automatic Document Processing, Prentice Hall (1971).

16. Samtani, G.: B2B Integration – A Practical Guide to Collaborative E-commerce, Imperial College Press (2002).

17. Sycara, K., Widoff, S., Klusch, M. and Lu, J.: LARKS: Dynamic Matchmaking Among Heterogeneous Software Agents in Cyberspace, *Autonomous Agents and Multi-Agent Systems*, Vol. 5, pp. 173–203 (2002).

18. Tewari, G. and Maes, P.: Design and Implementation of an Agent-Based Intermediary Infrastructure for Electronic Markets, *Proceedings of the 2nd ACM conference on Electronic commerce*, pp. 86–94 (2000).

19. Thompson, K.N.: Scaling Evaluative Criteria and Supplier Performance Estimates in Weighted Point Prepurchase Decision Models, *International Journal of Purchasing and Materials Management* , Vol. 27, No. 1, pp. 27–36 (1991).

20. Tully, S.: Purchasing's New Muscle, *Fortune* , February 20, pp. 75–83 (1995).

21. Veit, D., Müller, J.P. and Weinhardt, C.: Multidimensional Matchmaking for Electronic Markets, *Journal of Applied Artificial Intelligence* , Vol. 16, No. 9-10, pp. 853–869 (2002).

Price Determination and Profit Sharing for Bidding Groups in Agent-Mediated Auctions

Ming-Chih Hsu and Von-Wun Soo

Department of Computer Science, National Tsing Hua University, Hsin Chu, Taiwan 30043
{scat,soo}@cs.nthu.edu.tw

Abstract. It is a common behavior that a group of rational agents cooperate together as a bidder/seller to bid in an auction. How to determine the group bidding price and how to share the profit among the members in a group has been problems that are not studied thoroughly. In time-critical auctions, the problem is getting more complicated since the group has to decide new bidding prices within time limits. Conventional approaches used a centralized mechanism to assign profit share to each bidding agent in the group that usually lead to negative profit of individual bidding agent. We propose a distributed approach called Z-process that allows individual bidding agents to declare their compromised profit share based on their rationalities, and determines the group bidding prices simultaneously. We show that in Z-process there exists a dominant strategy for rational agents that can let them obtain maximum profit. We can also show that the compromised profit of each individual bidding agent by Z-process satisfies each agent's rationality.

1 Introduction

Auctions play important roles in human economics. Traditionally, buyers and sellers use many kinds of auctions to trade goods ranging from fishes to valuable antiques. Nowadays, auction mechanisms have been used to schedule tasks, find delivery route and allocate resources [1,2,3,4].

In micro-economics, different auction types, basic theorems and individual buyer/seller behavior analysis have been investigated in great depth [5,6].

Auctions can be considered as a market game of multiple agents. Each agent represents either a buyer or a seller. Of course in some settings an agent can be both a buyer and a seller. Although there are basically four kinds of auctions, the above settings still holds. In other words, we have a market game with all participants as rational agents. With this assumption, the dominant strategy, bidding price and even expected profit can be analyzed according to micro-economics.

However, situations in real life are becoming more complex. We can find cases where multiple agents collude together as one bidder or buyer group and bid in auctions. Companies of different capabilities join together as a coalition to bid for a government contract. Buyers of different needs join together to bid for a bunch of goods in order to get a better deal.

There are several issues about group bidding. In [7,8], the problem of how groups (or coalitions) are formed is discussed. Various techniques are proposed to cope with this problem such as negotiation [9], combinatorial auction [7,8], and others [10].

M.W. Barley and N. Kasabov (Eds.): PRIMA 2004, LNAI 3371, pp. 81–91, 2005.

Another problem arises after groups (or coalitions) are formed. How should the resource/profit/cost be distributed among the members of the group? What are the criteria for distributing resource/profit/cost? There are also works such as resource sharing [11,12], surplus/cost sharing [13,14] which are related to these problems.

As the importance of the rationality of individual bidders is being addressed, distributed solutions of the above problems are proposed [15].

In this work we focus on the problem of how to determine prices and share profits for group bidding using individual agent rationality. We don't address how the bidding group is formed. For example, if a group of companies (all the companies in the group are necessary) cooperate together to bid for a government contract in an English auction, then the problem of how these companies find each other belongs to the problem domain of group (coalition) formation. The decision of the bidding prices of the group can be solved using resource sharing or surplus/cost sharing methods (which directly assigns a price share to each company). But directly assigning price shares to companies sometimes lead to negative profits. We propose an approach which allows individual company to decide its own price, therefore each company gets positive profit. This approach also fulfills the requirement of English auctions that new bids must be placed within a certain time constraint.

We want to answer the following questions: How a bidding group determine its bidding prices in a multi-round auction (for example: English auction)? Is it possible that a feasible bidding price be generated within the time bound of a multi-round auction? What is the best strategy for a rational agent to bid in a bidding group? What is the expected group price when using our approach?

In this paper, we propose a mechanism called Z-process (ZP) that allows multiple rational agents to bid as a bidding group in an auction. In Z-process, we design a group pricing and profit sharing mechanism. Using this mechanism a bidding group can determine the optimal bidding prices in reverse English auctions and simultaneous derives the profit share for each member agent.

This work is organized as follows. In section 2, the terms and definitions used in the work are defined. In section 3, the algorithm of the Z-process is described. In section 4, the proof of properties of Z-process is mentioned. Finally, the applications of Z-process, discussion and conclusion are made in the fifth and sixth section respectively.

2   Terms and Definitions Used in Z-Process

We first define the terms used in this work (illustrated in Fig.1). Then the mechanism of the Z-process is described.

2.1   The Auction Scheme

We use a reverse English auction to demonstrate how Z-process works. In our reverse English auction setting there is a customer who wants to buy a service, so he opens an auction to have all possible service providers bid for his contract. The bidders (which are also sellers) in this auction are the service providers. The customer specifies his requirements of the service and the bidders bid the contract with the price of their service. The contract is given to the bidder with the lowest price.

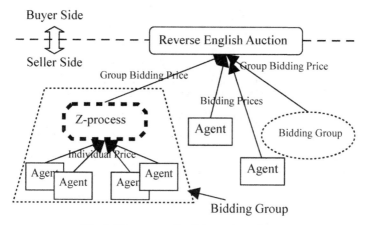

Fig. 1. The reverse English auction scheme

2.2 The Reservation Price

The reservation price of a service provided by an agent is defined by the following statements. *If a service is sold at its reservation price, the service providing agent gains zero profit. If a service is sold at a price lower than the reservation price, the service providing agent gets negative profit, and vice versa.* So a rational service providing agent will refuse to sell its service with a price under its reservation price to avoid negative profit. However, the reservation price of a service is only known by the service providing agent itself.

2.3 Bidding Group and Bidding Agents

A bidding agent is an agent who provides a certain type of service and knows how to bid in an auction. Each bidding agent knows the reservation price of its service and will try to maximize its profit by selling its service at a high price.

In some situations a single agent's service cannot fulfill buyers' requirements, so multiple service providing agents must cooperate together to bid for contracts. A bidding group consists of a set of bidding agents who cooperate together to provide an integrated service to win a contract in the auction. We assume each of the agents in a bidding group is necessary for the bidding group (e.g. no dummy or redundant bidding agent). If any one of the agents quits, the group is failed.

2.4 Individual Price and Group Bidding Price

The individual price denotes the price an agent declares to charge for the service it provides. The group bidding price (sometimes called group price) equals the summation of all the individual prices in the group.

2.5 Profit

The profit of a service provided by an agent denotes the difference between the individual price and the reservation price of the service (Fig.2).

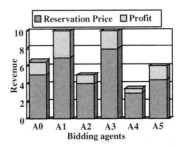

Fig. 2. The revenue distribution of the bidding agents of a bidding group

2.6 The Goal of Z-Process

The goal of Z-process is to have each bidding agents in a bidding group an incentive to maximize its group wining probability by reducing its price. Therefore the key issue to the goal is to balancing out these two factors: group wining probability and individual profit.

3   The Z-Process in a Reverse English Auction

In an English auction the dominant bidding strategy of a bidder (buyer) is to stay in the auction as long as the current bidding price is below its valuation of the service. This situation still holds for reverse English auctions where the bidders are sellers. The only difference is that the bidder should keep on bidding if its valuation is below the current bidding price. For a naive bidder the bidding decision is usually to compare the current price and its valuation. But if the bidder represents a group of bidding agents the situation is getting more complicated. For a bidding group the initial bidding price can be obtained easily by asking all the bidding agents of the group to declare their initial prices. But in the consequent bidding, the above method does not work. The bidding group needs to reduce its bidding price by a certain amount to stay in the auction. But do all the bidding agents of the group agree to bid this new group bidding price? Which bidding agents in the group should cut their individual prices to achieve such a group bidding price reduction? A certain procedure is needed to perform two tasks: to determine new bidding prices, and do it within the time bound sanctioned by the auction. And the Z-process does both (Fig.3).

The Z-process is an intermediate process that helps a bidding group to determine new group prices and profit sharing among bidding agents in the group. In a reverse English auction, if some other bidder places a winning bid, a bidding group will use the Z-process to determine if the bidding agents of the group agree to cut their prices to derive a new group bidding price that is lower than the winning price. And the decision must be made within the time bound of the reverse English auction. Z-process is a multi-round procedure. In each round Z-process asks all the bidding agents of the bidding group if some of them could cut their prices a certain amount. Z-process ends when the goal group price is reached (enough price cuts collected) or there is no bidding agent cuts its price in a certain round. If Z-process ends without achieving goal group price, it is failed and therefore the bidding group will not place the bid with the goal group price in the auction. However, if Z-process is successful, the group will bid in the reverse English auction. The bidding agents that agreed to cut their prices will receive profits that are decreased by the amount they promised to cut.

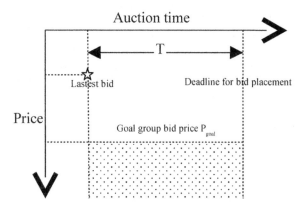

Fig. 3. In a reverse English auction, a bidding group has to decide within time limit T whether to place a bid with price P_{goal}. The dotted area represents the possible group bidding price and feasible bidding time

3.1 The Coordinator

The coordinator is a simple facility that performs the following task.
- Keep group information such as the list of bidding agents of the group.
- Keep known parameters
- Calculate unknown parameters
- Execute Z-process algorithm

3.2 Initial Condition

Before the Z-process is applied the following parameters are already known:
- A bidding group G
- Member bidding agents of G

3.3 Known Parameters

The values of these parameters are already known before Z-process.
- Total available time T
  The total time that is available to the Z-process execution. In reverse English auction, this parameter equals the clearing time.
- Initial group bid price P_{init}
- Goal group bid price P_{goal}
- Number of group members N
- Bidding agent response time t_i for agent I
  The time used to sending a message and receiving response to agent i. This parameter affects the execution speed of Z-process because we have to wait this much time to ensure that every bidding agent did receive messages.

3.4 Unknown Parameters

The values of these parameters are unknown before Z-process. These two parameters determine the speed and efficiency of Z-process.

- Number of rounds R
  The maximum number of rounds a Z-process can have.
- Price decrement dS
  This is the price reduction unit. Each time a bidding agent agrees to cut its price, its price is decreased by one price decrement dS.

3.5 Parameter Relations

- One round time constraint
  $$T/R \geq \max(t_i)$$
- Price constraint
  $$dS \times R \geq P_{goal} - P_{init}$$

From the above two constraints we derived the following relation which denotes the lower bound of dS:

$$dS \geq (P_{goal} - P_{init}) \times \max(t_i)/T$$

Now we have to determine the value of dS and R, thereafter the Z-process can proceed.

3.6 Parameter Decision Considerations

Upon determining dS two important factors must be considered: speed and resolution. The speed factor means that we need dS to be large enough to achieve P_{goal} in reasonable rounds. The resolution factor means that dS should be small enough to fit the difference of agent profit. For large dS some agents with profits smaller than dS will not want to cut their price to avoid negative profits.

Since we have derived the lower bound of dS, and dS needs to be as small as possible, we have

$$dS = (P_{goal} - P_{init}) \times \max(t_i)/T \text{ , and}$$
$$R = T/\max(t_i)$$

3.7 Z-Process Algorithm

With all the needed parameters in hand, the coordinator can carry out the Z-process algorithm. The steps of the algorithm are listed below.

```
**Main Steps of Z-process

Step 1:
    Calculate initial group bid price P_init
```

```
Step 2:
    Determine the known parameters
Step 3:
    Calculate unknown parameters
    • Bid increment
```

$$dS = (P_{goal} - P_{init}) \times \max(t_i)/T$$

```
    • Number of rounds
```

$$R = T / \max(t_i)$$

```
    • Round time
```

$$TR = T / R$$

```
Step 4:
  Repeat the following round operations until  no  bidding
agents agrees to cut its price.
```

**Z-process round operations*

```
GroupPrice = Pinit
CurrentRound=0
repeat
  AnswerBidderNumber = 0
  CurrentRound+1
  Repeat the following while time < TR
  • Accept incoming dS from bidding agents
  • Calculate the new individual price of the answering
    agent
  • AnswerBidderNumber+1
  • GroupPrice+dS
  End of repeat
while
  GroupPrice<Pgoal and
  AnswerBidderNumber > 0 and
  CurrentRound < R

if GroupPrice<Pgoal then return FAIL
Otherwise G can bid Pgoal in the reverse English auction
process
```

```
Extra Rule E:
  If a bidder decides not to cut its price at a certain
  round in a Z-process, it will not be able to bid at the
  following rounds.
```

4 Analysis of the Z-Process in a Reverse English Auction

The group bidding prices and profit sharing of Z-process is based on two factors: group wining probability and individual prices. We made an analysis from the view point of a single bidding agent in a bidding group.

4.1 Expected Profit and Dominant Strategy

For a bidding agent X in a bidding group in the reverse English auction settings, the only decision it has to make is "Should I bid (compromise) or not?" in each round in the Z-process. From simple strategy analysis in (Fig.4) we found that if the other bidding agents in the same group tend not to bid (compromise), then the agent X will have to bid (compromise) to prevent the bidding group from losing in the reverse English auction. But if the other bidding agents tend to bid for the benefit of the bidding group, the agent may not have to bid to obtain better profit for itself if doing this won't affect the wining probability of the group.

	Other Agents Bid	Other Agents No Bid
Agent X Bid	Initial Profit-dS	Initial Profit-dS
Agent X No Bid	Initial Profit or 0	0

Fig. 4. Strategy analysis (expected profit of agent X) of different bidding behavior

Let's consider a simple scenario. Suppose a bidding agent X who wants to decide whether to bid at the first round in a Z-process. If X places a bid at the first round, then it will have to reduce its profit by dS but will be allowed to join the next round. If X does not bid at the first round, its profit will not be reduced but it will not be allowed to join the remaining rounds. So X has to evaluate the expect profits of these two decisions.

Let p be the probability that a bidding agent places a bid at a round in a Z-process, u is the total number of bids needed for the Z-process to succeed, and r is the initial profit of X. We assume that all the other bidding agents are homogeneous and have the same p. Then if X refuses to bid at the first round, the expected profit of X in the whole Z-process will be

$$r \times p^u \tag{1}$$

If X agrees to bid at the first round but refuses to bid in the second round, its expected profit will be

$$(r - dS) \times p^{u-1} \tag{2}$$

By subtracting (**2**) from (**1**), we have

$$p^{u-1} \times (dS - r \times (1 - p)) \tag{3}$$

In the following paragraph we will have an inspection on (**3**) to see if X should choose to bid. If (**3**) > 0, then X will be better off by give up bidding at the first round, otherwise it should place a bid at the first round. Following the above discussion the bidding strategy function (**3a**) is derived. If (3a) >= 0 then agent X should bid, otherwise X should not bid.

$$Bid(r, p) = r \times (1 - p) - dS \tag{3a}$$

From (**3a**), we know that if X's profit is close to dS (dS must be larger than r, otherwise X will has nothing to worry about!), agent X should bid (expression (**3a**) > 0) when the other bidding agents have low probability to bid (small p). If X's profit is much greater than dS, X should bid even when the other bidding agents have very high probability to bid (large p). This result is compatible with (Fig.4).

From (**3a**) we find that the dominant strategy for X at the first round is adaptive: agent X's willingness to bid is proportional to its current profit. In other words, *agent X should places bids in a Z-process if its profit is larger than dS*.

The relation between r and p is illustrated in (Fig.5). Since the bidding strategy for agent X in the first round of Z-process has been derived, we can use a similar approach to prove that the same strategy still holds for the other rounds.

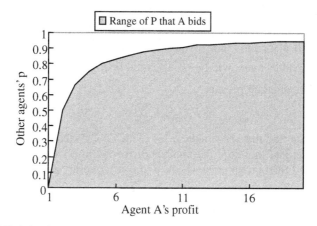

Fig. 5. Relation between agent X's profit and other agents' bidding probabilities

4.2 Heterogeneous Bidding Agents

If the bidding agents are not homogeneous, the bidding probabilities of them will not be the same and hence the formulas derived above should be modified. Let $p(u)$ denotes the cumulative product of the probabilities of all needed u bids. We have a modified version of formula (1) and (2) as

$$r \times p(u) \tag{1m}$$

$$(r - dS) \times p(u - 1) \tag{2m}$$

By subtracting (**2m**) from (**1m**), and let p denotes the term that only exist in $p(u)$ but not in $p(u-1)$ we have

$$p(u - 1) \times (dS - r \times (1 - p)) \tag{3m}$$

Since we only care about the sign (negative or positive) of (3m), the term $p(u-1)$ is ignored because it is always positive. Following a similar procedure mentioned above, we can derive a similar result and therefore the dominant bidding strategy for a bidding agent of a group is the same one that was mentioned above: an agent should places bids in a Z-process if its profit is larger than dS.

4.3 The Expected Final Group Price

If we apply Z-process to a bidding group repeatedly until Z-process fails, and if all the agents in a bidding group are rational, the expected final group bidding price can be derived in the following way. We know that

Initial group price P_{init} =
$\qquad$ *Group reservation price $P_{reserve}$ + Initial group profit R.*

For each bidding agent

Initial agent price p_{init} =
$\qquad$ *Agent reservation price $p_{reserve}$ + Initial agent profit r.*

The initial agent profit for agent i:

$r_i = u_i \times dS + ss_i$, u_i is an integer, $0 <= ss_i < dS$. So u_i can be interpreted as the maximum number of bids the bidding agent will place in a Z-process. Each rational bidding agent will place bids until its profit is below or equal to dS. The expected final profit of individual agent will be ss_i. The total final group profit is $R' = \sum ss_i$.

The expected final group price is

$$P_{expected} = P_{reserve} + \sum ss_i \qquad (4)$$

From (4) we can find that the smaller dS is (which means that the time bound for a Z-process is large, and therefore the number of rounds in a Z-process is large), the closer the expected final group price will be to the group reservation price.

5 Applications of Z-Process

In [15] we have applied the Z-process to a travel planning system. We use graph theory to find a suitable travel route that meets user preference. Then the transportation companies that provide transportation services of the route segments are informed and assigned the same group. Therefore each transportation company in a group is necessary. Any company quits and the entire group is failed because of incomplete travel route.

In order to get a better deal in travel transportation expense, the travel agent asks all the groups attend a reverse English auction. The Z-process is used when a group tries to win the travel contract by decreasing it price.

By using Z-process, bidding groups can refine their group bidding prices based on the progress and situation of an auction. In the same time the rationalities of individual bidding agents are still preserved.

6 Conclusion and Future Work

We figure out the problem of price determination and profit sharing for group bidding. The focus of this work is on the situation when a bidding group wants to change their group bidding price in response to the progress of the auction the group attend. A mechanism call Z-process is constructed to deal with this problem. In Z-process the rationalities of the bidding agents of a bidding group is used to make the agents cut their prices in order to maximize group winning probability. Using Z-process a bidding group can derives new group bidding prices within the time bound sanctioned by English auctions. The final group bidding price obtained by repeatedly applying Z-process to a bidding group is also prove to be optimal when the individual rationality and privacy preservation properties are to be fulfilled.

We have found that with minor modification the Z-process can be used in other types of auctions (Vickrey, first-price sealed bid, Dutch). The properties of such modification are being studied.

References

1. www.e-bay.com
2. http://wireless.fcc.gov/auctions/
3. Allard, Nicholas W.: The New Spectrum Auction Law. 18 Seton Hall Legis. J. (1993), 13-58
4. Cramton, Peter: The Efficiency of the FCC Spectrum Auctions. 41 J. L. & Econ. (1998), 727-735
5. Andreo Mas-Colell, Michael Whinston and Jerry R. Green, Microeconomic Theory, Oxford University Press, 1995.
6. P. Preston McAffe and J. McMillan, Auctions and Bidding, Journal of Economic Literature, 25:699-738, 1987.
7. C. Li and K. Syacara, Algorithm for Combinatorial Coalition Formation and Payoff Division in an Electronic Market Place, in Proc. of International Conference on Autonomous and Multi-agent Systems, 2001.
8. W. Conen and T. Sandholm, Partial Revelation VCG Mechanism for Combinatorial Auctions, National Conference on Artificial Intelligence (AAAI), 2003.
9. Onn Shehory, Sarit Kraus, Coalition formation among autonomous agents: Strategies and complexity, From Reaction to Cognition --- Fifth European Workshop on Modelling Autonomous Agents in a Multi-Agent World, MAAMAW-93 (LNAI Volume 957)
10. Kevin Leyton-Brown, Yoav Shoham, Moshe Tennenholtz, Bidding Clubs: Institutionalized Collusion in Auctions, ACM Conference on Electronic Commerce, 2000
11. Gelman, A. D., and Halfin, S., Analysis of Resource Sharing in Information Providing Services, Proceedings of IEEE Global Telecommunications Conference and Exhibition 1990, Vol. 1, 1990. resource sharing
12. A. Lazar and N. Semret. Auctions for Network Resource Sharing. CTR Technical Report, Columbia University, February 1997
13. Friedman, E. and H. Moulin (1995). "Three Additive Cost Sharing Methods: Shapley-Shubik, Aumann-Shapley, and Serial". Mimeo, Duke University. Shapley, L. S. #1981#. Discussant's Comments. In Moriarity, S., editor, Joint Cost Allocation. Oklahoma Press, Tulsa, Oklahoma, U.S.A.
14. T. Sandholm, Distributed Rational Decision Making, In the textbook Multiagent Systems: A Modern Approach to Distributed Artificial Intelligence, Weiss, G, ed. MIT Press, pp. 201-258, 1999.
15. Ming-Chih Hsu, Hsueh-Min Chang, Yi-Ming Wang and Von-Wun Soo, Multi-Agent Travel Planning through Coalition and Negotiation in an Auction, PRIMA 2003.

Agent Based Risk Management Methods for Speculative Actions

Yasuhiko Kitamura[1] and Takuya Murao[2]

[1] School of Science and Technology, Kwansei Gakuin University,
2-1 Gakuen, Sanda, Hyogo 669-1337, Japan
ykitamura@ksc.kwansei.ac.jp
http://ist.ksc.kwansei.ac.jp/~kitamura/
[2] Osaka City University, Osaka 558-8585, Japan
murao@kdel.info.eng.osaka-cu.ac.jp

Abstract. In multiagent systems, a cooperative action requires the mutual agreement of multiple agents which is generally achieved by exchanging messages. Any delay in message transfer will, however, delay the realization of agreement, and this may reduce the effectiveness of the cooperative action. One solution is to use speculative actions, actions taken before agreement is reached with the goal being to "lock in" the benefits of the cooperative action; its downside is the penalty incurred in unwinding the speculative actions if indeed the agents do not reach agreement. In this framework, we have two risks; the risk of losing the benefits of the cooperative action and the risk of unwinding the speculative actions. It is clear that some form of risk management is needed. In this paper, we propose two risk management methods, the hybrid method and the leveled method, which are viewed as a single agent approach and a multiagent approach, respectively. We discuss their advantages using the meeting room reservation problem.

1 Introduction

Generally speaking, concluding a cooperative action between multiple agents requires agreement and the agreement is normally achieved by exchanging messages among the agents [5, 6]. Agreement may, however, be delayed by either communication in the channels connecting the agents or by the agents themselves.

The first problem reflects the congestion or interruption of the communication channels that connect the agents. The second one is more subtle. In multiagent systems, we often assume that each agent behaves autonomously and rationally to maximize its profit. When the profit to the agent depends on the reply, it may take some time to gather all the information needed to maximize its profit.

This paper considers only the second problem and focuses on cases where the delay reduces the effectiveness or value of the cooperative action. For example, consider the meeting room reservation problem in which a host agent and a member agent must reach agreement about when to have a meeting; the room

M.W. Barley and N. Kasabov (Eds.): PRIMA 2004, LNAI 3371, pp. 92–103, 2005.
© Springer-Verlag Berlin Heidelberg 2005

for the meeting is to be reserved in advance by the host agent. When they succeed in having a meeting, the host agent receives a reward from some external party and the member agent receives some share of the reward from the host agent. We assume that the more time the agents take to reach agreement, the more difficult it is to reserve a room, and that a cost is charged when an agent cancels a reserved room. In this problem, if the agents take a long time to reach agreement (when to hold a meeting), they risk having no room in which to meet.

Speculative action [4] is one solution to the delay in reaching agreement. It is an action taken before agreement is reached later that attempts to lock-in the reward of having the meeting. If agreement is reached, the speculative action is effective. On the other hand, if agreement is not reached, the action should be cancelled or rolled back which would, we assume, incur some penalty. For example, in the problem considered, let us assume that the host agent reserves a room as a speculative action before reaching agreement with the member agent. If agreement is reached, the two agents can have the meeting without the need to worry about the room reservation. On the other hand, if no agreement is reached, the host agent has to cancel the reserved room and pay a cancellation charge. When an agent takes a speculative action, it accepts the risk of needing to cancel the action. This illustrates the need for an effective risk management method.

This paper proposes two risk management methods for speculative actions: the hybrid method and the leveled method. In the hybrid method, the host agent estimates the probability of agreement and decides whether to initiate a speculative action. This method can be viewed as a single agent approach because the decision is made by a single agent. In the leveled method, the host agent concludes a pre-agreement with the member agent and either agent can cancel the pre-agreement by paying a penalty. This method can be viewed as a multi-agent approach because it is based on pre-agreement among the agents involved.

In Section 2, we define the meeting room reservation problem and two fundamental agreement methods called the basic method and the speculative method and discuss these methods from the viewpoint of expected profit. Section 3 introduces the hybrid method and the leveled method and discusses the circumstances under which the agents would accept the leveled method. We mention related works in Section 4 and conclude this paper in Section 5.

2   Meeting Room Reservation Problem

2.1   Definition

To make the discussion of speculative action concrete, we use the meeting room reservation problem. There exist a host agent and a member agent, and they negotiate to decide when to have a meeting in a room to be reserved in advance by the host agent.

For the negotiation, the agents exchange messages following a protocol like the Contract Net Protocol [5]. Initially, the host agent sends an announcement of the meeting date to the member agent. The member agent sends a reply of agreement or disagreement to the host agent. Finally the host agent reserves a meeting room if they reached agreement as to when to have the meeting.

The host agent receives a reward a from some external party when the meeting takes place and the member agent receives a share, value ρ, of the reward from the host agent. The value amount is specified in the announcement message. The member agent receives announcements not only from the host agent but also other agents, and decides whether it accepts to have a meeting with the host agent considering the shares offered by the other agents. Announcements sequentially reach the member agent, and the probability of getting a better share monotonically increases as the time goes by. Hence, the member agent does not reply promptly to the host agent, but rather waits as long as possible to increase its profit, which delays the agreement. If the agents follow the Contract Net Protocol, the host agent can set an time limit for receiving replies to the announcement and the member agent sends a reply within the limit. For convenience, we fix the time interval of expiration to T. Hence, after the member agent receives an announcement, it waits T for to receive announcements from the other agents. The probability, P_m, that the member agent agrees with the host agent to have the meeting on the date specified is given by

$$P_m = \int_0^\rho f(b)db,\tag{1}$$

where b is the best share offered by the other agents up to the expiration time, $f(b)$ is the probability distribution function of b, and is the share offered by the host agent.

We assume that the probability of successfully reserving a meeting room decreases as time goes by. For convenience, we set the probability to be 1 when the host agent sends the announcement, and P_r when the host agent receives a reply after time interval T.

2.2   Agreement Formation for Meeting Room Reservation Problem

We discuss two naive agreement formation methods, the basic method and the speculative method, for the meeting room reservation problem.

In the basic method, shown in Fig. 1(a), the host agent first sends an announcement message which indicates the date and share ρ to the member agent. After it receives an agreement message from the member agent, it tries to reserves a meeting room and succeeds with probability P_r.

In the basic method, after the member agent agrees to have the meeting, the host agent may fail to reserve a room because of the delay. When it fails in this manner, the host agent must pay share ρ to the member agent.

In the speculative method, shown in Fig. 1(b), the host agent sends the same announcement message as well as reserving a room. We assume that this reservation will always succeed. If the reply is 'agree', then the meeting will be held. Otherwise, the host agent has to cancel the reservation and pay cancellation charge c.

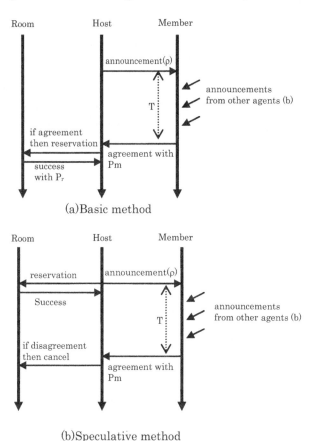

(a)Basic method

(b)Speculative method

Fig. 1. Basic method and speculative method.

2.3   Expected Profit of Agents in Meeting Room Reservation Problem

The profit tree in Fig. 2 shows the expected profits of the host and member agents in the meeting room reservation problem. If the host agent and the member agent agree to have a meeting by using the speculative method, the host agent receives reward a and pays share ρ to the member agent, so the profit of the host agent is $a - \rho$ while that of the member agent is ρ. If the member agent does not agree, the host agent has to pay c to cancel the meeting room, so the profit of the host agent is $-c$ and that of the member agent is 0. Hence, the expected profit of the host agent and the member agent using the speculative method is calculated as

$$profit_{SM}^{h} = P_m \cdot (a - \rho) + (1 - P_m) \cdot (-c) \tag{2}$$

and

$$profit_{SM}^{m} = P_m \cdot \rho \tag{3}$$

respectively.

If the host agent and the member agent agree to have a meeting and the host agent succeeds to reserve a meeting room by using the basic method, the host agent receives reward a and pays share ρ to the member agent, so the profit of the host agent is $a - \rho$ while that of the member agent is ρ. If the host agent fails to reserve a meeting room, it receives no reward and pay ρ, so the profit of the host agent is $-\rho$ while that of the member agent is ρ. Hence, the expected profit of the host and member agents using the basic method is calculated as

$$profit_{BM}^{h} = P_m \cdot P_r \cdot (a - \rho) + P_m \cdot (1 - P_r) \cdot (-\rho) \tag{4}$$

and

$$profit_{BM}^{m} = P_m \cdot \rho \tag{5}$$

respectively.

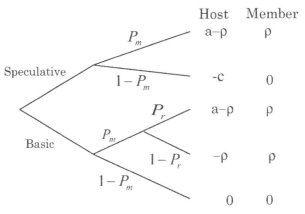

Fig. 2. Profit tree of the host and member agents.

Fig. 3 shows the expected profit of the host agent using the basic and speculative methods with $a = 50$, $\rho = 35$, and $c = 10$.

In the basic method, when P_r is large, the profit of the host agent increases with P_m. When P_r is small, it is difficult to reserve a room, which negates the value of the member agent's agreement. The profit of the host agent decreases as P_m increases because it has to pay ρ to the member agent even though it receives no reward.

The speculative method never fails to reserve a meeting room, and the profit of the host monotonically increases as the probability of the member's agreement increases. However, if the probability is low, the host agent has to pay the cancellation charge.

In conclusion, the speculative method has no risk of failing to reserve a room, but has the risk of canceling the reservation. Especially when the probability of agreement is low and $c > 0$, the basic method returns a better profit than the speculative method. Hence, we need a risk management method for speculative actions that can increase the profit. To that end, we propose two methods in the next section.

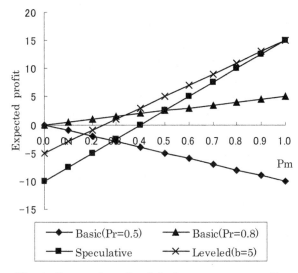

Fig. 3. Expected profit of the host agent versus P_m.

3   Risk Management Methods for Speculative Actions

The speculative method eliminates the risk of causing the failure of the cooperative action, while creating the risk of having to unwind the speculative action. We here propose two risk management methods called the hybrid method and the leveled method to balance these two risks according to the situation.

3.1   Hybrid Method: A Single Agent Approach

As shown in Fig. 3, the speculative method should be used if the probability of the member's agreement is high while the basic method should be used if the probability is low. The hybrid method switches between the speculative method and the basic method by estimating the probability of the member's agreement. If the probability is estimated to be high, it uses the speculative method, otherwise the basic method. Because it is based on an estimation performed by the host agent, it is viewed as a single agent approach.

In this method, it is important to decide the timing to switch from one method to another. The condition in which the speculative method is superior to the basic method is given as

$$P_m \cdot (a - \rho) + (1 - P_m) \cdot (-c) \geq P_m \cdot P_r \cdot (a - \rho) + P_m \cdot (1 - P_r) \cdot (-\rho), \quad (6)$$

considering the expected profit of each method.

When we pay attention to the probability, P_m, of the member's agreement, the inequality can be rewritten as

$$P_m \geq \frac{c}{(1 - P_r) \cdot a + c}. \quad (7)$$

Fig. 4 shows the expected profit of the host agent using the hybrid method when $a = 50$, $\rho = 35$, $c = 10$, and $P_m = 0.5$. If the host agent can accurately estimate P_m, the hybrid method returns a better profit regardless of P_r than the basic method or the speculative method. If, however, the host estimates P_m incorrectly, the profit decreases. For example as shown in Fig. 4, if the host agent wrongly estimates $P_{m}*$ to be 0.3, it uses the speculative method in the interval of $0.53 < P_r < 0.8$ inappropriately which reduces the profit. Likewise, if P_m is wrongly estimates to be 0.7, the host agent uses the basic method in the interval of $0.8 < P_r < 0.91$ inappropriately and the profit reduces.

We need to discuss how the host agent estimates the probability of the member's agreement. As suggested in Section 2, the probability can be estimated from ρ, the share given by the host, and $f(b)$, the probability distribution function of the maximum shares offered by other agents. The host agent does not know $f(b)$ accurately. However, it may be able to estimate $f(b)$ by using the history of past agreements.

We need to discuss how the host agent estimates the probability of the member's agreement. As mentioned in Section 2, the probability can be estimated from ρ, the share given by the host, and $f(b)$, the probability distribution function of the maximum shares offered by other agents. The host agent does not know $f(b)$, but it may be able to estimate $f(b)$ by using the history information of agreements in the past. If the member agent has agreed 5 times out of 10 invitations, the host agent can estimate that $P_m = 0.5$. The agreement made by the host agent actually depends on ρ. If the agent records the history according to ρ, its estimation will be more accurate. Generally speaking, if the host agent

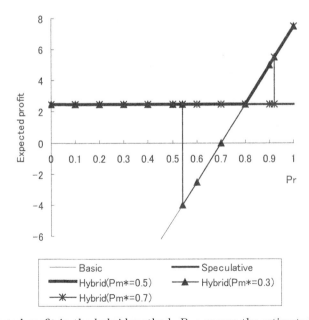

Fig. 4. Expected profit in the hybrid method. $P_{m}*$ means the estimated value of P_m.

fails to estimate P_m correctly, its profit reduces. This means a limitation of the hybrid method in which the host agent switches between two methods based on the estimation of agreement.

3.2   Leveled Method: A Multi-agent Approach

In the leveled method, the host agent and the member agent make a pre-agreement, and either can cancel it by paying a penalty. By making a pre-agreement, the host agent can reduce the risk of unwinding the speculative action when the member agent disagrees. The leveled method is a risk management method based on a pre-agreement made by the host and member agents and so is viewed as a multi-agent approach.

The protocol of the leveled method is shown in Fig. 5. The host agent initiates the speculative action after it concludes the pre-agreement. When the expiration limit of the main agreement is reached, the member agent replies whether it agrees or not to the host agent. If the member agent disagrees, the member agent pays penalty d and the host agent cancels the room by paying cancellation charge c. The profit tree of the leveled method is shown in Fig. 6.

The profit of the host agent in the leveled method, given as

$$profit_{LM}^h = P_m \cdot (a - \rho) + (1 - P_m) \cdot (d - c) \tag{8}$$

is more than that in the speculative method for $(1 - P_m) \cdot d$. This is because the member agent offsets some of the cancellation charge. Fig. 3 shows that the expected profit of host agent with the leveled method is better than that with the speculative method at any P_m. When P_m is low, the basic method is superior

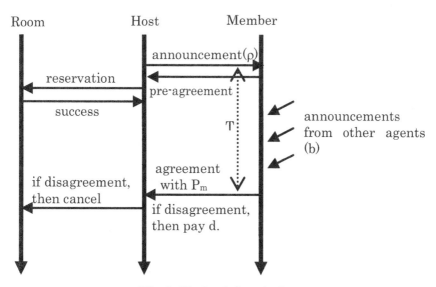

Fig. 5. The leveled method.

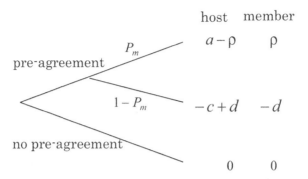

Fig. 6. The profit tree of the leveled method.

to the leveled method. If we can estimate P_m properly, we can switch between the basic method and the leveled method as in the hybrid method.

If we increase d, the expected profit of the host agent increases but that of the member agent decreases. Since this obviously involves a tradeoff, the next section examines the conditions under which the host and the member agents enter into the pre-agreement.

3.3   Entering into Pre-agreement

In the leveled method, the condition under which the host agent should accept the pre-agreement is given as

$$profit^h_{LM} \geq 0. \tag{9}$$

That for the member agent is given as

$$profit^m_{LM} \geq E[b], \tag{10}$$

and only if both conditions are satisfied, the host and member agents make pre-agreement.

For example, let us consider a case when $a = 45$, $c = 10$, and

$$f(b) = \begin{cases} 0.01 & (0 \leq b \leq 100) \\ 0 & (\text{otherwise}) \end{cases} \tag{11}$$

If b is less than ρ, the member agent keeps the pre-agreement, otherwise, it breaks it, so the host's expected profit is calculated as

$$profit^h_{LM} = (45 - \rho) \int_0^\rho f(b)db + (d - 10) \int_\rho^{100} f(b)db$$

$$= (45 - \rho) \cdot \frac{\rho}{100} + (d - 10) \cdot \frac{100 - \rho}{100} \tag{12}$$

The member's expected profit is calculated as

$$profit_{LM}^m = \rho \int_0^\rho f(b)db + \int_\rho^{100} (b-d) \cdot f(b)db$$

$$= \frac{\rho^2}{100} + \frac{1}{100}[(5000 - 100d) - (\frac{\rho^2}{2} - d\rho)]$$

$$= \frac{1}{200}(\rho^2 + 2d\rho + 10000 - 200d) \tag{13}$$

Fig. 7 and Fig. 8 depict the condition in which both agents are happy with the pre-agreement. Fig. 7 shows the expected profit graph when we fix $d = 10$ and change share ρ. Fig. 8 shows that when we fix $\rho = 40$ and change penalty d. These figures show that the agents will accept the pre-agreement only in a limited range of ρ or d.

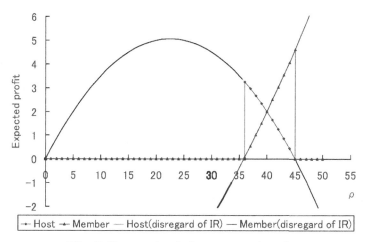

Fig. 7. Share ρ that balances agents' profits.

Fig. 7 shows that the host agent maximizes its profit if the pre-agreement uses $\rho = 45/2$. This, unfortunately, imposes a loss on the member agent, who would thus reject the pre-agreement. Pre-agreement is feasible only when $34.20 < \rho < 45$.

A similar discussion can be made for d. When d is too large, the member agent is not satisfied, and when too small, the host agent is not satisfied. Fig. 8 shows that the pre-agreement is possible when $6.67 < d < 13.33$.

4   Related Work

The idea of speculative action is based on the work on speculative computation [2, 1]. Speculative computation has been proposed as a method to accelerate the processing speed of pipelined parallel computers. A pipelined parallel computer can pre-fetch as many commands as there are processors and execute them in parallel. However, if a branch command is included in the pre-fetched

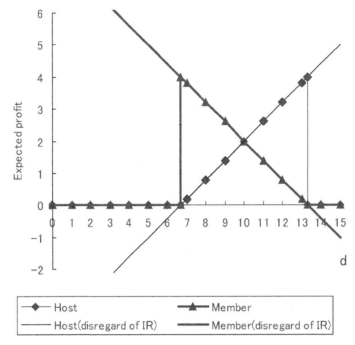

Fig. 8. Penalty d that balances agents' profits.

commands, the following sequence of commands to be executed changes depending on the result of the branch command. Speculative computation attempts to choose the most plausible command and to execute it speculatively. It runs the risk of choosing a wrong command, which must be canceled or rolled back.

Satoh et al. [4] introduced the idea of speculative computation into the field of multi-agent systems. They discussed the issue of communication delay in multi-agent systems and dealt with it by using a default reasoning technique, which is viewed as a variant of speculative computation.

In previous works, the failure of speculative computation is recovered simply by canceling the computation and no side effects are assumed to occur. In this paper, we assume that unwinding a speculative action has a cost. The leveled method described here is based on the leveled commitment method proposed by Toumas Sandholm et al. [3].

5   Conclusions and Future Work

Speculative actions are effective if agreement cannot be reached rapidly. Since we assume that unwinding them incurs a cost, they are not a universal palliative. We proposed two methods in this paper to reduce the risk of unwinding a speculative action: the hybrid method, which switches between the speculative method and the basic method based on the estimated probability of agreement;

and the leveled method, which makes the host and the member agents enter a pre-agreement and forces them to pay a penalty when they break the pre-agreement. We showed the advantages and disadvantages of these methods by using the example of the meeting room reservation problem. The hybrid method has better performance than either of its constituents, the basic method and the speculative method, if the probability of agreement is correctly estimated. Otherwise, its performance is degraded, so estimation accuracy is a critical issue. The leveled method is based on establishing a pre-agreement between the two agents, so the logic of why the agents would accept the pre-agreement is a critical issue. We discussed the settings in which the two agents would accept a pre-agreement.

In this paper, we used the meeting room reservation problem as a case study to discuss speculative actions, but we need to further discuss how we can apply the proposed methods in more general contexts. We also need to deal with cases where there are more than two agents.

Acknowledgement

This work is partly supported by the Grant-in-Aide for Scientific Research (No.13358004) from Japan Society for the Promotion of Science. We would to like to show our thanks to Ken Satoh, Chiaki Sakama, Katsumi Inoue, Koji Iwanuma, and anonymous reviewer for their helpful comments.

References

1. Burton, F.W.: Speculative Computation, Parallelism, and Functional Programming, IEEE Transactions on Computers, Vol. C-34, pp.1190-1193 (1985)
2. Halstead, R.H.Jr.: Parallel Symbolic Computing, IEEE Computer, Vol.19, No.8, pp.35-43 (1986)
3. Sandholm, T. and Lesser, V.: Leveled Commitment Contracting: A Backtracking Instrument for Multiagent Systems, AI Magazine, Vol.23, No.3, pp.89-100 (2002)
4. Satoh, K., Inoue, K., Iwanuma, K., and Sakama, C.: Speculative Computation by Abduction under Incomplete Communication Environments, Proceedings of the Fourth International Conference on MultiAgent Systems, pp. 263-270 (2000)
5. Smith, R.G.: The Contract Net Protocol: High-Level Communication and Control in a Distributed Problem Solver, IEEE Trans. on Computers, Vol. 29, No. 12, pp.1104-1113 (1980)
6. Smith, R. G. and Davis, R.: Frameworks for Cooperation in Distributed Problem Solving, IEEE Trans. on System, Man, and Cybernetics, Vol. SMC-11, No. 1, pp.61-70 (1981)

Handling Emergent Resource Use Oscillations*

Mark Klein[1], Richard Metzler[2], and Yaneer Bar-Yam[2]

[1] Massachusetts Institute of Technology
m_klein@mit.edu
[2] New England Complex Systems Institute
{richard,yaneer}@necsi.org

Abstract. Business and engineering systems are increasingly being created as collections of many autonomous (human or software) agents cooperating as peers. Peer-to-peer coordination introduces, however, unique and potentially serious challenges. When there is no one 'in charge', dysfunctions can emerge as the collective effect of locally reasonable decisions. In this paper, we consider the dysfunction wherein inefficient resource use oscillations occur due to delayed status information, and describe novel approaches, based on the selective use of misinformation, for dealing with this problem.

1 The Challenge

Business and engineering systems are increasingly being created as collections of many autonomous (human or software) agents cooperating as peers. The reasons for this are simple: the challenges we now face are simply too large, both in scale and complexity, to be handled by hierarchical control schemes. In many cases, moreover, political or other concerns exclude the possibility of centralized control even when it is technically feasible.

In such systems we face, however, the potential of highly dysfunctional dynamics emerging as the result of many locally reasonable agent decisions [1]. Such "emergent dysfunctions" can take many forms, ranging from inefficient resource allocation [2] [3] to chaotic inventory and price fluctuations [4] [5] [6] [7] to non-convergent and sub-optimal collective decision processes [8]. The properties of these dysfunctions often appear paradoxical, and their solutions often require new kinds of thinking.

In this paper we focus on one type of emergent dysfunction: resource use oscillation in request-based resource sharing. Imagine that we have a collection of consumer agents faced with a range of competing providers for a given resource (e.g. a piece of information, a sensor or effector, a communication link, a storage capability, or a web service). Typically, the utility of a resource is inversely related to how many consumers are using it. Each agent strives to select the least-utilized resource, and resources are allocated first-come first-served to those who request them. This is a peer-to-peer mechanism: there is no one 'in charge'. This kind of resource allocation is widely used in settings that include markets, internet routing, and so on. It is simple to im-

---

* This is a revised version of a paper submitted to the Agents for Business and Engineering Systems track of the 2004 Conference on Autonomous Computing and Agents for Business Automation.

M.W. Barley and N. Kasabov (Eds.): PRIMA 2004, LNAI 3371, pp. 104–114, 2005.

plement, makes minimal bandwidth requirements, and - in the absence of delays in resource status information – allows consumers to quickly converge to a near optimal distribution across resources.

Consumers, however, will often have a delayed picture of how busy each resource is. Agents could imaginably poll every resource before every request. This would cause, however, a N-fold increase in number of required messages for N servers, and does not eliminate the delays caused by the travel time for status messages. In a realistic open system context [9], moreover, consumers probably cannot fully rely on resource providers to accurately characterize the utility of their own offerings (in a way that is comparable, moreover, across providers). Resource providers may be self-interested and thus reluctant to release utilization information for fear of compromising their competitive advantage. In that case, agents will need to estimate resource utilization using other criteria such as their own previous experience, consulting reputation services, or watching what other consumers are doing. Such estimates will often lag behind the actual resource utility.

When status information is delayed in some way, we find that resource use oscillations emerge, potentially reducing the utility achieved by the consumer agents far below optimum [10].What happens is the following. Imagine that we have two resources, R1 and R2. We can expect that at some point one of the resources, say R1, will be utilized less than the other. Consumers at that point will of course tend to select R1. The problem is that, since their image of resource utilization is delayed, they will continue to select R1 even after it is no longer the less utilized resource, leading to an "overshoot" in R1's utilization. When the agents finally realize that R2 is now the better choice, they will tend to select R2 with the same delay-induced overshoot. The net result is that the utilization of R1 and R2 will oscillate around the optimal equilibrium value. The amplitude of the oscillations, moreover, increases with the delay, to the extent that all consumers may at times select one resource when the other is idle:

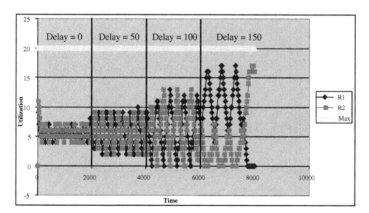

Fig. 1. The utilization of two equivalent resources with and without delays in status information

Such oscillations have two undesirable effects. One is that they can increase how long consumers have to wait for resources (i.e. reduce system throughput), because some resources may lay idle even when there are consumers not being served. The other is that they can increase the *variability* in how long consumers have to wait for a resource, which may be significant in domains where consistency, and thus predictability, is valued.

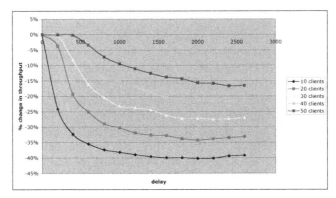

Fig. 2. Decline in throughput as a function of number of consumers (5 resources)

This problem is influenced, in seemingly paradoxical ways, by changing the number of resources and consumers. Figure 2 shows the decline in throughput for a system with 5 resources as a function of status delay and number of consumers. We see that reducing resource utilization actually *worsens* the decline in throughput, and causes throughput losses to occur at *lower* status delay values. The throughput reduction can be substantial, reaching as high as 40% Figure 3 shows the decline in throughput for systems with differing numbers of resources, where the number of consumers per resource is fixed.

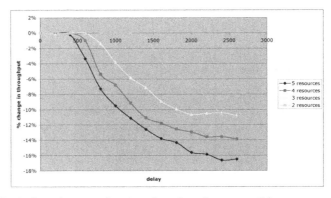

Fig. 3. Decline in throughput as a function of number of resources (10 consumers per resource)

We find that the throughput losses increase and come at shorter status delays, as we increase the number of resources. The traditional 'fix-all' of increasing system capacity thus actually makes this emergent dysfunction worse. Despite their apparently counter-intuitive nature, these results can be explained simply. When the utilization of a resource is low, even small amplitude oscillations can cause it to go idle. And since all consumers shift to what they believe is the least-utilized resource, many resources can potentially go idle as a result of delay-induced oscillations.

Another paradox is that the more aggressive agents are at requesting only the least-utilized resource, the worse the problem gets. This strategy, moreover, is the individually rational one despite the throughput losses that can result. The incentives follow a prisoner's dilemma game [11]. While everyone would be better off if all consumers occasionally selected what they believe to be the more heavily utilized resource (i.e. if everyone 'cooperated') the temptation is for agents to 'defect' (i.e. only request the least-utilized resource) to take advantage of the cooperators and/or avoid being taken advantage of themselves. Self-interested agents will thus find themselves driven to behaviors that cause resource use oscillations.

Resource use oscillations have been studied, primarily for the two resource case, in the literatures on "minority games" and distributed systems. The minority games literature [12] [13] has investigated how to design agents, typical using evolutionary techniques, so that their local decisions do not interact to produce oscillations. While this approach does work under some conditions, it is unrealistic in an open systems context where agents are developed independently, so their resource request strategies are not subject to centralized control. The distributed computing work took the approach of creating an ecology of agents that each look at resource status information with some characteristic additional delay. Those agents whose total status delay matches the period of the resource use oscillation will, in theory, do a superior job of estimating current utilization and will come to dominate the population [14]. This approach has several disadvantages. First of all, it is a closed systems approach, in that it assumes that agents adhere to a centrally defined decision function. It also assumes that the delay in status information (and thus the oscillatory period) changes slowly or not at all. If the status delay changes more quickly than the agent population can evolve, the population will tend to be dominated by agents with inappropriate additional delays. It has been shown, in addition, that such systems are prone to sporadic bursts of strategy instability that can affect the period of resource use oscillations even in the absence of changes in actual status delays [15]. Finally, this work was only evaluated for the two resource case, so it's value for larger numbers of resources is unknown. Our challenge, therefore, is to find an approach that moderates or eliminates oscillatory resource utilization dynamics without needing to control the design or operation of the consumer agents.

2   Efficiency Through Misinformation

As we have seem emergent dysfunctions often have counter-intuitive properties. The solutions for emergent dysfunctions can, similarly, grow out of behavior that seems locally sub-optimal. This is the case with the techniques we have investigated. Our approach is predicated on resources (selectively) *misinforming* consumers about how busy the resource is. Paradoxically this can lead, as we show below, to superior resource allocation performance, including greater throughput and reduced variability.

The Scenario: All the approaches were evaluated in a scenario with multiple (from 20 – 50) consumers and multiple (2 – 5) resources. Consumers submit requests to the resource that they judge is the least heavily utilized. Resources differ in how quickly they can complete requests. When a request is received by a resource, it is placed on a queue and, once it reaches the front of the queue, the resource is allocated to the consumer for a length of time inversely proportional to the speed of the resource. When that period is over, a notification message is sent to the consumer. Messages take a fixed amount of time to travel from sender to receiver. Consumers wait a randomly selected amount of time, after a notification is received, before submitting a new request. The value of a resource to a consumer (though not of course the time it takes to access the resource) is independent of the resource's utilization. The case where utilization does affect resource value is considered in [16]. The two metrics of interest to consumers in this scenario include (1) the aggregate throughput of the system, in terms of requests processed per time unit, and (2) the variability in request processing times. In our simulations, messages took 20 time units to propagate, the time gap between receiving a completion notification and a sending a subsequent request was normally distributed with an average of 40 and a standard deviation of 10, one server took 80 time units to service a request, and the other took 160 time units. Each simulation run was 10,000 time units long.

The dynamics of this system can be described analytically [17]. We can show that queue lengths will follow a triangle function where the frequency is determined only by the delay in status information, and the amplitude, for a given scenario, is determined only by the ratio of the delay time to the time it takes a resource to process a request. Message travel time has the same impact as status delays, because both increase the lag between a change in resource utilization and the response by consumers. When oscillations become so strong that the resources go idle periodically, the throughput of the system is inversely proportional to the status delay.

Status Misinformation: Let us assume that the resources have control over the status information that the consumers are given when they decide which resource to request. Let us further assume that consumers have a probability **p** of being given information that leads them to select the 'wrong' (more heavily utilized) resource. The notion that agents can have somewhat 'corrupted' status information was broached in [14], but that work did not investigate how status misinformation can be beneficial by dampening delay-induced oscillations. Oscillations are damped because misinformation causes requests are spread to some extent to both resources, irregardless of which one is actually less utilized. In the following figure, for example, we can see how the oscillations in resource queue lengths were substantially reduced when resource status misinformation (**p** = 0.5) was introduced at time = 10000:

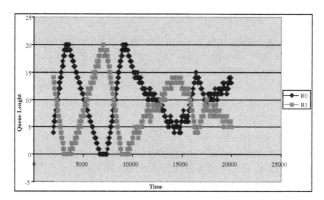

Fig. 4. Effect of introducing status misinformation with delay-induced resource use oscillations

It can be shown analytically [17] that for small levels of **p**, the variability in resource utilization is reduced linearly with **p**. As **p** approaches 1, however, consumers get less and less 'real' information, and are increasingly likely to choose resources without regards to their actual utilization, so resource utilization performs a 'random walk' [18], increasing the variability in request processing times and raising the possibility that the queue for one of the resources will empty out, thereby reducing throughput. So we are faced with a tradeoff. Small levels of **p** reduce the oscillatory amplitude, but larger ones increase it again due to the impact of random fluctuations. These insights are confirmed by simulations:

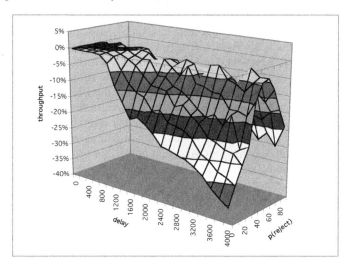

Fig. 5a. Throughput as a function of delay and misinformation probability **p**

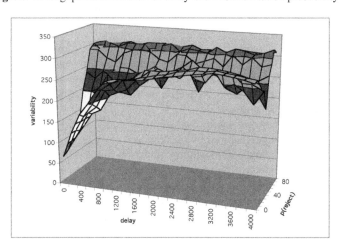

Fig. 5b. Variability in completion time as a function of delay and misinformation probability **p**

When **p** is zero, we find that the variability in how long an consumer must wait for a resource increases, as we would expect, with the status information delay, due to periodic oscillations. When the delays get large enough to cause queue emptying, throughput drops. For intermediate values of **p**, throughput is returned to near-optimal levels even with large delays, but variability is high. As **p** approaches 1, throughout drops off again (due to queue emptying caused by random walk fluctuations) and variability becomes higher yet. Throughput is maximized when **p** is about 0.7. Remarkably, performance is improved by imposing substantial misinformation.

Stochastic Request Rejection: The approach just discussed relies on the ability to control the information that consumers use to decide which resources to request. This is an unrealistic assumption, however, for many domains. In an open system, we do not have the control of consumer design that would be necessary to assure this. This approach also assumes that messages with resource status information are sent to consumers, either periodically (with a frequency at least as high as that of the delay-induced oscillations) or when they are about to make a resource request. This can substantially increase the message traffic required by the resource sharing protocol. This motivated us to explore an alternative approach for alleviating delay-induced resource use oscillations. The idea is simple: some fixed fraction of resource requests are rejected, at random, by resources. When a consumer receives a rejection message, it is (reasonably) assumed to send its request to some other server instead. The net effect is the same as with the previous approach in that, for some constant fraction of requests, consumers are misled about which resource is the least utilized. In the scenario we studied, throughput was maximized when 1/2 of all requests were stochastically rejected.

The stochastic request rejection approach can, however, reduce throughput if resource demands are low enough that the resource queues are forced to empty out due a request rejection. It also increases message traffic due to the addition of reject messages. Using this technique, the average number of rejections for a request is given by:

$$\sum_{i=1} p^i$$

where p is the probability of a request being rejected by a resource. For $p = 0.5$ this value is 1, so an average of 2 requests will be needed to access a resource, increasing total required message traffic from 2 (one request and one notification) to 4 (two requests, one reject, and one notification).

Both of these disadvantages can be substantially ameliorated by adopting a load-dependent rejection scheme, inspired by the 'random early drop' scheme proposed for avoiding send-rate synchronization among network router clients [19]. Instead of using a fixed request rejection frequency, resources reject requests with a frequency proportional to how full their queue is. The number of rejection messages generated is less (because high rejection rates are only incurred at the utilization peaks) and very few rejections occur when the resources are under-utilized, making it unlikely that throughput will be reduced because a request was rejected when a resource was available. Load-dependent rejection also offers the bonus of somewhat higher throughout than fixed-rate rejection; because the rejection rate (and thus the degree of damping) increases with the amplitude, the oscillations have a rounded shape that results in a smaller peak amplitude.

The average rate of rejection needs to be tuned to the current average load. There is a tradeoff involved. If the rejection regime is too aggressive, we incur excessive reject message traffic, and the possibility of causing queue emptying by rejecting requests when a resource is lightly utilized. If the rejection regime is not aggressive enough, however, there will be insufficient damping which can also led to queue emptying and throughput loss. The following figure shows a typical tradeoff:

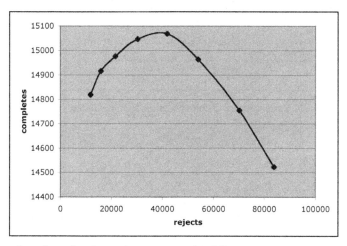

Fig. 6. Throughput (completes) vs reject messages for different levels of load-dependent rejection. For 5 resources, 50 consumers, and a status delay of 1000

Each point on the curve represents a different level of load-dependent rejection: a relatively mild rejection regime (i.e. where the rejection rate increases slowly with load) on the left, and increasingly aggressive rejection to the right. As we can see, there is an optimum rejection 'strength', beyond which throughout begins to decrease.

The impact of the schemes we have discussed can be summarized and contrasted as follows:

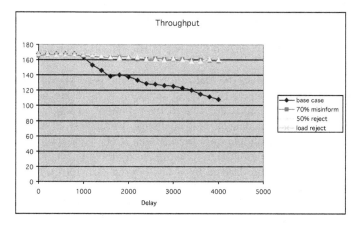

Fig. 7a. Throughput for different oscillation remediation schemes

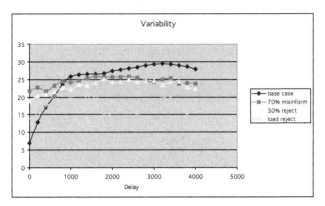

Fig. 7b. Variability for different oscillation remediation schemes

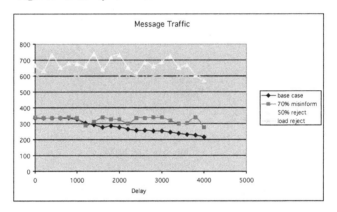

Fig. 7c. Message traffic for different oscillation remediation schemes

Misinformation-based techniques substantially increase throughput and reduce the variability in the time it takes to get a consumer request satisfied, for a wide range of delays, relative to the base case where these techniques were not used. Load-based rejection is the best technique in terms of throughput and variability, with the additional advantage of not assuming we can control the status information received by consumer agents, but incurs increased message traffic. These effects were statistically significant ($p < .01$).

One final refinement involves the realization that there is no point in incurring the increased message traffic caused by request rejection if there are no resource use oscillations, or if the oscillations are caused by variations in *aggregate* consumer demand rather than by status delays. This challenge, fortunately, is easy to address. Stochastic request rejection should only be activated if (1) there are significant periodic oscillations in resource utilization (determined by looking for above-threshold values in the power spectrum derived by a fast Fourier transform), and (2) the resource utilization across servers is *negatively* correlated (positive correlation would imply that aggregate demand is varying). We have implemented this approach and found that it successfully avoids being triggered by aggregate demand variations while remaining effective in responding to delay-induced oscillations.

The load-dependent stochastic rejection approach has also been shown, in our simulations, to effectively reduce the impact of status delay-induced oscillations when there are more than 2 resources.

3 Contributions and Future Work

We have presented a novel and promising approach for mitigating the deleterious effects of delay-induced resource-use oscillations on request-based resource sharing, by exploiting the paradoxical power of selectively misinforming consumers. The approach is designed to be appropriate for the important context of distributed systems with peer-to-peer coordination, where we can not rely on being able to control the design or operation of the resource consumers.

Our future efforts will include empirical and analytic work. We will extend our analytic treatment to cover more than two resources. We also are developing an analytic way to determine the correct rejection regime for different contexts; we have done this empirically to date. We also plan to use our models to predict the degree of resource oscillation, as well as the potential benefits of selective misinformation, for real-world resources such as competing web sites.

Acknowledgements

This work was supported by the NSF Computational and Social Systems program as well as the DARPA Control of Agent-Based Systems program.

References

1. Jensen, D. and V. Lesser. *Social pathologies of adaptive agents. in Safe Learning Agents Workshop in the 2002 AAAI Spring Symposium.* 2002: AAAI Press.
2. Chia, M.H., D.E. Neiman, and V.R. Lesser. *Poaching and distraction in asynchronous agent activities. in Proceedings of the Third International Conference on Multi-Agent Systems.* 1998. Paris, France.
3. Hardin, G., *The Tragedy of the Commons. Science,* 1968. 162: p. 1243 - 1248.
4. Youssefmir, M. and B. Huberman. *Resource contention in multi-agent systems. in First International Conference on Multi-Agent Systems (ICMAS-95).* 1995. San Francisco, CA, USA: AAAI Press.
5. Sterman, J.D., *Learning in and about complex systems.* 1994, Cambridge, Mass.: Alfred P. Sloan School of Management, Massachusetts Institute of Technology. 51.
6. Kephart, J.O., J.E. Hanson, and A.R. Greenwald, *Dynamic pricing by software agents.* Computer Networks: the International Journal of Distributed Informatique, 2000. 32(6): p. 731-52.
7. Ranjan, P., et al. *Decision Making in Logistics: A Chaos Theory Based Analysis. in AAAI Spring Symposium on Diagnosis, Prognosis and Decision Making.* 2002.
8. Klein, M., et al., *The Dynamics of Collaborative Design: Insights From Complex Systems and Negotiation Research.* Concurrent Engineering Research & Applications, 2003. 11(3): p. 201-210.
9. Hewitt, C. and P.D. Jong, *Open Systems.* 1982, Massachusetts Institute of Technology.
10. Hogg, T., *Controlling chaos in distributed computational systems.* SMC'98 Conference Proceedings, 1998(98CH36218): p. 632-7.

11. Osborne, M.J. and A. Rubinstein, *A course in game theory*. 1994, Cambridge, Mass.: MIT Press. xv, 352.
12. Challet, D. and Y.-C. Zhang, *Emergence of Cooperation and Organization in an Evolutionary Game*. arXiv:adap-org/9708006, 1997. 2(3).
13. Zhang, Y.-C., *Modeling Market Mechanism with Evolutionary Games*. arXiv:cond-mat/9803308, 1998. 1(25).
14. Hogg, T. and B. Huberman, *Controlling chaos in distributed systems*. IEEE Transactions on Systems, Man & Cybernetics, 1991. 21(6): p. 1325-32.
15. Youssefmir, M. and B.A. Huberman, *Clustered volatility in multiagent dynamics*. Journal of Economic Behavior & Organization, 1997. 32(1): p. 101-118.
16. Klein, M. and Y. Bar-Yam. *Handling Resource Use Oscillation in Multi-Agent Markets*. in AAMAS Workshop on Agent-Mediated Electronic Commerce V. 2003. Melbourne Australia.
17. Metzler, R., M. Klein, and Y. Bar-Yam. *Efficiency Through Disinformation*. 2004. New England Complex Systems Institute. http://www.arxiv.org/abs/cond-mat/0312266
18. Bar-Yam, Y., *Dynamics of complex systems*. 1997, Reading, Mass.: Addison-Wesley. xvi, 848.
19. Braden, B., et al., *Recommendations on Queue Management and Congestion Avoidance in the Internet*. 1998, Network Working Group.

The Role of Agents in Intelligent Mobile Services

Fernando Koch[1] and Iyad Rahwan[2]

[1] Institute of Information and Computing Sciences,
Utrecht University, Utrecht, The Netherlands
`fkoch@acm.org`
[2] Department of Information Systems,
University of Melbourne, Parkville, VIC, Australia
`i.rahwan@pgrad.unimelb.edu.au`

Abstract. In this paper we argue that the agent paradigm offers promising techniques for dealing with the challenges of building intelligent mobile services. We present Agent Oriented Software Engineering as a solution for the problems in designing a new generation of mobile services. To illustrate our position, we present a brief agent-oriented analysis of a mobile commerce scenario.

1 Introduction

Existing commercial mobile services are only scratching the surface of what is possible. As pointed out by the survey presented in [23], the main problems against technology adoption are lack of interest, unappealing services and communication costs. Hence, in a new generation of mobile services, human-device interaction must become more useful and concise, reducing the number of user interventions while providing appealing value.

The power of pervasive computing is unleashed when the application has the intelligence to process contextual information about the user and the environment in order to provide the user with the *right information at the right time*. A framework for building these applications must provide the means to handle the distribution inherent in the environment and, at the same time, allow the easy mapping of human knowledge into computer applications. We call this class of applications as *Intelligent Mobile Services*.

To address these requirements we must deal with new issues in the field of Distributed Computing and Artificial Intelligence. Mobile computing introduces new elements of complexity [20]: dynamic environments, changes in actual and relative location, constrained computing power, connectivity latency and unreliability, limited battery power, and constrained input and output interfaces. These constraints are not artefacts of current technology, but are intrinsic to mobility.

We argue that agent-based computing [25] is a promising enabling technology for second-generation mobile services. The agent paradigm offers methodologies for creating distributed, intelligent, integrated and cooperative applications. This paper tries to link the requirements of the new generation mobile services to the

M.W. Barley and N. Kasabov (Eds.): PRIMA 2004, LNAI 3371, pp. 115–127, 2005.
© Springer-Verlag Berlin Heidelberg 2005

solutions provided by agent-oriented software paradigm. This exercise serves as a guide for analysing existing systems and as a mean for identifying new opportunities.

This work is structured as follows: section 2 describes the requirements for mobile services and presents key definitions like context-awareness; the section 3 presents the agent technology and its relationship to the development of intelligent mobile services; section 4 presents the exercise of building an agent-based solution based on the presented ideas, then conclude in section 5.

2   Requirements

Mobile service provision imposes two major challenges: the *infrastructure challenge*, which is concerned with building robust hardware and software technology that facilitate mobile connectivity, location-identification, service discovery, fault tolerance, etc. [9]; second is the *services challenge*, which is concerned with how we can use the infrastructure available in order to provide new and useful services, such as trip planning or and mobile commerce [20]. In this study, our focus is on the latter. In particular, we are interested in high-level *intelligent services*, which take advantage of the processing power of mobile devices in order to provide users with context-aware support.

Zambonelli and Parunak [27, 26] argue that *situadedness*, *openness*, *locality in control* and *locality in interaction* are fundamental characteristics of future software systems. We argue that these characteristics are intrinsically related to known issues in mobile computing:

- **Situatedness:** This property means that the software system is situated in an *environment*, which it can influence and be influenced by. A mobile device aimed at providing support to the user in a dynamic environment would benefit from representing and processing information about this environment in order to provide appropriate support.
- **Openness:** This property refers to the system's ability to accommodate changes in the system structure as when, for example, new components enter the system or existing components leave. In the world of mobile services, new services and devices might appear and disappear due to changes in connectivity, user location, and because users' availability itself changes [16]. The software needs to adapt to such changes appropriately.
- **Locality in Control:** This means that software components may be required to operate 'autonomously' based on local policies. In mobile services, this may be a necessity to ensure service robustness, for example if connectivity is lost when outside a coverage area. This may also be required for cost reduction because contacting a service on a centralised server might be expensive. To deal with this, devices must be capable of tracking their execution and interaction states when communicating to external services.
- **Locality in Interactions:** This refers to a software component's ability to interact with other components in local geographical or logical neighbourhoods. In mobile services, such interaction is needed for reliability and quality related reasons. Interaction between different mobile devices or between a

device and other services takes place over unstable and unreliable communication channels, and hence must be endowed with the ability to recover such interaction appropriately in case of error.

A key feature of the above characteristics is *context-awareness*. *Context* is any information that can be used to characterize the situation of an entity [6]. Context-awareness involves the means to capture, represent and process context information. In Figure 1, we demonstrate the typical processes involved in a mobile service environment: collecting raw data about the device, user and network, combining this data into context information, and inferring some appropriate action to take.

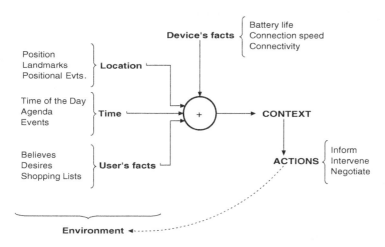

Fig. 1. Context-awareness in mobile services workflow.

3   Agents and Mobile Services

Ultimately, the new generation of mobile services must deliver an enhanced user experience. The human-device interactions must become more concise, reducing the number of user interventions. Pervasive software applications should make use of local processing to reason about the user's context and predict user's intents, actions and location, behaving as an always present personal assistant, available anytime, anywhere. A framework for building these applications must provide the means to handle the distribution inherent in the environment and at the same time allow the easy mapping of human knowledge into computer applications.

3.1   The Role of Agents

Agent-based computing is becoming increasingly popular because it enables building modular software systems capable of operating in dynamic, unpredictable environments. The agent paradigm has produced a wide variety of concepts and tools for constructing sophisticated autonomous software and structuring high-level interaction patterns that facilitate cooperative behaviour [12]. In addition, a set of methodologies have been developed that enable system designers to distil domain knowledge and transform it into agent or multi-agent system specifications [10]. Hence, agents seem to offer a set of features that are very closely aligned with the requirements of service delivery challenge in pervasive computing.

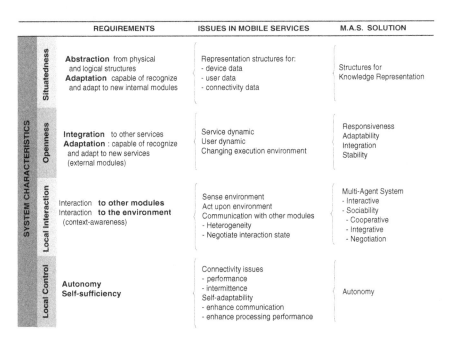

Fig. 2. Role of Agents in Mobile Services.

In Figure 2 we summarise the characteristics of mobile services discussed in the previous section, and demonstrate how the *agent paradigm* can provide solutions to support these characteristics, and hence address the requirements of mobile computing. We detail this in the following:

– **Structures for Knowledge Representation:** Existing agent systems can provide an answer to the situadeness requirement. The agent paradigm has produced a variety of methods for explicit representation of the environment, and for reasoning about this environment to produce decisions [24]. We denote, however, that agent systems are not the only paradigm to provide this ability. Nonetheless it is an intrinsic problem in multi-agent systems, and hence inherent in agent architectures.

– **Responsiveness and Adaptivity:** Jennings and Wooldridge [13] pointed out that responsiveness and adaptivity are inherent features provided by agent systems; agents should be able to adapt to constantly changing execution environments, one of the predictable problems of mobile computing.

– **Sociability and Locality of Interaction:** As also pointed out by Jennings and Wooldridge [13], agents are able to interact with other agents or humans when needed. Sophisticated interaction mechanisms have been developed in the agent community to facilitate information exchange [4], coordination [8], collaboration [17], and negotiation [1]. Such mechanisms offer great potential to address the local interaction requirement in mobile service delivery.

– **Autonomy:** As we argued in an earlier paper [14], the agent paradigm offers mechanisms that address varying degrees of autonomy, from basic reactive architectures based on a set of pre-determined rules, to mechanisms for proactive behaviour [3] considering the context and user preferences and behaviours. This inherent feature is useful to configure agents to react to and plan for changes in a mobile service environment.

Another important feature of the agent paradigm is that it provides an infrastructure for *decomposition* and *abstraction* [11]. Jennings describes *decomposition* by stating that "the most basic technique for tackling large problems is to divide them into smaller, more manageable chunks, each of which can then be dealt with in relative isolation."

3.2   Relevant Aspects of Agents

Having outlined the different roles an agent can play in mobile service delivery, it would be useful to have a perspective through which to look at existing agent-based mobile applications and to recognise opportunities for further work.

Agent-based services can be analysed on several different dimensions. We find the following classification, due to Jennings et al. [13], useful for our purposes. Agent systems can be classified according to the: *sophistication of the application*, from agents work based on well-defined, pre-specified rules and assumptions, to service performing and the more complex predictive/proactive agents; *role of the agent*, like decision support and problem solving automation, and; *granularity of the view*, from single-agents to more complex multi-agent systems. By correlating these aspects of agent-based applications and the roles of agents in mobile service applications, we came up with a taxonomy based on the aspects of *granularity*, *role* and *level of autonomy*, as described below. This taxonomy is one way to describe the different aspects of using agents in mobile service delivery:

– **Granularity:** An agent-based application can provide *single user* support or *multi-user* interaction support. The decision about whether to adopt a single-agent or multi-agent approach is generally determined by the domain and is similar in nature to decisions about whether monolithic, centralized solutions or distributed, decentralized solutions are appropriate.

– **Role:** Agents running on mobile devices can play different roles, offering varying levels of support to the user. Sheridan [22] presents a taxonomy of four main stages of complex human-machine tasks: (a) *acquiring information*, where the application gathers information and saves it for future processing; (b) *analysing and displaying results* is where the application analyses and displays the collected information, considering the context and tailoring the output information to the user's preferences; (c) *deciding on an action or sequence of actions* means the application suggests actions based on the analysis of environmental information; and (d) *implementing decided actions*, where the application is responsible for carrying out the steps required for the task completion.

– **Autonomy:** An agent application may behave in a *reactive* manner to environment stimuli based on a set of pre-determined rules or user commands. Instead, an agent may act *proactively* considering the context and user preferences and behaviours. Different levels of autonomy exist between these two extremes, and the degree of this autonomy may be adjustable by the user [21].

Using the above taxonomy, we look at some existing agent-based mobile services in the next section.

4   Some Early Attempts

Several efforts in building applications that utilize agent-based techniques to provide services to mobile users have been conduced by other groups. Our aim is to provide the reader with a snapshot of current developments, and to describe these within the above taxonomy.

– **MyCampus** [19] is a Semantic Web environment for context-aware mobile services at Carnegie Mellon University. In this project, the agent-based approach provides autonomous discovery of services and personalized services based on users' preferences and contextual attributes. According to the taxonomy we have given above, MyCampus would be classified as *single-user support*, with the role of *acquiring information* to *analyse and display*. Essentially, MyCampus is a *reactive system*, as it works by responding to environment changes.
– **AbIMA** [18] is an agent-based intelligent mobile assistant that runs on a hand-held device and assists the user through the execution of individual tasks. AbIMA uses a set of pre-programmed plans for executing different tasks. These plans can be distilled from domain knowledge, or learned through observation of user behaviour. AbIMA offers agent-based support for a *single user*, acting by performing *analysis and displaying suggestions* to the user. It exhibits *proactive behaviour* by providing proactive advice to the user when things go wrong and initial plans cannot be executed.
– **Paurobally et al.** [15] proposed an agent-based framework for providing personalised mobile services. Producers and consumers of services are viewed as software agents, some of which are located on users' mobile devices. These agents use negotiation as a mechanism for reaching agreement on the terms of a transaction in a mobile-commerce scenario. As per our taxonomy, this infrastructure would be classified as *multiple-user* support, as it supports a community of users and their inter-operations with the environment; the role would be *implement action* and on autonomy it would classify as *pro-active*.

- **The Electric Elves project** [2] exploits agent technology to support human organisation. Teams of agents help users conduct routine, well structured tasks, such as organising meetings. Each person has their own proxy agent running on a mobile device. The Electric Elves project is based on a multi-agent approach to coordinating multiple mobile users. Agents' roles range from *deciding what information to acquire*, to *analysing situations* using decision-theoretic planning, to making suggested actions. Agents exhibit varying degrees of autonomy based on the type of situation at hand and learned user preferences

In Figure 3 we present which depicts the classifications given above.

	Granularity		Role				Autonomy	
	Single	Multi	Acquire	Display	Decide	Implem.	React	Proact
Mycampus		X	X	X			X	
ElectricElves		X	X	X			X	X
Abima	X			X				X
Paurabally's		X				X		X

Fig. 3. Classification of early attempts.

5   Engineering Agents-Based Mobile Services: Mobile Computing Example Scenario

Our long-term aim is to provide an agent-based approach to specifying and constructing intelligent mobile services. In this section, we take a preliminary step in this direction through a brief case-study. Our aim is not to give a comprehensive *methodology* but rather to outline a coherent sequence of steps for building agent-based intelligent mobile services and discuss the agent-based techniques that can prove useful. The steps start from scoping the problem to defining the requirements and functional specifications, to defining the various processing components, processing rules and their interaction. We go through these steps through an illustrative scenario (depicted in Figure 4).

Define the Problem

Purpose: *Provide a clear definition of the problem to guide subsequent steps.*

The problem in the proposed example is to create a context-aware mobile commerce application that utilises pervasive computing technologies in order to deliver the right information (shopping list quotation) at the right time (while nearby a grocery store).

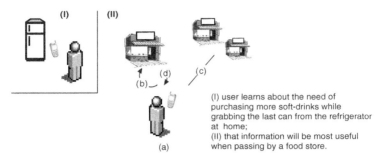

Fig. 4. Mobile commerce scenario.

Define the Requirements and Functional Specification

Purpose: *Scope the aimed level of automation, assess the available enabling and support technology, what context-awareness support infrastructure is available, and describe the requirements from the service with regards to feedback loops, human-computer integration and group of participants.*

The requirements for running this mobile service are: (1) a location-based system, with landmark event generation, which detects the user's device nearby a setup landmark and sends a notification; (2) the interface definition between the device-based application and the grocery store server; (3) connectivity; (4) plan resolution while the user is walking nearby the store; (5) interfacing to present the solution (e.g. price quote) to the user.

Considering these requirements, this application's architecture can be model as either client-server or local-processing applications, depending on the available device connectivity.

Decompose the Problem

Purpose: *to define the autonomous entities in the problem and how they can be distributed. Decomposition is the most basic technique for tackling large problems is to divide them into smaller, more manageable chunks, each of which can then be dealt with in relative isolation, as described by Jennings [11].*

By decomposing the problem into the *minimum* parts, we came up with an abstract sketch of a multi-agent system where each module addresses one specific part of the problem. The modules are presented in Figure 5 and described below.

- **Location Agent:** knows about the user's position and processes landmark events. Although at first glance it may look unnecessary to have an agent dedicated to location-based services, for the sake of this exercise we are decomposing the problem to the minimum components. This agent would contain the skills necessary to interface with location-based services, to handle the landmark table and to related positioning information (coordinates) to landmarks proximity.
- **Calendar Agent:** keeps track of user's appointments and provide the functions to check user availability;

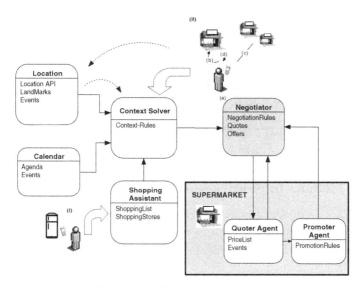

Fig. 5. Application architecture.

- **Shopping Assistant Agent:** keeps track of user's shopping lists and pre-ferred stores;
- **Context Solver Agent:** implements the context inferencing and triggers the selected actions;
- **Negotiation Agent:** implements the negotiation strategies and functions.

Define the Processing Rules

Purpose: *describing the process events and, specially for Mobile Services, the relationship between events, context and actions. For context-aware computing, these are the context inference rules, as described by Dey [5, 7].*

The *Context Solver Agent* receives the landmark event and must process it accordingly. For example, it should check if there is a shopping list available, if the user's agenda allows a visit to the nearby shopping store and, if possible, compare the received quote with the quotes provided by the user's preferred stores. Finally, it should present the quote along with a suggest of action to the user. This context resolution rule is presented in the pseudo-code below.

Event: Near a Supermarket

EVENT –
    location(near, supermarket(SUPER-A))
CONTEXT –
    location(near, supermarket(SUPER-A)) AND
    Agenda(available, next(30mins)), AND
    ShoppingList(supermarket, SHOPPINGLIST))

ACTION –
  setContext(NegotiatingList, SHOPPINGLIST),
  Negotiate(SHOPPINGLIST, SUPER-A, QUOTE),
  Store(quote(SUPER-A,QUOTE)),
  ShoppingStores(supermarket, STORESLIST),
  Negotiate(SHOPPINGLIST, STORESLIST, LISTQUOTES),
  Store(quotes(STORESLIST, LISTQUOTES)),
  Compare(QUOTE, LISTQUOTE, RESULT),
  Display(RESULT)

Define the Modules Interdependencies and Interoperations

Purpose: *This phase leads to the distribution problem and the developer must decide where each module will execute (server-based, client-server, local-processing and/or mobile code) and the interactions between the modules.*

In this environment, when the user passes by a food store the *Location Agent* detects the landmark and throws an event to the *Context Solver Agent*. The system checks for time availability and presence of a shopping list. If there is a positive context (i.e. if a certain condition is satisfied based on the observation of the environment), the system triggers the negotiation process, which will interact with the supermarkets' agent, bargain and display the best price quote it could find. The modules interdependencies are presented in the Figure 5.

Exercise Conclusions

Other steps include lower level definitions such as the specification of the graphical user interface, aspects of human-computer interactions, application programming interfaces to access contextual data and connectivity and networking issues. These stages are essential for the development of the final product but as they enter into lower-level details and technological issues we regard them as beyond the scope for this paper.

Several other factors could be improved and extended in this architecture sketch, such as perception of device and network conditions. For example, if the battery level is low or the network is expensive or unreliable then the agent may not conduct the time-consuming price bargaining process. This would address an extra requirement in mobile computing: *local control.*

In our classification system, the *Personal Assistant* described in the above scenario would be classified as a *single-user support* for granularity, has the role of *suggesting action* and is *pro-active* in terms of autonomy. Several other possibilities are feasible, and here are some examples:

– *Acquire Information, Analyse and Display* and *Reactive:* The agent could be reactive in the sense that it only responds to an explicit request for quotes by the user based on the given shopping list and, once processed, the quote information is acquired and displayed to the user. This is a rather simplistic agent and would not require location-based context-awareness infrastructure.

- *Decide Action* and *Reactive:* The user can delegate the act of bargaining and finalising a deal to the agent. For instance, the agent collects the quotes from the nearby and remote store. It also checks for alternative brands that the user configured as acceptable and compile the best quote from every store, based on what user preferences. The agent will work to find the best deal possible to the customer and direct him to a particular food store to shop. This solution requires connectivity but, since the action is initiated by the user, does not require a location-based service that proactively initiates interaction via detecting user location. This scenario can be engineered using a client-server architecture with the context rules processing in the server.
- *Decide Action* and *Proactive:* In this variant, the user's agent starts to bargain by itself when it detects the food store's proximity and if the stored shopping list and other scheduled activities permit (it wouldn't make sense to spend processing power and communication if the user doesn't have time availability for shopping at that time). Moreover, the proativiness could also take place on the *merchant side*, for example, as the merchant's agent detects the customer's proximity and the amount it intends to shop, it could provide a discount coupon valid for a period of time, teasing this customer to step in. Of course, this raises privacy issues worthwhile of serious separate investigation.

Although simplistic, this exercise demonstrates some solutions provided by the agent-oriented approach, and provides the reader with a hands-on feel for building a mobile service using agent-oriented software engineering.

6   Conclusions

We hope to have demonstrated that the agent paradigm provides useful tools and abstractions for addressing the requirements of the new generation of mobile services. We also hope that our classification would help future research in the area by enabling the identification of opportunities to extend existing efforts. We described a recipe for engineering agent-based mobile applications and presented a quick hands-on exercise utilizing agents for mobile services.

The use of context information will be important for mobile services. Agent-based software development could provide the structures for building context-aware systems. It is important to create better methods to collect, represent and process contextual information. Agent-oriented approaches can supply the tools for such development.

Our future work includes extending our classification model and use it to analyse other existing systems. We also plan to engineer more elaborate mobile service architectures based on these classifications. Finally, we will work on the implementation of the proposed examples, creating proof-of-concept applications.

Acknowledgement

This work was conducted while Fernando Koch was a visitor at the Department of Information Systems, University of Melbourne.

References

1. M. Beer, M. d'Inverno, M. Luck, N. Jennings, C. Preist, and M. Schroeder. Negotiation in multi-agent systems. *Knowledge Engineering Review 14*, pages 285–289, 1999.
2. H. Chalupsky, Y. Gil, C. A. Knoblock, K. Lerman, J. Oh, D. V. Pynadath, T. A. Russ, and M. Tambe. Electric elves: Applying agent technology to support human organizations. In H. Hirsh and S. Chien, editors, *Proceedings of the 13th International Conference of Innovative Application of Artificial Intelligence (IAAI-2001)*. AAAI Press, 2001.
3. M. Dastani, F. Dignum, and J.-J. Meyer. Autonomy and agent deliberation. In M. Rovatsos and M. Nickles, editors, *The First International Workshop on Computatinal Autonomy - Potential, Risks, Solutions (Autonomous 2003)*, pages 23–35, Melbourne, Australia, July 2003.
4. F. de Boer, R. M. van Eijk, W. van der Hoek, and J.-J. Meyer. A fully abstract model for the exchange of information in multi-agent systems. *Theoretical Computer Science*, 290(3):1753–1773, 2003.
5. A. K. Dey. *Providing Architectural Support for Building Context-Aware Applications*. PhD thesis, Georgia Institute of Technology, November 2000.
6. A. K. Dey and G. D. Abowd. Towards a better understanding of context and context-awareness. Technical Report GIT-GVU-99-22, College of Computing, Georgia Institute of Technology, June 1999.
7. A. K. Dey, G. D. Abowd, and D. Salber. A conceptual framework and a toolkit for supporting the rapid prototyping of context-aware applications. *Human Computer Interaction Journal*, 16:97–166, 2001.
8. E. H. Durfee. Practically coordinating. *Artificial Intelligence Magazine*, 20(1):99–116, Spring 1999.
9. K. Henricksen, J. Indulska, and A. Rakotonirainy. Infrastructure for pervasive computing: Challenges. In K. Bauknecht, W. Brauer, and T. A. Mück, editors, *Informatik 2001: Wirtschaft und Wissenschaft in der Network Economy - Visionen und Wirklichkeit*, volume 1 of *Tagungsband der GI/OCG-Jahrestagung*, pages 214–222, Universität Wien, September 2001.
10. N. R. Jennings. Agent-oriented software engineering. In F. J. Garijo and M. Boman, editors, *Proceedings of the 9th European Workshop on Modelling Autonomous Agents in a Multi-Agent World : Multi-Agent System Engineering (MAAMAW-99)*, volume 1647, pages 1–7, Spain, 30– 2 1999. Springer-Verlag: Heidelberg, Germany.
11. N. R. Jennings. An agent-based approach for building complex software systems. *Commun. ACM*, 44(4):35–41, 2001.
12. N. R. Jennings, K. Sycara, and M. J. Wooldridge. A roadmap of agent research and development. *Journal of Autonomous Agents and Multi-Agent Systems*, 1(1):7–38, 1998.
13. N. R. Jennings and M. J. Wooldridge. Applications of intelligent agents. *Agent technology: foundations, applications, and markets*, pages 3–28, 1998.

14. F. Koch and I. Rahwan. Classification of agents-based mobile assistants. In *Proceedings of the AAMAS Workshop on Agents for Ubiquitous Computing (UbiAgents)*, New York, USA, Jul 2004.

15. S. Paurobally, P. J. Turner, and N. R. Jennings. Automating negotiation for m-services. *IEEE Trans. on Systems, Man and Cybernetics (Part A: Systems and Humans)*, 33(6):709–724, 2003.

16. G. P. Picco, G.-C. Roman, and A. L. Murphy. *The future of Software Engineering*, chapter Software Engineering for Mobility: A Roadmap, pages 241–258. ACM Press, 2000.

17. D. Pynadath and M. Tambe. Multiagent teamwork: Analyzing key teamwork theories and models. In C. Castelfranchi and L. Johnson, editors, *Proceedings of the 1st International Joint Conference on Autonomous Agents and Multiagent Systems (AAMAS-2002)*, pages 873–880, New York, USA, 2002. ACM Press.

18. T. Rahwan, T. Rahwan, I. Rahwan, and R. Ashri. Agent-based support for mobile users using agentspeak(l). In P. Giorgini, B. Hederson-Sellers, and M. Winikoff, editors, *Agent Oriented Information Systems*, Lecture Notes in Artificial Intelligence. Springer Verlag, Berlin, Germany, 2004.

19. N. Sadeh, T.-C. Chan, L. Van, O. Kwon, and K. Takizawa. Creating an open agent environment for context-aware m-commerce. In Burg, Dale, Finin, Nakashima, Padgham, Sierra, and Willmott, editors, *Agentcities: Challenges in Open Agent Environments*, LNAI, pages 152–158, Heidelberg, Germany, 2003. Springer Verlag.

20. M. Satyanarayanan. Pervasive computing: vision and challenges. *IEEE Personal Communications*, 8(4):10–17, 2001.

21. P. Scerri, D. Pynadath, and M. Tambe. Towards adjustable autonomy for the real-world. *Journal of AI Research (JAIR)*, 17:171–228, 2002.

22. T. B. Sheridan. Rumination on automation. In *Proceedings of 7th IFAC/IFIP/IFORS/IEA Symposium on Analysis, Design and Evaluation of Man-Machine Systems*, Kyoto, Japan, 1998. Oxford: Pergamon Press. Plenary address.

23. M. Uncapher. M-commerce e-data: Jupiter media metrix says mobile transactions to comprise only a sliver of all online shopping. *ITAA E-LETTER*, page 2, July 2001.

24. G. Weiss. *Multiagent Systems: A Modern Approach to Distributed Artificial Intelligence*. The MIT Press, 1999.

25. M. J. Wooldridge. *An Introduction to MultiAgent Systems*. John Wiley & Sons, Chichester, England, 2002.

26. F. Zambonelli and H. V. D. Parunak. Towards a paradigm change in computer science and software engineering: a synthesis. *The Knowledge Engineering Review*, 2004. (to appear).

27. F. Zambonelli and H. Van Dyke Parunak. From design to intention: Signs of a revolution. In *Proceedings of the First International Joint Conference on Autonomous agents and Multiagent Systems*, pages 455–456. ACM Press, 2002.

A Trust/Honesty Model
in Multiagent Semi-competitive Environments

Ka-man Lam and Ho-fung Leung

Department of Computer Science and Engineering,
The Chinese University of Hong Kong,
Sha Tin, Hong Kong, China
{kmlam,lhf}@cse.cuhk.edu.hk

Abstract. Much research has been done on the calculation of trust, impression and reputation, as well as using these information to decide whether to cooperate with other agents in cooperative environments. However, little is about how to use these information to help agents make decision on whether to believe a particular message when the message sender has intention to be honest as well as dishonest, and make decision on whether to lie. In this paper, we describe a framework to help agents make these decisions in a semi-competitive environment, and show that agents adopting the proposed model have better performance than agents adopting previous models or strategies.

1 Introduction

Much research has been done on agents coordination [6–8, 12, 17, 22, 23]. Besides, the issues about honesty and trust among agents have also been addressed by various researchers [1–5, 9, 13–16, 19–21]. However, the discussions have been mainly concentrated on cooperative environments.

In this paper, we discuss the issues of trust and honesty in *semi-competitive* multi-agent environments. In purely cooperative environments, agents share their utilities, so there is no reason to lie to the partners. In strictly competitive environments such as zero-sum games, that one agent wins means that other agents lose, so there is no need to be honest to the competitors. In (semi-)competitive environments, agents compete with each other in some aspects, and at the same time, agents might cooperate with each other to increase their utilities. Therefore, there are reasons for the agents to lie as well as to be honest. Consequently, on receiving information from other agents, receivers need to decide whether to trust the messages. On the other hand, before sending information to other agents, senders need to decide whether to lie or not. Compared to those in purely cooperative or strictly competitive environments, the issues about trust and honesty among agents become more significant and complicated in semi-competitive environments. In this paper, we describe a framework to help receivers make decision on whether to believe a particular message, and help senders make decision on whether to be honest in a semi-competitive game.

M.W. Barley and N. Kasabov (Eds.): PRIMA 2004, LNAI 3371, pp. 128–147, 2005.

The rest of the paper is organized as follows. In the next section, we briefly review the background of this work. In sections 3 and 4, we introduce our model. We analyze the performance of agents employing this model in section 5, based on simulation results. We show that agents employing our trust model greatly outperform agents employing other trust models available in the literature. Section 6 concludes the paper and discusses possible future work.

2   Background

Marsh [13] is among the first to investigate trust in multiagent systems. In his thesis, he mentions that an agent decides to cooperate with another agent on a matter, if the trust it has on that agent in that matter is greater than a cooperation threshold, which is calculated from the risk and importance of the matter, as well as the competence of that agent on that matter. However, the risk of a matter and the competence of an agent on a particular matter are difficult to estimate in real practice. In addition, the framework is incomplete, as the way in which trust can be modified is not defined.

Mui *et al.* [14–16] use a Bayesian approach in the computational model of trust and reputation, in which they estimate the reputation of agent x in the eye's of agent y as the probability that agent x cooperates with agent y, that is the number of cooperation that agent x has made toward agent y out of the previous encounters. The reputation defined there is an opinion that a single agent has about a particular agent, rather than the opinion that a group of agents have about a particular agent. This deviates from the definitions in the dictionaries [10, 11]. In the computational model, they define trust as the expected probability that agent x will cooperate the next time, given a history of encounters. There is a problem with this approach. Agents adopting this model can be cheated easily. For example, out of 10 encounters, agent x cooperates with agent y in 9 rounds bringing a utility gain of 10, but it does not cooperate in 1 round bringing a utility loss of 100, the expected probability that agent x will cooperate the next time is 0.9, so agent y will still trust agent x. However, agent x actually brings much more harm than gain to agent y, that is agent y is trusting a harmful agent. The reason for this is that this model only calculates the expected probability for cooperation, but does not include the utility that the interacting agent brings.

Sabater and Sierra [19] propose another reputation model. There they define *impression* that an agent has on another agent as the subjective evaluations made by an agent on certain aspects of the agent being evaluated, and they calculate *individual-experienced reputation* that an agent has on another agent, directly from an agent's impression database. For example, to evaluate the reputation of being a trustworthy sender, agent will consider the reputation of telling the truth. In this model, there is a *group-experienced reputation* that a group of agents have on a particular agent being evaluated. This is calculated by the weighted sum of the individual-experienced reputation that the member agents in the group has, on the agent being evaluated. This matches the definition from the dictionary [10, 11]. However, this work mainly concentrates on the calculation of impression and reputation, rather than showing how to use these information to make decisions.

On the other hand, Rubiera *et al.* [18] propose a fuzzy model of reputation rather qualitatively. Castelfranchi and Falcone [1, 3] also describe the importance of trust and explain what trust is in a qualitative way. Much other research [4, 9, 20, 21] has been done on the application of trust, impression, reputation, and reputation management, rather than a framework for decision making.

3   The Trust Model

3.1   A Motivating Example

Consider the example semi-competitive scenario depicted in Fig. 1. In this environment, the agents R_1, R_2 and R_3 interact to maximize their respective payoffs. There are three goals, G_1, G_2 and G_3. Agents have four possible actions: obtaining G_1, obtaining G_2, obtaining G_3, or staying still. Note that R_2 will not be able to obtain G_3 as it does not know that goal. The costs for agents to obtain the goals are shown besides the arrows in the figure, and the cost for staying still is zero. The payoff for agent R_i to obtain goal G_j is defined to be the worth of the goal (if R_i wins the worth of G_j) minus the cost for the agent to obtain the goal (denote as $cost(R_i \rightarrow G_j)$). When more than one agent decides to obtain the same goal, the worth of the goal will be completely given to one agent among all the full-cost paying agents. To decide which agent can win the worth of a certain goal, different systems may apply different mechanisms. For ease of presentation and without loss of generality, it is assumed that for each goal, there is an associated priority ordering of agents, which is shown in the figure. For example, if R_1 decides to obtain G_1, it can win the worth only if both R_3 and R_2 do not compete with it. There are several rounds in this game, one round proceeds after another. In each round, agents are free to communicate until all agents openly announce their choices of actions, then the round ends and the worths of the goals are given to the winning agents. Each agent can only choose one action in each round. An agent knows which messages it received from other agents are true, and which are lies, only after the round ends.

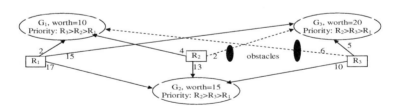

Fig. 1. Example scenario of interacting agents in a semi-competitive environment.

Using Lam and Leung's extension [12] to the Recursive Modeling Method (RMM) of Gmytrasiewicz and Durfee [6–8], R_1 can determine that before any communication, R_2 will choose to obtain G_1, and R_3 will choose to obtain G_2, so R_1 will choose to obtain G_3.

Motivation to Tell the Truth: Invitation to Cooperate. Agents are self-interested, and always want to maximize their own respective utilities. Therefore, in the semi-competitive environment, it is not always good for an agent to share all of its information with other agents. In the decision-making process, we note that R_1 can increase its payoff if R_2 chooses to obtain G_3. To invite R_2 for cooperation, R_1 considers it rational to send R_2 the information about G_3, which is unknown to R_2. This message, M_1, should look like this: "You can obtain the goal G_3, with worth 20, $cost(R_1{\to}G_3) = 15$, $cost(R_2{\to}G_3) = 2$, $cost(R_3{\to}G_3) = 5$ and G_3's priority is $R_2 > R_3 > R_1$." After communication, if R_2 believes the message M_1, it will choose to obtain G_3. This is because R_2 can get a payoff of 18 by obtaining G_3, no matter what actions other agents take. In fact this payoff is also the best payoff it can get among all its possible actions. This shows an example in which agents can benefit mutually by cooperation. This also shows that agents have incentives to tell the truth.

Motivation to Tell a Lie: To Prevent Competition. At the same time, we can see that R_3 can maximize its payoff by obtaining G_3. However, it has a lower priority than R_2, which means that it needs to compete with R_2. So, to prevent competition with R_2, R_3 considers it rational lying to R_2 and directing it to a fake goal. This message, M_2, should look like this: "You can obtain the goal G_4, with worth 24, $cost(R_1{\to}G_4) = 50$, $cost(R_2{\to}G_4) = 4$, $cost(R_3{\to}G_4) = 50$ and G_4's priority is $R_2 > R_1 > R_3$." This shows an incentive for an agent to lie.

To Believe, or Not to Believe, That Is the Question. Now R_2 receives two messages: M_1 from R_1 and M_2 from R_3. If R_2 believe M_1, it will choose to obtain G_3. If R_2 believe M_2, it will choose to obtain G_4. Otherwise, it will choose to obtain G_1. The payoffs of R_2 with respect to its trust on M_1 and M_2 as well as the nature of M_1 and M_2 are summarized below:

		Nature					Nature	
		M_1 is True	M_1 is False				M_2 is True	M_2 is False
R_2	Believe	18	−2		R_2	Believe	20	−4
	Not Believe	6	6			Not Believe	6	6

Now, R_2 faces a difficult question. If R_2 makes the simple assumption that the probability for R_1 or R_3 telling the truth to be $\frac{1}{2}$, then the following expected utilities result:

	Expected Utility		Expected Utility
believe M_1	$\frac{1}{2} \times (18 - 2) = 8$	Not Believe M_1	$\frac{1}{2} \times (6 + 6) = 6$
believe M_2	$\frac{1}{2} \times (20 - 4) = 8$	Not Believe M_2	$\frac{1}{2} \times (6 + 6) = 6$

Since both the expected utilities of believing M_1 and M_2 are higher than that of believing neither M_1 nor M_2, R_2 will believe either M_1 or M_2, or both. However, the two messages lead R_2 to two different actions, but each agent can only choose one action. So, R_2 has to choose to follow either M_1 or M_2, but not both. As the expected utilities of believing M_1 and M_2 are the same, R_2 cannot determine whether to follow M_1 or M_2. In this example, we show that agents have incentives to tell the truth as well as to tell lies in semi-competitive environments. Besides, we show in the example that considering only the expected utility is not enough in making the decision on which message to believe. To solve the problem, we need to consider trustworthiness in addition to expected utilities[1].

3.2   Impression

- From Cambridge Dictionaries Online [10], *Impression* is "the opinion you form when you meet someone or see something."
- From Merriam-Webster Online [11], *Impression* is "a telling image impressed on the senses or the mind."

We suggest that in semi-competitive environments, each receiver agent should maintain an impression on each sender agent about based on its experience. A sender gives a good impression to a receiver if and only if the former has told truths to the latter, which has brought the latter benefits. We define the *impression* that receiver i has towards sender j to be a real number in $[-1, 1]$:

$$imp_{ij} = f_i(\sum gain_{ij}, \sum loss_{ij}, p, n)$$

where $\sum gain_{ij}$ ($\sum loss_{ij}$) is the sum of the utility that agent i has gained (lost) by having believed the truths (lies) from agent j, p is the number of times that agent j has told truth, and n is the total number of messages that agent i has received from agent j. The function f_i must satisfy the following axioms:

Axiom f_{i1}: f_i is continuous.
Axiom f_{i2}: f_i strictly increases as p increases.
Axiom f_{i3}: f_i increases as $\sum gain_{ij}$ increases.
Axiom f_{i4}: f_i decreases as $\sum loss_{ij}$ increases.
Axiom f_{i5}: $f_i = 0$ when $n = 0$.
Axiom f_{i6}:   For $\sum gain_{ij} = \sum loss_{ij}$, $f_i = 0$ when $p = n - p$, $f_i > 0$ when $p > n - p$, and $f_i < 0$ when $p < n - p$.
Axiom f_{i7}: $f_i > 0$ when $\sum gain_{ij} > \sum loss_{ij}$ and $p \geq n - p$.
Axiom f_{i8}: $f_i < 0$ when $\sum gain_{ij} < \sum loss_{ij}$ and $p \leq n - p$.
Axiom f_{i9}: $f_i < 0$ when $\sum gain_{ij} > \sum loss_{ij}$ and $p < n - p$.
Axiom f_{i10}: $f_i < 0$ when $\sum gain_{ij} < \sum loss_{ij}$ and $p > n - p$.

It is rational that receiver will have better impression on a sender if the sender tells much truth, or the sender brings much gain, but receiver will lower the impression on the sender if it brings much loss. These are expressed by axioms

---

[1] In this paper, we assume that if an agent believes a message, the agent believes all the information provided by the message. Choosing to believe only some parts of the message will much complicate the discussion and we leave it to the future work.

f_{i2}, f_{i3}, and f_{i4}. Impression will be neutral if agent i receives no message from agent j (axiom f_{i5}). Axiom f_{i6} states that if a sender brings the same amounts of gain and loss, then impression will be neutral if the sender has told the same number of truths and lies, or positive if the sender has told more truths than lies, or negative otherwise. From axioms f_{i7} and f_{i8}, if a sender brings more gain than loss and has told more truths than lies (or the same number of truths and lies), this means that the sender is good to the receiver, so the receiver will have a positive impression on the sender and vice versa. Axiom f_{i9} says that if a sender brings more gain than loss, but has told more lies than truths (for example, a sender tells a truth bringing a utility of 100 to the receiver at the first encounter, but the sender lies and makes the receiver lose a utility of 90 in total in the following nine encounters), it is obvious that the sender is doing harm to the receiver. So, the impression in this case should be negative. Axiom f_{i10} shows that impression is also negative if a sender has told more truths than lies, but brings more loss than gain.

The following is an example function satisfying the above axioms and the intuitive meanings:

$$
imp_{ij} = \begin{cases}
0 & n = 0 \\
\frac{p-(n-p)}{n} & \sum gain_{ij} = \sum loss_{ij} \\
-(\frac{p-(n-p)}{n})(\frac{\sum gain_{ij} - \sum loss_{ij}}{\sum gain_{ij} + \sum loss_{ij}}) & \sum gain_{ij} < \sum loss_{ij} \wedge p \le n - p \\
(\frac{p-(n-p)}{n})(\frac{\sum gain_{ij} - \sum loss_{ij}}{\sum gain_{ij} + \sum loss_{ij}}) & \text{otherwise}
\end{cases}
$$

3.3   Reputation

- From Cambridge Dictionaries Online [10], *Reputation* is "the opinion that people in general have about someone or something, ..., based on past behavior or character."
- From Merriam-Webster Online [11], *Reputation* is the "overall quality or character as seen or judged by people in general."

Following the definition in the dictionaries, we define the reputation of an agent to be an averaged impression that the population has towards that agent. However, the only way for an agent to access other agents' impressions on a particular agent is to ask other agents for their impressions on that particular agent. It is possible that an agent can lie in answering the query, so a weight could be introduced to the answer. In an N agents environment, we define *reputation* of a sender j, as seen by a receiver i, as a weighted sum of individual impressions of a subset of the population:

$$
rep_{ij} = \frac{\sum_{k=1}^{k=n} imp_{kj} \times W_{ik}}{n}
$$

where W_{ik} is the weight that agent i attaches to agent k's impression on agent j and $n \le N$. Note that each receiver can choose its own subset of population and decide the corresponding weights in calculating the reputation of a particular sender. Much research has been done on this issue [16, 18, 19]. In the absence of any knowledge about other agents' honesty and trustworthiness, the weights can be assumed to be 1.

3.4   Risk Attitude and Trustworthiness

In human interaction, different people have different reactions when they are cheated by the same lie, and the degree of trust that different people have towards the liar will be different. For example, one will consider not trusting the liar anymore once he is cheated, while another person may continue trusting the liar even he is cheated. This is because different people have different *attitudes towards risk*: some do not mind taking any risk, some do not want to take any risk, while others are neutral. To model this, we propose to include the *risk attitude* of the receiver agent in calculating its trustworthiness on the sender. The risk attitude here does not mean the risk undertaken by the agent, but rather an index, which reflects the amount of risk that the agent is willing to undertake. Here, we define *risk attitude*, r, of an agent to be a real number in [0,1]. Agents with risk attitude being 0 is the most risk-averse while agents with risk attitude being 1 is the most risk-seeking. A risk-averse agent prefers messages from a sender with high trustworthiness, while a risk-seeking agent prefers messages with high utilities. This risk attitude is determined by the agent itself, like the personality of human, and can change over time.

In section 3.1, we show that considering expected utility alone is not enough for an agent to determine which message(s) to believe when multiple messages are received. In fact, it is dangerous for an agent to believe a message just because the expected utility of the message is attractive: the agent can be cheated easily. We propose that in a multi-agent semi-competitive environment, each receiver should maintain a *trustworthiness* to every sender of the messages it receives.

- From Cambridge Dictionaries Online [10], *Trustworthiness* is the property of being "able to be trusted," while *trusting* is "to have belief or confidence in the honesty, goodness, skill or safety of a person, organization or thing."
- From Merriam-Webster Online [11], *Trustworthiness* is the property of being "worthy of confidence."

We define *trustworthiness*, t_{ij}, that receiver i has towards sender j as a function of the impression that agent i has about agent j, agent i's calculation on the reputation of agent j as well as the risk attitude of agent i:

$$t_{ij} = f_t(imp_{ij}, rep_{ij}, r_i)$$

The function f_t returns a real number in $[-1, 1]$, and must satisfy the following axioms:

Axiom f_{t1}: f_t is continuous.
Axiom f_{t2}: f_t decreases as imp_{ij} decreases and vice versa.
Axiom f_{t3}: f_t decreases as rep_{ij} decreases and vice versa.
Axiom f_{t4}: f_t decreases as r_i decreases and vice versa.

Axioms f_{t2} and f_{t3} state that it is rational that if the receiver's impression on the sender, or the sender's reputation, decreases, then trustworthiness of the sender decreases, and vice versa. Axiom f_{t4} states that if the risk attitude of the receiver decreases, which means the receiver becomes more risk-averse and thus less willing to trust other agents, the evaluated trustworthiness of the sender will decreases.

An example function satisfying the above axioms and the intuitive meanings is shown below, which attaches the same degree of importance to impression and reputation, and is in proportion to the agent's risk attitude.

$$t_{ij} = \frac{imp_{ij} + rep_{ij}}{2} \times r_i$$

3.5   Persuasiveness of a Message vs. Stubbornness of the Receiver

On determining whether to believe a particular message, besides considering the expected payoffs that the receiver can gain by believing the message, trustworthiness of the message sender should also be considered. Formally, a receiver makes use of a *persuasiveness function* f_p to rank the messages and choose to follow the message that has the highest value of persuasiveness. The *persuasiveness*, p_M, of a message M is defined by:

$$p_M = f_p(r_i, t_{ij}, u_k)$$

Intuitively, the function f_p takes the risk attitude r_i of receiver i as the first argument, the trustworthiness t_{ij} of the message sender j, as seen by receiver i, as the second argument and the expected utility u_k of the message k as the last argument, and returns a real number in $[-1, 1]$ as the rank of the message. The function f_p must satisfy the following axioms:

Axiom f_{p1}: f_p is continuous.
Axiom f_{p2}: (*Adventurousness of risk-seeking agents*) There exists a
        value $r_0 \in \Re$ such that $f_p(r, t_2, u_1) > f_p(r, t_1, u_2)$ if and only
        if $r > r_0$, $t_1 > t_2$ and $u_1 > u_2$.
Axiom f_{p3}: (*Cautiousness of risk-averse agents*) There exists a value
        $r_0' \in \Re$ such that $f_p(r, t_2, u_1) < f_p(r, t_1, u_2)$ if and only if
        $r < r_0'$, $t_1 > t_2$ and $u_1 > u_2$.
Axiom f_{p4}: if $u_1 \geq u_2$, $f_p(r, t, u_1) \geq f_p(r, t, u_2)$.
Axiom f_{p5}: if $t_1 \geq t_2$, $f_p(r, t_1, u) \geq f_p(r, t_2, u)$.
Axiom f_{p6}: if $r_1 \geq r_2$, $f_p(r_1, t, u) \geq f_p(r_2, t, u)$.

It is obvious that the domains of the inputs of f_p are continuous, so f_p should be continuous. Besides, it is reasonable that utility will be more attractive than the trustworthiness of the message sender to a risk-seeking agent, and vice versa to a risk-averse agent. These bring about Axioms f_{p2} and f_{p3}. Axiom f_{p4} states that if an agent receives two messages from senders with the same trustworthiness, but with different payoffs, it is rational that the receiver is more willing to follow the message with the higher payoff. Axiom f_{p5} states that if an agent receives two messages from senders with different trustworthiness, but with same payoffs, it is rational that the receiver is more willing to follow the message from sender, which is more trustworthy. Axiom f_{p6} means that the persuasiveness of the same message from the same sender, with the same trustworthiness, decreases if the receiver become more risk-averse.

Theorem 1 r_0 *(in axiom f_{p2}) equals r'_0 (in axiom f_{p3}).*

Proof. Assume r_0 is not equal to r'_0, this results in the following two cases:

Case 1. $r'_0 > r_0$ By axiom f_{p2}, if $r > r_0$, $t_1 > t_2$ and $u_1 > u_2$, $f_p(r, t_2, u_1) > f_p(r, t_1, u_2)$. By axiom f_{p3}, if $r < r'_0$, $t_1 > t_2$ and $u_1 > u_2$, $f_p(r, t_2, u_1) < f_p(r, t_1, u_2)$. As a result, for $r_0 < r < r'_0$, $f_p(r, t_2, u_1) > f_p(r, t_1, u_2)$ and $f_p(r, t_2, u_1)$ ¡ $f_p(r, t_1, u_2)$, which is a contradiction.

Case 2. $r'_0 < r_0$ By axiom f_{p2}, $f_p(r, t_2, u_1) > f_p(r, t_1, u_2)$ if and only if $r > r_0$, $t_1 > t_2$ and $u_1 > u_2$, so for $r < r_0$, $f_p(r, t_2, u_1) \leq f_p(r, t_1, u_2)$. By axiom f_{p3}, $f_p(r, t_2, u_1) < f_p(r, t_1, u_2)$ if and only if $r < r'_0$, $t_1 > t_2$ and $u_1 > u_2$, so for $r > r'_0$, $f_p(r, t_2, u_1) \geq f_p(r, t_1, u_2)$. As a result, for $r'_0 < r < r_0$, $f_p(r, t_2, u_1) \leq f_p(r, t_1, u_2)$ and $f_p(r, t_2, u_1) \geq f_p(r, t_1, u_2)$, which is a contradiction.

So r_0 equals r'_0.

A simple example satisfying the above axioms, f_p can be defined as follows[2]:

$$f_p(r, t, u) = \begin{cases} \frac{r}{1-r}u + t & \text{for } r \neq 1 \\ u & \text{for } r = 1 \end{cases}$$

With this function, the most risk-averse agent, with zero risk attitude, considers only trustworthiness of the sender in making decision. The most risk-seeking agent, with risk attitude 1, considers only utilities of the messages, while agents with other risk attitudes consider trustworthiness of the sender and utility of the message in a certain ratio.

If a receiver receives only one message, it should believe the message only if the persuasiveness of the message is higher than a certain threshold. We call this the *stubbornness* of the receiver to the sender, which is a real number in $[-1, 1]$. Each agent maintains a stubbornness to each message sender, which can change over time, like personality of human. If more than one message is received at a time, as an agent can only choose one action in one single round, the receiver should believe the message with the greatest persuasiveness, among those messages having a persuasiveness greater than the corresponding stubbornness to the senders.

From the definition of the f_p function, it is easy to see that it is possible that two messages have the same value of persuasiveness. This means that the two messages are having the same expected utility and both are from sources with the same degree of reliability. In this case, the effect on believing and following which message will have no difference, so the agent can simply throw a dice to determine which message to believe. Another problem is that a message with an extremely high utility will cause an agent to follow. First, we note that this

---

[2] In this formula, the utility is assumed to be in the range $[-1, 1]$.

actually mimics a real-life phenomenon occurring in human community. Second, a cheated agent will decrease the trustworthiness of a message sender who lied to it. Possibly, the agent will also become more risk-averse. Consequently, an agent will be cheated for only the first few times, and will not believe further messages from the same message sender. This will be discussed in future work.

Theorem 2 *If two messages M_1 and M_2, with expected utilities u_1, u_2 and trustworthiness of message senders t_1, t_2, respectively, where $u_1 > u_2$ and $t_2 > t_1$, are sent to all agents with different risk attitudes. Then there exists a constant $r_0 \in \Re$ depending only on u_1, u_2 and t_1, t_2, such that all the agents with risk attitude $r > r_0$ will choose to believe M_1 and all the agents with risk attitude $r < r_0$ will choose to believe M_2.*

Proof. Agent uses a function f_p to rank the messages and choose to believe and follow the message that has the highest value of f_p, where f_p must satisfy axioms f_{p1} to axioms f_{p6}. Since $t_2 > t_1$ and $u_1 > u_2$, by axiom f_{p2}, there exists a value $r_0 \in \Re$ such that $f_p(r, t_1, u_1) > f_p(r, t_2, u_2)$ if and only if $r > r_0$. And by axiom f_{p3}, there exists a value $r'_0 \in \Re$ such that $f_p(r, t_1, u_1) < f_p(r, t_2, u_2)$ if and only if $r < r'_0$. By Theorem 1, $r = r'_0$. So, for $u_1 > u_2$ and $t_2 > t_1$, there exists a value $r_0 \in \Re$ such that if $r > r_0$, then $f_p(r, t_1, u_1) > f_p(r, t_2, u_2)$, which means the agent will choose to believe and follow message M_1, and if $r < r_0$, then $f_p(r, t_1, u_1) < f_p(r, t_2, u_2)$, which means the agent will choose to believe and follow message M_2.

Theorem 3 *Suppose there are two agents R_1 and R_2, with risk attitudes r_1 and r_2 respectively, where $r_1 > r_2$, that is agent R_1 is more risk-seeking than agent R_2. Then there exist two messages M_1 and M_2, with expected utilities u_1, u_2 and trustworthiness of message senders t_1, t_2, respectively, where $u_1 > u_2$ and $t_2 > t_1$, such that when these two messages are sent to R_1 and R_2, R_1 will choose to believe message M_1 and R_2 will choose to believe message M_2.*

Proof. By theorem 2, for any two messages M_1 and M_2, with expected utilities u_1, u_2 and trustworthiness of message senders t_1, t_2, respectively, where $u_1 > u_2$ and $t_2 > t_1$, there exists a constant $r_0 \in \Re$ depending only on u_1, u_2 and t_1, t_2, such that all the agents with risk attitude $r > r_0$ will choose to believe and follow M_1 and all the agents with risk attitude $r < r_0$ will choose to believe and follow M_2. In other words, proving theorem 3 is to find the two messages such that $r_2 < r_0 < r_1$. We do this by first initialize two messages M_1 and M_2, with expected utilities u_1, u_2 and trustworthiness of message sender t_1, t_2, respectively, where $u_1 > u_2$ and $t_2 > t_1$. When these two messages are sent to the two agents, one of the following four cases will result:

Case 1. Both of R_1 and R_2 choose to believe and follow message M_1. In this case, generate another two messages M'_1 and M'_2, with expected utilities u'_1, u'_2 and trustworthiness of message sender t'_1, t'_2, respectively, where $u'_1 > u'_2$, $t'_2 > t'_1$, $t'_2 > t_2$ and $t'_1 < t_1$.

Case 2. Both of R_1 and R_2 choose to believe and follow message M_2. In this case, generate another two messages M'_1 and M'_2, with expected utilities u'_1,

u'_2 and trustworthiness of message sender t'_1, t'_2, respectively, where $u'_1 > u'_2$, $t'_2 > t'_1$, $u'_1 > u_1$ and $u'_2 < u_2$.

In case 1 and case 2, the process is continued by sending the new messages M'_1 and M'_2 to the agents, replacing the old messages M_1 and M_2. As r is a real number, as long as $r_1 > r_2$, there exists $r_0 \in \Re$, such that $r_2 < r_0 < r_1$. So, eventually, the process converge and case 3 will results.

Case 3. R_1 chooses to believe and follow message M_1 and R_2 chooses to believe and follow message M_2. In this case, the theorem is proved.

Case 4. R_1 chooses to believe an follow message M_2 and R_2 chooses to believe and follow message M_1. In fact, this case will never happen. Suppose R_1 and R_2 choose to believe and follow different messages, as $r_1 > r_2$, and by theorem 2, $r_2 < r_0 < r_1$, which means R_1 will choose to believe and follow message M_1 and R_2 will choose to believe and follow message M_2.

The following theorem states that it is rational for an agent to believe a message with a higher utility and from a more trustworthy source, rather than a message with a lower utility and from a less trustworthy source.

Theorem 4 *For risk attitude r, trustworthiness t_1 and t_2, and utilities u_1 and u_2, where $t_1 \geq t_2$ and $u_1 \geq u_2$, $f_p(r, t_1, u_1) \geq f_p(r, t_2, u_2)$.*

Proof. From axiom f_{p4}, if $u_1 \geq u_2$, $f_p(r, t_1, u_1) \geq f_p(r, t_1, u_2)$. From axiom f_{p5}, if $t_1 \geq t_2$, $f_p(r, t_1, u_2) \geq f_p(r, t_2, u_2)$. So, $f_p(r, t_1, u_1) \geq f_p(r, t_1, u_2) \geq f_p(r, t_2, u_2)$. That is $f_p(r, t_1, u_1) \geq f_p(r, t_2, u_2)$.

Intuitively, if an agent becomes more risk-averse and lowers the trustworthiness of the message sender after it is being cheated, then when this agent receives the same message from the same sender (with trustworthiness lowered), it should be less willing to follow the message. This phenomenon is confirmed by the following theorem.

Theorem 5 *For risk attitudes r_1 and r_2, trustworthiness t_1 and t_2, and utility u, where $r_1 \geq r_2$ and $t_1 \geq t_2$, $f_p(r_1, t_1, u) \geq f_p(r_2, t_2, u)$.*

Proof. From axiom f_{p6}, if $r_1 \geq r_2$, $f_p(r_1, t_1, u) \geq f_p(r_2, t_1, u)$. From axiom f_{p5}, if $t_1 \geq t_2$, $f_p(r_2, t_1, u) \geq f_p(r_2, t_2, u)$. So, $f_p(r_1, t_1, u) \geq f_p(r_2, t_1, u) \geq f_p(r_2, t_2, u)$. That is $f_p(r_1, t_1, u) \geq f_p(r_2, t_2, u)$.

A dual of Theorem 5, Theorem 6 shown below has no intuitive meaning; it is shown here only for completeness.

Theorem 6 *For risk attitudes r_1 and r_2, trustworthiness t, and utilities u_1 and u_2, where $r_1 \geq r_2$ and $u_1 \geq u_2$, $f_p(r_1, t, u_1) \geq f_p(r_2, t, u_2)$.*

Proof. From axiom f_{p6}, if $r_1 \geq r_2$, $f_p(r_1, t, u_1) \geq f_p(r_2, t, u_1)$. From axiom f_{p4}, if $u_1 \geq u_2$, $f_p(r_2, t, u_1) \geq f_p(r_2, t, u_2)$. So, $f_p(r_1, t, u_1) \geq f_p(r_2, t, u_1) \geq f_p(r_2, t, u_2)$. That is $f_p(r_1, t, u_1) \geq f_p(r_2, t, u_2)$.

4 The Honesty Model

4.1 Motivation: To Lie, or Not to Lie, That Is the Question

For naive receiver agents that do not employ any trust model, it is rational for a sender to lie, if it can model that the receiver will believe the message and change its action accordingly, which brings the sender an increase in utility. In fact, a sender agent can lie that the worth of a fake goal is extremely large, so that it can always be sure that the receiver will believe the message as receivers with no trust model consider only expected utility. This means that agents will always choose to lie. However, the receivers become less easy to be cheated after employing a trust model. In addition to the expected utility, a receiver also takes into account the trustworthiness of the message sender, when it decides whether to believe the received message. As a result, a sender also needs to consider if the receiver will actually be cheated before telling lies. So, whether or not to lie becomes a question.

4.2 Impression

In semi-competitive environments, each sender also maintains an impression on each receiver, based on its past experience. We define the *impression* that sender i has towards receiver j to be a real number in $[-1, 1]$:

$$imp_{ij} = f_i(\sum gain_{ij}, \sum loss_{ij}, p, n)$$

where $\sum gain_{ij}$ is the sum of the utility that agent i has gained by successfully cheating agent j, $\sum loss_{ij}$ is the sum of the utility that agent i has lost by unsuccessfully cheating agent j, p is the number of times that agent j has been successfully cheated by agent i, and n is the total number of times that agent i lie to agent j. This function follows the same set of axioms as described in section 3.2:

Axiom f_{i1}: f_i is continuous.
Axiom f_{i2}: f_i strictly increases as p increases.
Axiom f_{i3}: f_i increases as $\sum gain_{ij}$ increases.
Axiom f_{i4}: f_i decreases as $\sum loss_{ij}$ increases.
Axiom f_{i5}: $f_i = 0$ when $n = 0$.
Axiom f_{i6}: For $\sum gain_{ij} = \sum loss_{ij}$, $f_i = 0$ when $p = n - p$, $f_i > 0$ when $p > n - p$, and $f_i < 0$ when $p < n - p$.
Axiom f_{i7}: $f_i > 0$ when $\sum gain_{ij} > \sum loss_{ij}$ and $p \geq n - p$.
Axiom f_{i8}: $f_i < 0$ when $\sum gain_{ij} < \sum loss_{ij}$ and $p \leq n - p$.
Axiom f_{i9}: $f_i < 0$ when $\sum gain_{ij} > \sum loss_{ij}$ and $p < n - p$.
Axiom f_{i10}: $f_i < 0$ when $\sum gain_{ij} < \sum loss_{ij}$ and $p > n - p$.

Axioms f_{i2} and f_{i3} state that sender will have a better impression on the receiver if the number of times that the receiver is cheated by the sender increases, or the sum of utility that the sender has gained from the receiver increases. On the other hand, axiom f_{i4} states that impression decreases when the sum of utility that the sender has lost increases due to the receiver's distrust on it.

Axioms f_{i5} and f_{i6} say that impression will be neutral if there is no inter-action between the sender and the receiver, or if the sender gains as much as loses and the receiver is cheated successfully and unsuccessfully for the same number of times, while impression will be positive if the number of times that the receiver is cheated successfully is more than that of unsuccessfully, and vice versa.

From axioms f_{i7} and f_{i8}, impression is positive if the sender gains more than loses and the number of times that the receiver is cheated successfully is more than (or equal to) that of unsuccessfully and vice versa. Axiom f_{i9} state that even if the sender gains more than loses but the number of times that the receiver is cheated successfully is less than that of unsuccessfully, the sender should be cautious for this receiver and the impression is negative. Similarly, impression should also be negative if the sender loses more than gains even if the number of times that the receiver is cheated successfully is more than that of unsuccessfully, which is axiom f_{i10}.

The following is an example function satisfying the above axioms and the intuitive meanings:

$$imp_{ij} = \begin{cases} 0 & n = 0 \\ \frac{p-(n-p)}{n} & \sum gain_{ij} = \sum loss_{ij} \\ -(\frac{p-(n-p)}{n})(\frac{\sum gain_{ij} - \sum loss_{ij}}{\sum gain_{ij} + \sum loss_{ij}}) & \sum gain_{ij} < \sum loss_{ij} \wedge p \leq n - p \\ (\frac{p-(n-p)}{n})(\frac{\sum gain_{ij} - \sum loss_{ij}}{\sum gain_{ij} + \sum loss_{ij}}) & \text{otherwise} \end{cases}$$

4.3   Reputation

Similarly, each sender also maintains a reputation on each receiver about ease of being cheated by asking other agents for their impressions on that particular agent. It is also possible that an agent can lie in answering the query, so a weight could be introduced to the answer. In an N agents environment, we define *reputation* of a receiver j, as seen by a sender i, as a weighted sum of individual impressions of a subset of the population:

$$rep_{ij} = \frac{\sum_{k=1}^{k=n} imp_{kj} \times W_{ik}}{n}$$

where W_{ik} is the weight that agent i attaches to agent k's impression on agent j and $n \leq N$. In the absence of any knowledge about other agents' honesty and trustworthiness, the weights can be assumed to be 1.

4.4   Risk Attitude and Deceivability

A dual of the trustworthiness in the trust model, a *deceivability* is maintained by each sender to each receiver, which shows how easily the receiver can be cheated as seen by the sender. We define *deceivability*, c_{ij}, of receiver j from sender i's point of view, as a function of the impression that agent i has about agent j, agent i's calculation on the reputation of agent j as well as the risk attitude of agent i, which returns a real number in $[-1, 1]$:

$$c_{ij} = f_c(imp_{ij}, rep_{ij}, r_i)$$

The function f_c must satisfy a similar set of axioms for function f_t as stated in section 3.4:

Axiom f_{c1}: f_c is continuous.
Axiom f_{c2}: f_c decreases as imp_{ij} decreases and vice versa.
Axiom f_{c3}: f_c decreases as rep_{ij} decreases and vice versa.
Axiom f_{c4}: f_c decreases as r_i decreases and vice versa.
    Axioms f_{c2} and f_{c3} state that it is rational that the deceivability of the receiver decreases if the sender's impression on it decreases, or the receiver's reputation decreases and vice versa. If the risk attitude of the sender decreases, which implies that the sender becomes more risk-averse and thus less willing to cheat other agents, then the evaluated deceivability of the receiver will decrease. This is axiom f_{c4}.
    An example function satisfying the above axioms and the intuitive meanings is shown below, which attaches the same degree of importance to impression and reputation, and is in proportion to the agent's risk attitude.

$$c_{ij} = \frac{imp_{ij} + rep_{ij}}{2} \times (1 - r_i)$$

4.5   Temptation of Lying vs. Sincerity of the Sender

For a sender to decide whether to tell a lie, besides considering the expected payoffs that the agent can gain by lying, it should also consider the deceivability of the receiver. Formally, a sender makes use of a *temptation function* f_{tp} to calculate the temptation of lying. The *temptation*, t_L, of a lie L is defined by:

$$t_L = f_{tp}(r_i, c_{ij}, u_k)$$

Intuitively, the function f_{tp} takes the risk attitude r_i of sender i as the first argument, the deceivability c_{ij} of receiver j as seen by agent i as the second argument and the expected increase in utility u_k as the last argument, and returns a real number in $[-1, 1]$ as the temptation of lying. The function f_{tp} must satisfy a similar set of axioms for function f_p as stated in section 3.5:

Axiom f_{tp1}: f_{tp} is continuous.
Axiom f_{tp2}: (*Adventurousness of risk-seeking agents*) There exists a
         value $r_0 \in \Re$ such that $f_{tp}(r, c_2, u_1) > f_{tp}(r, c_1, u_2)$ if and only
         if $r > r_0$, $c_1 > c_2$ and $u_1 > u_2$.
Axiom f_{tp3}: (*Cautiousness of risk-averse agents*) There exists a value
         $r_0' \in \Re$ such that $f_{tp}(r, c_2, u_1) < f_{tp}(r, c_1, u_2)$ if and only if
         $r < r_0'$, $c_1 > c_2$ and $u_1 > u_2$.
Axiom f_{tp4}: if $u_1 \geq u_2$, $f_{tp}(r, c, u_1) \geq f_{tp}(r, c, u_2)$ for $r > r_0$ and
         $f_{tp}(r, c, u_1) \leq f_{tp}(r, c, u_2)$ for $r < r_0'$.
Axiom f_{tp5}: if $c_1 \geq c_2$, $f_{tp}(r, c_1, u) \geq f_{tp}(r, c_2, u)$.
Axiom f_{tp6}: if $r_1 \geq r_2$, $f_{tp}(r_1, c, u) \geq f_{tp}(r_2, c, u)$.

Axiom f_{tp2} and f_{tp3} state that it is rational for a risk-seeking sender to consider expected gain in utility to be more important than deceivability of the receiver, and vice versa to a risk-averse sender. At the same time, temptation of lies that bring more utility should be higher for a risk-seeking sender, but lower for a risk-averse sender, as it is rational for a risk-averse sender to be hesitate to tell a lie with higher utility. This brings about axiom f_{tp4}. In addition, the temptation of lying a more deceivable receiver should be higher, which is axiom f_{tp5}. However, the temptation of lying decreases if the sender becomes more risk-averse, which is axiom f_{tp6}.

A simple example satisfying the above axioms, f_{tp} can be defined as follows[3]:

$$
f_{tp}(r, c, u) = \begin{cases} \frac{(r-1)u+c}{2} & \text{for } r < 0.5 \\ \frac{u+c}{2} & \text{for } r = 0.5 \\ \frac{(r+1)u+c}{3} & \text{for } r < 0.5 \end{cases}
$$

With this function, the more risk-averse the sender is, the more important the deceivability of the receiver is in making decision. The more risk-seeking the sender is, the more important the utility of the lie is, while senders with neutral risk attitude consider deceivability of the receiver and utility of the lie to be the same important. Note that the functions suggested in this paper are only example satisfying the axioms, anyone can use other functions in the model if the functions satisfy the axioms.

A sender should decide to tell a lie only if the temptation of lying is greater than a certain threshold. We call this the threshold the *sincerity* of the sender to the receiver, which is a real number in $[-1, 1]$. Each sender maintains a sincerity to each receiver, which can change over time. If more than one lie can be chosen from, the sender should send the lie with the greatest temptation, among those lies having a temptation higher than the corresponding sincerity to the receivers. Since agents can only choose one action in each round, and the aim of lying is to change the competitor's action so as to make its own action compatible, agents will only choose at most one lie to send.

The function f_{tp} also have a set of theorems similar to that stated in section 3.5:

Theorem 7 r_0 *(in axiom f_{tp2}) equals r_0' (in axiom f_{tp3}).*

Theorem 8 *If two lies M_1 and M_2 are available to all senders with different risk attitudes, while M_1 and M_2 have expected utilities u_1, u_2 and deceivability of receivers c_1, c_2, respectively, where $u_1 > u_2$ and $c_2 > c_1$. Then there exists a constant $r_0 \in \Re$ depending only on u_1, u_2 and c_1, c_2, such that all the senders with risk attitude $r > r_0$ will choose to send out M_1 and all the senders with risk attitude $r < r_0$ will choose to send out M_2 if temptation of the lies are greater than the senders' sincerity.*

Theorem 9 *Suppose there are two senders R_1 and R_2, with risk attitudes r_1 and r_2 respectively, where $r_1 > r_2$, that is sender R_1 is more risk-seeking than*

---
[3] In this formula, the utility is assumed to be in the range $[0, 1]$.

sender R_2. Then there exist two lies M_1 and M_2, with expected utilities u_1, u_2 and deceivability of receivers c_1, c_2, respectively, where $u_1 > u_2$ and $c_2 > c_1$, such that when these two messages are available to R_1 and R_2, R_1 will choose to send message M_1 and R_2 will choose to send message M_2 if temptation of the lies are greater than the senders' sincerity.

It is rational for a risk-seeking sender to send out a lie with a higher utility to a more deceivable receiver, rather than a lie with a lower utility and to a less deceivable receiver. For a risk-averse sender, as it will be hesitate to tell a lie with a higher utility, which lie it chooses to send depends on the actual values of the deceivability, utilities, risk attitude and sincerity. This is represented by the following theorem.

Theorem 10 *For risk attitude $r > r_0$, deceivability c_1 and c_2, and utilities u_1 and u_2, where $c_1 \geq c_2$ and $u_1 \geq u_2$, $f_{tp}(r, c_1, u_1) \geq f_{tp}(r, c_2, u_2)$.*

The following theorem confirms that if a sender becomes more risk-averse and lowers the deceivability of the receiver after it fails to cheat the receiver, then it should be less willing for the sender to tell the same lie to the same receiver (with deceivability lowered).

Theorem 11 *For risk attitudes r_1 and r_2, deceivability c_1 and c_2, and utility u, where $r_1 \geq r_2$ and $c_1 \geq c_2$, $f_{tp}(r_1, c_1, u) \geq f_{tp}(r_2, c_2, u)$.*

5   Performance Analysis

Simulation is done to compare performance of agents employing our Trust/Honesty model with performance of agents adopting other models or strategies. The setting of the simulation is as follows. We include receivers and senders adopting our Trust/Honesty model. In addition, we include receivers and senders adopting other models or strategies. For receivers adopting our Trust/Honesty model, a negative stubbornness and a risk attitude of 0.2 are used[4]. For receivers adopting Sabater and Sierra's REGRET model [19] and Mui *et al.*'s computational model of trust and reputation [16], reputation and trust are calculated with the parameters suggested in these papers. Receivers adopting the "choose maximum reputation" strategy choose to believe the message from a sender with the maximum reputation when several messages are received at a time. If only one message is received, it chooses to believe the message if and only if the reputation of the message sender is greater than 0.5, where the reputation is normalized to 1. Similarly, receiver adopting the "choose maximum utility" strategy choose the message with maximum utility to believe when several messages are received at a time, and chooses to believe the message if the utility of the message is greater than 0.5, where the utility is normalized to 1. Finally, receivers adopting the random strategy randomly choose to believe a message when several messages

---

[4] This is the best value we obtain in previous experiments, which are not shown here due to lack of space.

are received at a time, and randomly choose to believe or not to believe the message when only one message is received.

In each round, a random semi-competitive scenario is virtually generated. Each sender decides whether to tell a lie to a receiver according to its adopted strategy. Therefore, it is possible that a receiver receives more than one message at a time. Each receiver then chooses whether to believe the message according to its adopted strategy. Note that a receiver adopting the Trust/Honesty Model may believe no message at all if the persuasiveness of the messages it receives are all less than its stubbornness. At the end of each round, a receiver gains if it has believed a true message, or loses if it has believed a lie. On the other hand, a sender gains if the receiver has believed its message, or loses if the receiver has not. Then all agents update the impressions, reputations, trustworthiness, and deceivability accordingly. In this simulation, all agents' risk attitudes, stubbornness values, and sincerity values do not change throughout the game. Each game contains 5,000 rounds, and the average results of 100 games are shown in Table 1 and Table 2.

Table 1 shows the average utility gain[5] of receivers[6]. In the table, maximum possible utility means the maximum utility a receiver can possibly gain if it is so smart as to always choose the right message to believe, and has never been cheated. Note that this just serves as a benchmark for the comparison. Experiments show that receivers adopting our Trust/Honesty Model significantly outperform the others by at least 3 times. This is because the REGRET model and Mui *et al.*'s computational model do not take utility into account in making decisions. Utility of the receiver adopting the "choose maximum reputation" strategy is similar to those of the receivers adopting Sabater and Sierra's REGRET model and Mui *et al.*'s computational model. The receivers adopting the Choose maximum utility strategy and the random strategy end up with negative utilities, because they are easily cheated.

Table 1. Average utility gain of receivers.

Models/strategies	Utility gain
Maximum possible utility	1980
Trust/Honesty Model	1502
Sabater and Sierra's REGRET model [19]	521
Choose maximum reputation	508
Mui *et al.*'s computational model [16]	499
Random	-724
Choose maximum utility	-812

---

[5] Rounded up to the nearest integer.

[6] We have not implemented Marsh's model [13] because agents' competence is irrelevant in our model, and the way trust should be modified is not defined, as discussed in section 2. Also, Mui *et al.*'s Reputation Tic-for-tat [14] is not implemented, either. This is because it cannot handle the case when a receiver receives more than one message at a time. Mui *et al.*'s another model [16] is used for comparison instead.

Table 2. Average utility gain of senders.

Models/strategies	Utility gain
Maximum possible utility	1868
Trust/Honesty Model	1230
100% truth	616
Mui et al.'s computational model [16]	540
Sabater and Sierra's REGRET model [19]	501
Random 50% truth	-678
Always lie	-1769

Table 2 shows the average utility gain of senders. Again in the table, maximum possible utility means the maximum utility that a sender can possibly get if it can always gain receivers' trust. Again, this serves only as a benchmark for comparison. Among all senders, sender adopting our Trust/Honesty Model with risk attitude 0.4 and sincerity 0.8 has the highest utility. The sender adopting the 100% truth strategy always tells the truth. However, receivers may not believe it if the utility brought by the messages is not attractive, so its performance is not the best. Senders adopting the REGRET model and Mui et al.'s model choose to tell lies if the target receiver has good reputation of being deceivable. Their results are similar but not very good as they only take reputation into account, but do not consider utility in making decision. The sender adopting the Random 50% truth strategy randomly tells 50% of truth and the one adopting the Always lie strategy always tells lies. As a result, their utilities are negative, as their reputations are low and no receiver believe them.

These experiments show that our Trust/Honesty model significantly outperforms other trust models. It helps agents to achieve a utility that is about two to three times better than that achieved by agents adopting other trust models reported in the literature. Experiments also show that considering only reputation or only expected utility cannot achieve high utility.

6   Conclusion

In semi-competitive environments, agents have intentions to be honesty and have intentions to lie. This paper introduces a Trust/Honesty Model for receivers to decide whether to believe a received message, and for senders to decide whether to be honest. In the model, risk attitude, stubbornness and sincerity of agents are similar to personality of human, which will be altered in gaining experiences. Experiments show that our Trust/Honesty model significantly outperforms other trust models reported in the literature.

We note that the utility gain much depends on the choice of the parameters of risk attitude, stubbornness and sincerity, etc. In addition, choice of parameters depends on the types of opponents and the actual environment. However, agents in general cannot know the types of opponents and environment in advance. Worse, one set of parameters excelling in a particular environment might not work well in others. To solve this problem, we are developing adaptive agents, which can adjust the parameters autonomously according to their experience. We shall present the adaptive Trust/Honesty Model in another paper.

References

1. C. Castelfranchi and R. Falcone. Principles of trust for mas: Cognitive anatomy, social importance, and quantification. In *Proceedings of the Third International Conference on Multiagent Systems*, pages 72–79, 1998.
2. C. Castelfranchi, R. Falcone, and G. Pezzulo. Trust in information sources as a source for trust: A fuzzy approac. In *Proceedings of The Second International Joint Conference on Autonomous Agent and Multiagent Systems*, pages 89–96, 2003.
3. R. Falcone and C. Castelfranchi. Social trust: A cognitive approach. In *Trust and Deception in Virtual Societies*, pages 55–90. Kluwer Academic Publishers, 2001.
4. A. Glass and B. Grosz. Socially conscious decision-making. In *Proceedings of the Fourth International Conference on Autonomous Agents*, pages 217–224, 2000.
5. P. J. Gmytrasiewicz and E. H. Durfee. Toward a theory of honesty and trust among communicating autonomous agents. *Group Decision and Negotiation*, 2:237–258, 1993.
6. P. J. Gmytrasiewicz and E. H. Durfee. A rigorous, operational formalization of recursive modeling. In *Proceedings of the First International Conference on Multi-Agent Systems*, pages 125–132, 1995.
7. P. J. Gmytrasiewicz and E. H. Durfee. Rational coordination in multi-agent environments. *Autonomous Agents and Multi-Agent Systems*, 3(4):319–350, 2000.
8. P. J. Gmytrasiewicz and E. H. Durfee. Rational communication in multi-agent environments. *Autonomous Agents and Multi-Agent Systems*, 4:233–272, 2001.
9. N. Griffiths and M. Luck. Coalition formation through motivation and trust. In *Proceedings of The Second International Joint Conference on Autonomous Agent and Multiagent Systems*, pages 17–24, 2003.
10. http://dictionary.cambridge.org/. Cambridge dictionaries online.
11. http://www.webster.com/. Merriam-webster online.
12. K. M. Lam and H. F. Leung. An infinite belief hierarchy based on the recursive modeling method. In *Proceedings of Sixth Pacific Rim International Workshop on Multi-Agents*, pages 25–36, 2003.
13. S. Marsh. *Formalising Trust as a Computational Concept*. PhD thesis, University of Stirling, 1994.
14. L. Mui, A. Halberstadt, and M. Mohtashemi. Notions of reputation in multi-agent systems: A review. In *Proceedings of Autonomous Agents and Multi-Agent Systems*, 2002.
15. L. Mui, M. Mohtashemi, C. Ang, P. Szolovits, and A. Halberstadt. Ratings in distributed systems: A bayesian approach. In *Workshop on Information Technologies and Systems*, 2001.
16. L. Mui, M. Mohtashemi, and A. Halberstadt. A computational model of trust and reputation. In *Proceedings of 35th Hawaii International Conference on System Science*, 2002.
17. J. S. Rosenschein and M. R. Genesereth. Deals among rational agents. In *Proceedings of the Ninth International Joint Conference on Artificial Intelligence*, pages 91–99, 1985.

18. J. C. Rubiera, J. M. M. Lopez, and J. D. Muro. A fuzzy model of reputation in multi-agent systems. In *Proceedings of the Fifth International Conference on Autonomous Agents*, pages 25–26, 2001.
19. J. Sabater and C. Sierra. Regret: A reputation model for gregarious societies. In *Proceedings of Fourth International Workshop on Deception, Fraud and Trust in Agent Societies*, 2001.
20. B. Yu and M. P. Singh. Towards a probabilistic model of distributed reputation management. In *Proceedings of Fourth International Workshop on Deception, Fraud and Trust in Agent Societies*, pages 125–137, 2001.
21. B. Yu and M. P. Singh. Detecting deception in reputation management. In *Proceedings of The Second International Joint Conference on Autonomous Agent and Multiagent Systems*, pages 73–80, 2003.
22. G. Zlotkin and J. S. Rosenschein. Negotiation and task sharing among autonomous agents in cooperative domains. In *Proceedings of the Eleventh International Joint Conference on Artificial Intelligence*, pages 912–917, 1989.
23. G. Zlotkin and J. S. Rosenschein. Negotiation and conflict resolution in non-cooperative domains. In *Proceedings of the National Conference on Artificial Intelligence*, pages 100–105, 1990.

An Image Annotation Guide Agent

Chen-Yu Lee, Von-Wun Soo, and Yi-Ting Fu

Department of Computer Science
National Tsing Hua University, HsinChu, 30043, Taiwan
{leoli,soo,mr916792}@cs.nthu.edu.tw

Abstract. The performance of retrieving an image in terms of text-type of queries depends heavily on the quality of the annotated descriptive metadata that describes the content of the images. However, the effective annotation of an image can often be a laborious task that requires consistent domain knowledge. Annotators may annotate features in the images that could not contribute much to retrieval of the images. For effective annotation, an annotation guide agent (AGA) is proposed to aid annotators. Basically AGA monitors the annotator's behaviors and based on the common sense induced from previous annotation instances as well as the domain ontology suggests critical property that will yield the most valuable information for image retrieval. We showed by experiments that the critical property and common sense heuristics used by AGA to aid the annotation of images could significantly lead to the improvement of the recall and precision of image retrieval.

1 Introduction

Retrieving an image from a large set of images based on its content cannot be an easy task. One way to reduce the task is to allow the image content to be described in advance in terms of natural language descriptive metadata so that a text-based retrieval method can match the descriptive metadata with the text-based query to retrieve the image with the described content. We call the process of associating the descriptive metadata with an image as the image annotation process. However, since it is difficult for machines to deal with natural language in the retrieval of images, we had established a case-based learning framework for facilitating image retrieval based on domain ontology and the annotated descriptive metadata of the images [1,2]. We had developed techniques to automate the process of converting the natural language descriptive metadata of an image into machine-readable format that conforms by the semantic web RDF (resource description framework) standards. However, even with these tools, the annotators can still have the difficulty of knowing how to efficiently annotate an image. This is because, first of all, as "an image is worth more than a thousand words" that there are so many details to say for an image. "What details should be annotated and what should not?" can sometimes be a non-trivial decision. On the other hand, if all the details of an image are to be annotated, it could become a tedious task if not an impossible one. On the other hand, when there are common descriptions shared by similar images the annotators may have to go through the redundant annotation process by simply complete the descriptive metadata one by one. Thirdly, when it comes to the domain that an annotator is unfamiliar with, the annotator might accidentally annotate with descriptive metadata that is inconsistent with the domain concepts or ontology.

M.W. Barley and N. Kasabov (Eds.): PRIMA 2004, LNAI 3371, pp. 148–161, 2005.
© Springer-Verlag Berlin Heidelberg 2005

Fourthly, when different annotators who possess different partial point of views of the domain are annotating a set of images, they might annotate the images in terms of quite different set of vocabularies that make coherent annotation of an image impossible and consequently might jeopardize the image retrieval as well.

In order to process a huge amount of annotated images, the automatic semantic tagging system that can convert the descriptive metadata into machine-readable format is a necessary step for the annotated images to be retrieved easily by intelligent retrieval agents. More specifically speaking, the annotator can annotate images with descriptive metadata in natural language statements but the system can automatically convert them into machine-readable format based on the domain ontology. Therefore, the intelligent retrieval agents can share the same domain ontology with the annotator. However, if an annotator has an incomplete or wrong knowledge and ontology, the annotation may become a problem for intelligent retrieval agent to retrieve the correct image. The ideal annotated image base for an image retrieval system is that every image is fully annotated (complete annotation) with correct ontology; which means that all the relations in the domain ontology that are associated with the image have to be completely expressed and specified. But this is a difficult goal to achieve in reality. Human annotators without complete knowledge! Therefore how to make an annotation more precise and complete without requiring a human annotator to completely specify and annotate all possible relations in the image has become an important issue.

Due to the above reasons, we design of an annotator guide agent (AGA) who could guide an annotator to decide what to annotate for an image in a more effective and coherent manner. In section 2 we describe an overview of an automatic semantic annotation system and its relation to AGA. In section 3, we describe the notion of critical property that is used by AGA to guide annotation. In section 4, we describe the experiments that were used to evaluate performance of image retrieval of the annotation results guided by AGA. In section 5, we discuss and make conclusions.

2   Overview of Automatic Semantic Annotation Systems for Image Retrieval

The semantic web [3-14] proposed a knowledge representation framework that enabled the sharing of the domain knowledge on web in terms of XML-based (Extensible Markup Language) ontology languages such as RDF/RDFS (Resource Description Framework/Schema) and OWL [12-14]. The ontology languages provide a well-defined set of relational terms that are essential for building domain concepts. They also provide the semantic interoperability at different platforms that allow knowledge exchange in machine-readable format. RDF/RDFS represents each semantic relation as an information resource in terms of a triple of Subject, Predicate, and Object.

In Figure 1, we showed an automatic image annotation and retrieval system that can help to convert annotator's natural language descriptive metadata of an image into RDF/OWL format so that the image retrieval users can retrieve images in terms of natural language queries. In our previous work [1,2,15] we have implemented a case-based learning parser that can convert the natural language descriptive Meta data as well as the retriever's queries into RDF/OWL format so that the annotation and retrieval can be shared with the same domain ontology. The image retrieval process can therefore be conducted by matching the user's query descriptions with the image descriptions at the structural and semantic level. However, since the performance of retrieving an image in terms of text queries depends heavily on the quality of the annotated descriptive metadata that describes the content of the images, we have proposed in this paper an Annotation Guide Agent to ensure an image be annotated effectively and coherently.

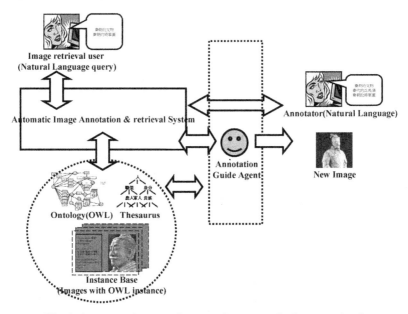

Fig. 1. An automatic semantic annotation system for image retrieval

2.1   The Annotation Guide Agent

As mentioned above, an annotation process requires an annotator to describe image content in natural language descriptive metadata and the AGA can convert it into OWL instances with the aid of sharable thesauri and ontology. And we also mentioned that images should be annotated in a complete and error-proof manner to ensure the performance of image retrieval. But we can't guarantee that annotators always have the same complete knowledge with the system's domain ontology or be patient enough to annotate all the details in the image. Therefore, Annotation Guide Agent should help human annotators to deal with the difficulties.

As in Figure 2, an Annotation Guide Agent (AGA) should keep track of the annotation behaviors of annotators, infer domain common sense from previous annotation instances, record and analyze the queries of image retrievers and prompt an annotator with appropriate suggestions of annotation at an appropriate moment. AGA could provide three possible aids: 1) request the value of a critical property to make images distinguishable in retrieval, 2) provide a set of well-known property-value pairs based on domain common sense to save annotator's effort, and 3) detect and resolve the possible conflicts or inconsistencies. Since the page is limited, the conflict resolution tasks of AGA won't be discussed in this paper.

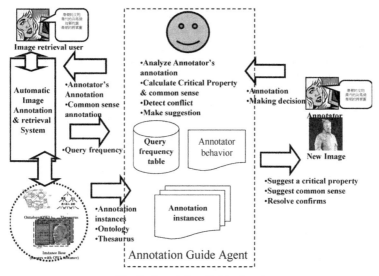

Fig. 2. Annotation Guide Agent

3   The Notion of a Critical Property

In our system, it does not require an annotator to know or learn the system's ontology before annotation; this could reduce the burdens and restrictions of the annotator. However, annotators without knowing the system's ontology may end up with similar annotations for different images. For example, a naive annotator may describe all the terracotta soldier's images in terms of only viewpoints of such as "material", "functionality", and "gender". In the terracotta soldier domain, the material, functionality and gender of a terracotta soldier tend to be the same. The kind of annotation would not be good from the point of view of image retrieval because the images cannot be distinguished from the retrieval point of view. Second, different annotators may annotate the same image from different partial point-of-view, for example, an annotator may annotate the terracotta soldier's images from the viewpoint of "name", "birthday", "Occupation", and "gender", yet another one could annotate from the viewpoint: of "material", "age", and "functionality". This makes the image retrieval difficult also, namely, users interested in "occupation" of terracotta soldiers cannot retrieve the image at all if it is simply annotated with "materials", "age" and "functionality" viewpoints. Since the natural language annotation descriptions have been converted by AGA into RDF format, the descriptions of images are composed of many RDF relation triples. The critical property is an attribute in the RDF triple in the ontology that makes the annotation of an image more precise and easy for retrieval. We evaluate a property as a critical property based on three factors: degree of scatter, common sense inducibility and query effect that will be discussed as following sections.

3.1   The Degree of Scatter

The degree of scatter is a measure based on the annotator's previous annotations. In general, two sub-factors Multiplicity and Equalization are considered. Multiplicity is a property that possesses more different value types for a property, and Equalization is a property whose values types tend to have the same probability of occurrences. A property with above two sub-factors would be regarded as higher degree of scatter and thus tends to be a critical property. For example, if an annotator annotates a human image, an AGA may suggest the annotator to fill in the value of "hasOccupation" based on pervious instances due to the reason that the property "Occupation" tends to have more value types whose occurrences are equally probabilistically distributed. Therefore we calculate the following formula to estimate the degree of scatter for each property, the higher the expected number of values of a property, the lower the degree of scatter.

$$\text{Degree of scatter} = \text{Sum } (P_i^2), \ i = 1 \text{ to } n \qquad (1)$$

Where P_i denotes the occurrence probability of ith value type, and n denotes the number of all different value types in this property.

Figure 3 shows a case of 30 annotated image instances and AGA had recognized that the object under annotation was a "Person". The ratio attached to each property value represents the number of instances that the property has the corresponding value. For example, the degree of scatter for property "hasSkinColor" (the third property from the top in Figure 3) is estimated as $1(1^2)$ and for property "hasDuty" (the last property in Figure 3) is estimated as $0.36 \ [(11/30)^2+(2/30)^2+(14/30)^2+(1/30)^2+(1/30)^2+(1/30)^2]$. It implies that "hasDuty" has a higher degree of scatter than "hasSkinColor". (Note: The lower the ratio the higher the degree of scatter).

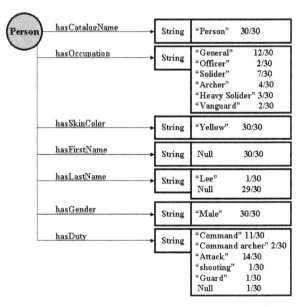

Fig. 3. An example of the data-type properties for the class of a "person"

3.2   The Common Sense Inducibility

The common sense [16] inducibility of a property is a measure of how much chance the property can make the annotation more complete. We estimate the common sense inducibility of a property as the expected number of associated common sense relations that can be inferred by the property. For example, the class "Person" in Figure 3 has several associated properties. Supposed that "hasOccupation = General" can always infer "hasGender=male" and "hasDuty = command" based on previous annotation instances, then AGA estimates that "hasOccupation= General" can infer on average two more common sense relations. The concept of common sense features is to reduce the efforts that might be needed in annotating an image for a human annotator. If AGA could automatically infer common sense, a human annotator does not need to describe the trivial well-known facts, namely the domain common sense features, all the time. The method to acquire the common sense features is to find those triples that are of the same value in a particular class of objects based on their appearance frequencies. For example, supposed that an annotator is annotating an image of a "general" and the AGA had recorded many of its image annotation instances with the following annotation information as: 1.This is a "person", and the person's occupation is a "General". According to the information, AGA may infer that the "gender" of a general should be a "male" because almost all instances that are annotated as "generals" turned out to be a "male" also.

A threshold is used to decide if a property-value pair is a common sense feature. If the occurence frequency of a property-value pair in a triple exceeds a threshold, AGA can infer the corresponding property as a common sense feature in the class of objects. This leads to the method to decide a property-value pair as a common sense feature by calculating the expected frequency of triples whose property-value pairs are the same and check if it exceeds a threshold. We ignore those properties with null values.

Fig. 4. An interface of AGA that can assist an annotator to find the critical property and common sense

In Figure 4, we show an interface of AGA that assists an annotator to annotate an image. AGA showed a subject "person" that the annotator was focusing and showed probability distribution of different properties attached to the person as well as the domain common sense. It shows that most persons have the skin color as "yellow" and the gender as "male". When the annotator hits the button "Find critical property", AGA would suggest the critical property as shown. However, the interface in Figure 4 is suitable for the system development purpose only, not for the actual annotation usage.

Using default rules is another way to express domain common sense. But the human experts need to first establish a set of default rules based on their own domain knowledge. The advantages of using expert default rules are that it can yield nice performance at the outset without any training data and it responds faster to user in comparison to probabilistic or statistical estimation approaches. But it has several drawbacks too:

1) It requires domain experts to write down the default rules first.
2) The default rules cannot guarantee to cover all possible cases and are difficult to adapt.
3) Extra space for the default rules and a parser are needed.

Therefore the statistical estimation approach was adopted in calculating the commonsense in this paper.

3.3 The Query Effect

Query effect of a property is estimated from user's (image retriever) query. Because the annotation process is usually independent of the user queries, the critical property determined by degree of scatter and common sense inducibility does not take the user query into consideration. For example, the image size (bits that an image is encoded) is a very scattered property. But, generally a user would not use the query "I want to find images whose sizes are one Megabits." This means even a property that is scattered in nature might not always lead to useful information for image retrieval. AGA records the frequencies of properties used in the retrieval queries. AGA can guide annotators to annotate by taking into consideration of the properties that are often queried by image retrievers.

3.4 Normalization

In order to calculate the overall degree of criticality of a property, a normalization process is proposed. The degree of scatter will fall into the range [0...1] because the sum of all probability's range is [0...1]. Common sense inducibility and query effect can also be normalized by dividing themselves with the maximum amount so that their values will range within [0...1] interval. Finally, AGA will get its reciprocal after normalization (lower value is better than higher value).

So the degree of criticality of a property p can be calculated as

$$\text{Degree of criticality (p)} = \text{degree of scatter (p)} + \text{common sense induciabilty (p)} + \text{Query effect (p)}$$

4 Experimental Results

Two Experiments were conducted in this paper. The first one was to examine the effectiveness of annotation using the critical property as the guide to annotate an image. The second experiment was to evaluate the effectiveness of domain common sense as a guide to annotate an image.

4.1 Experimental Design and Data Collection

We used the images and their metadata description texts from First Emperor of China CD ROM [17] of Prof. Ching-Chih Chen and website of Museum of Qin Shihuang Terracotta Warriors and Horses [18]. The domain ontology defines domain concepts and schemas in terms of the objects and relations among the objects. The objects and relations are described in terms of classes and properties. Currently there are 14 classes and 129 properties for the whole terracotta soldier domain. 30 images of terracotta soldiers including generals, officers, solider, and archers are collected as the training cases for AGA. The descriptive metadata texts were converted into OWL instance format by AGA using the domain ontology. The descriptive metadata are taken from the domain ontology of terracotta soldier domain, which include the background information about a person (such as occupation, duty, and gender...etc.), the body descriptions (such as dressing, equipments, direction, and gesture... etc), and the item attribute descriptions (such as color, shape, material, and texture...etc.). The training data of 30 images were annotated as complete as possible since we filled in all possible property-value (feature) pairs that are applicable to each image. In Figure 5, a terracotta general image with its OWL annotation is illustrated.

Fig. 5. An image of a terracotta general with its OWL format annotation

4.2   Experiment 1

Six students were asked to annotate fifty images (all belong to the terracotta soldier pictures). The annotators were allowed to use only six simple feature descriptions for each image. The experiments were conducted in two groups: Group 1 (Normal) the annotators annotated the image without the aid of AGA1, and Group 2 (AGA1), the last feature annotation would be suggested by AGA. Namely, the AGA suggested a critical property as the sixth feature after the annotator had given five feature annotations. Only the sixth feature was suggested because AGA must base on the annotator's behavior to make suggestions. Then 20 user queries for the terracotta soldier image domain were collected from five different users that were used as the test queries to retrieve the images from the two groups of the fifty annotated images. We calculated and compared the recall and precision of the image retrieval between the two groups based on the 20 test queries. The recall and precision results are shown in Figure 6 (recall) and 7 (precision) respectively, where the x-coordinate indicates queries and y-coordinate indicates the recall and precision.

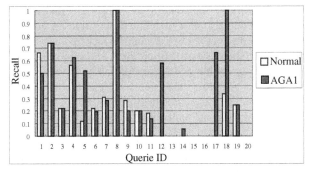

Fig. 6. Recall of experiment 1: Normal vs AGA1

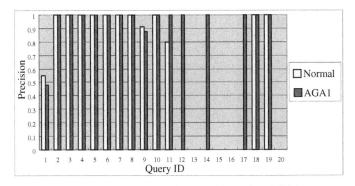

Fig. 7. Precision of experiment 1: Normal vs AGA1

The experimental results show that the average recall in the Normal group is 0.254 with an average precision of 0.613 while that in the AGA1 group is 0.359 with an average precision of 0.767. The average recall and average precision are of 10.5 percent and 15.4 percent difference respectively. Why did the group in AGA perform better than the group in Normal? We analyzed the annotator's annotated features and found that most annotators described images in terms of the same properties (fewer properties are used by annotators), and kept on using those properties to describe what they saw in the images. So although sometimes some useful sixth feature of the original annotator may be replaced by AGA and thus decreased the performance (as in the query #1 and #11 in Figure 6), but more likely the useless sixth features will be replaced with appropriate one (at query #12, #14, and #17 in Figure 7) that's why AGA1 group outperformed Normal group. Thus, we concluded that the annotation guided by AGA could significantly improve the annotation performance in the sense of recall and precision of image retrieval.

4.3   Experiment 2

By further evaluation of the performance of AGA using domain common sense heuristic, we used the same experimental design as Experiment 1. But AGA used the common sense heuristic as the basis to make annotation recommendation (where the common sense threshold is chosen as 0.8). It would automatically augment the annotation by recommending all possible property-value pairs implied by the domain common sense based on AGA1's sixth property. In this way, the number of property-value pairs to be annotated would increase. As shown in Figure 8, in the case study the average number of property-value pairs (common sense inferred) increased was 3.86 property-value pairs on average for each image.

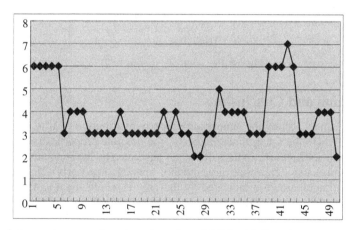

Fig. 8. Increasing property-value set number of AGA with Domain common sense

We use the same set of 20 queries to calculate the recall and precision of image retrieval from the 50 images. These experimental results are shown in Figure 9 (recall) and Figure 10 (precision), where AGA2 indicate AGA are using critical property as well as augmented by the domain common sense.

The experimental results show that the average recall in AGA2 group was 0.516 and the average precision was 0.965. Thus, we concluded that on the AGA2 group significantly outperformed the Normal group by about 26.2 percent for recall and 35.2 percent for precision.

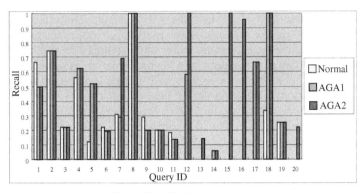

Fig. 9. Recall of experiment 2

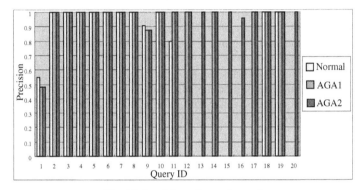

Fig. 10. Precision of experiment 2

5 Discussion and Conclusions

Figure 11, 12 and 13 show the annotation property distribution of fifty images in the experiments, where the x-coordinate indicates the possible properties in ontology and the y-coordinate indicates the indices of images annotated by the annotators, each dot in the figures represents a case that the annotator annotated property x in image y, the frequencies of annotation are indicated by the grey levels of the dots that vary from black (many times) to white (zero time), and the horizontal lines in Figure 11 separate different annotators.

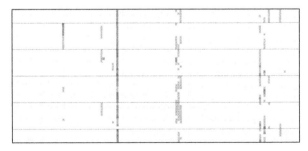

Fig. 11. The property distribution of fifty images by six human annotators

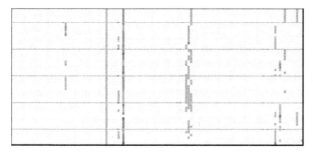

Fig. 12. The property distribution of fifty images by six human annotators with the aid of AGA1

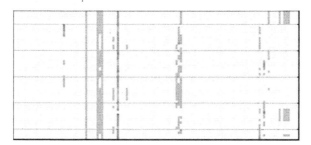

Fig. 13. The property distribution of fifty images by six human annotators with the aid of AGA2

In Figure 11, two phenomena were observed. Firstly, all annotators tended to annotate using similar properties as indicated by the black vertical lines. Secondly, annotators tended to use similar properties to describe different images. Figure 12 shows the annotation property distribution of AGA1. It indicated that the phenomenon of repeating annotation properties was decreased by the fact that the black lines became lighter. The annotation properties tended to become more scattered by the fact that the number of darker (black) spots were decreased. The second vertical line from the left became the most critical property suggested by AGA1 because the property turned into a solid line (e.g. most images were suggested to annotate with this property) in comparison to the sparse dots in Figure 11. Figure 13 shows the annotation property distribution of AGA2 (augmented with domain common sense). It indicated that gray areas spread much wider because totally 193 property-value pairs were taken into consideration.

Due to the possible discrepancy of the domain knowledge of image annotators and image retrieval, the annotation results cannot always be effective from the point of view of image retrieval. In designing an automated semantic annotation system for image retrieval, we have realized that an annotation guide agent (AGA) is necessary to mediate in the loop to aid human annotator to describe the images in terms of more effective features so that the images could be much easier to retrieve later on. Our experimental results had justified our conjectures that using both critical property and domain common sense heuristics could help annotators to annotate the image more effectively. From Figure 11, 12, 13 and the experimental results reported in section 5, we concluded that AGA tended to guide the annotator to annotate an image with more discriminating and relevant properties that lead to a better performance of image retrieval.

The Annotation and Retrieval Integration Agent (ARIA)[19] is a interface agent proposed by MIT media Lab. ARIA system assists an annotator suggested all possible annotations and common senses for an image and retrieve relevant images in the context, but ARIA did not guide an annotator how to annotate, what to annotate and the annotation tended to be personalized that can't be shared in open web environment. Instead, AGA analyzes the annotator's behavior and can provide not only possible common sense but also can guide the annotator to make better annotation that can be shared by most of people based on their own domain ontology.

Although in the experiments, we had tentatively restricted the number of annotation features to only six and allowed only the sixth feature to be modified or recommended by the AGA. In practice, AGA could be invoked at any proper time.

In the performance evaluation experiments we did not include the query effect in the guidance of suggesting the critical property, this is because in doing so it will bias the evaluation on the test query we prepared. But if we allow AGA to use the query effect, the performance should be more effective from the sense of image retrieval because the AGA would recommend those properties that tend to be used for retrieval queries. Also, in this paper, we did not show the actual performance of AGA in resolving the conflicts. They should be invoked whenever the conflicts are detected. However, when will be the most appropriate time to invoke AGA so that the annotation process of the annotators will not become annoying will be the future work.

Acknowledgment

This research is supported in part by Taiwan Ministry of Education Program for Promoting Academic Excellence of Universities under grant number 89-E-FA04-1-4.

The images and image illustration that we used in our experiment were authorized by:

1. Ching-chih Chen, "The First Emperor of China", CD-ROM, Voyager, 1991[17], and
2. Museum of Qin Shihhuang Terra-catta Warriors and Horses, Xi'an city, China [18].

The ontology we constructed is using the Protégé-2000 that developed by Stanford Medical Informatics at the Stanford University School of Medicine [20].

References

1. Von-Wun Soo, Chen-Yu Lee, Chung-Cheng Li, Shu Lei Chen and Ching-chih Chen, "Automated Semantic Annotation and Retrieval Based on Sharable Ontology and Case-based Learning Techniques", in Proc. of ACM/IEEE International Joint Conference of Digital Library, pp. 61 - 72, 2003.
2. Von-Wun Soo, Chen-Yu Lee, Chao-Chun Yeh and Ching-chih Chen, "Using Sharable Ontology to Retrieve Historical Images", in Proc. of ACM/IEEE International Joint Conference of Digit al Library, pp.197-198, 2002.
3. James Hendler, Tim Berners-Lee, and Eric Miller, "Integrating Applications on the Semantic Web," Journal of the Institute of Electrical Engineers of Japan, Vol 122(10), October, 2002, pp. 676-680, http://www.w3.org/2001/sw/.
4. Stephen Cranefield, "Networked Knowledge Representation and Exchange using UML and RDF", Journal of Digital Information, Vol.1, Issue 8, 2001.

5. Boris Motik and Vlado Glavinic, "Enabling Agent Architecture through an RDF Query and Inference Engine", 10th Mediterranean Electro-technical Conference, MeleCon, 2000.
6. Steffen Staaba and Michael Erdmann, "An Extensible Approach for Modeling Ontologies in RDF(S)", in Proc. of ECDL Workshop on the Semantic Web, pp.11-22, 2000.
7. Stefan Decker and Sergey Melnik, "The Semantic Web: The Roles of XML and RDF", IEEE Internet Computing, Vol. 4(5), pp. 63-74, October 2000.
8. B. Amann and I. Fundulaki, "Integrating Ontologies and Thesauri to Build RDF Schemas", Third European Conference ECDL'99, Paris, France, Springer Verlag, pp. 234-253, September, 1999.
9. "Resource Description Framework (RDF) Model and Syntax Specification W3C Recommendation 22, February, 1999", http://www.w3.org/RDF/.
10. Stefan Decker, Frank Van Harmelen and Jeen Broekstra, "The semantic Web - on the respective Role of XML and RDF", http://www.ontoknowledge.org/.
11. "The DARPA Agent Markup Language Homepage", http://www.daml.org/.
12. Deborah L. McGuinness and Frank van Harmelen, "OWL Web Ontology Language Overview", W3C Candidate Recommendation 18 August 2003, http://www.w3.org/TR/2003/CR-owl-features-20030818/.
13. Michael K. Smith, and Deborah McGuinness, "Web Ontology Language (OWL) Guide Version 1.0", http://www.w3.org/TR/owl-guide/.
14. Peter F. Patel-Schneider, and Patrick Hayes, "Web Ontology Language (OWL) Abstract Syntax and Semantics", http://www.w3.org/TR/owl-semantics/.
15. Yi-Jia Chen and Von-Wun Soo, "Ontology-based Information Gathering Agents", in Proc. of Web Intelligence, pp.423-427, 2001.
16. Henry Lieberman ,"Common Sense Reasoning for Interactive Applications", MIT Media Lab Course - Fall 2002, http://web.media.mit.edu/~lieber/Teaching/Common-Sense-Course-02/Common-Sense-Course-Intro.html.
17. Ching-chih Chen, "The First Emperor of China", CD-ROM, Voyager, 1991.
18. The museum of Qin shihuang terra-cotta warrior and horses, http://www.bmy.com.cn/.
19. Aria, http://web.media.mit.edu/~lieber/Lieberary/Aria/Aria-Intro.html.
20. Protège 2.0 with OWL Plugin, http://protege.stanford.edu/.

A Dedicated Approach
for Developing Agent Interaction Protocols

Ayodele Oluyomi and Leon Sterling

Department of Computer Science and Software Engineering
The University of Melbourne, 111 Barry Street, Carlton, Victoria 3053, Australia
{aoo,leon}@cs.mu.oz.au

Abstract. Much current research is focussed on developing agent interaction protocols (AIPs) that will ensure seamless interaction amongst agents in multi agent systems. The research covers areas such as desired properties of AIPs, reasoning about interaction types, languages and tools for representing AIPs, and implementing AIPs. However, there has been little work on defining the structural make up of an agent interaction protocol, or defining dedicated approaches for developing agent interaction protocols from a clear problem definition to the final specification. This paper addresses these gaps. We present a dedicated approach for developing agent interaction protocols. Our approach is driven by an analysis of the application domain and our proposed structured agent interaction protocol definition.

1 Introduction

Interaction is generally recognized as an important characteristic of multiagent systems (MAS) [1, 5]. A widely acceptable view conceptualizes an agent as an autonomous agent possessing the ability to *interact* with other agents to achieve its goals and that of the multiagent system. Agent Interaction Protocols (AIPs) are used for managing and controlling the interactions in MAS [3].

There are two issues that are important in thinking about AIPs. The first one is that an AIP within a MAS has its particular identity, that is, a component part of the MAS that is present to serve the interaction needs of the agents while remaining separate from the individual agents within the system. Secondly, interaction in a MAS is context sensitive. The nature and structure of interaction, and therefore the structure and properties of the AIPs that will achieve a specific interaction, are dependent on the purpose and peculiarities of the domain of application of the MAS in which the specific interaction takes place.

Several Agent Oriented Software Engineering (AOSE) methodologies have been and are still being developed [2, 1, 4]. However, a review of these AOSE methodologies reveals that most of them do not have a clear process for developing AIPs that will be used in the MAS to be developed [1, 4].

The existing body of research work on AIP is largely focused on areas such as AIP specification methods [18, 19]; analysis of interaction types e.g. negotiation, argumentation, persuasion, etc and their underlying philosophies [12, 21, 6]; AIP concatenation and extension issues [22]; languages and tools for representing AIPs [7]; implementing AIPs [13], and so on. In as much as they all have their significant contributions to the agent world, they seem to be going in their individual directions

M.W. Barley and N. Kasabov (Eds.): PRIMA 2004, LNAI 3371, pp. 162–177, 2005.

with no convergence of these efforts and their results, because there is not much effort yet in developing a dedicated approach to engineering AIPs.

Further, a good number of the existing AIPs have weaknesses. A common major weakness is that AIPs do not have important properties such as termination and rule-consistency, which may limit their suitability for their application [6]. It is also important to note that different AIP properties or different combinations of these properties are required for different domains of MAS applications.

Interaction in MAS is high level and significantly context sensitive when compared with data communication protocols. The aspiration of the agent community is to make these interactions as close as possible to human interactions. This conceptual view and the aspiration therefore emphasize the context sensitivity of interagent interaction and therefore the AIPs that will guide these interactions [2]. The contexts of the domain of MAS applications determine the structure and properties of AIPs necessary to achieve effective and efficient interactions within the MAS. Issues such as time criticality, safety criticality, concurrency, control hierarchy, goal diversity and so on are domain dependent and these all influence the way and manner in which effective interaction in such systems should occur.

Most of the MAS development methodologies that consider interaction identify the interaction needs of the system and then implement an existing AIP. For instance, a MAS that requires a *Negotiation* type interaction may implement the FIPA Contract Net Protocol [8]. Although this suggests the software engineering concept of reuse, it does not always achieve desired results due to the following possibilities: the AIP chosen may be too generic for the intended application making it inefficient; the AIP chosen may not be comprehensive enough for the intended application; the AIP chosen may not have the desired properties such as safety, confidentiality, or timing constraints, to ensure rich context based interaction that are well suited for the intended application. Also, it is well accepted that inadequately planned reuse is counter productive.

To address these inadequacies, we propose a comprehensive and dedicated approach for developing AIPs with the aim of generating readily customizable and well structured AIPs that will be appropriate for their domains of application. There are two main drivers for this approach.

1. The first driver is the recognition of the impact of the peculiarities of individual domains of application on the AIP being designed. Based on this recognition, a comprehensive analysis of the domain of application of a MAS is necessary for the development of appropriate AIPs.
2. The second driver is the need for a structure for AIPs. Apart from the concepts of micro and macro protocols, nested protocols and concatenation of protocols, it is necessary to appropriately conceptualize the definition of agent interaction protocols. This will facilitate reusability as it will make it easy to customize a protocol where there is a clear structure to its definition.

In this paper, we present a new dedicated approach for developing AIPs.

The remainder of this paper is organized in the following way. Section 2 discusses the motivation for this work. The drivers for the proposed approach are presented in section 3 with a description of the proposed structure for defining AIPs. Section 4 presents a description of the new approach for engineering AIPs. In Section 5, we present an example of the use of our protocol structure in specifying the analysis of a domain. Section 6 is a brief discussion of AIPs and the open problems surrounding them. Section 7 concludes the paper.

2 Motivation

In principle, a MAS is a system of *interacting* agents. Regardless of the complexities or sophistication or simplicity of the individual agents in any MAS, a common characteristic of such systems is interaction amongst the different agents within the system. According to [1], interaction is arguably the most important single characteristic of complex software which constitute a MAS. According to [15], interaction is identified as an essential component of the dynamics of the MAS. The significance of interaction in MAS is expressed in fundamental attributes of a software agent. An agent in a MAS that will be reactive and proactive in its sphere of operation, its environment, will do so via interaction with the other agents. Interaction Protocols are the concrete definition and means of implementation of the interactions in a MAS. Interaction Protocols give context and direction to the interactions in a MAS. Interaction is a driver of the overall behaviour of a MAS since an agent's perception of its environment is modified by results of interactions, and these modifications influence the agent's decision process [6]. Therefore AIPs are crucial aspects of the development, implementation and operation of the MAS.

AIPs are a somewhat different component of the MAS. Unlike the individual agents which take up specific roles [16, 4], AIPs have no function without at least two agents, and two agents cannot interact effectively without an AIP. Hence an AIP is defined in the light of a minimum of two agents engaged in an interaction. So where agents require attributes that will ensure the achievement of their goals, AIPs require attributes that will ensure that two or more agents with similar or divergent goals interact effectively in order to achieve their respective objectives. Examples of these properties include rule consistency, rule simplicity, inclusiveness, architecture independence, etc. These attributes define the identity of the AIPs and determine their success in achieving interaction in the domain of application.

The significance and peculiarity of AIPs in MAS as described above, demands a dedicated approach to the development of AIPs when building MAS. However many (if not most) of the existing AOSE methodologies do not define specific processes for developing AIPs [1, 6, 5]. Though there is doubtless a large body of research work in the area of AIPs, to the best of our knowledge, very little work is focussed on defining a dedicated process for the development of AIPs [5, 11, 3].

In consideration of the existing work on AIP development, we are of the view that:

1. AIPs resulting from a general approach may not be well suited to the particular application for which they were intended.
2. Assumptions about the character of AIPs are implicit, and not separate from the actual rules guiding the sequencing of the messages in the conversation [14].
3. A proper understanding of the essence of a protocol is lacking, for instance describing the same message structure only with different parameters as separate protocols.
4. A proper understanding of a protocol structure is lacking, for instance, the difference between a protocol and a performative is unclear.
5. Reuse of existing AIPs is hard to achieve.

The process of developing appropriate AIPs requires that the *problem* be well-defined [10]. A problem should be carefully defined before design tasks are undertaken. For the problem definition to be able to solve the problem appropriately, it needs to be expressed in the light of the problem domain.

Our dedicated approach for developing AIPs is motivated by the fact that interaction and therefore AIPs describe the peculiar characteristics and overall behaviour of a domain of MAS application. The consideration is, *negotiation* in a business to business transaction is different in some attributes from *negotiation* in a business to consumer transaction. While one may be critical on time, for instance a business to business transaction for raw materials required for production scheduling, the other may not be. Another example is the difference in the *cooperation* that is required amongst a set of agents assisting surgeons in a critical operation when compared to the *cooperation* among a set of telecommunications service provider agents in a bid to present a common tariff regime to their customers. We see from these two examples that the nature of the interaction reflects the peculiar characteristics of the domains. Hence, the right applicability of MAS to these domains is dependent on how the interagent interactions in the system are conceptualized and implemented. Also, these two examples also show that the differences in similar interaction types needed for different domains could either be subtle, requiring certain attribute modifications or fundamental, impacting on the entire structure of the interaction.

This proposed AIP development approach is situated in the context of the ROADMAP methodology [4, 9] for building MAS. This approach is an extension of the Interaction model component of the methodology. However, it is being designed with the concept of an AOSE feature [17] in mind such that it can be used for developing AIPs alongside other AOSE methodologies as well.

3 Structured AIP Definition

As expressed by the examples in the preceding section, we believe that understanding the domain of application of a MAS, in order to determine its peculiar features, is pivotal to the success of interaction in the MAS. Domain understanding should be the primary driver for the AIP development process. A clear analysis of the domain of application will provide the features of the AIPs required for interaction within the system. These features will define the identity of the AIP during the design to ensure adequate applicability and also, provide a proper basis for the verification of any AIP specified for the system.

We highlight three conceptual issues informing our work on AIP. The first is determining the component parts of a complete protocol. The second is how these component parts are related to or dependent on one another in describing a complete protocol. The third is specifying the mandatory and optional components for a protocol to be complete.

These issues relate to *protocol definition,* the secondary driver of our approach. Protocol definition significantly impacts on how AIPs are designed and serves as a basis for assessing the completeness of the protocol specified.

Our new structured definition states that an AIP is made up of two broad components. These are the *Protocol Structure* and the *Protocol Property Suite*. Our work on protocol structure is based on work on communication protocols [10]. However, we present this in the concept of interagent interaction. We also show the way in which the component parts of the protocol structure are connected to model a complete AIP, see figure 1. The protocol property suite on the other hand, defines the collection of the values of the properties of a particular protocol being specified. Our claim is that a protocol changes to become another protocol by changes to its properties, as these define the protocol's structural component and therefore its function and identity.

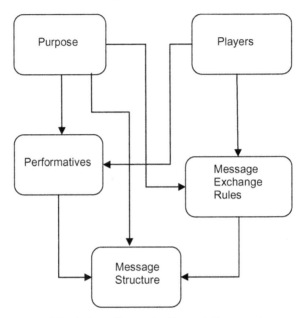

Fig. 1. Agent Interaction Protocol Structure

3.1 AIP Structure

Purpose: the purpose component of the protocol structure is the most significant component. It is the representation of the analysis of the interaction that the protocol is being designed to implement. This component provides a basis for the specification of the interaction model (specified in the Players component) in the light of the characteristic features of the interaction domain. It is not just a description of the essence of the AIP to be built, it is a structured specification that describes the interaction behind the AIP. Hence, this component determines the kind and structure of the messages and the rules that will guide the exchange of these messages amongst the interacting agents. The purpose specification also describes the properties of the protocol and these influence the other components of the protocol structure. See Table 1 for the definition of the elements of the Purpose component.

Players: the agents involved in the interaction are described as the players. This component of the protocol structure documents the interacting agents and their roles within the MAS. The relationships between these agents are also specified in this component. These relationships include organizational hierarchies, buyer/seller, competitor relationships and so on. Based on the relationships, restriction on interaction

Table 1. Elements of the Purpose component

Interaction:	A statement of the interaction e.g. Stocks Transaction
Related System Goal:	A statement of the system goal that requires the interaction e.g. optimize investments
Domain of application:	A specification of the domain stratification e.g. Business-Stock Exchange-Stock Market
Domain type:	A specification of the type of the domain e.g. open, distributed, closed, real-time, etc
Interaction objective:	A description of the essence of the interaction within the system and in the context of the domain
Interaction type:	A specification of the type of interaction e.g. negotiation, collaboration, competition, etc
System Safety:	A statement of the impact of this interaction on the physical safety of the system
Pre conditions:	A specification of the system state necessary to trigger the interaction e.g. presence of an open order on the stock exchange
Post conditions:	A specification of the expected system state (or possible states) after a successful completion of the interaction e.g. the stock is purchased

involvement to either any or specific instances of certain agent roles are specified in this component as well as the part (initiator, participant or responder) to be played by particular agents in the interaction. The players component also describes the interaction mode i.e. bilateral or multilateral interaction. See Table 2 for the definition of the elements of the Players component.

Performatives: this component is a listing of all the performatives that will be used in the AIP and their meanings. It is important to clearly define the meaning of the performatives in order to avoid misinterpretation by the interacting agents. Connections between a performative and an agent or interaction part (initiator or responder) are specified in this component, for instance, the specification that a performative is an interaction initiating performative. Also, the number of times it is permitted to have a performative in an interaction is specified in this component.

Message Structure: a message is defined by a performative, however, the structure of each message in the interaction is a specification of the information that the message will carry when it is sent. The different fields that each message should have and a representation of information in each field are specified in this component of the protocol structure.

Message Exchange Rules: this component of the protocol structure defines the characteristic behaviour of the interaction. This presents a specification of the different guidelines that direct how messages are exchanged in order to efficiently and effectively realize the interaction. The specification includes how an interaction should be initiated, how the interaction should end, message exchange mode, timing constraints between receiving and sending of messages, and so on.

Table 2. Elements of the Players component

Interacting agents:	A specification of the type of agents involved in the interaction
Initiator:	A specification of the agent that initiates the interaction
Responder(s):	A specification of the agent(s) allowed to respond to the Initiator
Inter-agent Relationships:	A description of the association between the interacting agents e.g. Client/Server, Buyer/Seller
Priviledges:	A specification of the permission given to one of the participants to change the rules of the interaction
Number of agents:	A specification of the number of agents to be involved in the interaction if known(or range i.e. Greater than two, if the number is not known)
Diversity of agents:	A description of the source of the agents in the interaction i.e. Heterogeneous or Homogeneous agents
Distribution:	A description of how the initiator(s) connect with the responder(s) based on the number of each category of agents interacting i.e. One-to-Many, Many-to-One, Many-to-Many, etc
Accessibility:	A specification of the initiator agent's awareness of the other participants and how to contact each of them (addresses). There could be Complete or Partial or No Accessibility
Inclusiveness:	A specification whether the number of participating agents is fixed or variable at the start of the interaction

The different components of the protocol structure are connected to one another, as shown in figure 1, to show how one component influences the content of another one. These connections reveal the part a component plays in specification of other components. These connections present a relationship amongst the components and they give a better conceptualization of the motivation for this proposed AIP definition. This relationship provides a guide for the sort of information and specification that should be stated in the different components.

The purpose component determines the content of the performatives, message structure and message exchange rules components. The purpose of the interaction dictates the number and type of performatives required to achieve such an interaction. The message structure is affected by the purpose as some of the information to be included or not included in the message structure will be determined by the purpose of the interaction. For instance, a purchase interaction between a buyer and a seller requires settlement details in one of the messages while an advertisement interaction between a seller and potential buyer may or may not include only modes of payment and not settlement details. The major determinant of the message exchange rules is the purpose component since the purpose details what the interaction seeks to achieve, how critical it is to the system, how quickly the interaction should happen, how it should end, how it should handle errors in the interaction, and so on.

The players specification influences the performatives and the message exchange rules since some of the players may have overriding roles in the interaction, hence considerations will be given to such roles where they exist, in defining the performatives and the message exchange rules. Performatives affect message structure since a performative gives meaning to a message. Also, message exchange rules in some cases influence the message structure, an example is where a message exchange rule states that 'the interaction initiating message must state the purpose of the message' (where this is not part of the performative's semantic meaning), the structure for such a message will therefore include a field for this information.

It is needful to specify these details explicitly because it helps in achieving uniform protocol interpretation and also in appropriate interaction error handling. For instance, if a responder is sending a *cfp* message, which has been declared in the performatives component to be an initiator performative or if a performative that is defined to be used only once is being used a second time within the same interaction, it indicates a high likelihood of an error or an exception in the interaction being executed.

3.2 AIP Property Suite

The properties of a protocol are the features or attributes that define the protocol's identity. Each of these properties has more than one possible value. The set of values of the properties applicable to an AIP make up the Protocol Property Suite, according to our definition. As the interaction is analyzed in the context of the domain, the properties that are applicable to the protocol to be designed are identified. The values of the identified properties make up the protocol property suite for this particular protocol. See Table 3 for a brief description of the properties.

We differentiate the protocol properties which are integral to our definition, from the quality attributes that the protocol is expected to have in the larger context of the MAS that the protocol is a part of. It is needful to separately represent the protocol property suite because it makes it a lot easier to modify and upgrade a protocol and also to make another protocol out of an existing one easily.

To illustrate some of the concepts we introduce here and the claim that two AIPs with the same protocol structure will differ in function by their properties, we present the following example:

Consider two AIPs P_A and P_B. They both have the same set of performatives *ask, tell* and *end* with the message sequence in the order *ask – tell – end* (an example of a subset of their protocol structure). A property *timing sensitivity* with values *False* for P_A and *True* for P_B (the values *False* and *True* for property *timing sensitivity* represent the protocol property suite) will differentiate the behaviour of the protocols by defining the following message exchange rules for the two protocols.

P_A: An agent A that sends the message *ask* to another agent B does not send the message *end* to close the interaction until it receives the message *tell* within a time interval of $0 – 300$ seconds, after which it may close the interaction with the message *end*.

P_B: If an Agent A does not receive a message *tell* within a time interval of $0 – 5$ seconds after sending the message *ask* to an agent B, A should send the message *ask* to another agent C. If A receives a *tell* message from either of B or C within 5 seconds of sending to C, A closes both interactions by sending *end* messages to B and C, otherwise it closes interaction with B alone.

Table 3. Elements of the Protocol Property Suite component

Timing con-straint:	A description of the impact of time in achieving the interaction objective e.g. bid submission is deadline constrained
Security concerns:	A specification of the impact of this interaction on the security concerns of the system (e.g. confidentiality of information exchanged)
Error sensitivity:	A description of the sort of error (content and control) that the interaction can cope with e.g. high error sensitivity in air traffic control related interaction
Messaging mode	A specification of the message sequencing mode i.e. Asynchronous or Synchronous
Messaging mechanism	A specification of method of sending messages to the intended recipients i.e. broadcast, multicast
Interaction mode	A specification of the number of agents that an agent can simultaneously connect with for message exchange i.e. Multilateral, Bilateral
Ontology	A specification of the uniformity or otherwise of the participating agents' representation of the real world

This is a clear instance of how the values of a property, will differentiate the functions of two AIPs with the same structure. AIP P_B represents a time critical system, while P_A represents a system that is not time critical. The essence of expressiveness is evident by this illustration as the level of details in specifying the protocols will reduce ambiguity in the protocol interpretation.

Our protocol definition is conceptualized as follows. The Purpose and Players specifications *generate* the Protocol Property Suite as well as the Performatives, Message Exchange Rules and Message Structure. The protocol property suite is used to *define* the Message Exchange Rules, the Performatives and the Message structure, see Figure 2. This presents a clear relationship amongst the different aspects of our protocol definition and is useful in specifying an approach for protocol engineering.

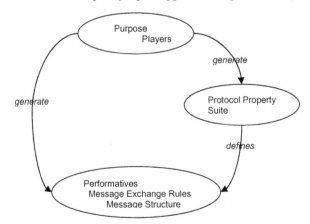

Fig. 2. Relationship between Protocol Structure and Protocol Property Suite

4 Our Dedicated Approach for Developing AIPs

In the preceding section, we presented the structured AIP definition, one of the drivers for this approach. Here, we present a brief description of the new approach. Our approach to AIP engineering is a 2 phase model consisting of the domain-directed analysis and the design/verification phases, see figure 3. This approach focuses on analysis and design since an AIP can not be implemented outside of a MAS implementation. Also, it is our intention that this AIP development approach will be applicable to different MAS development methodologies.

4.1 Domain-Directed Analysis Phase

The analysis phase of the AIP engineering process is divided into two stages. The first stage is the actual analysis which is carried out in the context of the domain of application. The characteristics of the domain are the basis for the analysis in order to draw out the requirements of the AIP to be engineered. Identity is given to the protocol developed and its appropriate applicability is assured when its requirements are analyzed in the context of the domain. Examples of domains of application of MAS technology include the smart home (a network of intelligent appliances), air traffic management, medical applications, internet based e-markets and so on. The domain-directed analysis is carried out using the following process:

1. At the completion of the MAS requirements analysis, identify the system goals that require more than one agent to achieve them.
2. For system goals that require more than one agent to fulfill them, define if the agents need to interact with one another or with external sources in order to achieve the goal.
3. For system goals that are achievable by only one agent, define if the agent requires information or assistance (resources) from other sources in order to achieve the goal.
4. Where interaction is identified to be necessary from steps 2 and 3 above, analyze the goal and the domain of application in order to define the elements of the Purpose component for each interaction required.
5. Identify the agents that are required for each interaction.
6. Analyze the goal, the domain of application and the agents involved in each interaction in order to define the elements of the Players component for each interaction.
7. Using the Purpose and the Players component and analysis of the domain of application, define the Protocol Property Suite.

The outcomes of this phase of the engineering process are the specifications of the Purpose and Players components and the Protocol Property Suite of our protocol definition. These components present a detailed and structured representation of the analysis in the context of the domain such that it can be effectively translated into design with very minimal ambiguity.

The second stage in the analysis phase of our approach is the search for existing AIPs. This is separately represented and emphasized to show our recognition of the existing body of work on AIP specifications and to emphasize our consideration for reuse. The specifications generated from the analysis are used as a basis to search for an existing AIP that is most suited to the AIP to be developed. The outcome of the directed search could be an existing AIP that suits the intended AIP, an existing AIP that needs to be modified to suit the intended AIP or no existing AIP that is close to the intended AIP, hence requiring design from scratch.

4.2 Design/Verification Phase

The design phase of our AIP development approach has two possible paths depending on the outcome of the directed search in the analysis phase. Where a similar existing AIP is found, the reuse path is taken. If no similar AIP is found, the develop path is followed. Where an AIP that matches the intended AIP is found after the directed search, the process proceeds to the Verification phase, Figure 3.

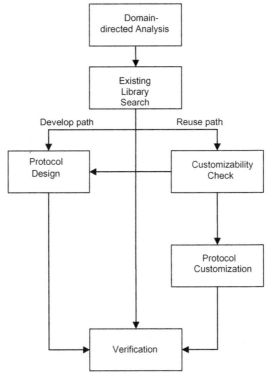

Fig. 3. Proposed AIP engineering process

Where the design follows the reuse path, the first stage in reuse is to determine if the existing AIP can be modified to make it fit into the requirements of the intended AIP. A major consideration at this stage is to assess the *cost* of modifying in terms of time and effort, against that of developing the protocol from scratch. Some of the things to consider in determining if an existing protocol can be readily modified include method of specification, understanding of the heuristics or logic behind the design, complexity of the protocol, etc. If it is determined that this existing protocol can be readily modified, the next stage along this design path is to customize the protocol using the specifications from the analysis phase.

Where there is no existing AIP that matches the intended AIP, or the existing AIPs are not customizable, the develop path is followed i.e. the intended AIP is designed from scratch. The develop path of the design phase starts by defining the set of performatives to be used by the AIP and their semantics using the specifications from the analysis phase. Then the message exchange rules are defined and a model of the message structure for each of the performatives is also defined. Subsequently, the protocol is graphically specified. Here, we propose the use of Scenario-Based Programming (SBP) for graphically specifying the protocol. Scenario-Based Programming is based on the formal language of Live Sequence Charts [20]. SBP representation of an AIP creates expressive specifications of AIPs.

Verification of the AIP developed (specified or modified) and the unmodified existing AIP is the final stage of the design/verification phase of our AIP engineering process. The verification process is dependent on the method used in specifying the AIP. SBP has automated techniques for carrying out the verification of the accuracy of the specified agent interaction protocols. The design/verification phase is iterative. It is repeated until the verification proves that the protocol has been properly specified.

The relationship between our protocol definition and the protocol engineering process is shown in figure 4. The analysis phase of the *Process* generates the three *Products* Purpose and Players specifications and the Protocol Property Suite. The design/verification phase generates the performatives, message structure and message exchange rules.

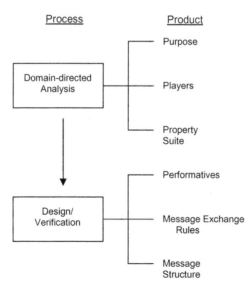

Fig. 4. Relationship between Protocol definition and Protocol development process

5   Example

In this section, we illustrate the use of our protocol structure in describing the domain analysis for developing an AIP. The AIP used for this illustration is the Provisional

Agreement Protocol (PAP) for Global Transportation Scheduling [23] developed for interaction in military operations transportation scheduling. According to [23], a typical military transportation operation is to move large quantities of resources on a global scale. As a result, a transportation operation may require the services of many transportation organizations. Each of these transportation organizations is usually only capable of moving a portion of the quantity of the resource through only a portion of the distance to be covered. The domain is open and dynamic. Transportation organizations enter and leave the system at will with the possibility of their capabilities continually changing.

We present the specifications of the Purpose, Players and Protocol Property Suite components of the PAP in the following tables, 4, 5, and 6:

Table 4. PAP Purpose component

Interaction:	Transportation Scheduling
Related System Goal:	Plan Logistics
Domain of application:	Military Operations – Transportation
Domain type:	Decentralized, Open, Dynamic
Interaction objective:	Efficient scheduling for transporting large quantities of resources globally
Interaction type:	Complex negotiations (allowing partial quantity and route bids and backtracking)
System Safety:	Interaction has no direct impact on the physical safety of the system
Pre conditions:	A minimum quantity q of resources is to be moved over a minimum distance d over a time t
Post conditions:	A comprehensive schedule within time frame A conclusion that task is not feasible within time frame

Table 5. PAP Players component

Interacting agents:	Manager Agents – Military Organization Transportation Agents – Transportation Organizations
Initiator:	Manager Agent
Responder(s):	Transport Agents
Inter-agent Relationships:	Client / Service Provider
Priviledges:	None
Number of agents:	Greater than two
Diversity of agents:	Heterogeneous
Distribution:	One-to-Many
Accessibility:	Complete
Inclusiveness:	Variable

6 Discussion

AIP is a peculiar kind of software as it serves as the software *infrastructure* for interacting agents in a system that seeks to closely model real world interactions. The behaviour of the real world system being modeled is represented and implemented by

Table 6. PAP Protocol Property Suite component

Timing constraint:	Time sensitive. Bids are deadline driven
Security concerns:	Low
Error sensitivity:	High
Messaging mode	Asynchronous
Messaging mechanism	Broadcast
Interaction mode	Multilateral
Ontology	Uniform

the AIP. AIPs are different from communication protocols as AIPs bring contextual dimension into the interactions they implement instead of merely transporting data packets with some convention. The context of an application domain is a fundamental consideration in conceptualizing and developing AIPs. Therefore, a dedicated approach is required to develop well suited AIPs in a manner that makes them readily reusable.

Most of the existing work on AIPs focus on either design or implementation without a dedicated approach for developing AIPs. Also, the crucial aspect of application domain analysis is not given the attention it demands. As a result, existing AIPs, which may not necessarily be appropriate in modeling the particular system interactions, are plugged into MAS development projects. Software quality attributes depend on the context of the application domain. To achieve good software quality, dedicated engineering approaches are required for the aspect of the software being developed [17], in this case, AIPs.

7 Conclusions

This paper presents a new dedicated approach for developing agent interaction protocols. This approach, which specifies the Analysis and Design/Verification phases of the development process, is driven by the analysis of the characteristics/peculiarities of the domain of application as they affect interaction. We also propose a new structured definition for agent interaction protocols as a second driver for the new approach. Our aim is to present a well defined and reusable process for the design and development of AIPs based on an AIP structure that facilitates productive reusability. This paper presents the description of the proposed protocol structure, establishing the link between the components of the structure. Also, we present a brief description of the approach in this paper. Work continues to further describe the process, procedures and products of the approach.

References

1. Wooldridge, M. and Ciancarini, P. Agent-Oriented Software Engineering: The State of the Art. In Agent-Oriented Software Engineering. Ciancarini, P. and Wooldridge, M. (eds), Springer-Verlag Lecture Notes in AI Volume 1957, 2001.
2. S Bussman, N.R. Jennings, M. Wooldridge. Re-use of interaction protocols for agent-based control applications 73-87 Electronic Edition (Springer Link). AOSE 2002, Bologna Italy.

3. J. L. Koning. Compiling a conversation policy's Implementation from its validated specification model. International Conference on Parallel and Distributed Processing Techniques and Applications, Las Vegas, USA, June 2000.

4. Juan, T., Pearce, A. and Sterling, L., ROADMAP: Extending the Gaia Methodology for Complex Open Systems, Proceedings of the 1st Int. Joint Conference on Autonomous Agents and Multi-Agent Systems (AAMAS), p3-10, Bologna, Italy, July 2002.

5. M.-P. Huget and J.-L. Koning. Requirement analysis for interaction protocols. In V. Marik, J. Mueller, and M. Pechoucek, editors, Proceedings of the Third Central and Eastern European Conference on Multi-Agents Systems (CEEMAS 2003), Prague, Czech Republic, June 2003.

6. P. McBurney, S. Parsons, and M. Wooldridge. Desiderata for agent argumentation protocols. In Proceedings of the First International Conference on Autonomous Agents and Multiagent Systems (AAMAS-02), Bologna, Italy, July 2002.

7. S. Paurobally and R. Cunningham. Achieving common interaction protocols in open agent environments, AAMAS, 2002.

8. FIPA Specification. Foundation for Intelligent and Physical Agents, http://www.fipa.org/repository

9. Juan, T. and Sterling, L., A Meta-model for Intelligent Adaptive Multi-Agent Systems in Open Environments (Poster), Proceedings of the Second International Joint Conference on Autonomous Agents and Multi-Agent Systems (AAMAS), Melbourne, Australia, July 2003.

10. G.J. Holzmann. Design and Validation of Computer Protocols. Prentice Hall, November 1990.

11. J.L. Koning, M.P. Hugget, Interaction Protocol design: Application to an agent-based teleteaching project. The Second IEEE International Conference on Cognitive Informatics (ICCI'03). August, 2003

12. J.L. Koning. Designing and testing negotiation protocols for electronic commerce applications. 34-60 Electronic Edition (Springer LINK)

13. R. König: State-Based Modeling Method for Multiagent Conversation Protocols and Decision Activities. Agent Technologies, Infrastructures, Tools, and Applications for E-Services 2002: 151-166

14. M. Greaves, H. Holmback, and J. Bradshaw. What is a conversation policy? In F. Dignum and M. Greaves, editors, Issues in Agent Communication, Lecture Notes in Artificial Intelligence 1916, pages 118--131. Springer, Berlin, Germany, 2000

15. A. E F-Seghrouchni, S. Haddad, H. Mazouzi. A formal study of interactions in multi-agent systems. In Proceedings of ISCA International Conference in Computer and their Applications (CATA `99), April 1999.

16. Wooldridge, M., Jennings, N. and Kinny, D. The Gaia Methodology for Agent-Oriented Analysis and Design. Journal of Autonomous Agents and Multi-Agent Systems 3 (3). 2000, 285-312.

17. Juan, T., Sterling, L., Martelli, M. and Mascardi, V.,Customizing AOSE Methodologies by Reusing AOSE Features, Proc. 2nd Int. Conference on Autonomous Agents and Multi-Agent Systems (AAMAS), Melbourne Australia, July, 2003, pp. 113-120.

18. S. Paurobally, R. Cunningham, and N. R. Jennings. Developing agent interaction protocols using graphical and logical methodologies. In Workshop on Programming MAS, AAMAS, 2003.

19. J. Odell, H.V.D. Parunak, B. Bauer. Representing Agent Interaction Protocols in UML. Agent-Oriented Software Engineering, P. Ciancarini and M. Wooldridge eds., Springer-Verlag, Berlin (2001), 121--140.

20. D. Harel and R. Marelly. Come, Let's Play: Scenario-Based Programming using LSCs and the Play-Engine. Springer-Verlag, 2003.

21. C. Bartolini, C. Preist, N.R. Jennings. Architecting for reuse: a software framework for automated negotiation. Proc. 3rd Int Workshop on Agent-Oriented Software Engineering, Bologna, Italy, 87-98.
22. M.H. Nodine, A Unruh. Constructing robust conversation policies in dynamic agent communities. Technical Report MCC-INSL-020-99, Microelectronics and Computer Technology Corporation, 1999
23. Don Perugini, Dale Lambert, Leon Sterling, and Adrian Pearce. Provisional Agreement Protocol for Global Transportation Scheduling. In Workshop on agents in traffic and transportation held in conjunction with the International Conference on Autonomous Agents and Multi Agent Systems (AAMAS), New York, 2004.

Introducing
Participative Personal Assistant Teams
in Negotiation Support Systems

Eric Platon and Shinichi Honiden

National Institute of Informatics, 2-1-2 Hitotsubashi, Chiyoda, Tokyo 101-8430, Japan
{platon,honiden}@nii.ac.jp

Abstract. This paper introduces teams of personal agents that support users individually in electronic negotiations. These agents listen to the running negotiation and to each other to point out relevant information and compile advice for the user. In this frame, we first describe the architecture of this system and propose assistance interaction protocols to specify agent external behaviours in performing their tasks. Then, we discuss the semantic representation of agent communication and describe an abstraction layer to let agents understand user message issues. Our future work aims at improving these mechanisms and enriching them toward a full-fledged implementation.

1   Introduction

The last decade reveals a multiplication of software agents that organize our time, advice in booking airplane tickets, perform auctions on our behalf, or maintain business process [1–4]. In most systems, a central mechanism is the negotiation between cooperative or conflicting agents that need ways to reach an agreement in the fulfilment of their tasks. Most projects also have in common to assign a single agent to each user and to concentrate on the challenging concept of delegated negotiation in which agents autonomously act on behalf of their owners, under customised constraints. The restriction to one agent is natural as users need to deal with one entity at a time, but it seems also limiting when comparing standalone agents to multi-agent systems (MAS). We argue that teams of specialised agents can ease both the understanding of the system behaviours for the user and the engineering of smaller interactive software for the system designer. Delegated negotiation is a very active discipline in multi-agent systems [3, 5, 6], but we think potential users are still reluctant to delegate any power to artificial agents in affairs concerning personal issues. Assistants that act *with* the user should be more easily trusted, since they mainly suggest possibly relevant information or anticipate user needs rather than negotiate automatically.

In this context, we introduce a *personal assistance system* (PAS) that features assistant teams to participate to negotiation processes aside the user, rather than on her behalf. This intermediate stance between manual mode (no support) and delegated negotiation should steadily strengthen user trust in artificial assistance, and probably lead to higher acceptance in delegation. Such PAS have

M.W. Barley and N. Kasabov (Eds.): PRIMA 2004, LNAI 3371, pp. 178–192, 2005.

already been partially explored with single assistants [2, 7], but we will describe active teams that clarify the system reactions to the user, and permit flexible management of the agent population in terms of available service (user point of view) and software engineering (incremental population of more simple units).

The paper is organised as follows: we first situate and motivate our research in the field of Negotiation Support Systems (NSS) in section 2. After presenting our settings and assistant teams in section 3, we introduce in section 4 our methodology describing team protocols and participative features that address the system issues. In section 5, we detail work related to NSS and assistance, and finally compile our current concerns and future work in section 6.

2 Negotiation Support and Participative Assistance

This section is first devoted to the description of our concept of PAS relative to NSS and the motivations to propose another model for assisted negotiation. Then, we highlight the issues we address in conducting this research.

2.1 Personal and Participative Assistance in Negotiation

Online negotiation becomes a standard so that NSS appear in numerous projects. For most researchers, agent-mediated solutions represent appropriate models, mainly for the challenging delegated negotiation. However, user reluctance stems from the idea of transferring decision power to artificial agents, since delegation-based software usually do not reach the 'trust threshold', as shown on Fig. 1. We think this threshold is shifting and people will accept such a support in the future, when solutions are robust enough to deaden most worries about automated processes. The work of Klein et al. advances in this direction [8], and steady introductions in the industry should encourage for acceptance.

Fig. 1. Our distribution of participation and delegation on the trust ladder.

Meanwhile, we suggest an intermediate stance to address this user reluctance. PAS are NSS that negotiate *aside* rather than *for* users, so that it solves intrinsically the delegation concern. We reuse the term and concept of *participation* exploited by Drogoul in Agent-Oriented Simulation [9] to refer to our type of negotiation assistance, where user and assistants are paired and bound with the same aim. If this approach is accepted by users, we think it may reduce the gap for eventually accepting delegated negotiation. Little work already exists [7], and the proposal we introduce should lead farther. Indeed, our vision of assistant is strongly akin to human one. For example, a secretary initially executes exactly chief's orders, provides few valuable feedbacks, and has no power.

After bilateral adaptation, the chief increasingly trusts the secretary and delegates more power; the secretary learns about chief's methods and can anticipate some requests and give relevant information. Hence, some secretaries negotiate efficiently the real business schedule of chiefs that trust them. Thus, PAS aim at designing assistants that reply to user requests, and also take such meaningful and understandable initiatives that can serve the user in its activity. The latter functions include searching non-requested information related to the context, suggesting alternatives, and so forth.

Second, NSS solutions are restricted to one single assistant. Standalone agents can become fairly monolithic in this situation and cannot leverage the potential of MAS. One central requirement from users to accept an artificial agent is to sufficiently understand and predict its behaviours. In complex knowledge-based systems, explanation facilities are exploited, but we think a team of simpler agents can generate easier justifications of their actions, in addition to explain their interactions. Moreover, the engineering of simple agents that cooperate allows dividing design over specialised entities and their interaction patterns, i.e. a multi-agent system.

Beyond the case of negotiation assistance, we finally see personal agent teams as the future of user interfaces. Trends like ubiquitous computing show software belongs to our private daily life through our mobile phones or PDA. One day users might head a family of persistent agents that assist them in their digital life. A specialised team like our proposal can lead to an appropriate foundation.

2.2   Research Issues

The purpose of this work is first to design adequate interaction protocols that orchestrate agents to reply to user requests, and enact the initiative feature of efficient assistants. These protocols must deal with both the assistance provided by one single agent (e.g. simple smart search on Internet) and a group of cooperative agents (e.g. the search agent initiates a search on its own to assist another agent – itself assisting the user) to provide advanced services and straightforward identification of actors by users.

Once protocols set up the required infrastructure, assistance needs representing and reasoning about events and their semantics. This provides an appropriate knowledge of the current affairs and allows agents reacting accordingly. In addition to simply communicate directly as in most current MAS, we think agents should be endowed with mechanisms to listen to others' interactions. Indeed, the recent concept in MAS named *overhearing* [10, 11] provides much more knowledge resources that agents can exploit to improve their services.

Such mechanisms emphasize the issue of communicative act semantics with assistants. Natural Language Processing (NLP) is a very active field, but free communication with computers remains a technical challenge. Computer-based assistants suffer from the poor meaning that we can currently embed in user interfaces. An abstraction layer for communication should normalise the form and semantics of messages input to the system, in a specialised and restricted way of the Semantic Web [12]. Such an alternative could convey human- and machine-understandable meaning among assistants and users. In our context, it should be a compromise between *simplicity* to bypass most NLP challenges and *richness* for our purpose of negotiation support.

Finally, our future view of daily life assistants requires flexibility for users and software designers. One may want a dynamic population of communicative agents to add or remove services, upgrade or customise heterogeneous components. This is directly related to an incremental design approach that allows such dynamism and also reduces the complexity of each piece of agent. This flexibility at runtime represents one major reason to consider MAS. In the scope of this paper, we describe PAS as a solution to address those above issues, the least advanced state being the knowledge management part.

3   Assistant Team Model

3.1   Architecture

The central mechanism of our negotiation assistance model is the interaction among agents and humans. Our infrastructure is laid out on Fig. 2 among three negotiation participants, together with their assistant teams.

Conversely to most NSS (see Sect.5), agents do not substitute users but participate to the overall process discussing, listening to exchanged messages, and reacting for their owner's sake. Rather than delegating the negotiation performance to their agents, users act directly with other parties and keep full control of their strategy. Assistants stay aside and intervene as necessary on

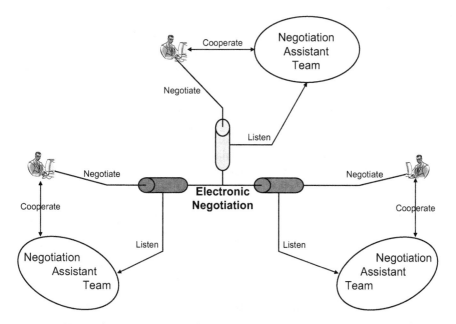

Fig. 2. Architecture view: online negotiation and assistant teams.

user invocation or key event occurrence (detection of irregularities, discovery of relevant information or even some comparison results with past events).

Each user is endowed with a *team* of assistants, i.e. a set of agents that collaborate to provide support. Services first consist in individual activities of each assistant (such as search, history, or strategy advice) that produce local arguments for the system and perform tasks directly required by the user. Second, the service features a system-level argumentation synthesising individual grounds to deduce a global argument. The user can access both individual and global information depending on the strategy (one may prefer peculiar types of data) and the will to trust system conclusions. The main idea is to consider this team as a board of advisors in a meeting room. All participants discuss the agenda under ruling of the chairman, who is the user in our present case, and they provide personal opinions to allow the chairman synthesising all viewpoints to define the company's strategy.

3.2   Illustrative Example

This section describes a negotiation assistant team through an example. Our illustrative scenario is stated as follow: John in Australia and Takezo in Japan have decided to meet in front of Victoria station, London on their common free day and agree upon the details by email. The email client has an interface that allows assistant teams performing their service. They both come by different airports. *The negotiated issue is to decide the meeting time.*

The agent team that intervenes in this example features three different specialists:

- *Presentation Agent* manages the user interface (proxy), interprets user events as communication acts, broadcasts events, and compiles global arguments.
- *Search Agent* can access the Internet to feed agent peers with fresh and parsed information, and can initiate complementary search on its own.
- *Strategic Agent* computes information and events under the essential negotiation point of view and breeds strategic arguments.

First, users negotiate along with their required Presentation Agent and one single Search Agent. We then run the scenario once more, introducing a strategic agent dynamically to the assistance population. The Presentation Agent plays the unique role to bridge the actual communication between user and assistants, albeit each agent virtually interacts with all peers and the user. When other agents 'talk' to the user, they indeed talk to the Presentation Agent. This allows treating all interactions similarly. Initial beliefs of our agents are stated in Table 1.

The first run starts with this initial knowledge when John writes a proposal:

$$I \text{ will be at Heathrow at 8am, so let's meet at lunch time.} \quad (1)$$

Before relaying the message to Takezo, the Presentation Agent (P) broadcasts it in the system. The Search Assistant (SE) knows from its beliefs the context of meeting organisation and switches to the schedule issue. Typically,

Table 1. Initial Agent Beliefs.

	John's Assistants	Takezo's Assistants
Search Agent	1. Internet time table search engine	
	2. In meeting issues, users usually need time table information	
	3. Meeting place: Victoria Station	
	4. User schedule (Heathrow 8am)	4'. User schedule (Gatwick 10am)
Strategic Agent	1. User intention to organise a meeting	
	2. Check inconsistencies in schedules (overlapping, etc.)	
	3. Meeting place: Victoria Station	
	4. User schedule (Heathrow 8am)	4'. User schedule (Gatwick 10am)

it autonomously checks online time tables for transportation means and times along John's itinerary. John can ask for all the results directly to this assistant and require farther search. On its own initiative, SE can also inform John about any relevant result it may find (strikes, track engineering, etc.). A timeout ends the system deliberation if nothing occurs, then P can relay the message. At this point, John's assistants have no belief regarding Takezo for the meeting time question.

When Takezo receives the message, the Presentation Agent listens to this virtual discussion and broadcasts the incoming information. While Takezo is considering the new elements, assistants update their beliefs, infer intermediate results and verify the applicability. For instance, SE gets information to reach Victoria station at noon and suggest its results automatically. Takezo can exploit this behaviour and answer back to accept, deny or propose an alternative.

The second situation introduces a strategic agent in the assistant population. This can be a new run of the above scenario or users can dynamically activate the new service in the system. From the same first proposal sent by John, P and SE have the same reaction. The Strategic Assistant (ST) infers from (1) that John must be at Victoria station by noon, so it checks that John is free on this period and can reach the meeting point on time. The former check is immediate as the schedule is empty. For the second check, ST needs search support. It forwards the verification request argument to SE and waits for its reply. John can consult ST to check its trace of reasoning and perhaps find inconsistencies in the offer (1). In the case where SE replies in a timely fashion (the timeout managed by P ensures system reactivity for the user), ST completes its concern verification and validates John's idea as there is no apparent reason to fail, so that P eventually sends the proposal.

On the side of Takezo, the same analysis is performed by P and SE. ST also listens to the discussion and to SE, since the critical strategic point is the schedule here. ST deduces from its beliefs and SE results that the schedule is a little tight. Takezo can consult each agent trace or their compiled advice, and can reply:

I am not sure to reach Victoria Station by noon. How about 1pm?   (2)

Before relaying this message, assistants process it as stated for John and the negotiation process continues.

From this basic example, we intend to build a system that address general negotiation situations including buying, organising time and solving conflicts. It appears from the example that interactions between assistants imply part of the system 'intelligence' and performance, while the incremental and dynamic agent population serves both users and software engineers.

4 Protocols and Participation Methodology

In this section we first present our models of assistance protocols to orchestrate the system. Then, interactions carry messages that specialise assistance in negotiation, so we describe how agents participate by exploiting message semantics.

4.1 Interaction Protocols

The assistant team should behave as a coherent whole at the user level. Agents in teams have the common goal to individually and collectively serve the owner by local and global interventions that can be described by interaction protocols. In our research, we aim at protocols that verify properties related to the concept of participative personal assistance. First, protocols must depict interactions representing both user services and cooperation among agents. This last feature details how specialised agents build up arguments they cannot produce independently, and consequently better serve the user while their actions remain understandable and dynamic. Second, the agent population must be freely decided by the user so that protocols should be as much as possible independent from the number of actors (our proposal do not currently fulfil this point). Finally, protocols must enforce agent reactivity with time management. Indeed, the agent debate is meaningful to the user only when available in a timely fashion. For instance, we address this issue in our protocol by endowing the Presentation Agent with a timeout. All system agents must submit their results on time, if relevant. This constraint binds the reasoning cycles, so that users receive support on time at the cost of shallower performance. Although most simple agents can complete their individual tasks on time, crossing and revising arguments can be time-consuming. Time bounds mostly limit the revision depth. Experimental results to explore this claim are required and consist in part of our future endeavours.

From these properties, we split interaction protocols into two connected parts. First, the *assistance diagram* presented on Fig. 3 intends to formalise with the FIPA syntax [13, 14] how assistants and users are situated. This first schema refers to the second part that describes the *assistant team diagram* deployed on Fig. 4 in the case of our example. It is the effective interaction protocol between assistants. Messages exchanged in these diagrams do not follow exactly the FIPA Communicative Acts recommendation [14]; we chose mnemonics instead of the FIPA language for space and readability reasons. For example, 'invoke' message refers to the 'request' in FIPA and could be defined as in Code 1.

Fig. 3 shows the Presentation Agent as user proxy, i.e. a relay interface with other assistants. The user may invoke the system intentionally (Alternative 1;

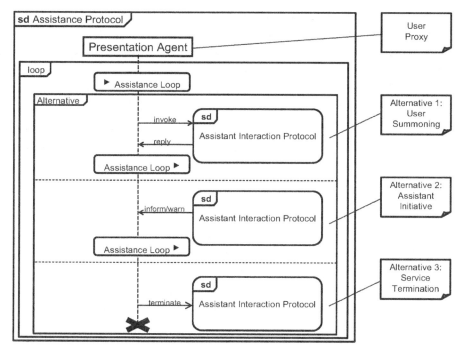

Fig. 3. Assistance Protocol: the Presentation Agent is the user proxy.

e.g. consult the Search Agent), trigger its invocation by issuing an event (Alternative 1: send a message to other parties), or terminate the agent service (Alternative 3). Furthermore, real assistants would take initiatives (inform about sudden bad weather conditions, strikes, etc.) and this is modelled with Alternative 2 in the diagram. Invocation and agent initiative activate the external protocol 'Assistant Interaction Protocol', partially laid out on Fig. 4.

Code 1. FIPA 'request' to formalise the message 'invoke'.

```
(request
    :sender (agent-identifier :name PresentationAgent)
    :receiver (set (agent-identifier :name SearchAgent))
    :content
        ''(search list route A B)''
    :language lisp)
```

The FIPA recommendation reuses the gates from UML2.0 to connect two diagrams. As the standard has no explicit representation of the gate, we present it on Fig. 4 similarly to an agent and its lifeline as it can be confounded with the Presentation Agent. Cases presented on this schema are limited to the 'invoke' and 'terminate' messages from P. In the global invocation process, agents act in

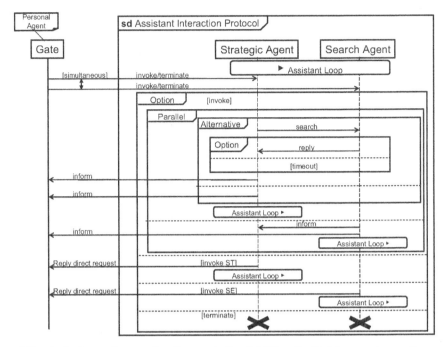

Fig. 4. Assistant Interaction Protocol, Partial View limited to user invocation.

parallel, as described in our example scenario. If the invocation targets only one agent, other agents listen to the event and only intervene in case they can infer critical arguments.

When the user sends a message to another one (initial invocation on top of Fig. 4), the Strategic Agent (ST) may ask for a search to the Search Agent (SE), and wait for an answer before informing P about its results (possibly after revision exploiting SE information). Otherwise, ST may already hold sufficient results and directly contact P. Concurrently, SE can inform on its own initiative ST about relevant events (strikes, etc.) and reports to P. The individual invocations are limited here to reply to user's requests. Extensions of our model will allow the polled agent to send messages to peers in this case. Finally, the termination case ends the assistant protocol and asks for shutdown.

The assistant diagram is designed to be a generic assistance model. Our current status for the assistant team diagram is still idiosyncratic and our endeavour is to deduce a generic protocol that still validates the previous properties, independently of the agent population.

4.2   Assistance and Participation

Besides interaction protocols, our system requires semantic process to carry on user assistance. The semantics is expressed at two levels, namely the interaction patterns and the message content carried by these interactions. Although our illustrative scenario was detailed with natural-language syntax for readability, formal communication and argumentation are needed, such as the typical illustrations by Parsons, Ramchurn [15, 16]. Implementation of these semantics enables constructing automatically sound, pragmatic, and both user- and machine-understandable arguments.

First, interaction patterns may carry meaningful information about the behaviour and intention of agents, such as cases where one can infer that running interactions follow the contract net protocol or an intimidation process. Hence, our agents should identify some recurrent or unusual patterns in the user-user, user-agent, and agent-agent discussions. The method of Sabouret allows one agent extracting knowledge from its interaction patterns with peers by compiling and integrating relevant information in *chronicles* [17]. These time-dependent internal representations contain summaries of interactions by grouping similar events in behaviours. Regular and essential features of patterns are maintained so that the agent can reason about them, react in accordance, and explain their occurence. Agents can answer common sense questions such as 'why do you turn left?' or 'what is on the table?'. Our model will extend this method so that agents are furthermore able to process knowledge from any multi-agent interaction patterns they can listen or observe, say 'overhear', as in the simplest case depicted on Fig. 5. The mechanisms rely on the assumption that listening agents receive 'copies' of interaction messages so that they can integrate them and intervene when they consider it necessary and on time. The concept of assistant team is here a fundamental requirement as these copies imply cooperative agents.

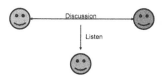

Fig. 5. Listener Agent.

Fig. 6. Semantic Mapping.

Second, the participation of agents to the user activity needs one more important brick at the interface level to exploit message content. From well-defined semantic languages and ontology, one can build user-readable arguments automatically. However, the converse action to understand user input is a stumbling block. Our abstraction layer to address this issue aims at appropriate compromise between expressive power and complexity alleviation by well-formed arguments mapping. It is mostly based on a MAS version of the project in [18] that exploits Natural Language packages. The Presentation Agent (P) filters all messages issued and received by the user and builds up with her a temporary ontology of the running negotiation. In the case of multiple negotiation threads, the assistant selects the corresponding ontology by extracting case data from the message (who, what, etc.). The ontology serves to write down standard FIPA-ACL messages so that all agents can acquire the appropriate knowledge. This process starts with the negotiation initiation. The user sends or receives a natural language message from a peer negotiator. P parses this message and extracts term candidates for the negotiation context (communicative acts, who, what, issues, etc.) in the local ontology. These candidates are then validated by the user so that P is sure the semantic mapping is correct. To reduce the inconvenience of this participative process, we think a proper presentation to the user is required. Thus, the original message is shown to the user with highlighted term candidates and semantic annotation. Figure 6 lays out this interface. The user can click on incorrect mappings and specify the right ones. Once the agent understanding is ensured, P can compile its ontology for reuse with next messages (learning stage), translate the message into ACL, forward the original message to the recipient, and the ACL message to system agents. For a given process, P is increasingly efficient as it learns the right semantics and requires fewer user interruptions (like the secretary we introduced earlier). This method maintains sufficient expressive power for our case and bypasses the language processing barriers. It however lacks convenience for humans and need the definition of a rough natural language parsing.

5 Related Work

This section comments work akin to assistance systems and current NSS technology in comparison with our assistant team.

5.1 Assistance Projects

The Helper Agent (HA) from Isbister et al. [19] has similarities with the model we presented in this paper. In computer-supported communication, instant messaging is very popular and HA aims at improving and motivating its usage to better connect people. The main differences with PAS are that HA is standalone middleware that communicates with all actors of the communication channel, and is designed in the context of friendly relationship between actors. Our assistants form a *personal* multi-agent system that supports only one user, and will interact with outside agents in the future. So there is no assumption about the relationship between human users. Our example with John and Takezo would be similar if they are friends, client/provider, or competitors (the process would certainly end with different results).

The main common point between HA and our assistants is the behaviour extraction issue. HA reacts to silence detection and when the communication channel is idle for a too long time, HA contacts both users to figure out a new topic of discussion, if desired. Our assistants listen to all messages transferred to the system to extract as much information as possible, then to revise their beliefs and possibly react.

Another project is from Helmy et al. [20] about their Kodama agents assisting web search. Kodamas form an assistant team, specialised in retrieving information on Internet. Their collaboration and underlying interactions allow certain information retrieval performance and a flexible load distribution. The main difference with our project is most Kodamas serve different users simultaneously as local infrastructure. Also, Kodamas do not provide explicit explanation facilities so that users have no insight of the system mechanisms. They mainly exploit the user browsing history and the static profile to refine their search.

5.2   Negotiation Support Systems

Much recent work relies on agents that negotiate on behalf of human users. The typical protocol collects information from the user, performs the negotiation, confirms results with the user, and eventually commits the transaction [5]. These systems often improve time- and cost-efficiency in any kind of negotiation [1, 5], so that successful simple industrial versions were derived as EBay^{TM} [21]. The reason of this simplification is that most users lack faith in most types of automation that reduce their feeling of control. Consequently, users are often reluctant to the idea of letting artificial agents negotiate for real personal affairs and prefer self-performance with possible assistance as our proposal. In the commerce-centric NSS domain, Kasbah, AuctionBot and MAGMA are three reference architectures. Other solutions feature either similar functions or less expressive properties, so we focused only on these three ones. In addition, we discuss the particular case of ASPIRE as it has a similar stance as ours in NSS.

To begin, Kasbah is the first attempt to design an agent-mediated negotiation platform [6]. Buying and selling users send their negotiation agents with constraints. Agents negotiate by following a decay function (defining the 'strategy' of the agent depending on the function profile). This first platform was innovative but suffers from its early model. Agents just follow a function, and although they can autonomously complete negotiations, their lack of reactivity limits the range of application and we cannot really trust them. The work of Klein at al in [8] shows the drawbacks of that type of framework in terms of robustness and reliability.

AuctionBot is a client-server architecture that was used to organise online auctions between anyone endowed with a web-browser [3]. In this platform, buyers and sellers participate to auctions either with simple agents (idea of a proxy) that just inform owners about the state of their auctions (no autonomy), or exploit their self-developed agents based on the AuctionBot API to negotiate on their behalf. Users can join or create auctions, and choose the type among the most frequents. Although very flexible and comprehensive auction performer, this platform suffers from the same drawbacks as Kasbah. However, the strict auction protocols often allow enforcing the rules. As stated in [22], one important feature of the AuctionBot is its neutral stance toward sellers and buyers. This third-party ensures strict compliance to the auction protocol and so breeds higher trust in that kind of automated negotiation.

MAGMA represents one attempt to implement the marketplace metaphor in computing environments for the future electronic commerce world [5]. The framework aims at comprehensive models of actors and entities of marketplaces and so relies on multi-agent systems. Built on the experience acquired from the previous Kasbah and AuctionBot platforms, MAGMA embodies agents that negotiate for users and a complete environment including banks, balanced communication infrastructure (no central 'hub'), advertising, and software representation of physical goods to ensure coherence with real products and prevent from defrauding. The negotiation process exploited for this experiment is only the Vickrey auction, described in detail in their paper. The realistic virtual market goal lets perform direct negotiations, but the main focus is on agent-brokered processes that act similarly to the AuctionBot. The comprehensive set of features implemented by MAGMA clarifies the concept of electronic automated negotiations. The experimental restriction actually ensures higher degree of trust in the agent reactions owing to the strict auction rules, and perhaps because the Vickrey protocol best practice to maximise one's utility is 'to be honest'. This project shows trust can be achieved by clear rule enforcement in a dedicated electronic institution. However, such infrastructures is still in the long term and the participative assistance can be an alternative meanwhile.

Finally, ASPIRE turns delegated negotiation into collaborative negotiation [7]. This collaboration seems matching better the idea of assistant that provides support or aid (inspired from Merriam-Webster online dictionary) rather than the 'proxy' represented by the delegated negotiation agent. Thus, ASPIRE provides an asynchronous negotiation platform enabling two parties negotiating any goods by exchanging messages and negotiation field values (price, etc.). Personal assistants intervene for instance when a user submits a message. Before letting the system relaying the message to the opponent, the agent detects some inconsistencies or unusual negotiation behaviours such as an over- or underevaluated offer compared to the previous one. The agent features other functions that allow correcting potential strategic errors. ASPIRE is in the direction of our work and shows promising results along practical experiments conducted in simulations. However, we think the engineering of ASPIRE may be a limiting factor. The project intends to extend the personal assistant abilities to larger 'communication channels' (multimodal) with the owner but also other agents. Our multi-agent framework encompasses inherently these functions with assistant teams that intrinsically interact with both human, team members, and soon other agents. Furthermore, it covers more issues including user service, explanation facilities and other engineering concerns.

6   Conclusion

In this paper, we presented a team of personal agents that supports one user in electronic negotiations. The agent team replies to user request and also takes initiatives as would do efficient assistants. The latter functions rely on the principle of listening to user interactions with the outer world, by means of the recent concept of overhearing. Teams offer the advantage to diversify functions of agents, exploit the intelligence emerging from their interactions, and engineer incrementally the agent population, i.e. extend and modify available services. Through an example, we laid out our current status in describing the key mechanisms in the interaction protocols of these MAS.

As stated along this paper, the present model of our assistant teams for negotiation support is an original platform compared with both NSS systems and with assistance solutions. We identified the central endeavours as the study of interactions, knowledge representation and extraction from these interactions and the consequent reasoning issues.

Our ongoing work first addresses the development of a generic assistant interaction protocol verifying the properties introduced in section 4. Second, the example presented in this paper featured three agents. We are investigating which services are pertinent in the negotiation process to answer user needs. Thus, we intend to integrate for example a history agent as negotiation requires knowledge of the past to both avoid reproducing errors and adapt to new situations [23]. Also, the abstraction layer we proposed in this paper to let agents understand the semantics of natural language messages from users suffers from its interfering process. We aim at a more transparent mechanism that would interrupt the user only on critical dilemma and to base parsing on pre-defined negotiation ontology. Finally, agents cooperate with each other and the user in our present model. Next, they will be authorised to compete with other systems on issues the owner considers secondary and releasable to agents, thus bridging participative and delegated negotiation techniques.

Acknowledgement

We would like to thank Nicolas Sabouret for our fruitful discussions on this research, the anonymous members of the PRIMA'04 program commitee that reviewed this paper, and the editors and authors of this volume for their advice.

References

1. Chalupsky, H.; Gil, Y.; Knoblock, C.A.; Lerman, K.; Oh, J.; Pynadath, D.V.; Russ, T.A.; Tambe, M.: 'Electric Elves: Applying Agent Technologies to Support Human Organisations', 13th IAAI Conference, pp.51-58, 2001.
2. Rich, C.; Sidner, C.: 'COLLAGEN: When Agents Collaborate With People', First International Conference on Autonomous Agents, 1997.
3. Wurman, P.R.; Wellman, M.P.; Walsh, W.E.: 'The Michigan Internet AuctionBot: A Configurable Auction Server for Human and Software Agents', Second International Conference on Autonomous Agents, 1998.
4. Alty, J. L.; Griffiths, D.; Jennings, N. R.; Mamdani, E. H.; Struthers, A. and Wiegand, M. E.: 'ADEPT - Advanced Decision Environment for Process Tasks: Overview and Architecture', BCS Expert Systems 94 Conference, pp.359-371, 1994.
5. Tsvetovatyy, M.; Gini, M.; Mobasher, B.; Wieckowski, Z.: 'MAGMA: An Agent-Based Virtual Market for Electronic Commerce', Journal of Applied Artificial Intelligence, Vol. 11, $N°6$, pp.501-523, 1997.
6. Chavez, A.; Maes, P.: 'Kasbah: An Agent Marketplace for Buying and Selling Goods', First International Conference on the Practical Application of Intelligent Agents and Multi-Agent Technology, 1996.
7. Kersten, G.; Koszegi, S.T.; Vetschera, R.: 'The Effects of Culture in Anonymous Negotiations: Experiments in Four Countries', 35th HICSS, 2002.

8. Klein, M.; Faratin, P.; Sayama, H.; Bar-Yam, Y.: 'Protocols for Negotiating Complex Contracts', IEEE Intelligent Systems, pp.32-38, Nov./Dec. 2003.
9. Drogoul, A.; Vanbergue, D.; Meurisse, T.: 'Multi-Agent Based Simulation: Where are the Agents?', MABS02 Workshop, AAMAS'02 Conference, 2002.
10. Busetta, P., Donà, A., Nori, M.:'Channeled Multicast for Group Communications', First International Conference on Autonomous Agents and Multi-Agent Systems, AAMAS'02 Conference, 2002.
11. Gutnik, G. and Kaminka, G.: 'Towards a Formal Approach to Overhearing: Algorithms for Conversation Identification', AAMAS'04 Conference, 2004.
12. World-Wide Web Consortium: The Semantic Web: http://www.w3.org/2001/sw/
13. FIPA Specifications: FIPA Modelling: Interaction Diagrams, Working Draft, 2002.
14. FIPA Specifications: FIPA Communicative Act Library Specification, 2002.
15. Parsons, S. and Jennings, N.R.: 'Negotiation through argumentation - a preliminary report', Second International Conference on Multi-Agent Systems, 1996.
16. Ramchurn, S.D.; Jennings, N.R.; Sierra, C.: 'Persuasive Negotiation for Autonomous Agents: A Rhetorical Approach', IJCAI Workshop on Computational Models of Natural Argument, 2003.
17. Sabouret, N.: 'Representing, requesting and reasoning about actions for active components in human-computer interaction', LIMSI-CNRS, Report 2002-09, 2002.
18. Vargas-Vera, M.; Motta, E.; Domingue, J.; Buckingham Shum, S; Lanzoni, M.: 'Knowledge Extraction by using Ontology-based Annotation Tool', ACM, 2000.
19. Isbister, K.; Nakanishi, H.; Ishida, T.; Nass, C.: 'Helper Agent: Designing an Assistant for Human-Human Interaction in a Virtual Meeting Space', CHI'00, 2000.
20. Helmy, T.: Amamiya, S.; Amamiya, M.: 'Collaborative Kodama Agents with Automated Learning and Adapting for Personalised Web Searching', 13th IAAI Conference, pp.65-72, 2001.
21. Ebay[TM] Web site: http://www.ebay.com
22. Han, B.; Lim, J.: 'Influence of Culture and Explanation Facility on Performance of Negotiation Agents', 35th HICSS, 2002.
23. Tzu, S.: 'The Art of War', Oxford Press, June 1971.

A Distributed Workflow System with Autonomous Components

Maryam Purvis, Martin Purvis, Azhar Haidar, and Bastin Tony Roy Savarimuthu

Information Science Department, University of Otago, Dunedin, New Zealand
{tehrany,mpurvis,tonyr}@infoscience.otago.ac.nz

Abstract. This paper describes the architecture of a distributed workflow management system in a dynamic environment. The system features autonomous agent components that can adapt to both structural changes in business processes and changes in system parameters, such as the number of available resources. This adaptation could be a permanent adjustment that should be reflected in all the incoming work cases, or be associated with a particular instance of a work case. In addition, parts of the system can be modified by observing the behaviour of the system for possible shortcomings due to a non-optimal distribution of resources or faulty inter-process dependencies which could result in bottlenecks. Because of the autonomous nature of subsystem components, the workflow system can adapt to changes without the necessity of centralized control. The architecture of the system is described in the context of a distributed workflow example.

Keywords: dynamic workflow, autonomous components, interaction protocols, coloured Petri nets, adaptability

1 Introduction

Workflow management systems (WfMS) [1-3] are increasingly being used to manage business processes associated with distributed global enterprises. Some of the benefits of using a WfMS are

- ability to visualize the overall process and interdependencies between various tasks,
- automation of the processes, and
- coordination and collaboration between various business entities.

Traditionally, however, most WfMSs have had centralized control architectures along with fixed process model specifications. The current research trend is in the direction of (a) more distributed architectures which can reduce potential bottlenecks with respect to particular system components and (b) more flexible process model specifications, which can accommodate dynamic and changing requirements that occur in today's business environment [4,5].

It is often desirable to have the capability of modifying the existing process model due to changing external influences or of dealing with exceptional cases in which the normal processes may not be appropriate. In the past WfMSs were used in well-defined activities, such as manufacturing, where the processes tend to be more established and stable. But in the current climate WfMS may be used in connection with more fluid business processes, such as e-commerce, or in more complicated processes

M.W. Barley and N. Kasabov (Eds.): PRIMA 2004, LNAI 3371, pp. 193–205, 2005.
© Springer-Verlag Berlin Heidelberg 2005

involving human interactions, such as the software development process. In such situations, at times, it is not always possible to predict in advance all parameters that may be important for the overall processes. In addition, it is often appropriate for certain groups within a distributed organisation to be autonomous and not always under centralized control. Consequently it would be helpful if we could design WfMS systems that could cope with these dynamic requirements and provide some level of process modification. It is important to make the workflow system dynamic and adaptable, since workflows of multi national companies span across countries. For example the main workflow might be present in New Zealand and the sub processes could be distributed in countries like India and Germany.

One of the benefits of using a WfMS is to be able to streamline processes associated with an organization and be able to visualize some of the interdependencies between various tasks or various processes in a larger context. It is desirable to represent these processes in a formal way that could be used for further analysis and at the same time have a graphical and intuitive representation. The coloured Petri net (CPN) notation [6] meets this requirement. In the past, the CPN formalism has been used successfully to model the dynamic behaviour associated with particular processes representing various activities of a complex system, such as business processes. In the context of the WfMS, CPNs have been used to specify the process model of a WfMS component [2,7], and CPNs have been used to model processes generally, since they offer a well-established modelling technique that combines expressiveness, simplicity and formal semantics. However, in the present work we are extending this idea so that the various sub-processes associated with a large enterprise could be distributed on different hosts, while at the same time being interconnected with one another according to the overall process model associated with a given organization.

An advantage of having a formal representation that is executable is that one can examine the behaviour of the system according to various what-if scenarios that may be considered as a result of potential changes to the process or some of the model parameters such as the various constraints that might affect the outcome. By simulating the model for typical scenarios, it is possible to analyse the outcome of the simulation and fine-tune the specified resources or constraints so that more favourable results can be achieved; and this is also possible with coloured Petri nets.

2 Architecture of the System

To accommodate this level of adaptability, the system should be flexible and made of loosely coupled modules. Our workflow system uses JFern [8], a Java-based tool for the enactment and simulation of coloured Petri nets. We are also using the Opal agent framework [9], which conforms to the Foundation for Intelligent Physical Agents (FIPA) specifications [10] and which provides an agent-based infrastructure for the support of distributed, adaptable computing.

The system architecture (shown in Figure 1) is based on a framework that was developed by the NZDIS research group [11]. In this framework various agents are responsible for performing their tasks by executing a model of their activity specified with Petri nets. The open and dynamic nature of the agents facilitate the incorporation of adaptable process models. Each model is associated with a sub-process associated with the overall workflow.

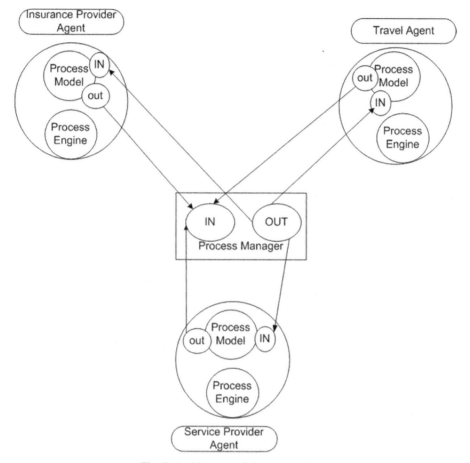

Fig. 1. Architecture of the agent system.

Each agent runs an instance of JFern for Petri net protocol enactment. The agents interact by sending messages to other agents as specified in their protocol model. When an agent receives a message, the appropriate information is deposited in an *In* place in its Petri net, and this may enable transitions to be fired that are associated with the protocol model. Similarly any message going to another agent is deposited in the *Out* place. All these nodes are fused with the *out* place of the process manager. The process manager dispatches the messages to the appropriate agents as specified in the message content.

An agent can receive a proposal for a new or modified interaction protocol, associated with its participation in the overall workflow, from another agent by means of a FIPA-specified *propose* message. The content of this message contains the proposed interaction protocol encoded in XML format. The interaction protocol actually comprises a coloured Petri net and the associated ontology, which describes the terms used in the model and their relationships. The ontology is represented in UML, and both the Petri net and the UML-encoded ontology information are encoded in XML and sent together as the overall interaction protocol. Because the agents are autonomous, they may not agree to the new proposed protocol and may inform the proposing agent of their refusal to agree. Under certain circumstances, such as in loosely-organised confederations of service providers that are distributed across the Internet, this option of refusing the newly proposed protocol may be appropriate. The system architecture described here provides support for this kind of semi-autonomous workflow structure.

The agent-based architecture also supports the notion of incorporating new agents appearing on the scene (joining the agent group) and offering new services on the fly. These new agents will be informed on arrival of current interaction protocols for the group by means of the same *propose* message mentioned above.

The governance of the interaction protocols is handled by one or more 'manager' agents, which maintain a model repository. At the present stage of technology, such manager agents are expected to be interfaces to human managers. Thus if it is determined during the middle of workflow execution that a new model is required, the manager or workflow designer would have the opportunity to create a new model and register it with the 'manager' agent's model repository which can then be distributed to the appropriate agent that may require an alternative protocol.

A separate workflow designer component can exist on different hosts. The workflow administrator of a branch of an organisation can design the process associated with that particular office and send the model and the associated work cases to a specific agent.

The system architecture comprises several components including the workflow engine, workflow modeller, and various services such as an XML-to-Petri net (in Java) translator, and generic service provider agents that can locate a resource and provide a service for a particular task.

This architecture allows for monitoring of the system based on a set of predefined conditions such as availability of resources, which could be used as a feedback mechanism for human administrators.

2.1 The Workflow Modeller

This workflow modeller component is used to specify the processes associated with performing a particular activity. Coloured Petri nets are used to model workflow systems, due in part to their sound mathematical foundation and to the fact that they have been used extensively for modelling of distributed systems [12]. Coloured Petri nets consist of the following basic elements:

tokens which are typed markers with values - the type can be any Java class.
places (circles), which are typed locations that can contain zero or more tokens.
transitions (squares), which represent actions whose occurrence (firing) can change the number and/or value of tokens in one or more of the places connected to them. Tokens may have guards which must evaluate to TRUE in order for the transition to fire. In a workflow model a transition may represent a task.
arcs (arrows) connecting places and transitions. An arc can have associated inscriptions, which are Java expressions whose evaluation to token values affects the enabling and firing of transitions.

Some reasons for preferring Petri net modelling in connection with workflow modelling to other notations are:

\# They have *formal semantics*, which make the execution and simulation of Petri net models unambiguous.

\# It can be shown that Petri nets can be used to model workflow primitives identified by the Workflow Management Coalition (WfMC) [13]

\# Typical process modelling notations, such as dataflow diagrams, are event-based, but *Petri nets can model both states and events.*

\# There are *many analysis techniques* associated with Petri nets, which make it possible to identify 'dangling' tasks, deadlocks, and safety issues.

Other standardization protocols do not cater to expressiveness, simplicity and formal semantics. The comparison of high-level Petri nets with other proposed standardization protocols can be found in [15].

The Petri net models created using the JFern engine are instantiated as workflow components in our system.

2.2 Workflow Engine

The workflow engine is the component that executes the interaction protocol that has been modelled using Petri nets. The JFern tool can be used as a process modeller and also the execution engine.

2.3 Conversation Manager

The conversation manager is the component that organizes the interaction between various interaction protocols. It is responsible for dispatching the messages from the "in" and "out" places and the ontology component which defines the terms that appear in the model (the places, transitions and the arc expressions). The conversation manager plays the role of the resource manager. It identifies the list of resources that can perform a certain task. These resources can be chosen from a pool of resources available in the form of 'agent societies' [17]. The conversation manager can choose a service provider agent that is less flexible and less expensive than some other provider that offers more expensive services. Each agent in the society has certain capabilities inscribed as attributes.

3 Example Scenario

In order to show the operational aspect of the system, as well as how it can adapt to changes, an example scenario is described. In this scenario, various sub-nets associated with different sub-processes of the system are discussed. This model has been adapted from a travel agent model example discussed by Van der Aalst [2].

3.1 A Distributed Process Model

In this scenario the interactions involving a customer, a travel agent, a transport ticket seller (travel service provider) are described. Figure 2 depicts a simplified version of the interaction protocol for the travel agent. The protocol is initiated when a customer's request has been submitted to the travel agent, indicated in the model by the placement of a token at the *In* place of the net. The travel agent then searches some external database (not shown in the diagram) to come up with some possible trip options (the *Prod Opts* transition). The result of the search is placed in the *Opts* place. These options are then placed in the *Out* place so that they can be sent back to the customer. At this point the customer is contacted (the customer interaction is not shown in this diagram). When the customer responds, the travel agent's *Get Cus Res* transition will fire. Either the customer will select an option for purchasing a ticket (an external travel service provider will have to be contacted for the purchase of such a ticket) or the customer will not be satisfied with the options he was sent and will need more options (*Need More Opts*). Assuming that the customer does select one of the options for purchase (as indicated by the value of the token in the *Cus Res* place), the *Res Tick* transition is enabled, causing the travel agent to send a ticket reservation request to a travel service provider, such as a bus company or sightseeing operation. A copy of the customer's ticket reservation request is kept in the *Res Sent* place for later consultation. The travel service provider will either send back a notification that a reservation has been made (enabling the *Get Tick Res* transition) or send back notification that there are no tickets available (enabling the *Get Rej* transition, which will cause a notification of that fact to be sent back to the customer). If the travel service provider *does* return a confirmed ticket reservation, it is matched with the ticket reservation request stored in the *Res Sent* place and then deposited in the *Tick Res* place. This will, in turn, enable the *Send Bill* transition, causing a bill to be sent to the customer for payment. After payment is received, the travel agent will send the payment to the service provider, get the ticket from the service provider, and then forward the ticket on to the customer.

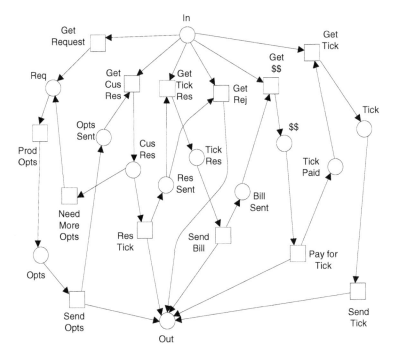

Fig. 2. Interaction protocol for the travel agent.

Note that information is stored in the *Opts Sent, Res Sent, Bill Sent, and Tick Paid* places for matching up with later messages that arrive. This enables the travel agent to conduct activities with many customers and travel service providers concurrently.

Figure 3 shows the interaction protocol[1] for the customer. This protocol has a *Start* place that has a token placed in it (specifying the customer's travel interests) when the customer wants to initiate a conversation with the travel agent. The *Send Request* transition causes the request to be placed in the *Out* place for sending a message to the travel agent and a copy of the request is stored in the *Req Sent* place. Later, the customer expects to receive a set of options for selection from the travel agent, and these options should match his or her travel request. After an option is selected, this is placed in the *Out* place for sending back to the travel agent, and a copy of the reservation selected is stored in the *Res Sent* place. Subsequently, the customer expects to get a bill, pay it, and ultimately get tickets matching what he or she has paid for.

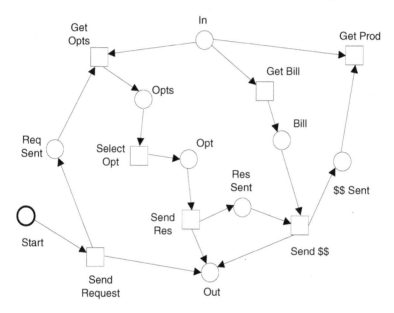

Fig. 3. Interaction protocol for the Customer.

Figure 4 shows the interaction protocol for the travel service provider. The travel service provider might supply any kind of travel service, such as boat passage, tramping guides, etc. The travel service provider initially receives a message from the travel agent indicating that a reservation has been requested for his or her service, such as a transport ticket. The service provider must then see if the requested resource (usually a ticket booking) is available. So both the *Prep Prod* and *Send Reject* transitions examine the single token located in the *Available Resources* place. The single token in the *Available Resources* place contains a list of available resources, and information

---

[1] At times we use the term protocol to refer to the activities of individual participants and at other times to the collection of activities of all participants. The context should make clear the difference.

for the list in this token is maintained by access to an external database. The *Prep Prod* transition is enabled if the relevant information (*i.e.* what is desired, for example, a bus ticket) on the reservation request token in the *Res* place matches up with one of the resources listed on the token in the *Available Resources* place. On the other hand, the *Send Reject* transition is enabled if the information on the token in the *Res* place fails to match up with an item listed on the token in the *Available Resources* place. In the case where there are tickets available, the service provider then prepares the product (a ticket, say) and sends the bill back to the travel agent and keeps a copy of it in the *Bill Sent* place. When payment is received later, the service provider will send the product that has been stored in *Prod Ready*. In the simplified scenario described here, there is only a single generic protocol for a travel service provider shown, but there could be many such protocols that are used for particular service providers. There could also be more complicated interactions with the customer. In our example, payment is made directly to the travel agent. But there could be other options available, including having the travel agent act as a broker, with payment transactions ultimately taking place directly between the customer and the travel service provider.

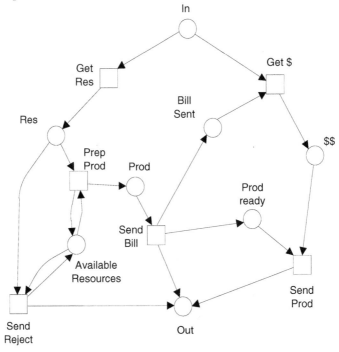

Fig. 4. Interaction protocol for the service provider.

Figure 5 shows how all the interaction protocols are created and executed. The human manager can create interaction protocols using the JFern process modeller and store them in the system using the storage agent. The stored protocols can be viewed querying the storage agent. When sets of interaction protocols are to be executed, the protocols are selected and submitted to the workflow engine.

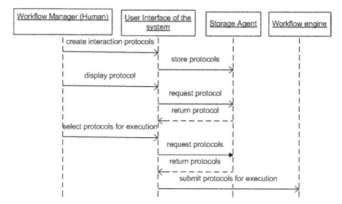

Fig. 5. Creation and execution of the interaction protocols.

The conversation manager plays the important role of the co-ordinating agent between various interaction protocols. It is responsible for matching the "in" and "out" tokens from various agents. Figure 6 shows the interaction between a customer agent, travel agent, service provider and the conversation manager.

The customer agent executes the interaction protocol and places a request for reserving a ticket to the travel agent through the conversation manager. The conversation manager transfers the requests to the travel agent from the customer agent. This corresponds to the transfer of a token from the *out* place of the customer agent to the *in* place of conversation manager. The token is then placed at the *out* place of the conversation manager which is appropriately moved to the travel agent's *in* place by the conversation manager.

The travel agent could then get the appropriate service provider to perform a particular task from the resource agent. All these interactions are co-ordinated through the conversation manager.

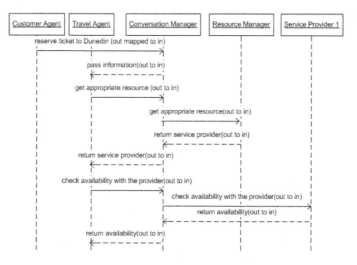

Fig. 6. Interaction protocol for the service provider.

3.2 Adaptive Workflow Process Operation

Consider now an international travel agency with individual travel agents spread across the globe (or region). The individual agents may be using an interaction protocol associated with customers and service providers such as we have described in Figures 2-4. These sets of interaction protocols represent the workflow cases for the travel agents of the agency. Suppose, now, that a health crisis emerges in some regions of the world, and that the global manager of the travel agency decides to recommend a new interaction protocol for some of his or her travel agents.

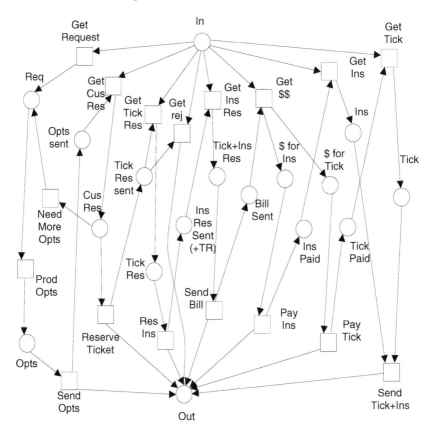

Fig. 7. New interaction protocol for travel agent involving two coupled service providers (for tickets and insurance).

The newly proposed protocol is to require that all ticket transactions must be bundled with a health insurance policy that is offered by some recommended health insurance agents. This new interaction protocol is now recommended for those travel agents in parts of the world that are affected by the health crisis, and the new travel agent protocol is shown in Figure 7. The entire protocol is sent to all travel agents in the organisation in the form of an encoded XML expression in the body of a FIPA *propose* message. Those travel agents that are dealing with customers in affected areas would be urged to adopt the new protocol. For a resilient and adaptive global organisation, this kind of autonomy may be essential for success in a competitive environment.

In the new protocol, there is now a ticket selling travel service provider and an insurance service provider. For this new scenario, we assume that the customer and both service provider protocols remain as shown in Figures 3 and 4, respectively. Both of the service provider agents use the interaction protocol depicted in Figure 4: they prepare a product when requested by the travel agent, and that product is delivered to the travel agent when payment is received. The protocol for the travel agent is modified, though, as shown in Figure 7. When the initial request comes in from the customer, the early stages of interaction are as before in Figure 2. However after the ticket reservation request is confirmed by receipt of a message from the ticket selling service provider, the travel agent proceeds to request purchase of insurance from an insurance provider (a message to the insurance provider is prepared in connection with the *Res Ins* transaction, and a token for the message is placed in the *Out* place). Information about the insurance request and the confirmed ticket reservation is stored in the *Ins Res Sent (+TR)* place. Later when the bill is sent to the customer and payment is received, the travel agent arranges to pay both the ticket selling service provider and the insurance provider. After the travel agent receives authorisation from both the ticket selling agent (in the form of tickets) and the insurance provider (possibly just some authorisation number) these vouchers are bundled together and forwarded on to the customer.

4 Discussions and Future Work

The ability to design and update interaction protocols that, together, represent workflow scenarios enables an organisation of semi-autonomous entities or agents to respond and adapt to changing conditions in a distributed environment. For illustrative purposes, we have described a distributed example involving travel agents. This is an appropriate example, because the conditions and available service providers are constantly changing in the travel and tourism industry, and it can be difficult to maintain an organised sense of workflow activities under these conditions. As new types of service providers become available, there can be new types of interaction protocols that are appropriate for those service providers, and all the agents that interact with them would need to be informed about those interactions protocols.

Another application domain can be in the area of distributed software development, where many independent, autonomous software developers are working together on a large, possibly open-source, development project. Integration, testing, and acceptance activities can be adapted to deal with changing scheduling requirements, customer-imposed constraints, or preferences among the distributed collection of team members.

This work is also applicable in those areas that are less human-dominated and in which electronic agents are performing most of the work. In these environments, it is essential to be able to monitor and coordinate the activities of groups of autonomous agents. Facilities such as those we are developing can offer more choice in the organisation of distributed enterprises, because they can provide coordination facilities while, at the same time, allowing individual entities to retain more autonomy.

The following enhancements to the existing system are planned for future work in this research.

\#   Provide more explicit facilities for resource management so that conventional workflow models can be incorporated.

\#   Provide a direct interface to one of the exiting analysis tools so that process models can be analysed on the spot. The resulting analysis can lead to improved system performance.

\#   Improve the monitoring capability so that various performance statistics and throughput information is available graphically.

\#   Improve the visualization of linked and hierarchical models.

\#   We are in the process of extending the proposed prototype and evaluating various process model scenarios. In particular we are examining the integration of the web services as discussed by Paul et al [16].

The authors would like to acknowledge the technical support and consultation provided by Mariusz Nowostawski and Peter Hwang of the University of Otago.

References

1. Schael, T.: Workflow Management Systems for Process Organisations. Springer-Verlag. (1998)
2. Van der Aalst, W., Van Hee, K., Schmidt, J. W.: Workflow Management: Models, Methods, and Systems. MIT Press. (2002)
3. Meilin, S., Guangxin, Y. , Yong, X. , Shangguang, W.: Workflow Management Systems: A Survey. In: Proceedings of IEEE Intl. Conf. On Communication Technology, Beijing, (1998)
4. Borghoff, U.M. , Bottoni, P. , Mussio, P., Pareschi, R.: Reflective Agents for Adaptive Workflows. In: Proc. 2nd Conf. on the Practical Application of Intelligent Agents and Multi_Agent Technology (PAAM'97), London, U.K., (1997) 405-420
5. Stormer, H.:A Flexible Agent-Based Workflow Systems. In: Workshop on Agent-Based Approaches to B2B, Fifth International Conference on Autonomous Agents, Montreal, Canada (2001)
6. Jensen, K.: Coloured Petri Nets - Basic Concepts, Analysis Methods and Practical Use, Vol. 1: Basic Concepts. Springer-Verlag, Berlin (1992).
7. van der Aalst, W.M.P.: The application of Petri nets to workflow management. In: The Journal of Circuits, Systems and Computers vol. (1998) 8(1), 21-66.
8. Nowostawski, M.: JFern, version 1.2.1, http://sourceforge.net/project/showfiles.php?group_id=16338 (2002).
9. Purvis, M., Cranefield, S., Nowostawski, M., and Carter, D.: Opal: A Multi-Level Infrastructure for Agent-Oriented Software Development. In: *Information Science Discussion Paper Series*, No. 2002/01, ISSN 1172-6024, University of Otago, Dunedin, New Zealand.
10. FIPA. Foundation For Intelligent Physical Agents (FIPA). FIPA 2001 specifications, http://www.fipa.org/specifications/ (2003)
11. Purvis, M. K., Huang, P., Purvis, M. A., Cranefield, S. J., and Schievink, M.: Interaction Protocols for a Network of Environmental Problem Solver. In: Proceedings of the 2002 iEMSs International Meeting: Integrated Assessment and Decision Support (iEMSs 2002), Volume 3, Andrea E. Rizzoli and Anthony J. Jakeman (eds.), The International Environmental Modelling and Software Society, Lugano, Switzerland (2002) 318-323

12. van der Aalst, W.M.P.: Three good reasons for using a Petri-net-based workflow management system. In: Navathe, S., Wakayama, T. (eds.): Proc of International Working Conference on Information and Process Integration in Enterprises (IPIC'96),. Massachusetts Institute of Technology, Cambridge, Massachusetts, (1996) 179-201.
13. Workflow Management Coalition: The Workflow Reference Model, Document No. TC00-1003, Issue 1.1. (1995)
14. Theoretical Foundations Group and Distributed Systems Group of the Department of Informatics, University of Hamburg. Renew – The Reference Net Workshop, Release 1.2, (2000)
15. van der Aalst, W.M.P.: Don't go with the flow: Web Services composition standards exposed, Jan/Feb 2003 issue of IEEE intelligent systems.
16. Paul Buhler and José M. Vidal. Enacting BPEL4WS specified workflows with multiagent systems. In *Proceedings of the Workshop on Web Services and Agent-Based Engineering*, 2004.
17. B.T.R Savarimuthu and M.Purvis, A Collaborative mulit-agent based workflow system. In: M. G. Negoita, R. J. Howlett, L. C. Jain (eds.), Knowledge-Based Intelligent Information and Engineering Systems, 8th International Conference, KES2004, Wellington, New Zealand, September 2004, Proceedings, Part II, Springer LNAI 3214, pp. 1187-1193, 2004.

Evaluation of a Multi-agent Based Workflow Management System Modeled Using Coloured Petri Nets

Maryam Purvis, Bastin Tony Roy Savarimuthu, and Martin Purvis

Department of Information Science, University of Otago,
P O Box 56, Dunedin, New Zealand
{tehrany,tonyr,mpurvis}@infoscience.otago.ac.nz

Abstract. Workflow management systems (WfMS) should address the needs of rapidly changing business environments. We have built a multi-agent based framework, JBees, which addresses these needs. We evaluate our agent-based workflow system, which employs coloured Petri net workflow modeling, with the proposed standards for various workflow patterns and communication patterns. The coloured Petri net models support the workflow patterns and the agent-based framework supports the communication standards developed by the Foundation for Intelligent Physical Agents (FIPA). The agent-based communication technology patterns along with the workflow patterns equip the workflow management system with a comprehensive set of capabilities, such as adaptability and distribution.

1 Introduction

Most of the commercially available workflow management systems do not offer sufficient flexibility for distributed organizations that participate in the global market. These systems have rigid, centralized architectures that do not operate across multiple platforms [8]. Employing a distributed network of autonomous software agents that can adapt to changing circumstances would result in an improved workflow management system technology. In the past, workflow management systems (WfMS) were used in well-defined activities, such as manufacturing, where the processes tend to be more established and stable. But in the current climate WfMS may be used for more fluid business processes, such as e-commerce, or in processes involving human interactions, such as the software development process. In such situations it is not always possible to predict in advance all the parameters that may be important for the overall processes. This gives rise to the need for adaptive WfMS. Our previous work ([2] and [17]) describes issues addressed by our agent-based framework JBees.

In this paper we evaluate our agent based workflow system, JBees, in two ways. We first evaluate our system for various workflow patterns. Secondly we compare the communication patterns supported by our system. These comparisons are made with reference to the patterns described in previous work by van der Aalst ([10], [11], [12], [13], [14] and [15]). The paper is organized as follows. Brief descriptions of various notations used and our agent-based framework are given in Section 2. The third section describes how we evaluate our system using various workflow and communication patterns. The concluding remarks are presented in the fourth section.

M.W. Barley and N. Kasabov (Eds.): PRIMA 2004, LNAI 3371, pp. 206–216, 2005.
© Springer-Verlag Berlin Heidelberg 2005

2 System Technology Background

In this section we discuss system technologies on which our work is based, which includes (a) the use of coloured Petri nets, which are used to design the process models and (b) the multi-agent system on which our workflow system has been built.

2.1 Coloured Petri Nets

The sound mathematical foundation behind Coloured Petri nets (CPN) [16] offers advantages for modelling distributed systems. Petri nets consist of four basic elements. The *tokens* which are typed markers with values, the *places* that are typed locations that can contain zero or more tokens, the *transitions* which represent actions whose occurrence can change the number and value of tokens at the places, and the *arcs* that connect places and transitions. When a transition occurs (fires), the placement and values of tokens can be changed depending on expressions specified on the arcs connected to that transition. Some reasons for preferring Petri net modeling to other notations used for workflow modeling are given by [20]:

- They have formal semantics, which make the execution and simulation of Petri net models unambiguous.
- It has been shown that Petri nets can be used to model workflow primitives identified by the Workflow Management Coalition (WfMC) [21]
- Unlike some event-based process modeling notations, such as dataflow diagrams, Petri nets can model both states and events.
- There are many analysis techniques associated with Petri nets, which make it possible to identify 'dangling' tasks, deadlocks, and safety issues.

2.2 Agent Systems

Sycara [25] identifies several benefits associated with using multi-agent systems for building complex software. For example, multi-agent systems can offer a high level of encapsulation and abstraction. Some commonly accepted characteristics of agents are listed in [22, 23, 24]. Because agents are independent, every agent can have its own strategy for solving a particular problem. Different developers can build agents and as long as these agents understand each other through agent communication, they can work together. A second important benefit is that multi-agent systems offer distributed and open platform architecture. Agents can support a dynamically changing system without the necessity of knowing each part in advance. This requires, however a matchmaking infrastructure. Our system is based on the Java-based agent platform Opal [7], developed at the University of Otago since 2000. It meets the standards of the Foundation for Intelligent Physical Agents (FIPA) [6] for agent platforms and incorporates a modular approach to agent development [26].

2.3 Related Work

In the context of WfMSs, agent technology has been used in different ways [27]. In some cases the agents fulfill particular roles that are required by different tasks in the workflow. In these cases the existing workflow model is used to structure the coordination of these agents [28, 29]. An example of this approach is the work by M. Nissen in designing a set of agents to perform activities associated with the supply chain process in the area of e-commerce [29].

In other cases, the agents have been used as part of the infrastructure associated with the WfMS itself in order to create an agent-enhanced WfMS [30, 31]. These agents provide an open system with loosely coupled components, which provides more flexibility than the traditional system architectures. Some researchers have combined both of these approaches [32], where an agent-based WfMS is used in conjunction with specialized agents that provide appropriate application-related services. We have taken the latter approach, which provides sufficient flexibility required for a dynamic and adaptive system.

Adaptive workflows have been discussed for some time, and many people have discussed the problem [10, 32]. Only a few have proposed techniques to manage adaptability and only a small number of actual implementations have been made that tackle some aspects of adaptability [32]. Transferring running work cases to a new model is still a difficult issue. The work done in the paper [32] describes a prototype, which provides *some* adaptability by manual transfer of tokens in the new process model, as indicated in a comparison of current WfMS done by Van der Aalst et al [13].

2.4 Architectural Overview

Our research is focused on developing an agent-enhanced WfMS, where the work associated with running a WfMS has been partitioned among various collaborating agents that are interacting with each other by following standard agent communication protocols. JBees is based on Opal [7] and uses the CPN execution tool JFern [5]. A first description of JBees can be found in the previously published papers [2] and [17]. Our enhanced system consists of seven Opal agents, which provide the functionality to control the workflow. Figure 1 shows these seven agents and their collaboration.

The manager agent provides all functionality the workflow manager needs, such as creation and deletion of tasks, roles and process definitions, instantiation of new process instances, and creation of resource agents. The process agent executes a process instance. Each resource in the system has its own resource agent. Every resource in the system gets registered to one of the broker agents that allocate the resources to the process. The storage agent manages the persistent data that is needed. The monitor agent collects all the process-specific data and sends them to the storage agent. The control agent continuously looks for anomalies to the criteria specified by the human manager and reports the violations to these criteria to the manager agent. The manager agent provides information to the human manager, which can be used as a feedback mechanism.

2.5 Flexibilities of Our Workflow System

The flexibilities of our workflow system enable us to provide the support for distribution, adaptability, monitoring, and controlling of processes. JBees supports inter-organizational co-operation through the distribution of processes. For example, the

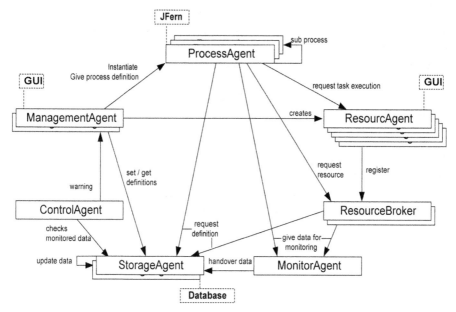

Fig. 1. Showing the architecture of JBees

main process could be present in Germany and the sub-process could be present in New Zealand. The use of multi-agent technology facilitates the distribution of such processes. Also, the persistent data can be distributed. The user of the system can decide to modify or change a running process [1]. Our system has also been endowed with the monitoring and controlling of processes. The process data is stored and the controlling agent constantly checks for anomalies for the criteria entered by the process manager.

3 Evaluation

Workflow systems are driven by the process models, which describe the workflow process. A sample process model for ordering a book is shown in figure 2. The activities associated with the process include order entry, inventory check, credit check, evaluation, approval, billing, shipping, archiving and the activity associated with writing a rejection letter. Evaluation of workflow systems are carried out on the basis of 20 workflow patterns described by Van der Aalst[13]. We evaluate our system for these workflow patterns (and also the communication patterns) and explain the features of the agent framework, which provide support for these patterns.

3.1 Workflow Patterns

Since we use coloured Petri nets [16] as the process-modeling tool, we satisfy the basic workflow patterns such as sequence, parallel split, synchronization, exclusive choice and simple merge [13]. Table 1 shows the categorization of patterns and shows the level of support that our system provides. The notation "++" is used when the pattern is supported by Petri nets, and "+" notation denotes that the pattern is not supported by Petri nets but can be achieved by using our agent-based framework. Van der Aalst categorizes workflow patterns into the following.

1. Advanced branching and synchronization patterns
2. Structural patterns
3. Patterns involving multiple instances
4. State-based patterns
5. Cancellation patterns

Out of these categories of patterns, the coloured Petri net formalism supports patterns described by categories 1, 2 and 4 [13].

3.1.1 Advanced Branching and Synchronization Patterns

The patterns in this category include the multiple-choice pattern, synchronization merge pattern, multiple merge pattern and the discriminator pattern. All the four of the above-described patterns can be achieved by examining the colour of the token. The token can have attributes, which can be evaluated so that the transition could be fired and one of the possible paths (branching or merging) can be chosen.

3.1.2 Structural Patterns

Structural patterns include the *Aribitrary cycles pattern*, which describes the point in a workflow process where one or more activities can be done repeatedly. This can be implemented in Petri nets.

The *Implicit termination pattern* occurs when the given sub-process should be terminated when there is nothing else to be done. Our framework supports implicit termination (refer to the example given in figure 4). The user can interact with the system to indicate the occurrence of an external event, which could trigger the termination of the process.

3.1.3 Patterns Involving Multiple Instances (MI's)

Patterns involving multiple instances are not directly supported through Petri nets[13]. But the same can be achieved by the combination of other patterns or through the agent framework. MI without synchronization is possible by using the arbitrary cycles pattern. In this case instead of having multiple instances of the same activity, the process is repeated for a certain number of cycles. Figure 3 shows a process (Case A), the MI described by Aalst (Case B), and the arbitrary cycles (Case C). It can be seen that the Case B described by Aalst can be modified into Case C, which uses the arbitrary cycles. This can be achieved by the arc expression, which would check the attribute of the token representing the number of times the task has to be repeated.

3.1.4 State Based Patterns

The *deferred choice* pattern describes the execution of one of the two alternatives paths. The choice of which path is to be executed should be determined by some environmental variables. The *interleaved parallel routing* pattern describes execution of two activities in random order, but not in parallel. The *milestone* pattern enables an activity until a milestone is reached. These patterns are inherently supported by coloured Petri nets [13].

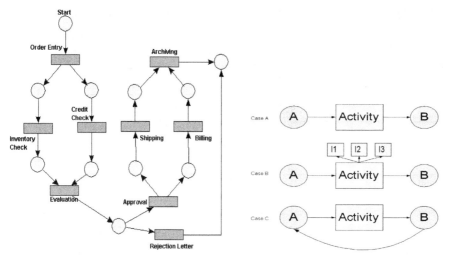

Fig. 2. Process model of ordering a book

Fig. 3. Showing processes with a single instance activity, multi instance activity and multi instance activity achieved through arbitrary cycles (iteration)

3.1.5 Cancellation Patterns

The *cancel activity pattern* is cancellation or disabling of an activity. The CPN will not be able to cancel an activity because, in CPN, we only have local control around a transition. Depending upon the value of tokens in the input places, the tokens on the output place can be generated. But this can be achieved using the higher-level language support that executes the process model. The agent-based framework can provide a user interface such as a stop activity button so that the activity can be cancelled. This is possible since a separate process agent executes every case.

The *cancel case pattern* is the cancellation of the entire case of a process. The same argument for the previous case holds good. The user interface of the agent framework can support it. Figure 4 shows how the framework can support the cancellation patterns. *Activity2* is the active activity. The user can now decide to cancel the activity or the entire case. There might be a few activities, which would need to be undone as the case is cancelled. Those activities which are to be undone can be modeled as compensation activities.

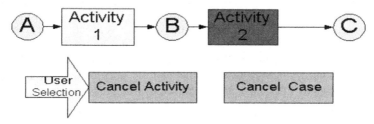

Fig. 4. Showing the user interface for cancellation of running case/activity of the Petri net process model

Table 1. Showing the categorization of workflow patterns and their support in JBees

Categorization of workflow patterns	Workflow Patterns	Support in JBees (++ or +)
Basic Patterns	Sequence	++
	Parallel Split	++
	Synchronization	++
	Exclusive Choice	++
	Simple Merge	++
Advanced branching and synchronization patterns	Multi Choice	++
	Synchronizing Merge	++
	Multi Merge	++
	Discriminator	++
Structural patterns	Arbitrary Cycles	++
	Implicit Termination	+
Patterns involving multiple instances	MI without Synchronization	+
	MI with a Priori Design Time Knowledge	+
	MI with a Priori Runtime Knowledge	+
	MI without a Priori Runtime Knowledge	+
State based patterns	Deferred Choice	++
	Interleaved Parallel Routing	++
	Milestone	++
Cancellation patterns	Cancel Activity	+
	Cancel Case	+

Table 2. Showing the categorization of communication patterns and their support in JBees

Categorization of communication patterns	Communication Patterns	Support in JBees (++ or +)
Synchronous	Request/Reply	++
	One-way	++
	Synchronous Polling	++
Asynchronous	Message Passing	++
	Publish/Subscribe	+
	Broadcast	+

3.2   Communication Patterns

Communication is realized by the exchange of messages between different processes. Our agent-based system is designed for sending and receiving messages based on the FIPA [6] protocols. In this section we evaluate JBees for the various communication patterns. An example (shown in figure 5) of the communication is how the sub-processes are executed. To execute a sub-process, the process agent of the parent process instantiates another process agent. The process-related communication takes place between the parent process agent and the sub process agent. Table 2 shows the categorization of communication patterns and shows the level of support that our system provides. The notation "++" is used when the pattern is supported by FIPA specification that our framework is built upon and "+" notation denotes that the pattern is not supported by FIPA but can be achieved by using our framework.

3.2.1   Synchronous Communication

The *request/reply pattern* is the communication pattern in which the sender sends a request and waits for a reply. The communication scenario shown in Figure 5 is an

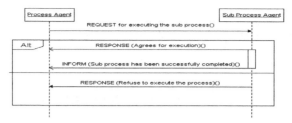

Fig. 5. Showing the communication between the parent process agent and the sub process agent executing the main and sub process respectively

example of this pattern. The *one-way pattern* is the pattern where a sender makes a request to a receiver and does not wait for response. The receiver sends the acknowledgement message but not the actual reply. Our FIPA compliant framework supports these patterns. The *synchronous polling pattern* occurs when the sender communicates a request to a receiver, but instead of blocking it continues processing and constantly checks for response. If a resource is not available at a point of time, the process agent continuously keeps checking with the resource broker whether any resource is available after a fixed interval of time. Figure 6 shows the communication between the process agent and the resource broker agent.

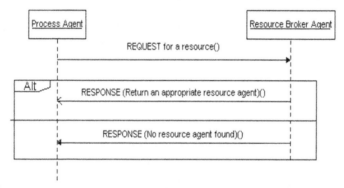

Fig. 6. Showing the communication between the process agent executing a process model and the resource broker agent

3.2.2 Asynchronous Communication

The *message passing pattern* is an asynchronous communication pattern in which the sender receives no response. When the request reaches the receiver, it processes the message and performs appropriate actions. Though our FIPA-compliant framework supports this form of communication, it is not used in the context of workflows, since the feedback from agents about the starting and completion of tasks/activities should have a reply/response. The *publish/subscribe pattern* is the asynchronous communication pattern in which the sender sends the message to those who have already expressed their interest in receiving the messages when an event has occurred. This pattern is not supported by FIPA yet, but it can be implemented in the framework by maintaining the list of all agents that would express their interest in receiving certain kinds of messages. The *broadcast pattern* is the form of communication in which all the participants receive a message. Though this has not been supported by the FIPA protocol, it can be achieved in our framework by sending messages to all agents that collaborate in a particular platform. The list of all collaborating agents can be obtained and the message can be sent to all agents individually.

3.3 Support for Workflow and Communication Patterns in JBees

It can be observed form sections 3.1, 3.2 and figure 7 that sixty five percent of the workflow patterns are supported directly by Petri nets, and the agent-based framework can support the rest of the patterns. We have also described the communication patterns that our system supports. Four out of the six communication patterns are supported directly by our agent-based framework and the other two can be supported with few changes.

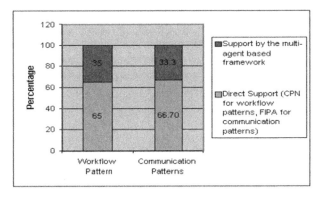

Fig. 7. Graph showing the support for workflow and communication patterns in JBees

4   Conclusion

We have evaluated the capability of our workflow system, both from a process modeling point of view, as well as the inter-process communication viewpoint. Through these patterns, the CPN models executed by the multi-agents have addressed issues on flexible workflow systems by supporting distribution and adaptability of processes. We agree with the viewpoints of van der Aalst [14] that Petri nets could be considered as a standard for modeling workflows, but they should be aided by multi-agents to provide the additional flexibilities associated with adaptability and the distribution of processes. Owing to the support of distributed and adaptive processes, workflow systems modeled using CPNs and managed by multi-agents have started emerging ([18] and [19]). Our described system is available under the GNU Lesser General Public License [3] on the Internet [9].

Acknowledgements

The authors wish to acknowledge the work of Lars Ehrler and Martin Fleurke in the implementation of the agent-based workflow system.

References

1. Martin Fleurke, JBees, an adaptive workflow management system – an approach based on Petri nets and agents, Master's thesis, Department of Computer Science, University of Twente, P.O. Box 217, 7500 AE Enschede, The Netherlands, 2004.
2. Martin Fleurke, Lars Ehrler, and Maryam Purvis, 'JBees - an adaptive and distributed framework for workflow systems', in Workshop on Collaboration Agents: Autonomous Agents for Collaborative Environments (COLA), Halifax, Canada, eds., Ali Ghorbani and Stephen Marsh, pp. 69–76, http://www.cs.unb.ca/~ ghorbani/cola/proceedings/NRC-46519.pdf, (2003). National Research Council Canada, Institute for Information Technology.
3. Free Software Foundation. GNU Lesser General Public License, 2000.
4. S. Meilin, Y. Guangxin, X. Yong, and W. Shangguang,' Workflow Management Systems: A Survey. ', in Proceedings of IEEE International Conference on Communication Technology, (1998).
5. Mariusz Nowostawski. JFern – Java based Petri Net framework , 2003.
6. FIPA, FIPA Communicative Act Library - Specification. 2002. http://www.fipa.org/specs/fipa00037
7. Martin K. Purvis, Stephen Cranefield, Mariusz Nowostawski, and Dan Carter, 'Opal: A multi-level infrastructure for agent-oriented software development', The information science discussion paper series no 2002/01, Department of Information Science, University of Otago, Dunedin, New Zealand, (2002).
8. J.W. Shepherdson, S.G. Thompson, and B. Odgers, 'Cross Organisational Workflow Coordinated by Software Agents', in CEUR Workshop Proceedings No 17. Cross Organisational Workflow Management and Coordination, San Francisco, USA, (1998)
9. Department of Information Science University of Otago. JBees. http://jbees.sourceforge.net, 2004.
10. W.M.P van der Aalst, ' Exterminating the Dynamic Change Bug: A Concrete Approach to Support Workflow Change ', Information Systems Frontiers, 3(3), 297–317, (2001).
11. W.M.P van der Aalst and K. van Hee, Workflow Management: Models, Methods, and Systems , MIT Press, 2002.
12. W.M.P. van der Aalst. The Application of Petri Nets to Workflow Management. *The Journal of Circuits, Systems and Computers*, 8(1):21–66, 1998.
13. W.M.P. van der Aalst and A.H.M. ter Hofstede Workflow Patterns: On the Expressive Power of (Petri-net-based) Workflow Languages. In: Kurt Jensen (Ed.): *Proc. of the Fourth International Workshop on Practical Use of Coloured Petri Nets and the CPN Tools, Aarhus, Denmark, August 28-30, 2002*, pages 1-20. Technical Report DAIMI PB-560, August 2002.
14. W.M.P. van der Aalst. Don't go with the flow: Web services composition standards exposed, IEEE Intelligent Systems, Jan/Feb 2003.
15. P. Wohed, W.M.P. van der Aalst, M. Dumas, and A.H.M. Hofstede. Pattern Based Analysis of BPEL4WS. QUT Technical report, FIT-TR-2002-04, Queens-land University of Technology, Brisbane, 2002.
16. Jensen, K., Coloured Petri Nets - Basic Concepts, Analysis Methods and Practical Use, Vol. 1: Basic Concepts. EATCS Monographs on Theoretical Computer Science. 1992, Heidelberg, Berlin: Springer Verlag GmbH. 1-234.
17. Savarimuthu, B.T.R., Purvis, M. and Fleurke, M. (2004). Monitoring and Controlling of a Multi-agent Based Workflow System. In Proc. Australasian Workshop on Data Mining and Web Intelligence (DMWI2004), Dunedin, New Zealand. CRPIT, **32**. Purvis, M., Ed. ACS. 127-132.
18. Vidal, J.M Buhler, P and Stahl, C (2004), Multi agent systems with workflows. IEEE computer society, Jan-Feb, *76-82*

19. K. Palacz and D.C. Marinescu. An agent-based workflow management system. In Proc. AAAI Spring Symposium Workshop "Bringing Knowledge to Business Processes", Standford University, CA
20. W.M.P. van der Aalst. Three Good reasons for Using a Petri-net based Workflow Management System. In S. Navathe and T. Wakayama, editors, Proceedings of the International Working Conference on Information and Process Integration in Enterprises (IPIC'96), pages 179– 201, Cambridge, Massachusetts, 1996.
21. The workflow management coalition. The workflow reference model, 1995.
22. J. Bradshaw. An Introduction to Software Agents . In J. Bradshaw, editor, Software Agents, pages 3–46. MIT Press, 1997.
23. M.J. Wooldridge. Intelligent Agents . In G. Weiss, editor, Multiagent Systems, pages 27– 77. MIT Press, 1999.
24. Y. Shoham. An Overview of Agent-Oriented Programming. In J. Bradshaw, editor, Software Agents, pages 271–290. MIT Press, 1997.
25. K.P. Sycara. Multiagent Systems . AI magazine, 19(2):79–92.
26. Mariusz Nowostawski, Geoff Bush, Martin K.Purvis, and Stephen Cranefield. A Multilevel Approach and Infrastructure for Agent-Oriented Software Development. In International Work-shop on Infrastructure for Agents, MAS and Scalable MAS, http://www.umcs.maine.edu/~wagner/workshop/01_nowostawski_bush_purvis_etal.pdf, 2001.
27. G. Joeris. Decentralized and Flexible Workflow Enactment Based on Task Coordination Agents. In 2nd Int'l. Bi-Conference Workshop on Agent-Oriented Information Systems (AOIS 2000 @ CAiSE*00), Stockholm, Sweden, pages 41–62. iCue Publishing, Berlin, Germany.
28. N.R. Jennings, P. Faratin, T.J. Norman, P. O'Brien, and B. Odgers. Autonomous Agents for Business Process Management. Int. Journal of Applied Artificial Intelligence, 14(2): 145–189, 2000.
29. M.E. Nissen. Supply Chain Process and Agent Design for E-Commerce. In 33rd Hawaii International Conference on System Sciences, 2000.
30. M. Wang and H. Wang. Intelligent Agent Supported Flexible Workflow Monitoring System . In Advanced In-formation Systems Engineering: 14th International Conference, CAiSE 2002, Toronto, Canada, 2002.
31. H. Stormer. AWA - A flexible Agent-Workflow System . In Workshop on Agent-Based Approaches to B2B at the Fifth International Conference on Autonomous Agents (AGENTS 2001), Montreal, Canada, 2001.
32. Q. Chen, M. Hsu, U. Dayal, and M.L. Griss. Multi-agent cooperation, dynamic work ow and XML for e-commerce automation. In fourth international conference on Autonomous agents, Barcelona, Spain, 2000.
33. Purvis, M. K. and Purvis, M. A. and Lemalu, S., "A Framework for Distributed Workflow Systems", Proceedings of the Hawai`i International Conference on System Sciences (HICSS-34), (CD-ROM) IEEE Computer Society Press, Los Alamitos, CA (2001).

Supporting Impromptu Coordination Using Automated Negotiation

Iyad Rahwan, Connor Graham, and Liz Sonenberg

Department of Information Systems, University of Melbourne,
Parkville, VIC 3010, Australia
i.rahwan@pgrad.unimelb.edu.au,
{cgraham,l.sonenberg}@unimelb.edu.au

Abstract. We are concerned with forms of interaction in which multiple users, with differing agendas and interests, may realise opportunities for useful synchronisation of their activities. We present a framework in which intelligent software agents act as semi-autonomous intermediaries among nomadic users. Agents capture and process information about situations (specifically about the environment, users and their activities) in order to jointly find and negotiate opportunities for coordinating the activities of their respective users. The interaction is structured using a negotiation protocol that exploits a hierarchical representation of tasks and goals.

1 Introduction

The use of mobile computing devices and services in everyday life is increasing largely due to the advancement of enabling technologies [13] as well as increasing efforts to make the technology more usable [16]. One of the challenges presented to the developer of such technologies is dealing with the complexity imposed by situations involving users who are mobile. Scenarios involving mobile technology usage often do not involve single, well-modeled users operating within a stable environment and interacting with stationary technologies. Part of the challenge for the developers of mobile technologies is to respond to a user's embeddedness in such situations in a sensible way. Opportunities exist to utilise new technologies to augment and alleviate the complexity of user situations, including the reconciliation of different interests and agendas among multiple parties. This might involve, for example, coordinating a meeting at a particular time in a particular place among many busy individuals.

An additional challenge for developing context-aware mobile systems is responding to actions and interactions that are neither planned nor routine [14] but evolving from interaction with an ever-changing environment. These actions and interactions are aligned to those well documented in computer-supported cooperative work that often form the cement that binds 'core' actions and interactions together: *spontaneous, lightweight interactions* [15, 17]. They are described as "impromptu," "quick and easy to initiate," "short and informal," "brief," "unplanned," and "intermittent" [ibid]. These interactions often manifest themselves as accidental, corridor conversations among work colleagues [4]. Thus they are not routine, as some reflection on work practice is often involved. Nor are they planned in a deterministic sense as they are often accidental. However, they are

M.W. Barley and N. Kasabov (Eds.): PRIMA 2004, LNAI 3371, pp. 217–227, 2005.
© Springer-Verlag Berlin Heidelberg 2005

related to individual actors' ongoing courses of action, or generic goals and they often involve negotiating multiple courses of action to achieve a shared goal. We dub these interactions *impromptu coordination*.

Impromptu coordination poses a challenge for technology support not only because of its unpredictability but due to the very nature of the mobile situations that form their backdrop: these situations involve physical movement or traversal through environments possessing multifarious agents (such as people and computational agents) and resources (such as digital displays and mobile phones). In addition, due to the nature of interaction investigated here (impromptu coordination) the demand on the effective exchange of information among agents is high and as a result there is a very high computational load for both the user and the supporting context-aware device. Here we suggest there is an opportunity to utilize specific agent technology to assist with these kind of interactions through the effective use of available resources by involved agents.

Research into computational multi-agent systems [18] has produced a variety of techniques for facilitating and controlling interaction among computational agents. In particular, a wide range of frameworks for automated negotiation have been presented [5].

In this paper, we explore the use of a novel automated negotiation technique, dubbed *interest-based negotiation* [11], to support impromptu coordination among mobile users. By doing so, the paper advances the state of the art in two ways. First, it is the first attempt at using negotiation techniques to support non-routine coordination of mobile users. Most existing work on agents for mobile devices focuses on supporting single users [12] or collaborative teams executing routine tasks [1]. Second, the paper introduces a novel coordination architecture, which integrates context-aware networked devices, agent-based reasoning, and automated negotiation. This approach may be used for building a variety of mobile coordination-support systems, that suit domains beyond that of the simple narrative used here for illustration.

Our argument for the possibility of using interest-based negotiation to support impromptu coordination proceeds as follows. In the next section, we outline key characteristics of mobile user coordination and how they require some form of negotiation. In section 3, we present our conceptual and technical framework for supporting mobile coordination through automated negotiation, and illustrate the use of the framework through an example. We conclude in section 4.

2   The Problem of Impromptu Coordination

We begin in section 2.1 by defining impromptu coordination. Then, in section 2.2, we describe some informal observations on the role of technology in facilitating interactions through which multiple users, with differing agendas and interests, may realise opportunities for useful coordination of their activities. To better understand the opportunities for technology intervention, we take Luff and Heath's [7] advice and "examine activities in which people engage with others when they are 'mobile' and how various tools and artefacts feature in those activities." To this end, we analyse an informal narrative in section 2.3 to distill essential characteristics of mobile use.

2.1   Impromptu Coordination

For mobile users, opportunities for collaboration arise more frequently than with static users due to the more diverse forms of context change, such as change in the user's location or the proximity of multiple users. Such opportunities usually cannot be anticipated a priori. Negotiation is a way of dynamically realising and taking advantage of such opportunities[1]. This also relates to the findings of Perry et al [8], who build on the Luff and Heath [7] study through the examination of 17 mobile workers in the United Kingdom. Specifically, they recommend that technologies supporting mobile workers should "allow more effective planning of activities and flexible allocation of resources" and "allow the location, use of, and access to locally available resources."

2.2   Supporting Impromptu Coordination

In the settings of interest, the user is mobile, connected, and engaged in complex interactions. This creates an opportunity for technology to support the user. In Table 1, we list different levels of support that technology could provide, and compare the extent to which different technologies go. The most basic approach would be to provide connectivity, for example, using mobile telephones. However, when support only takes the form of communication facilitation, users would, 'in their heads,' need to keep track of all changes to their context, manage the complexity of identifying opportunities as events unfold, deal with multiple interaction partners, and so on. This places great cognitive load on mobile users, and it is precisely for this reason that support software such as calendar applications are appropriate tools.

When a mobile phone is endowed with a calendar functionality, the user can 'outsource' the storage of large amounts of information about activities (meetings, special occasions, etc.) to their device. This representation of *individual* activities can then be used to help a user coordinate with others. Applications allowing for group task representation, such as Microsoft Outlook with the Exchange Sever, go a step further by providing stationary users with representations of multiple users activities in a globally accessible manner.

One could envisage device support not only through *representation* of individual and group activities, but also *automation* to support the cognitive processes that exploit and manipulate those representations. Such automatic processes would use the available information about the user's situation as well as information available about other users in order to automatically negotiate agreements over collaboration and coordination of activities. Through more elaborate examples, in the following section we demonstrate that making explicit and available a representation of users' goals and task structures and some ability to view and configure these, through communication or automatically, can better support impromptu coordination.

2.3   Characteristics of Impromptu Coordination

We now discuss particular *characteristics of impromptu coordination* and how they require some form of negotiation. These characteristics emerged from discussions in a

---

[1] This characteristic stresses the contrast between the focus of this paper and the objectives of intelligent scheduling applications.

Table 1. Levels of support for impromptu coordination.

Feature Technology	Connected while mobile	Represent tasks	Manual task manipulation		Auto task manipulation	
			Individual tasks	Group tasks	Individual tasks	Group tasks
Phone	✓					
Ph/Calendar	✓	✓	✓			
MS Outlook		✓	✓	✓		
All above + automated negotiation	✓	✓	✓	✓	✓	✓

multi-disciplinary focus group and among the authors of a narrative based on a diary of an actual PhD student renamed Omar, generated over a period of three days. The narrative approach has been used in order to understand individual mobile activities in other projects, such as ActiveCampus [3]. An approach grounded in broader and more systematic data collection would be desirable in the future, c.f. [4].

Narrative 1 *I realized I had not set up a lift home so I called my wife. I couldn't get through, so I left her a message and asked her to call me when she was close. While waiting for her to reply, I continued work. Then I called Jack to discuss our Wednesday meeting. Jack happened to be in his car on his way in a direction not too far from my home. He was short on time because he needed to pick up a book from the city first. I managed to get myself a lift by offering to borrow a copy for him from the University library.*

In the narrative above, Omar being connected to Jack was critical to him being able to capitalise on the opportunity presented by Jack's proximity. The phone did not allow him to predict the possible chances of the success of this opportunistic interaction through a representation of Jack's goals or tasks.

Fluidity. Kakihara and Sorenson [6] describe how the interaction experienced by mobile individuals is 'fluid'. Thus "human interaction is becoming ambiguous and transitory. The patterns of social interaction are dynamically reshaped and renegotiated through our everyday activities significantly freed from spatial, temporal and contextual constraints" [ibid]. Fluidity is apparent in the narrative above, describing Omar's activity.

Fluidity in the narrative above suggests that interaction can be rather occasional during impromptu coordination among mobile individuals, since the environment in which these portable devices operate changes more frequently than with stationary computers. Thus, for the agents involved, well-established, long-term relationships, in which task structures are well-defined and agreed upon, are less likely. In addition, the dynamism in the presence of resources within the immediate environment (such as a car) as a result

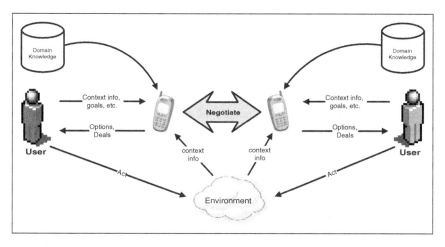

Fig. 1. Conceptual framework for mobile coordination through automated negotiation.

of mobile situations involving impromptu coordination makes it even more difficult for the agents involved to reduce uncertainty. Negotiation is one way of reaching temporary agreement in such dynamic situations.

Heterogeneity. When the modelling of situations involving impromptu coordination among mobile individuals is to take into account varying location, time, user profiles, tasks, interaction history, etc., we are confronted with a much greater variety of agent (and user) types. Each individual agent may achieve tasks in a different way. It is un-likely that information about this heterogeneity will be available a priori. Negotiation is a natural way to exchange information and reach useful agreement or compromise with collaborators (or in collaboration settings) not known before.

In the above narrative, Omar's coordination could have been made easier by a repre-sentation of Jack's and, at the very least, his availability. Given the complexity of these representations, some automation of the process of reconciling goals and availability among the multiple parties involved would also have been desirable.

Privacy and Connectivity. Mobile users who are involved in impromptu coordination are constantly confronted with different interaction partners that want to obtain infor-mation about them. Users may be unwilling to disclose all the information required to run a centralised algorithm for coordinating joint activity. They may be willing to do so only when interacting with particular partners, or when the they realise the potential benefit of exchanging such information. Negotiation is a natural way to reconcile one's own wish to protect private information with the potential benefit of interacting with others.

3   Negotiation for Impromptu Coordination

In the previous section, we argued that impromptu mobile coordination requires the ability to represent information about the tasks of different users, and the ability to in-teractively process this information. The situations in which these users are involved, as already discussed, are complex. In this section, we present how an automated negotiation framework can fulfill these requirements, and hence may be used in order to support interacting mobile users.

3.1   Conceptual Overview

Our conceptual framework for mobile coordination through automated negotiation is illustrated in figure 1. An agent running on a user's mobile device acts as an intermediary between the user and other potential collaborators. The agent gathers information from the environment (e.g., lecture times, location of user and colleagues) and from the user (e.g., availability, goals). The agent then uses this information, as well as domain-specific knowledge (e.g., procedures for borrowing books from the library) in order to negotiate with agents representing other users. Negotiations are motivated by the user's goals and aim at achieving 'deals' with other users and present the opportunity to alleviate the difficulties presented to mobile users involved in impromptu coordination. Negotiation may result in useful potential deals (e.g., appointment, lunch, lift home), these are proposed to the respective users, who might accept, reject, or modify these deals as they see suitable. To enable this kind of automated support, we need to encode information about users goals and use this information in the negotiation process. In order to address this issue, the automated negotiation framework we adopt enables agents to exchange information about their respective users' goals. As a result, agents are more likely to improve the likelihood and quality of a deal.

3.2   The Negotiation Framework

Since we require a negotiation mechanism that exploits representations of users' tasks and goals, we base our framework on the recently proposed *interest-based negotiation* framework [11]. We now give a brief overview of the framework.

Each computational agent has explicit representations of its *desires*. In order to achieve its desires, an agent decomposes these desires into less abstract *goals*, which may themselves be decomposable into other (sub-)goals, until concrete *actions* are reached (i.e., physical actions agents may execute directly in the world). This results in a hierarchical structure in which the top-level root nodes represent desires, intermediate nodes represent abstract goals, and leaf nodes represent concrete actions to be executed.

The framework involves a set $AGENTS$ of agents, a set $PROPS$ of belief propositions representing the agent's view of the world, and a set $ACTIONS$ of actions. The framework makes use of planning rules of the form φ_1 & $\ldots$ & $\varphi_n \to h$, where $\varphi_1, \ldots, \varphi_n \in PROPS \cup ACTIONS$ and $h \in PROPS$. Intuitively, a planning rule means that the agent believes that if actions or sub-goals $\varphi_1, \ldots, \varphi_n$ were realised, then h will be realised. We denote by $PRULES$ the set of all possible planning rules.

Definition 1. (Plan) A plan *for desire* $d \in PROPS$ *is a finite tree such that:*

– d *is the root of the tree.*
– *A non-leaf node is a proposition* $p \in PROPS$ *and has exactly* n *children* $\varphi_1, \ldots, \varphi_n$ *where* φ_1 & $\ldots$ & $\varphi_n \to p \in PRULES$.
– *The leaves of the tree are actions.*

An agent i may have more than one desire, defined in a desire set $\mathcal{D}_i$. Given a set of initial desires, the agent selects a consistent (sub-)set of these desires, which can also be achieved using a set of consistent plans[2]. The agent *intends* (i.e., becomes committed to) these desires as well as their corresponding plans. The exact mechanism by which the agent selects its intended desires and plans (e.g., based on desires' relative importance, or plans' relative costs) is outside the scope of our study[3].

Part (a) in Fig. 2 shows a sketch of (parts of) the plan structures for Omar and Jack from the narrative 1 above. Jack intends to go to the city because it is part of a plan for getting a book, which is, in turn, part of a larger plan for writing a research paper. To get a book, Jack needs to both get the book details and go to the city. To write the paper, Jack also needs to collect data, and possibly achieve other goals and actions. This is encoded in the following rules[4]:

$$getBookDetails \ \& \ goToCity \rightarrow getBook$$
$$getBook \ \& \ collectData \rightarrow writePaper$$

On the other hand, Omar wants to go home, and one way to do so is to get a lift.

Since agents are not always capable of achieving their goals individually, they may choose (or need) to negotiate with other agents in order to obtain their commitments towards achieving certain actions. A contract specifies what actions each agent has to perform.

Definition 2. *(Contract) A* contract *is an expression of the form*

$$Do(x_1, \alpha_1) \wedge \cdots \wedge Do(x_n, \alpha_n)$$

where $x_i \in AGENTS \mid 1 \leq i \leq n$ and where $Do(x_i, \alpha)$ denotes that agent x_i will execute action α.

Negotiation aims at achieving a *deal*: a contract that is acceptable by all agents required to perform actions within that contract.

Participants in the negotiation dialogue may exchange information about each others' plan structures according to a specific interaction protocol. They can then exploit and/or influence each others' plan structures in order to enable or improve agreement(s). Agents interact using a set of locutions (or primitive message types), which can be exchanged by agents according to a protocol. Due to space limitations, we only present the locutions along with an informal explanation.

L1 PROPOSE(i, j, Ω): Agent i proposes a contract Ω to agent j.
L2 ACCEPT(i, j, Ω): Agent i accepts contract Ω previously proposed by j.
L3 REJECT(i, j, Ω): Agent i states that contract Ω is not acceptable to it.
L4 ASSERT(i, j, X): Agent i states that it believes statement X.
L5 QUESTION(i, j, X): Agent i asks agent j whether it believes statement X.

---

[2] More details on the formal model can be found in [9].
[3] This may be operationalised, for example, using a hierarchical planner [2].
[4] Note that for the time being, we use a simple notation for describing rules. More realistically, one would need to express and reason about the temporal aspects of actions.

L6 CHALLENGE(i, j, X): Agent i asks agent j to provide a justification for formula X.

L7 RETRACT(i, j, X): Agent i retracts formula X that it previously asserted.

L8 REQ-PURPOSE(i, j, x): Agent i asks agent j to assert one of the super-goals of the action or goal denoted by x.

L9 REQ-ACHIEVE(i, j, x): Agent i asks agent j to explain how it intends to achieve the goal or desire denoted by x.

L10 QUIT(i): Agent i announces its withdrawal from the negotiation dialogue.

L11 PASS(i): Allows agent i to pass its turn in the dialogue.

Using locutions **L5**, **L8**, **L9** and **L4**, agents can exchange information about each others' plans. Then, they could influence each others' plans by doing one of the following:

– Argue that some of the beliefs or rules used in constructing a plan is incorrect. This may be achieved through a combination of challenges and counter assertions (using **L6** and **L4**);
– Introduce new beliefs or planning rules, by making new assertions;

These forms of influence may cause a variety of changes in the receiving agent's adopted plans and selected desires. Based on this, agents may be endowed with a variety of *strategies* that guide the way they influence each other. We do not further explore these issues here, but the reader may refer to [10, 11] for a more elaborate discussion.

3.3   Illustrative Example

Let us revisit the narrative introduced in section 2.3. Recall the situation where Omar fails to get in contact with his wife to secure a lift home. A device equipped with negotiation abilities could automatically attempt to find alternative ways to get a lift home by searching for nearby friends and checking (with their devices) for potential coordination. As soon as Omar's device detects that Jack is in a nearby area, it requests a lift from Jack's device. Upon inspection of the request, Jack's device discovers there is not enough time to drop by the university if Jack was to pick the book from the city on time; i.e., that there is some form of conflict between the two actions (in this case, the conflict is temporal). Omar's device could attempt to find out the reason behind the rejection, and suggest an alternative plan for getting the book (by Omar lending his copy of the book to Jack), in exchange for getting a lift.

Table 2 shows the dialogue sequence just described, using the locutions defined in the previous section, between Omar's and Jack's negotiation-enabled mobile devices. Part (b) in Fig. 2 shows Jack's modified plan, which now help achieve the desires of both himself and Omar.

There are other types of arguments that Omar could provide in an attempt to entice Jack to drop the goal of going to the library. For example, after acquiring more information about Jack's goal structure, Omar may attempt to disqualify Jack's ultimate goal of writing a paper, say by stating that data collection cannot be done on time anyway. See [11] for more details on arguments and locutions.

Table 2. Example negotiation dialogue.

Omar:	PROPOSE(*omar, jack, Do*(*jack, giveLift*)
Jack:	REJECT(*jack, omar, Do*(*jack, giveLift*)
Omar:	PASS
Jack:	ASSERT(*jack, omar,* conflict(*goToCity, giveLift*))
Omar:	REQ-PURPOSE(*omar, jack, goToCity*)
Jack:	ASSERT(*jack, omar,* prule(*getBookDetails* & *goToCity* → *getBook*))
Omar:	ASSERT(*omar, jack,* prule(*lendBook* → *getBook*))
Jack:	PASS
Omar:	PROPOSE(*omar, jack, Do*(*omar, lendBook*) & *Do*(*jack, giveLift*))
Jack:	ACCEPT(*jack, omar, Do*(*omar, lendBook*) & *Do*(*jack, giveLift*))

3.4 Characteristics Revisited

The framework we presented offers the features required to deal with the characteristics of impromptu mobile coordination discussed in section 2.3 above. In particular, the framework caters for the fluidity encountered in situations of mobile use involving impromptu coordination, since coordination does not assume predetermined and pre-negotiated task structures. Moreover, the focus on tasks and their underlying goals also enables impromptu realisation of opportunities for coordinating activities. By expressing the resources and objectives explicitly, it becomes possible to build technology that processes this information in order to "allow more effective planning and flexible allocation of resources" [8].

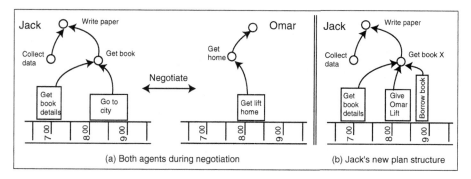

Fig. 2. An abstract view of negotiation.

4   Conclusions

In this paper, we have argued that automated negotiation technologies, from the multi-agent systems literature, are valuable for facilitating impromptu coordination among mobile individuals. We have grounded our discussion in current studies of mobile users and, through a narrative, identified key issues of mobile coordination and showed how they may be addressed using negotiation technologies. In particular, we argued for the suitability of negotiation frameworks that represent and manipulate users' goals. This is because negotiation allows coordination to be task-focused in the context of a user's current situation, and so no long term coordination structures are required (as is required, for example, in the Electric Elves project [1]). We have presented a framework for automated negotiation that exploits a hierarchical representation of tasks and goals, and demonstrated how it can be used to provide the required support.

In the longer term, future work includes experimenting with, testing, and validating various negotiation strategies within the negotiation framework in real usage situations involving interaction with the environment by users and computational agents. Other future research include detailed consideration of the design and usability issues surrounding the interaction with the user. There is also an opportunity to rationalise the environment in terms of resources and affordances that agents and users alike can interact with and utilise. For example, a GPS service running on the Internet can be seen as a resource-for-computational agent and a city building as an affordance-for-human agent. We hope to explore these notions in future work.

Acknowledgement

Thanks to Michael Rovatsos, Christine Satchell, Greg Wadley, Anton Kattan, and Fernando Koch for useful discussions. We thank Hewlett Packard's Philanthropy Division for donating equipment. Iyad Rahwan is grateful for the support of a Melbourne University Research Scholarship and a top-up scholarship from CMIS, CSIRO.

References

1. H. Chalupsky, Y. Gil, C. A. Knoblock, K. Lerman, J. Oh, D. V. Pynadath, T. A. Russ, and M. Tambe. Electric elves: Applying agent technology to support human organizations. In H. Hirsh and S. Chien, editors, *Proceedings of the 13th International Conference of Innovative Application of Artificial Intelligence (IAAI-2001)*. AAAI Press, 2001.
2. K. Erol, J. Hendler, and D. Nau. Semantics for hierarchical task network planning. Technical Report CS-TR-3239, UMIACS-TR-94-31, Department of Computer Science, University of Maryland, 1994.
3. W. G. Griswold, R. Boyer, S. W. Brown, T. M. Truong, E. Bhasker, G. R. Jay, and R. B. Shapiro. Using mobile technology to create opportunitistic interactions on a university campus. In *UbiComp 2002 Workshop on Supporting Spontaneous Interaction in Ubiquitous Computing Settings*, September 2002.
4. E. A. Isaacs, J. C. Tang, and T. Morris. Piazza: a desktop environment supporting impromptu and planned interactions. In *Proceedings of the 1996 ACM conference on Computer supported cooperative work*, pages 315–324. ACM Press, 1996.

5. N. R. Jennings, P. Faratin, A. R. Lomuscio, S. Parsons, C. Sierra, and M. J. Wooldridge. Automated negotiation: prospects, methods and challenges. *International Journal of Group Decision and Negotiation*, 10(2):199–215, 2001.

6. M. Kakihara and C. Sørensen. Mobility: An extended perspective. In R. S. Jr, editor, *Proceedings of the 35th Hawaii International Conference on Systems Sciences*, Big Island, Hawaii, USA, 2002. IEEE Press.

7. P. Luff and C. Heath. Mobility in collaboration. In *Proceedings of the 1998 ACM conference on Computer Supported Cooperative Work*, pages 305–314. ACM Press, 1998.

8. M. Perry, K. O'Hara, A. Sellen, B. Brown, and R. Harper. Dealing with mobility: understanding access anytime, anywhere. *ACM Transactions on Computer-Human Interaction*, 8(4):323–347, 2001.

9. I. Rahwan. *Interest-based Negotiation in Multi-Agent Systems*. PhD thesis, Department of Information Systems, University of Melbourne, Melbourne, Australia, 2004. (to appear).

10. I. Rahwan, P. McBurney, and L. Sonenberg. Towards a theory of negotiation strategy (a preliminary report). In S. Parsons and P. Gmytrasiewicz, editors, *Proceedings of the 5th Workshop on Game Theoretic and Decision Theoretic Agents (GTDT-2003)*, pages 73–80, 2003.

11. I. Rahwan, L. Sonenberg, and F. Dignum. On interest-based negotiation. In F. Dignum, editor, *Advances in Agent Communication*, volume 2922 of *Lecture Notes in Artificial Intelligence*, pages 383–401. Springer Verlag, Berlin, Germany, 2004.

12. T. Rahwan, T. Rahwan, I. Rahwan, and R. Ashri. Agent-based support for mobile users using AgentSpeak(L). In P. Giorgini, B. Hederson-Sellers, and M. Winikoff, editors, *Agent Oriented Information Systems*, volume 3030 of *Lecture Notes in Artificial Intelligence*, pages 47–62. Springer Verlag, Berlin, Germany, 2004.

13. N. M. Sadeh. *M–Commerce Technologies, Service, and Business Models*. Wiley, Hoboken NJ, USA, 2003.

14. A. Strauss. *The Continual Permutations of Action*. Aldine de Gruyter, New York NY, USA, 1993.

15. J. Tang, , E. Isaacs, and M. Rua. Supporting distributed groups with a montage of lightweight interactions. In *Proceedings of Conference on Computer Supported Co-operative Work, Chapel Hill NC, USA*, pages 23–34, New York NY, USA, 1994. ACM Press.

16. S. Weiss. *Handheld Usability*. Wiley, Hoboken NJ, USA, 2002.

17. S. Whittaker, G. Swanson, J. Kucan, and C. Sidner. Telenotes: Managing lightweight interactions in the desktop. *Transactions on Computer Human Interaction*, 4:137–168, 1997.

18. M. J. Wooldridge. *An Introduction to MultiAgent Systems*. John Wiley & Sons, Chichester, England, 2002.

Specification and Design of Multi-agent Applications Using Temporal Z

Amira Regayeg[1], Ahmed Hadj Kacem[1], and Mohamed Jmaiel[2]

[1] Faculté des Sciences Économiques et de Gestion de Sfax,
B.P. 1088, 3018 Sfax, Tunisia
{Amira.Regayeg,Ahmed}@fsegs.rnu.tn
[2] École Nationale d'Ingénieurs de Sfax,
B.P.W., 3038 Sfax, Tunisia
Mohamed.Jmaiel@enis.rnu.tn

Abstract. This paper proposes a formal approach, based on stepwise refinements, for specifying and designing multi-agent applications. This approach provides a specification language which integrates temporal logic in the Z notation allowing, in this way, to cover static, behavioural, as well as dynamic aspects of multi-agent systems. Moreover, it proposes a methodology giving a set of hints and principles which help and guide the design process. Indeed, this methodology enables the user to develop step by step, in an incremental way, an implementation starting from an abstract requirements (goal) specification. Finally, we illustrate our approach by developing an agent based solution for the *pursuit problem*.

1 Introduction

A multi-agent system is defined as a set of autonomous and distributed entities which cooperate in order to reach a common objective. This cooperation is essentially based on the exchange of data between these entities, on the one hand, and on the coordination of their activities particularly when they access to shared resources, on the other hand. In order to handle these aspects, autonomy, communication and coordination, the development of a multi-agent system should follow two ways diametrically opposite but closely dependent. The first focuses on the internal structure of agents (intra-agent), whereas the second concentrates only on the interactions between them (inter-agent). Considering intra-agent as well as inter-agent aspects makes the development of multi-agent systems an intricate task. Hence, mastering this complexity requires the application of rigourous approaches of software engineering.

In this paper we propose an approach which aims to facilitate the development of multi-agent applications while mastering its complexity. In order to achieve this objective, we follow two complementary principles of formal software design. The first principle stresses the need of a *requirements specification* phase. This phase makes use of formal specifications in order to perform rigourous reasoning. The second principle puts the emphasis on the *formal design*, in order to ensure the correctness of the design specification with respect to the requirements one. Our design process is based on *stepwise refinements* enabling us to

M.W. Barley and N. Kasabov (Eds.): PRIMA 2004, LNAI 3371, pp. 228–242, 2005.
© Springer-Verlag Berlin Heidelberg 2005

construct a detailed design specification, step by step, starting from an abstract requirements one. Doing so, we will be able to better follow the evolution of the design specification. In this context, refining a specification means enriching it, in the sense that it becomes closer to the implementation. An abstract specification may leave some design decisions open, which will be resolved in later refinement steps [8]. In order to guarantee the correctness of the design specification the refinement steps should preserve the properties of the applications to be developed. Accordingly, it is very important to define a *refinement relation* which states if a specification implements another.

In our approach, we suggest a formal specification language which allows to cover individual (static and behavioural) aspects of agents such as knowledge, goal, and role, as well as collective aspects of a multi-agent application like interaction protocols, organization structure and planning activities. This language is an integration of a first order temporal logic [5] in the framework of the Z notation [7]. In order to provide a formal interpretation for our temporal operators we suggest an operational semantics for multi-agent applications in terms of sequences of system states. The definition of this temporal model within the Z notation enables us to make use of tools supporting pure Z notation, such as Z/EVES [6]. These tools allowed us to perform syntax, type, and domain checking of our specifications as well as to reason about them by proving interesting properties. In the context of Z notation, a specification of a data structure includes two types of schemas in order to describe data and the operation on them. Generally, the refinement of such a specification requires *data* refinement as well as *operation* refinement respectively for data schema and operation schema. Since we do not use operation schemas (called also Δ schemas), we are only interested in refining Z schemas including data as well as behavioural description in terms of temporal properties. Accordingly, we define an appropriate data and behavioural refinement relation which extends the data one presented in [9].

This paper is organized as follows. Section 2 defines the specification language and its semantics. Then, in section 3 we present our development methodology. Thereafter, we illustrate our approach by developing a multi-agent solution for the pursuit problem. Finally, we conclude this paper with some future perspectives.

2   The Specification Language

We consider a multi-agent application as a collection of components which evolve in a continuously changing environment containing active agents and passive objects. Accordingly, the specification of a multi-agent application includes descriptions of the environment, the behaviour of individual agents (intra-agent), and the communication primitives as well as the interaction protocols (inter-agent). In addition, we may add to the collective part a description of the organizational structures and planning activities.

For the specification of multi-agent applications, we use an integration of temporal logic in Z schemas.

2.1   The Z Notation

The Z notation, as presented in [7], is a model oriented formal specification language which is based on the set theory and the first order predicate logic. This language is used to describe an application in terms of states which may change. A *basic type* is defined using one or several basic types. The definition of a *composed type*, with a collection of objects, needs a schema language. The latter is used to structure and to compose such specifications: collecting objects, encapsulating them, and naming them for reuse. A schema consists of two parts: a declaration part and a predicate part constraining the values of the declared variables. A Z schema has the following form:

$$
\begin{array}{|l}
\hline
\_\_ SchemaName _____ \\
Declaration \\
\hline
\quad Predicate, \ldots, Predicate \\
\hline
\end{array}
$$

2.2   The Temporal Logic

The linear temporal logic, as presented by Manna and Pnueli [5], is suitable for the specification and the verification of concurrent and interactive systems. Actually, there is a variety of temporal operators that can be used to express agents behavioural properties. However, all these operators can be defined in terms of two basic operators. In this paper, we make use only of the necessary operators for development of our multi-agent applications. In the following, we briefly present these operators with an intuitive explanation. Let P be a logical or a temporal formula:

∇P P holds "now"[1] (∇ may be omitted);
$\Box P$ "*always P*", i.e. P holds for the present and for all future points in time;
$\Diamond P$ "*eventually P*", i.e. P holds at some present or future point in time;
$\bigcirc P$ "*nexttime P*", i.e. P holds at the next point in time.

In order to integrate these temporal operators in the framework of the Z language, we give the following definition of temporal formulas according to the syntax of Z. We distinguish simple predicate formulas (*formula*), which are closely related to the application to specify, and temporal formulas (*Tempformula*) which connect predicate formulas with temporal operators.

$$Tempformula ::= \langle\!\langle formula \rangle\!\rangle \mid \bigcirc \langle\!\langle Tempformula \rangle\!\rangle \mid \Box \langle\!\langle Tempformula \rangle\!\rangle \mid$$
$$\Diamond \langle\!\langle Tempformula \rangle\!\rangle \mid \nabla \langle\!\langle Tempformula \rangle\!\rangle$$

We will see later that these operators are sufficient to express interesting properties of multi-agent applications.

---

[1] We explain the operators while being based on a concept of "time", but really the fundamental notion is the one of causality.

2.3   The Time Model

The basic unit of the underlying time model is the agent state. Let $[State]$ be the set of possible agent states. We define an entity state ($Entstate$) as a pair of a state and a point of time, where the time is specified as the set of natural numbers ($Time == \{x : \mathbb{N}\}$):

$$
\begin{array}{|l}
\hline
\_Entstate _____ \\
\quad time : Time \\
\quad state : State \\
\hline
\end{array}
$$

A system state ($Syststate$) is defined as the union of all agents states:

$$
\begin{array}{|l}
\hline
\_Syststate _____ \\
\quad syststate : \mathbb{F}\ Entstate \\
\hline
\end{array}
$$

A time structure ($StrTime$) is defined as an axiomatic function that associates to each point of time the corresponding system state:

$$
\begin{array}{|l}
StrTime : Time \rightarrow Syststate \\
\hline
\forall\, t : Time \bullet \exists\, s : Syststate \bullet \forall\, e : Entstate \mid e \in s.syststate \bullet \\
\quad StrTime(t) = s \Leftrightarrow e.time = t
\end{array}
$$

Based on this time structure we will be able to interpret any temporal formula.

2.4   The Semantics of Temporal Formulas

In this section, we define an evaluation function that associates the value true or false to any temporal formula. This step is very significant since it enables to translate temporal formulas into the pure Z notation[2]. In this way, it becomes easy to use the verification tools, such as Z/EVES or Isabelle, which accept the standard syntax of Z. First, we provide an axiomatic function ($Eval$) which evaluates a simple formula in a given system state:

$$
\begin{array}{|l}
Eval : formula \times Syststate \rightarrow bool \\
\end{array}
$$

Next, we define a similar axiomatic function for temporal formulas. This function gives a formal interpretation for the temporal operators $\triangledown$, $\square$, $\Diamond$, and $\bigcirc$ with respect to a given time structure. For each operator, the recursive function $TempEval$ defines a predicate which matches its intuitive meaning. In the following Z schema we present only the predicate defining the "always" operator. The predicates defining the other operators are similar.

---

[2] It should be stressed that temporal operators do not extend the expressive power of the Z notation based on the first order predicate logic.

$$TempEval : Tempformula \times StrTime \rightarrow bool$$

$$\forall f : Tempformula \bullet \forall t : Time \bullet \forall tt : Time \mid tt \geq t \bullet \forall S, SS : Syststate \bullet$$
$$TempEval(\square\ f, (t, S)) = T \Leftrightarrow SS = StrTime(tt) \wedge$$
$$TempEval(f, (tt, SS)) = T$$

Finally, in order to integrate the temporal operators in their usual notations (i.e. $\square$ for always) in the Z schema it is necessary to introduce them as axiomatic functions defined with the help of the interpretation function *TempEval*. In this way, we establish a logical equivalence between a temporal operator and the corresponding predicate specified in the above function *TempEval*. This equivalence is described for the $\square$ operator as follows:

$$[Tempformula]$$
$$\square\ :\ Tempformula \rightarrow bool$$

$$\forall f : Tempformula \bullet \exists\, present : Time \bullet \forall t : Time \mid t > present \bullet$$
$$\exists S : Syststate \bullet \square f = T \Leftrightarrow S = StrTime(t) \wedge$$
$$TempEval(\square f, (t, S)) = T$$

The other temporal operators are introduced with similar axiomatic functions.

3   Formal Design Approach

In order to be useful, a formalism or a set of tools have to be supported with a specification approach. This approach should provide some principles that help and guide the specification process. In this section, some of those principles are clarified.

Indeed, our approach is based on three principal phases. The first one is a specification phase in which we describe, in an abstract way, the user requirements. The second one is a design phase based on a succession of refinements in terms of collective behaviours (inter-agents) as well as individual behaviours (intra-agent). The requirements specification is thus presented by Z schemas which language is extended by temporal logic. The third phase consists of performing verification tasks by formulating and reasoning about the main properties of the multi-agent application to be developed.

3.1   Specification Phase

Generally, in this first phase we specify the requirements which correspond, in the context of multi-agent, to the common objective they have to achieve. It should be stressed that we are not interested, at this stage, in the manner of achieving this goal. In our approach, this stage includes also the description of the environment in which the agents evolve. This environment includes, generally, the work area, the passive objects, and the active entities representing the agents to be employed. The requirements specification is thus presented by a set of Z schema which properties language is extended by temporal logic.

1. *Specification of the Active Entities:* The description of an active entity (agent), at specification phase, consists in presenting, in terms of temporal formula, its static and dynamic original properties. These properties are the information acquired on the agents at the beginning. This description is given by a Z schema which declares the entity attributes, defines its static properties, in term of predicate logic, and its behavioural properties, in term of temporal logic.

$$
\begin{array}{|l}
\hline
\underline{\quad Entity} \\
atr_1 : Type_1, \ atr_2 : Type_2 \ \ldots atr_m : Type_m \\
\hline
Spr_1, \ldots, Spr_n \\
Cpr_1, \ldots, Cpr_{n'} \\
\hline
\end{array}
$$

Where atr_i corresponds to an attribute, Spr_i represents a static property and Cpr_i represents a behavioural property.

2. *Specification of the Environment:* The environment includes active entities (agents) as well as passive entities belonging to the operating field. This specification is given by a set formulas making in relation passive entities with those which are active. Generally, this leads to Z schema of the form:

$$
\begin{array}{|l}
\hline
\underline{\quad Environment} \\
obj_1 : TypeObject_1, \ obj_2 : TypeObject_2, \ \ldots, \ obj_k : TypeObject_l \\
Entities : \textbf{set of } Entity \\
\hline
Pr_1, Pr_2, \ldots, Pr_l \\
\hline
\end{array}
$$

Where obj_i corresponds to a passive entity, *Entities* represents a set of entities where cardinality is unknown at the beginning, and Pr_i represents a temporal formula.

3. *Specification of the Requirements:* This specification describes what we require from the system to develop. In the context of multi-agent, this corresponds to formulate, in term of temporal formula, a future environment state to be reached. According to the Z approach, such a specification is well expressed by a specialization of the schema specifying the environment. Generally, requirements specifications have the following form:

$$
\begin{array}{|l}
\hline
\underline{\quad Spec} \\
Environment \\
\hline
Tpr_1, Tpr_2, \ldots, Tpr_n \\
\hline
\end{array}
$$

Where Tpr_1 represents a temporal formula.

3.2   Refinement Phase

The basic idea consists in performing a succession of refinements in terms of specializations of Z schemas (data refinement) and deriving of temporal formulas (behaviour refinement).

Refinement Relation. First of all we define a refinement relation between specifications telling if a specification implements another. In the context of Z notation, we adopt the $\sqsubseteq$ relation defined in [9] with some restrictions. Concerning the data refinement, a schema S_j refines another schema S_i (written $S_i \sqsubseteq S_j$) if and only if the attributes of S_i are included in the declaration part of S_j. This inclusion of attributes can appear following a schema inclusion (S_j schema) or by a new declaration of these attributes (S_j' schema):

$$\begin{array}{|l}\hline S_i\;\underline{\hspace{6cm}}\\ Att_1 : Type_1\\ Att_2 : Type_2\\ \hline Operations\\ \hline \end{array}$$

$$\begin{array}{|l}\hline S_j\;\underline{\hspace{3cm}}\\ S_i\;(schema\;\;inclusion)\\ Att_3 : Type_3\\ \hline Operations\\ \hline \end{array} \qquad \begin{array}{|l}\hline S_j'\;\underline{\hspace{3cm}}\\ Att_1 : Type_1\;(attribute\;of\;S_i)\\ Att_2 : Type_2\;(attribute\;of\;S_i)\\ Att_3 : Type_3\\ \hline Operations\\ \hline \end{array}$$

Concerning the behavioural part which is specified in terms of temporal formulas the refinement relation is defined between temporal specifications. For this purpose, we adopt the refinement relation applied in [3] for designing communicating protocols using algebraic and temporal specifications. A temporal specification (set of temporal formulas) $TSpec = \{F_1, F_2, \ldots, F_n\}$ refines another one $TSpec' = \{F_1', F_2', \ldots, F_m'\}$, written $TSpec' \sqsubseteq TSpec$, if every formula F_i' in $TSpec'$ could be derived from $TSpec$, denoted $TSpec \vdash F_i'$, that is the validity of F_i' could be inferred from the validity of the formulas in $TSpec$ using the calculus of the first order temporal logic.

Refinement Process. The refinements are carried out at two complementary levels. The first, is the environment level which will be augmented by properties referring, primarily, to collective aspects (inter-agent) characterizing, in particular, organization and communication structures. The second level rather stresses on the individual aspects (intra-agent) by extending the specifications of the active entities provided in the first phase. The extensions of individual specifications have to remain consistent with the extensions made at the collective level.

Collective Level: Here we invent a suitable organization structure as well as a communication topology for the system to be developed. An organization structure assigns a role for each active entity belonging to the system. Furthermore, it implicitly defines a control strategy to be respected by these entities. This structure is, generally, defined in terms of temporal formulas referring to several entities at the same time. A sequence of Z schemas will be then generated:

$Implementation_1, \; Implementation_2, \; \ldots, \; Implementation_n$

The first schema corresponds to a direct refinement of the environment specification. It is of the form:

Where Org_i is a temporal formula that assigns roles to one or many entities. These formulas correspond to design decisions describing an organization structure. Each Z schema $implementation_i$ ($i > 1$) is a refinement (specialization) of the previous one $implementation_{i-1}$. These intermediate schemas may contain design decisions related to the communication topology and actions. It is obvious that the last schema $implementation_n$ is, by transitivity, a refinement of the initial environment schema.

Individual Level: Here we make use of the choices made at the collective level in order to refine, step by step, the internal structure and the behaviour of each agent. For each entity, we develop a succession of refinements as follows:

$$EntityImpl_1, \ EntityImpl_2, \ \ldots, \ EntityImpl_m$$

The first schema is an immediate refinement of the retained one at the specification phase. This schema is of the form:

```
__ EntityImpl_1 _____
   Entity
  _____
   Behav_1, Behav_2, ..., Behav_l
```

Where $Behav_i$ is a property describing a design decision related to the behaviour of the considered entity. These properties are given by individual temporal formulas referring to only one entity. Hence, each intermediate schema $Entityimpl_i$ is a refinement of the diagram $Entityimpl_{i-1}$. The design phase leads to a detailed specification of the environment and detailed behaviours of the active entities. The refinement specification corresponds to the schema for the environment (*Environment*) extended with the union of the properties added at both collective and individual levels.

3.3   Verification Phase

This phase allows to reason, according to the Z notation combined with temporal logic, about the schemas developed during the specification phase. Essentially, we are interested in proving the consistency and the completeness of the global specification resulting from the composition of the agent's individual specifications. On the basis of a set of abstract properties, which are specific to the application to be developed, we try to check the mentioned properties of consistency and the completeness of the global specification. Generally, we develop a schema Z which gathers a set of global and abstract properties:

```
┌─ Spec ──────────────────────────────────────────────────
│ ┌─ Environment ──
│ │
│ ├──────────────
│ │ Tpr₁, Tpr₂, ..., Tprₙ
```

$$\text{┌─ } Spec \text{ ─}$$

Where Tpr_1 represents a temporal formula. It is very important to use automatic tools which support the proof of the desired theorems. The temporal logic model that we proposed in the previous section makes possible the use of automatic tools, such as Z-Eves [6], while integrating temporal formulas in our specifications and theorems.

4   Case Study: The Pursuit Problem

We illustrate our approach by specifying a multi-agent solution for the pursuit problem. This application includes one prey and four predators. The prey moves randomly on a grid without perception of its environment. The predators cooperate to capture the prey using their perception and communication abilities.

Initially, each predator moves independently of the others. As soon as one predator perceives the prey, it follows the prey until its capture from the nearest side. This predator, which will play the *supervisor* role, will regularly inform the others about the current prey position. From this moment and based on the received information, each predator tries to capture the prey from the appropriate side, according to its position on the grid.

4.1   Specification Phase

Specification of the Environment: A box on the grid is defined by its abscissa and ordinate.

```
┌─ Box ───────────────────────────────────────
│ abs : ℕ
│ ord : ℕ
├──────────────
│ abs ≥ 0 ∧ ord ≥ 0
```

The basic concept, *Entity*, is characterized by its state (*Entstate*). So, we specify formally the entity state by the position (*pos*) that it occupies on the grid at a given time point.

```
┌─ Entstate ──────────────────────────────────
│ time : Time
│ pos : Box
```

A system state (*Syststate*) is defined as the union of the states of all agents:

Syststate

$syststate : \mathbb{F} \; Entstate$

An *Entity* is able to move randomly (*ChangePos*) on the grid. However, it can make at most one step (to the left, the right, the south, or the north) at a moment. This ability is formally specified in the following schema:

Entity

$state : Entstate$
$ChangePos : Box \times Box \rightarrow bool$

$\forall s_1, s_2 : Box \mid s_1 = state.pos \bullet \exists i, j : \mathbb{N} \mid i \in \{0, 1, -1\} \wedge j \in \{0, 1, -1\}$
$\quad \wedge \; (i = 0 \vee j = 0) \bullet ChangePos(s_1, s_2) = T \Leftrightarrow s_2.abs = s_1.abs + i \wedge$
$\quad s_2.ord = s_1.ord + j$
$\forall s_1, s_2 : Box \mid s_1 = state.pos \bullet next \; ChangePos(s_1, s_2) = T$

As mentioned in the previous section, atomic formulas are, generally, specific for the application to specify. So, we define, in the following, the set of atomic formulas relating to our application. An atomic formula may be a predicate describing an entity state. Formally:

$$formula == \{predicate : bool\} \tag{1}$$

A *Prey* is a simple entity, whereas a *Predator* is able to perceive other entities.

Predator

$Entity$
$Perception : \mathbb{F} \; Entity$

$Perception = \{e : Entity \mid$
$\quad (state.pos.abs - 2 \le e.state.pos.abs \le state.pos.abs + 2) \wedge$
$\quad (state.pos.ord - 2 \le e.state.pos.ord \le state.pos.ord + 2)\}$

An environment is composed of a grid, a prey and four predators. It has to meet two conditions. First, two entities cannot occupy the same box on the grid. Second, an entity should not leave the grid. Formally:

Environment

$X : \mathbb{N}$
$Y : \mathbb{N}$
$prey : Entity$
$pr_1, pr_2, pr_3, pr_4 : Predator$

$\forall e : Entity \bullet (e.state.pos.abs \le X) \wedge (e.state.pos.ord \le Y)$
$\forall e_1, e_2 : Entity \bullet (e_1.state.pos = e_2.state.pos) \Leftrightarrow (e_1 = e_2)$

Useful Definitions: In order to simplify our specifications and make them more readable, we provide some useful abbreviations. First, we define the *Side* type including exactly four values corresponding to the sides from which the prey can be captured.

$$Side ::= North \mid South \mid East \mid West$$

Second, we define an axiomatic function *SideCaptured* testing if the prey is captured by a predator from a given side. The following definition presents only the predicate relating to the *South* side. The predicates for the other sides are similar.

$SideCaptured : Entity \times Predator \times Side \rightarrow bool$

$\forall a : Entity \bullet \exists b : Predator \bullet$
$\quad SideCaptured(a, b, South) = T \Leftrightarrow b.pos.abs = a.pos.abs \wedge$
$\quad\quad b.pos.ord = (a.pos.ord + 1)$

The axiomatic function *Captured* abbreviates the fact that the prey is captured from all sides by the four predators.

$Captured : Entity \times \mathbb{P}\, Predator \rightarrow bool$

$\forall a : Entity \bullet \exists b_1, b_2, b_3, b_4 : Predator \bullet$
$\quad Captured(a, \{b_1, b_2, b_3, b_4\}) = T \Leftrightarrow SideCaptured(a, b_1, North) = T \wedge$
$\quad\quad SideCaptured(a, b_2, South) = T \wedge SideCaptured(a, b_3, East) = T \wedge$
$\quad\quad SideCaptured(a, b_4, West) = T$

Agent Actions: Before presenting the detailed specifications of the individual and collective aspects of our application, we introduce the set of possible actions which may be performed by a predator. We distinguish two kinds of actions: internal and external. Internal actions are instructions enabling a predator to update its mental state by revising its knowledge base or changing its local goal.

- Updating the knowledge base: *updateBase* $\langle\!\langle Predator \times Box \rangle\!\rangle$
  It consists in updating the knowledge base after receiving a new prey position.
- Updating the goal: *updateGoal* $\langle\!\langle Predator \times Side \rangle\!\rangle$
  Corresponds to updating the goal after receiving the information telling that the prey has been already captured from the envisaged side.
- Updating the destination: *updateDest* $\langle\!\langle Predator \times Box \times Side \rangle\!\rangle$
  It consists in updating the attribute destination following the reception of a captured side.

In our context, the communication actions which are considered as external are very essential. We identified three communication actions: *send*, *receive*, and *broadcast*.

- Send action: *send* ⟨⟨*Predator* × *Predator* × *Message*⟩⟩
  This action enables a predator to send some information to another predator.
- Diffusion action: *broadcast* ⟨⟨*Predator* × $\mathbb{P}$ *Predator* × *Message*⟩⟩
  This action allows to broadcast the same information to a set of predators.
- Receipt action: *receive* ⟨⟨*Predator* × *Predator* × *Message*⟩⟩
  This action enables a predator to receive an information sent by another predator.

A message may inform about the prey position (*Pos*), it may be a request made by a predator to the supervisor (*Request*), or it may be an assignment of a local goal made by the supervisor to a predator (*Assign*).

$$Message ::= Pos⟨⟨Box⟩⟩ \mid Request⟨⟨Box⟩⟩ \mid Assign⟨⟨Entity × Side⟩⟩$$

It is very important to note that we consider in our approach synchronous communication between agents. Moreover, we suppose that communication mediums are absolutely reliable. This is formally described by the following equivalences:

$$\forall\, a, b, b_1, ..., b_n : Predator \bullet \forall\, message : Message \bullet$$
$$broadcast(a, \{b_1, ..., b_n\}, message) = T \Leftrightarrow$$
$$\bigwedge_{i \in \{1,...,n\}} receive(b_i, a, message) = T$$
$$send(a, b, message) = T \Leftrightarrow receive(b, a, message) = T$$

4.2   Refinement Phase

In this section, we propose to design, in a first level, the individual aspect of the application and in a second level, the collective aspect. These two levels will be described by axioms that will be added to the schema of the predator.

Individual Aspect. During the game, the possible scenarios as well as the different acts of communication determine the agent mental state (knowledge base) and its future behaviour. This is represented in the different refinements that follow:

- The predator updates its knowledge base as soon as it perceives the prey:

```
┌─ Predator0 ──────────────────────────────────────────
│ Predator
│ ──────────────────────────────────────────────────
│ ∃ prey : Entity •
│     updateBase(prey.state.pos) = T ⇒ posprey = prey.state.pos
│ ∀ prey : Entity • ∃ s : Syststate | prey.state ∈ s.syststate •
│     prey ∈ Perception ⇒ ○ (updateBase(prey.state.pos), s) = T
```

- others updates of the knowledge base, the destination or the goal are done due to:
  - the receipt of an information about the prey position: *Predator1*
  - the receipt of an affectation of capture side: *Predator2*

– Another conceptual decision concerns the speed of predator displacement. The predator speed must be superior to the prey speed: *Predator3*
– Once a predator comes to capture the prey on one side, it is going to remain there always.

$$\underline{\;Predator4\;}$$
$$Predator3$$
$$\exists\, prey : Entity \bullet \exists\, side : Side \bullet$$
$$\exists\, s : Syststate \mid prey.state \in s.syststate \bullet$$
$$SideCaptured(prey, side) = T \Rightarrow \Box\,(SideCaptured(prey, side)), s) = T$$

These refinements constitute the description of the individual aspect of the MAS. This aspect concerns the properties referring to one agent whereas the proprieties in the collective aspect, subject of the next section, refer to many agents.

Collective Aspect. Our methodology consists in refining, step by step, the initial specification.

So, we give some modifications to *Environment* where we use the *Predator4* and where we describe the *Captured* predicate and the communication equivalence between *send* and *receive* actions.

- Definition of the organizational structure: In our example, we can distinguish between a supervisor predator (the first that perceives the prey) and the other predators. We define, then, a supervisor schema:

$$Supervisor == \{pr : Predator \mid \exists\, e : Entity \bullet e \in pr.Perception\}$$

The supervisor is charged to capture the prey of the nearest side and to distribute a request of information about the current positions of the other predators in order to affect the remaining sides. Thus, in this stage, a first implementation of the game is:

$$\underline{\;GameImpl0\;}$$
$$Environment0$$
$$pr_1 \in Supervisor$$

- In order to describe the communication structure, we will define the communication acts that could take place between the different predators referring to the following property:

$$a, b, b_1, ..., b_n : Predator$$
$$message : Message$$
$$broadcast(a, \{b_1, ..., b_n\}, message) = T \Leftrightarrow$$
$$\bigwedge_{i \in \{1, ..., n\}} receive(b_i, a, message) = T$$
$$send(a, b, message) = T \Leftrightarrow receive(b, a, message) = T$$

We can, further, refine the conception of the game : *GameImpl1* and *GameImpl2*.

Finally, the receipt of the capture side, by each predator, guarantees the sides affectation:

GameImpl3
GameImpl2

$\forall pr : Predator4 \mid pr \in \{pr_2, pr_3, pr_4\} \bullet \exists side : Side \bullet$
$\quad \exists S : Syststate \bullet pr_1.receive(pr, Pospr.state.pos) = T \Rightarrow$
$\quad \Diamond (pr_1.send(pr, Affect(prey, side)), S) = T$

4.3 Verification

In the verification phase, starting from a requirements specification, we try to prove the set of the theorems that may be generated from it. The requirements specification of the pursuit problem requires that the four predators eventually capture the prey from all sides. This is given by the following schema:

ReqSpec
Environment

$\Diamond \Box \, Captured(prey, \{pr_1, pr_2, pr_3, pr_4\}) = T$

To this schema leads the following theorem those we are charged to reduce to *true*:

Theorem 1. *axiom GameSpecFin*

$PreyPredSpec \Rightarrow \Diamond \Box \, Captured(prey, \{pr_1, pr_2, pr_3, pr_4\}) = T$

The proof of these theorems has been accomplished with the Z/EVES tool.

5 Conclusion

In this paper we proposed a formal approach for the development of multi-agent applications. Our contribution concerns, first, the definition of a formal language which covers the static and the behavioural aspects of agents by integrating temporal operators within Z notation. Then, we defined a methodology that permits to develop, step by step, in an incremental way, a design from an abstract specification. The investigation of the pursuit problem allowed a first illustration of our approach. Other case studies are under realization (e.g. the conflicts control in the air-traffic). However, it is necessary to point out that these first results, even original and promising, constitute a modest contribution to the problematic of multi-agent formal development. In a short term, we will proceed to automate the syntactic verification and the semantic validation of the well constructed specifications as well as the formal reasoning on these latest. Further, we plan to implement a tool-kit to deal with the steps of the proposed methodology. It is obvious that such tools must be coupled up with an environment that provides verification and reasoning about specifications such as Z/EVES [6] or Z-Hol [4].

References

1. M. d'Inverno, D. Kinny, M. Luck, and M. Wooldridge. A formal specification of dMARS. In *Intelligent Agents IV: Proceedings of the Fourth International Workshop on Agent Theories, Architectures and Languages*, 1998.
2. A. El Fallah. Représentation et manipulation de plans à l'aide des réseaux de Petri. *Actes des 2èmes Journées Francophones IAD-SMA*, 1994.
3. M. Jmaiel and P. Pepper. Development of communication protocols using algebraic and temporal specifications. *Computer Networks Journal*, 42:737–764, 2003.
4. R. Kolyang, T. Santen, and B. Wolff. A structure preserving encoding of Z in isabelle-Hol. In J. von Wright, J. Grundy, and J. Harrison, editors, *9th International Conference on Theorem Proving in Higher Order Logics*, LNCS 1125, pages 283–298. Springer Verlag, 1996.
5. Z. Manna and A. Pnueli. *The Temporal Logic of Reactive and Concurrent Systems*. Springer-Verlag, 1992.
6. I. Meisels and M. Saaltink. The Z/EVES 2.0 reference manual. Technical Report TR-99-5493-03e, ORA Canada, Canada, 1999.
7. M. Spivey. The Z notation (second edition). *Prentice Hall International*, 1992.
8. V. Von. *An Integration of Z and Timed CSP for specifying Real-Time Embedded Systems*. PhD thesis, 2002.
9. J. Woodcock and J. Davies. *Using Z: Specification, Refinement and Proof*. Prentice Hall, 1996.

Bio-inspired Deployment of Distributed Applications

Ichiro Satoh

National Institute of Informatics,
2-1-2 Hitotsubashi, Chiyoda-ku, Tokyo 101-8430, Japan
Tel: +81-3-4212-2546, Fax: +81-3-3556-1916
`ichiro@nii.ac.jp`

Abstract. This paper presents an approach to developing and managing self-organizing distributed computing systems. The approach is used to construct an application as a dynamic federation of mobile components that can migrate from computer to computer while the application is being executed. It also enables each component to explicitly define its own migration policy as the migration of other components. Therefore, a federation of components can be migrated and transformed according to its components' local policies, including bio-inspired deployment approaches. The approach was implemented as not only a test-bed system for the organization of multi-agents but also a middleware for real distributed systems. This paper describes a prototype implementation of the middleware built on a Java-based mobile agent system and its applications that illustrates the utility and effectiveness of the approach.

1 Introduction

Distributed computing systems are often composed of a number of software components, which run on different computers and interact with each other via a network. The complexity of modern distributed systems has already frustrated our ability to deploy components at appropriate computers through traditional approaches, such as centralized and top-down techniques. It is difficult to adapt such systems to changes in execution environments, such as adding or removing components and network topology, and to the requirements of users. This problem becomes more serious in ubiquitous computing as well as large-scale distributed systems, because ubiquitous computers are heterogeneous and their computational resources, such as processors, storage, and input and output devices, are limited so that they can only support their own initial applications. An application can execute on a group of one or more computers to satisfy its own requirements beyond the capabilities of individual computers. Moreover, such a group must be configurable in run-time because the goals and positions of users may change dynamically. We believe that the solutions to extreme dynamics and complexity in distributed systems, including ubiquitous computing environments, are based on metaphors drawn from biological processes.

Therefore, this paper presents a framework to adapt a federation of components, which may run on heterogeneous computers, to changes in user requirements and their associated contexts, such as locations and tasks. The framework is based on two key ideas. The first is to implement components as mobile agents that can travel from computer to computer under their own control. That is, each component can autonomously

M.W. Barley and N. Kasabov (Eds.): PRIMA 2004, LNAI 3371, pp. 243–258, 2005.

migrate to another computer and duplicate itself. The second is to facilitate the dynamic federation of one or more components as a virtual computer over distributed systems. The framework enables such a federation to be transformed and made mobile through bio-inspired self-organization, such as that undertaken by cells in their transforming and crawling locomotion.

This paper continues with a description of the issues we consider are necessary for the framework (Section 2) and a description of the design goals for it (Section 3). We then describe its design (Section 4) and a prototype implementation (Section 5). We also discuss our experience with two applications, which we used the framework to develop (Section 6), and briefly review related work (Section 7). We provide a summary and discuss some future issues (Section 8).

2   Approach

The goal of this framework is to provide a general infrastructure that enables applications on a distributed system to be deployed dynamically.

2.1   Distributed and Mobile Applications

The framework assumes that each application is composed of one or more software components, as we can see in Fig. 2. Each component corresponds to a motile unicellular structure since it is self-contained and self-mobile. An aggregation of components can also be treated as a pseudoplasmodium, because such an aggregation can change its structure and move over a distributed system according to changes in the underlying system and the requirements of the application (Fig. 1). The framework provides support for migration-transparent interactions between dynamically deployable components. It instructs components to migrate to computers that can satisfy their requirements. Where to deploy components is an application-dependent decision and a well-known practical policy is that any application that enables interaction with users should be executed at nearby computers to reduce network latency. For example, when the framework detects changes in a user's positions, it provides addresses of nearby computers by using the location information services we presented in our previous paper [17] and components then migrate to the closest of the computers.

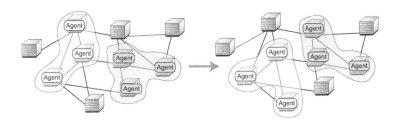

Fig. 1. Group migration.

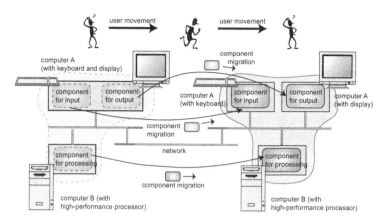

Fig. 2. Federation of Network-enabled Appliances.

2.2   Drawing Inspiration from Cell Transformation and Locomotion

Applications must not be bound to heterogeneous computers, which may have limited computational resources for specifics applications, but should be able to run on any computer that can satisfy their requirements and those of their users. However, it is difficult to deploy components at appropriate computers on a distributed computing system where computers are dynamically added and removed. Furthermore, the requirements of users or applications may vary. For example, mobile users may also want to constantly change the computers with which they interact. Consequently, applications should be able to move from computer to computer to follow their users. Therefore, our framework should enable a federation of partitioned applications, i.e., components, to partially or entirely migrate to suitable computers according to changes in user conditions and their associated context, e.g., locations, current tasks, and the number of components.

Federation Mobility of Components as Cell-Locomotion.   The framework is used to build an application as a set of mobile agent-based components and enables components to move to other computers while the application is running. As a result, the movement of one component may affect other components. For example, two components are required to remain at the same computer or nearby computers, when the first is a program that controls the keyboard and the second is a program that displays content on the screen. Since each component travels between computers under its own control, a federation of components tends to spread over a distributed system so that these distant components cannot efficiently coordinate with one another due to latency in communication. The framework therefore enables each component to explicitly specify its own constraints to migrate components. For example, if a component has a migration constraint dependent on another component, when the other component moves to another location, the former component decides its destination according to its own migration constraints, i.e., the source or destination of the other component. Such constraints are defined as policies within components and allow us to specify physical structures and mechanisms in motile cells, such as membrane and cytoplasmic streaming, and gel-to-sol transitions.

Speculative Deployment of Components as Cell-Lamellipodia. Lamellipodia are flattened and protrusive projections that periodically expand from the surface of a cell. Effective movement requires a motile cell to be polarised, so that its protoplasm membrane is relatively quiescent everywhere else except its leading edge where lamellipodia periodically project outward in all directions. As they pull on one another they create intervening regions in which the cortex is stretched. This tug of war continues until one lamellipodium aligns in a dominant direction and becomes unipolar, then migrates in that direction. Lamellipodia can be viewed in terms of speculative migration or expansion. Each component, however, should migrate to one of the most eligible computers that can satisfy its requirements as long as its migration constraints are valid. However, it cannot always establish precisely which destination is the most suitable. This framework permits a component to speculatively deploy its clones at multiple computers and to select one of the most appropriate clones. This mechanism corresponds to the process lamellipodia go through in motile cells.

2.3   Architecture

Our framework should be used as a general test-bed for providing various bio-inspired approaches in distributed systems as well as a middleware for adaptive distributed systems. There may also be one or more approaches to deploying components in a distributed system, because these are often application-specific. Therefore, the framework itself should be as independent as possible of any component-deployment approach and of any particular phenomenon in biological processes. By separating component-deployment approaches from infrastructures, the framework provides a general middleware for exchanging components between computers and enables such approaches to be implemented within components instead of the middleware. That is, each component can have its own deployment policy for specifying spatial constraints between its location and the locations of other components at neighboring computers. As a result, a federation of components is managed by each of the components' policies instead of any global policy.

3   Design and Implementation

The framework presented in this paper was implemented in Sun's Java Developer Kit version 1.4 and uses a Java-based mobile agent system to provide mobile components. It consists of two parts: mobile components and component hosts. The first defines partitioned applications. The second is a middleware and enables components to migrate from computer to computer.

3.1   Mobile Component

It is almost impossible to automatically partition existing standalone applications across multiple computers. Instead, this framework relies on the concept of a component-based application construction [21]. That is, an application is loosely composed of software components, which may run on different computers. In the current implementation of the framework, each component is a collection of Java objects in the standard JAR file format that can migrate from computer to computer and duplicate itself through mobile agent technology[1]. After arriving at its destination or being duplicated, each component can continue working without losing the accumulated work, such as the content of instance variables in the component's program, at the source computers. It is also equipped with its own identifier and that of the federation that it should belong to. It can explicitly specify the computational capability that its destination hosts must offer in CC/PP (composite capability/preference profiles) [23] form as we will discuss later. If a component is on a computer that cannot satisfy its requirements, its intent is to leave the computer.

As we will discuss in the following section, although the current implementation supports five several migration policies for the mobilities of two components, we will only present two typical policies as follows:

– When a component declares *follow* for another component, if the other component moves, the declarer or its clone migrates to the destination or a nearby proper host.
– When a component declares *fill* for another component, if the other component moves, the declarer or its clone migrates to the source of the latter component or a nearby proper host.

The first policy gathers components around specified components like aggregating dictyostelium and the second policy makes components track the footprints of other moving components like cytoplasmic streaming in cells. Fig. 3 and 4 have examples of the group migration of three components. When component B has a *follow* policy for component A and component C has a *dispatch* policy for component B, if component A moves, component B moves to component A's destination host because the host

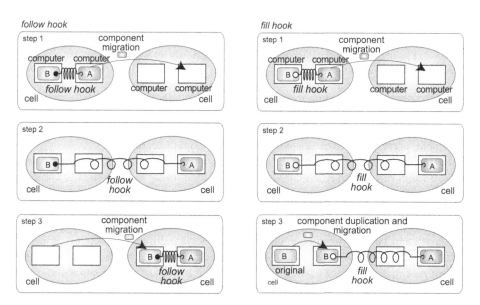

Fig. 3. Component migration with relocation policies.

---

[1] JavaBeans can easily be translated into components in the framework.

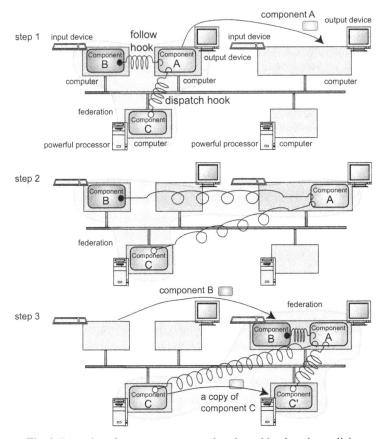

Fig. 4. Examples of component group migration with relocation policies.

satisfies component B's requirements and a copy of component C moves to component B's source host. Each component can change its policy while it is running. When some components in a federation alternately become mobile or stationary, their irregular movements correspond to the gel-to-sol transitions in motile cells.

Such policies may be similar to the dynamic layout of distributed applications in the FarGo system [9]. However, FarGo's policies aim at allowing a component to control other components, whereas our policies aim at allowing a component to describe its own migration, because our framework always treats components as autonomous entities that travel from computer to computer under their own control. Note that policies may conflict in FarGo when two components can declare different relocation policies for a single component. However, our framework is free of any conflict because each component can only declare a policy to relocate itself instead of other components.

Each component can have references to other components within the application federation that it belongs to. Each reference allows a component to interact with the component that it specifies, even when the former and latter components reside at different computers or move to other computers. The current implementation of the references provides mobility-transparent remote method invocation.

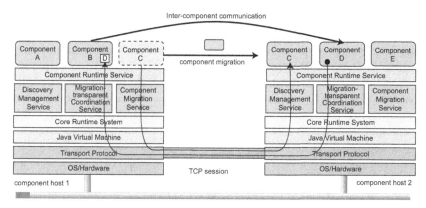

Fig. 5. Architecture of component host.

3.2   Component Host

Each component host provides a runtime system for executing components and migrating them to another place. Fig. 5 outlines the basic structure of a runtime system. Each host establishes at most one TCP connection to each of its neighboring hosts and exchanges control messages, components, and inter-component communications with the other hosts through the connection. Since it is constructed on the Java virtual machine, it can conceal differences between the platform architecture of the source and destination hosts, such as the operating system and hardware.

Component Runtime Service. Each runtime system governs all the components inside it and maintains the life-cycle state of each component. When the life-cycle state of a component changes, e.g. when it is created, terminates, or migrates to another host, the runtime system issues specific events to the component. This is because the component may have to acquire various resources or release them such as files, windows, or sockets, which it had previously captured.

The framework offers a language-based on CC/PP to describe the capabilities of component hosts and the requirements of components. For example, a description contains information on the properties of a computing device: the vendor and model class (PC, PDA, or phone), the screen size, the number of colors, CPU, memory, input devices, and secondary storage. Each host informs the components within it, or its neighboring hosts, about its profile specified with the language. Then, each of the components autonomously selects and migrates to one of the candidate destinations. Moreover, since each component can count coexisting components that are of the same type as it is, it can leave computers that have a high component density.

Component Migration Service. All component hosts can exchange components with others through the use of mobile agent technology. When a component is transferred over a network, the component host on the sending side marshals the code of the component and its state into a bit-stream and then transfers these to the destination. Another component host on the receiving side receives and unmarshals the bit-stream. The current implementation uses the standard JAR file format for passing components that can support digital signatures, allowing for authentication. It also uses Java's object seri-alization package for marshaling components, which can save the content of instance variables in a component program but does not support the stack frames of threads being captured. Consequently, component hosts cannot serialize the execution states of any thread objects. Instead, when a component is marshaled and unmarshaled, the component host propagates certain events to its components to instruct the components to stop their active threads, and then automatically stops and marshals them after a given period. Moreover, each host has a database on the locations of components it has received to support migration-transparent inter-component interactions. When a component moves, the source host forwards messages to the moved component and the destination host updates the databases of other hosts by multicasting control messages.

4   Component Programming

In this framework, each component is implemented as a collection of Java objects that are defined as subclasses of the Component class as follows:

```
class Component extends MobileAgent implements Serializable {
  void go(URL url) throws NoSuchHostException { ... }
  setPolicy(ComponnetProfile cref,
    MigrationPolicy mpolicy, boolean coexist) { ... }
  setTTL(int lifespan) { ... }
  void setGroupIdentifier(GroupIdentifier gid) { ... }
  GroupIdentifier getGroupIdentifier() { ... }
  void setComponentProfile(ComponentProfile cpf) { ... }
  ComponentProfile getComponentProfile(ComponentRef ref) { ... }
  boolean isConformableHost(HostProfile hfs) { ... }
  ....
}
```

We will explain some of the methods defined in the Component class. A component executes the go (URL url) method to move to the destination host specified as the url by its runtime system. The setTTL() specifies the life span, called Time-To-Live (TTL), of the component. The span decrements the TTL value as the passage of time. When the TTL of a component becomes zero, the component automatically removes itself. The setGroupIdentifier() method ties the component to the identity of the federation specified as gid. Each component can specify a requirement that its destination hosts must satisfy by invoking the setComponentProfile() method, with the requirement specified as cpf. The class has a service method called isConformableHost(), which the component uses to decide whether or not the capabilities of the component hosts specified as an instance of the HostProfile class can satisfy the requirements of the component. Each component can have more than one listener object that implements a specific listener interface to hook certain events issued by the runtime system before or after changes in its life-cycle state.

4.1   Migration Policy Programming

While each component is running, it can declare its own migration policy by invoking the setPolicy method of the Component class as follows:

```
setPolicy(cref, mp);
```

where the first argument is a reference to another component. The second argument is an instance of the `MigrationPolicy` class.

```
MigrationPolicy mp = new MigrationPolicy(int policy);
```

When a component specified as `cref` migrates from its source to its destination, the component creates an instance of the class with one of the following actions:

- If the second argument is `new MigrationPolicy(Policy.FOLLOW)`, the component migrates to the same destination computer.
- If the second argument is `new MigrationPolicy(Policy.DISPTACH)`, the component duplicates itself and migrates its clone to the same destination computer.
- If the second argument is `new MigrationPolicy(Policy.SHIFT)`, the component migrates to the source computer.
- If the second argument is `new MigrationPolicy(Policy.FILL)`, the component duplicates itself and migrates its clone to the source computer.
- If the second argument is `new MigrationPolicy(Policy.STAY)`, the component stays at the current computer.

where each component can have at most one policy. Figure 6 outlines four basic policies, where two components, B and C, have policies for component A.

These policies are related to phenomena in biological processes. For example, `Policy.FOLLOW` enables a component to come near another component. When multiple components declares a policy for a leader component, they can swarm around

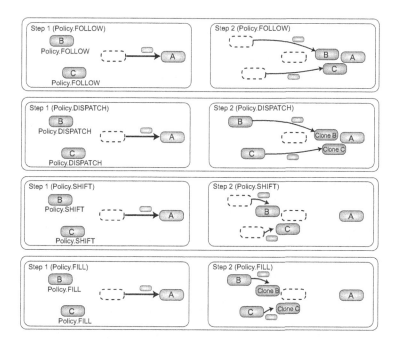

Fig. 6. Basic migration policies.

the leader component. `Policy.SHIFT` enables a component to follow the movement of another component. The former component can track the latter component as it moves. The policy thus corresponds to the phenomenon of cytoplasmic streaming. `Policy.DISPATCH`) enables a component to stay in the current location and then deploys its clone at the destination of another moving component. `Policy.DISPATCH`) can model the footprint of a motile cell. We have assumed that a component can declare the policy for another component and specify the TTLs of its clones as their life-spans. As the latter component moves, cloned former component are deployed at the footmark of the latter component and these clones are automatically volatilized after their life-spans are over. Therefore, the clone components can be viewed as a pheromone that is left behind after the latter component has moved on. `Policy.FILL` corresponds to the phenomenon of cell division. The framework is open to define policies as long as they are subclasses of the `MigrationPolicy` so that we can easily define new policies, including bio-inspired ones.

4.2 Component Coordination Programming

Component references are responsible for tracking possibly moving targets and for invoking the targets' methods. This framework provides the APIs for invoking the methods of other components on local or other computers with copies of arguments. Our programming interface to invoke methods is similar to CORBA's dynamic invocation interface and does not have to statically define any stub or skeleton interfaces through a precompiler approach, because our target is a dynamic computing system.

```
Message msg = new Message("print");
msg.setArg("hello world");
Object result = cref.invoke(msg);
```

The above code fragment is used to invoke a method of the component specified as the `cref` reference. Apart from this, the framework supports a generic remote publish/subscribe mechanism that enables subscribers to express their interest in an event so that they can be notified afterwards of any event fired by a publisher. This is implemented through Java's dynamic proxy mechanism, which has been a new feature of the Java 2 Platform since version 1.3[2].

5 Current Status

A prototype implementation of this framework was constructed with Sun's Java Developer Kit version 1.4 and although it was not built for performance, we measured the cost of component migration. For example, the cost of migrating the federation of three components in Fig. 4 is 180 ms, where the cost of migrating a component between two hosts over a TCP connection is 42 msec. This experiment was done with five computers (1.2-GHz Pentium III, with Windows XP and JDK 1.4.2) connected through a Fast Ethernet network. The latency included the costs of the following processes: transmitting

---

[2] As the dynamic creation mechanism is beyond the scope of the papers. we have left it for future publications.

the component's requirements from the source host to the LIS through TCP, transmitting a candidate destination from the LIS to the source host through TCP, marshaling the component, migrating the component from the source host to the destination host through TCP, unmarshaling the agent, and verifying security.

The current implementation can encrypt components before migrating them over a network and then decrypt them after they arrive at their destination. Moreover, since each component is just a programmable entity, it can explicitly encrypt its particular fields and migrate itself with these fields and its own cryptographic procedure. The Java virtual machine can explicitly restrict components to only access specified resources to protect hosts from malicious components. Although the current implementation cannot protect components from malicious hosts, the runtime system supports some authentication mechanisms to migrate components through mobile agent technology so that each component host can only send agents to and only receive from trusted hosts.

6   Initial Experience

This section presents three examples that illustrate how the framework works.

6.1   Desktop Teleporting in Ubiquitous Computing Environments

The first example is a mobile editor and is composed of three partitioned components. The first, called *application logic*, manages and stores text data and should be executed on a host equipped with a powerful processor with much amount memory. The second, called a *viewer*, displays text data on the screen of its current host and should be deployed at hosts equipped with large screens. The third is called a *controller* and forwards texts from its current host's keyboard to the first component. They have the following relocation policies. The application logic and control components have *follow* hook policies for the viewer component to deploy itself at the current host of the viewer component or nearby hosts. As we can see from Fig. 7, we assumed that the three components had been initially stored in two hosts.

The system can track the movement of the user in physical space through RFID-tag technology[3]. It also introduces a component, called a *user-counterpart*, since the component works as a virtual counterpart in cyberspace. The component can automatically move to hosts near the current location of the user, even while the user is moving. That is, a user-counterpart is always at a host near the user. Because the viewer component has a *follow* hook policy to move the user-counterpart component, it moves to a host that has a user-counterpart or nearby hosts. When a user moves to another location, the components can be dynamically allocated at suitable hosts without the loss of any coordination as we can see from Fig. 7. When application-specific components are animal cells, the counter component can be treated as a bait for those cells.

---

[3] An RFID-based location-dependent deployment of component was presented in our previous paper [17].

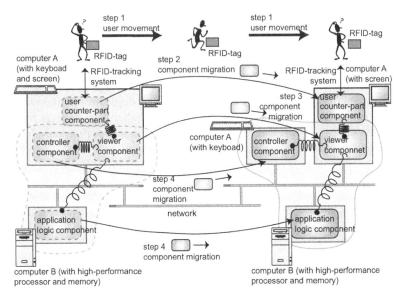

Fig. 7. Initial allocation of components for editor-application.

6.2 Ants-Based Routing Mechanisms

Ants are able to locate a path to a food source using trails of chemical substances called pheromones that are deposited by other ants. Several researchers have attempted to use the notion of ant pheromones for network-routing mechanisms [3, 20]. Our framework allows moving components to leave themselves on their trails and to become automatically volatilized after their life-spans are over. A mobile agent corresponding to an ant A corresponding to a pheromone is attached to another mobile agent corresponding to an ant according to the *fill* policy. When the latter agent randomly selects its destination and migrates to the selected destination, the former agent creates a clone and migrates to the source host of the latter. Since each of the cloned agents defines its life-span by invoking the `setTTL` method, they are active for a specified duration after being created. If there are other agents corresponding to pheromones in the host, the visiting agent adds their time spans to its own time span. When another agent corresponding to another ant migrates over the network, it can select a host that has the agents corresponding to pheromones whose time-spans are the longest from the neighboring hosts. We experimented on ant-based routing for mobile agents using this prototype implementation and eight hosts. However, we knew that it would be difficult to quickly converge a short-path to the destination in real systems, because routing mechanisms tend to be diverging.

6.3 Component Diffusion in Sensor Networks

The second example is the speculative deployment of components as is done with cell-lamellipodia. This provides a mechanism that dynamically and speculatively deploys components at sensor nodes when there are environmental changes. This mechanism was inspired by lamellipodia in cells. It assumes that the sensor field is a two-dimensional surface composed of sensor nodes and it monitors environmental changes, such as motion in objects and variations in temperature. It is a well known fact that after a sensor node detects environmental changes in its area of coverage, some of its geographically neighboring nodes tend to detect similar changes after a short time. Diffusion occurs as follows. When a component on a sensor node finds changes in its environment, the component duplicates itself and deploys the copy at neighboring nodes as long as the nodes have the same kinds of components (Fig. 8). Each component is associated with a resource limit that functions as a generalized Time-To-Live field. Although a node can monitor changes in interesting environments, it sets the TTLs of its components as their own initial value. It otherwise decrements TTLs as the passage of time. When the TTL of a component becomes zero, the component automatically removes itself. This example is still in the early stages of experimentation but we have developed a mobile agent-based middleware for sensor networks [22] and plan to extend this framework to the middleware.

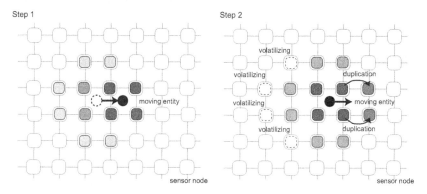

Fig. 8. Component diffusion in moving entity.

7 Related Work

The section discusses several bio-inspired approaches to distributed and multi-agents systems. Most of the work has been based on simulators. For example, Swarm [7] and MASS [6] are general simulators for multi-agent models. However, real systems are complex and varied. Our goal was also to provide a practical middleware for adaptive distributed systems. Unfortunately, we could not gain a rich experience with bio-inspired approaches in real systems because there have been few real systems based on approaches in the real world[4]. We still lack a lot of data that are essential to simulating the approaches accurately. Therefore, real experiments in a real distributed system must have priority over simulation-based experiments for actual experience to accumulate.

A few attempts have provided infrastructures for real distributed systems, like ours. The Anthill project [1] by University of Bologna developed a bio-inspired middleware

---

[4] In fact, several existing simulation-based results seem to be based on arbitrary hypotheses in the sense that various parameters in their experiments lack any technical grounds.

for peer-to-peer systems, which is composed of a collection of interconnected nests. Autonomous agents, called ants can travel across the network trying to satisfy user requests, like ours. The project provided bio-inspired frameworks, called Messor [11] and Bison [12]. Messor is a load-balancing application of Anthill and Bison is a conceptual bio-inspired framework based on Anthill. The main difference between Anthill, including its applications, and our framework is that it introduces agents as independent entities and ours permits components to be organized in a self-organized manner. The Co-Field project [10] by University di Modena e Reggio Emilia proposed the notion of a computational force-field model for coordinating the movements of a group of agents, including mobile devices, mobile robots, and sensors. However, the model only seems to be available within the limits of simulation and not within a real distributed system. Hive [8] is a distributed agent middleware for building decentralized applications and it can deploy agents at devices in ubiquitous computing environments and organize these devices as groups of agents. Although it introduced metaphors drawn from ecology, it cannot change the structure of agents dynamically whereas ours can.

We described an infrastructure for location-aware mobile agents in a previous paper [17]. Like the framework presented in this paper, this infrastructure provides tagged entities, including people and things, with application-level software to support and annotate them. However, since it cannot partition an application into one or more components, it must deploy and run an application within single instead of multiple computers. We presented an early prototype implementation of the federation mechanism presented in this paper in another previous paper [18].

8   Conclusion

This paper presented a middleware system for providing a dynamic federation of components on a distributed system. Since the middleware enabled each component to migrate over a distributed system under its own policy, the federation was mobile and able to be transformed in a self-organized manner. For example, it permitted components to follow other moving components and deployed their clones at different computers similar to what happens in the locomotion of motile cells. We designed and implemented a prototype middleware system and demonstrated its effectiveness in several applications.

To conclude, we would like to point out further issues that need to be resolved. The final goal of this middleware is to provide a general test-bed for various bio-inspired approaches for adaptive distributed systems. Although the current implementation focuses on the deployment of components, we plan to extend it so that it can be used to modify the behavior of each component, while they are running. Also, as its performance is not yet entirely satisfactory, further measurements and optimizations will be needed. The current migration policy for partitioned applications may still be naive. We have studied some higher-level routings for mobile agents in previous papers [14, 16, 19] and are interested in applying routing approaches to partitioned applications. We plan to develop a monitoring and testing system for components by using an approach where we test context-aware applications on mobile computers [15].

References

1. O. Babaoglu and H. Meling and A. Montresor, Anthill: A Framework for the Development of Agent-Based Peer-to-Peer Systems, Proceeding of 22th IEEE International Conference on Distributed Computing Systems, July 2002.
2. B. L. Brumitt, B. Meyers, J. Krumm, A. Kern, S. Shafer, EasyLiving: Technologies for Intelligent Environments, Proceedings of International Symposium on Handheld and Ubiquitous Computing (HUC'00), pp. 12-27, September, 2000.
3. G. Di Caro and M. Dorigo, AntNet: Distributed Stigmergetic Control for Communications Networks, Journal of Artificial Intelligence Research, vol.9, pp. 317-365, 1998.
4. K. J. Goldman, B. Swaminathan, T. P. McCartney, M. D. Anderson, R. Sethuraman The Programmers' Playground: I/O Abstraction for User-Configurable Distributed Applications, IEEE Transactions on Software Engineering, vol. 21, no. 9, pp.735-746, September 1995.
5. A. Harter, A. Hopper, P. Steggeles, A. Ward, P. Webster, The Anatomy of a Context-Aware Application, Proceedings of Conference on Mobile Computing and Networking (MOBICOM'99), pp. 59-68, ACM Press, 1999.
6. B. Horling, and V. Lesser, and R. Vincent, Multi-Agent System Simulation Framework Proceeding of IMACS World Congress 2000 on Scientific Computation, Applied Mathematics and Simulation, August 2000.
7. N. Minar, R. Burkhart, C. Langton, and M. Askenazi. The Swarm Simulation System, A Toolkit for Building Multi-Agent Simulations, Technical report, Swarm Development Group, June 1996.
8. N. Minar, M. Gray, O. Roup, R. Krikorian, P. Maes, Hive: Distributed Agents for Networking Things, International Symposium on Agent Systems and Applications / International Symposium on Mobile Agents (ASA/MA'99), 1999.
9. O. Holder, I. Ben-Shaul, and H. Gazit, System Support for Dynamic Layout of Distributed Applications, Proceedings of International Conference on Distributed Computing Systems (ICDCS'99), pp 403-411, IEEE Computer Society, 1999.
10. M. Mamei, L. Leonardi, F. Zambonelli, Co-Fields: A Unifying Approach to Swarm Intelligence, International Workshop on Engineering Societies in the Agents World (ESAW 2002), Lecture Notes in Computer Science, vol. 2577, Springer Verlag 2003.
11. A. Montresor, H. Meling, and O. Babaoglu, Messor: Load-Balancing through a Swarm of Autonomous Agents, Proceedings of International Workshop on Agents and Peer-to-Peer Computing, July 2002.
12. A. Montresor and O. Babaoglu, Biology-Inspired Approaches to Peer-to-Peer Computing in BISON Proceedings of International Conference on Intelligent System Design and Applications, Oklahoma, August 2003.
13. M. Román, H. Ho, R. H. Campbell, Application Mobility in Active Spaces, Proceedings of International Conference on Mobile and Ubiquitous Multimedia, 2002.
14. I. Satoh, Building Reusable Mobile Agents for Network Management, IEEE Transactions on Systems, Man and Cybernetics, vol.33, no. 3, part-C, pp.350-357, August 2003.
15. I. Satoh, A Testing Framework for Mobile Computing Software, IEEE Transactions on Software Engineering, vol. 29, no. 12, pp.1112-1121, December 2003.
16. I. Satoh, Configurable Network Processing for Mobile Agents on the Internet Cluster Computing (The Journal of Networks, Software Tools and Applications), vol. 7, no.1, pp.73-83, Kluwer, January 2004.
17. I. Satoh, Linking Phyical Worlds to Logical Worlds with Mobile Agents, Proceedings of IEEE International Conference on Mobile Data Management (MDM'2004), pp. 332-343, IEEE Computer Society, January 2004.

18. I. Satoh, Dynamic Federation of Partitioned Applications in Ubiquitous Computing Environments, Proceedings of IEEE International Conference on Pervasive Computing and Communications (PerCom'2004), pp.356-360, IEEE Computer Society, March 2004.

19. I. Satoh, Selection of Mobile Agents, Proceedings of IEEE International Conference on Distributed Computing Systems (ICDCS'2004), pp.484-493, IEEE Computer Society, March 2004.

20. R. Schoonderwoerd, O. Holland, and J. Bruten, Ant-like agents for load balancing in telecommunications networks, Proceedings of Conference on Autonomous Agents, pages 209-216. ACM Press, 1997.

21. C. Szyperski, Component Software, Addison-Wesley, 1998.

22. Umezawa T, Satoh I, Anzai Y. A Mobile Agent-based Framework for Configurable Sensor Networks. Proceedings of International Workshop on Mobile Agents for Telecommunication Applications (MATA'2002); Lecture Notes in Computer Science 2002; Springer; Vol. 2521: 128-140.

23. World Wide Web Consortium (W3C), Composite Capability/Preference Profiles (CC/PP), http://www.w3.org/TR/NOTE-CCPP, 1999.

How Agents Should Exploit Tetralemma with an Eastern Mind in Argumentation

Hajime Sawamura[1] and Edwin D. Mares[2]

[1] Department of Information Engineering and
Graduate School of Science and Technology,
Niigata University, 8050, 2-cho, Ikarashi, Niigata, 950-2181 Japan
sawamura@ie.niigata-u.ac.jp
[2] Philosophy Department, Victoria University of Wellington,
P. O. Box 600, Wellington, New Zealand
edwin.mares@vuw.ac.nz

Abstract. Argumentation is a ubiquitous but effective mode of interaction and dialogue in the human society. It has come to be known that argumentation has many implications to interaction among computational agents as well. After observing and discussing the tetralemma, which is said to characterize the Eastern thought, in this paper we propose an argumentation framework with the paraconsistent logic programming based on the tetralemma. It allows us to represent typical eastern modes of truth: $\top, \bot$ which are considered epistemic states of propositions. We introduce various notions for our argumentation framework, such as attack relations in terms of differences as a momentum of argumentation, argument justification, preferential criteria of arguments based on social norms, and so on, in a way proper to the four-valued paraconsistent logic programming. Finally, we provide the fixpoint semantics and dialectical proof theory for the argumentation framework. We illustrate our ideas with various argument examples.

1 Introduction

In this paper, we are concerned with a complex of the Western and Eastern thoughts and cultures in knowledge representation and reasoning. More specifically, we reconsider from an eastern point of view the paraconsistent logic programming of Blair and Subrahmanian [5] and intend to exploit it as a knowledge representation language, and then we build an argumentation model on top of this, taking into account Eastern meanings of the four truth values and the antagonism among them.

Argumentation is a ubiquitous form and way of dialogue in the human society. Recently in the fields of artificial intelligence and computer science, there has been a growing interest in argumentation as an effective means of interaction for intelligent systems [6], as a general framework for relating nonmonotonic logics of different styles [9] and so on. The underlying frameworks of argumentation have been mainly built using the normal logic programs or the extended logic programs (ELP) as knowledge representation languages (e. g., [8, 19, 6]) with which the belief and knowledge of each agent are described for argumentation.

M.W. Barley and N. Kasabov (Eds.): PRIMA 2004, LNAI 3371, pp. 259–278, 2005.

In this paper we propose an argumentation framework with the paraconsistent logic programming whose literals are annotated with four values. They are a set of truth-values $\{\mathbf{t}, \mathbf{f}, \top, \bot\}$ with a lattice structure. The apparatus of the four values is introduced to admit inconsistency (paraconsistency) and at the same time reject 'ex falso quodlibet'. Tolerance and acceptance of inconsistency that this logic has as its logical feature is useful to allow for arguments on inconsistent knowledge bases with which we are often confronted. The four-valued semantics was first introduced by Dunn for the logic of the first-degree entailments, and then advocated as a useful logic for computer applications [2, 3]. In this paper, we, however, pay much attention to the eastern meanings of the four values that has been originated in the era of the early Buddhism in India (more than 2500 years ago) and now called the tetralemma. The tetralemma is often said to characterize the Eastern thought. It is in general considered modes of truth or epistemic states of propositions. It further allows handling the inexpressible or inexplicable which are impredicative symbolically.

After observing and discussing the tetralemma in the first part of the paper, we will present an argumentation framework that has unique features induced by the paraconsistent logic programming language and the tetralemma. They include the argument definition, attack and defeat relations in terms of differences as a momentum of argumentation, argument justification, and preferential criteria of arguments based on conventional wisdom or standards and evidences. The notion, differences as a momentum of argumentation, is particularly outstanding as expressing disagreement among arguments since in the past argumentation models, the disagreement has been specified only for contradictory propositions of the form p and $\neg p$. In our model, "difference" is to be identified alike or fairly among the four truth-values, expecting a more versatile development of argumentation or dialogue. We provide the fixpoint semantics and dialectical proof theory for our argumentation framework along the line of Dung [8], and Prakken and Sarter [19]. We demonstrate our syncretic ideas on logic of argumentation based on the tetralemma, by applying it to many argument examples on worldly or unworldly issues.

Finally, as a significant extension, we consider how to incorporate dialectical reasoning or thought as a basic component of our argumentation model. According to Aristotle, argumentation consists of three components: deduction, rhetoric and dialectic. Three laws of the Hegelian and Marxist dialectics are particularly worthy to consider for agents' world as well as in our society: (1) the unity of opposites, (2) the transformation of quantity into quality, and (3) the negation of the negation.

The paper is organized as follows. In Section 2, tetralemma is revisited. In Section 3, the paraconsistent logic programming language for knowledge representation is outlined, and its features and significances in argumentation are discussed. In Section 4, an argumentation framework for paraconsistent logic programming language is described. In Section 5 and 6, a semantics for the argumentation framework and a dialogical proof theory for the argumentation framework are described respectively. In Section 7, our paraconsistent argumentation framework is illustrated using various argument examples. In Section 8, we consider incorporating Hegelian dialectics into argumentation as an effective form of attaining a consensus or reaching an agreement. Finally in Section 9, concluding remark and future work are described.

2   Tetralemma

In the early philosophical literature and text of Buddhism, the notion of four alternative positions (catuṣkoṭi in Sanskrit; shikufunbetsu in Japanese) appears very often in arguments on metaphysical questions such as whether Nirvāṇa is an existent, whether Tathāgata exists after death, in such a way that all conceptually imaginable positions are exhaustive and exclusive.

Nirvāṇa is an existent.
Nirvāṇa is a non-existent.
Nirvāṇa is both an existent and a non-existent.
Nirvāṇa is neither an existent nor a non-existent.

These represent four logical possibilities of the form: (1) affirmation, (2) negation, (3) both affirmation and negation, and (4) neither affirmation nor negation. The ancient Indians believed that the truth with regard to any matter lay in one of these alternatives. Over the last few decades, the logical structure of the four alternative positions has been the subject of a considerable amount of discussion and controversy, and also of some speculation in the context of what is sometimes called East-West philosophical comparison. Nowadays "the four alternatives (positions)" is also termed "tetralemma" or "tetrachotomy" in the literature [32, 22, 11, 4, 20].

Tetralemma is an epistemic state or way of recognizing things, beings, objects, propositions, etc. We use similar patterns of expressions very often in our daily life, for example,

Animals have moral rights.
Animals do not have moral rights.
Animals have moral rights and do not.
Animals neither have moral rights nor do not.

In his book, Logos and Lemma [32], Yamauchi Tokuryu contrasted Western and Eastern thought by characterizing the first as being determined by logos and the latter as being structured by the principles of the tetralemma, thereby conceiving of logos as a method of exclusion and of lemma as a way of friendly inclusion (even of the middle). The tetralemma, in fact, is closely related to the view of emptiness in Buddhism and the cultural idiosyncrasy such as holistic view on world, society and ecosystem in nature [18].

It would be helpful to speculate about the meanings of the third and fourth lemmas in more details since they are beyond simply saying either true or false, so that we could exploit them in applications to knowledge representation and argumentative reasoning.

2.1 The Third Lemma: 'It Is and It Is Not'

The third lemma obviously seems to violate the law of noncontradiction by Aristotle. It, however, often appears in the sutras of Buddhism and the eastern tradition of thought and culture. Daoists and Zen Buddhists, for example, see the two sides of any apparent contradiction existing in a harmony, opposed but interconnected, interpenetrating, and interdependent. In everyday situations where experience or desire is dominant, easterners are tolerant of contradictions. They have thought that the law of noncontradiction applies only to the realm of concepts and abstractions, which are merely reflections of things. In his recent book [18], a cultural psychologist, Nisbett has demonstrated tendency and evidence which indicate various differences of cognition and reasoning between Easterners and Westerners, including the preferential examination of acceptance or avoidance of contradictions.

Let us see some multi-faceted meanings of the third lemma since we think they are helpful to understand and use it in actual knowledge representation as well. Murti [16] says that the third lemma represents that we have the consciousness of the one-sidedness of mere is or mere is not, for example, God exist and does not. Jayatilleke [11] says that the historical examples show that the second alternative is the contrary and not the contradictory of the first, for example, west vs. east, knowledge vs. conduct. Then, the third asserts that the subject has a combination of the contrary characteristics. For example, when the statement 'universe is both finite and infinite' is made, it is intended that 'the universe is finite in one dimension (in some respects) and infinite in another. Here is a typical locution for 'it is and is not' in our daily life (or rather, politicians may use this): When they are asked a hard question to deal with, the answer would be 'yes and no'. Also in our daily life, we sometimes rhetorically use the oxymoron. It is a phrase that combines two words that seem to be the opposite of each other. For example, an open secret, too much of a good thing (bear's service), a happy scream, a deafening silence and so on. Oxymoron unites two opposing words into an expression with a single meaning, without contradiction.

The third lemma also can be found even in Western dialectics. It is a dialectical contradiction but not a contradiction in formal logic, being a form of the unity of opposites as a dialectical law in Hegelian and Marxist dialectics. The eastern style of reasoning is basically dialectical from scratch in the sense that it focuses on contradictions and how to resolve them or transcend them or find the truth in both. In either world, we need to invent concepts to both discard and absorb those contradictory propositions. Turning our eyes to the development in other traditional sciences, we can see that dialectical thought unites various opposite concepts, principles, and theories through mediating logical links in higher synthetic constructions.

We use the top symbol $\top$ for such an epistemic state or way of recognizing things, beings, objects, propositions, etc., and annotate propositions with the symbol $\top$ as in [5].

2.2   The Fourth Lemma: 'It Neither Is Nor Is Not'

Like the third lemma, the fourth lemma also appears very often in the sutras of Buddhism and the eastern tradition of thought and culture, such as in
Nāgārjuna's Mūlamadhyamakakārikā, which is one of the most influential work
in the history of Indian philosophy [17], and in the Heart Sutra.

Murti interprets it like this. It represents the full consciousness that no corresponding affirmation is available. This is an extreme form of non-committal.
It is not an attitude of decision, but of doubt. The competence of thought is
not questioned and reason is not transcended. It may correspond to the agnos-
tic position [16]. According to the interpretation of Jayatilleke, there is left a
part of the determinable constituting the universe of discourse which is referred
to by the fourth lemma since the second alternative is the contrary and not
the contradictory, and the third asserts that the subject has a combination of
some of the contrary characteristics [11]. Here is a good example illustrated by
Jayatilleke [11]:

A person is happy.
A person is not happy.
A person is both happy and unhappy.
A person is neither happy nor unhappy.

Happiness in this context is a determinate quality characterizing a person's
hedonic tone. When we remove the qualities of "happiness", "unhappiness", or
a mixture of the two, we are left with "neutral hedonic tone". So a person who is
"neither happy nor unhappy" comprises the class of people expressing a neutral
hedonic tone. Such a class need not necessarily be a null class, although it could
be so sometimes. Here is another similar type of locutions, which can be seen
in our daily life as well: His act is neither right nor wrong, or we are neither for
nor against his act.

The fourth lemma has had a wide spectrum of meanings or epistemic states
of things, beings, objects, and propositions. It would be worthy and useful to list
up it as follows for the knowledge representation and argumentation described
later: no commitment, no comment, no concern, no information, an attitude of
doubt, a neutral or transcendental epistemic state, and a view of Emptiness:
the Buddhist technical terms for the lack of independent existence, inherent
existence, or essence in things. We degenerate these into the bottom symbol $\perp$
and the context is supposed to specify a meaning of it.

3   Paraconsistent Logic Programming Language

We employ the paraconsistent logic programming language for knowledge representation language with which our argumentation model is to be built. This was
first introduced by Blair and Subrahmanian [5] and then extended to generalized annotated logic programming by Kifer and Subrahmanian [12], preserving
paraconsistency of a knowledge base. They formalized generalized Horn clauses

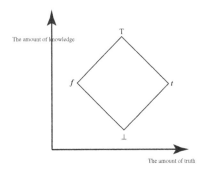

Fig. 1. 4-element lattice of truth values (epistemic states) $FOUR$ [2, 1].

(GHC) with annotations, and gave a fixpoint semantics and procedural semantics for GHC [5]. Below, we will outline it to the extent that it is needed in the paper.

Definition 1 (Truth-values [5] or Epistemic states). $\mathcal{T} = \{\top, \mathbf{t}, \mathbf{f}, \bot\}$ *is a set of truth values or epistemic states). Its partial order $\preceq$ is defined to be* $(\forall x, y \in \mathcal{T})\ x \preceq y \Leftrightarrow x = y \lor x = \bot \lor y = \top$. *(see Fig. 1).*

Definition 2 (Annotation, Annotated Atoms and Literals [5, 12]). *Let A be an atom, L a literal and $\mu \in \mathcal{T}$. Then μ is an annotation, $A : \mu$ is an annotated atom and $L : \mu$ is an annotated literal.*

Definition 3 (Rules [5, 12]). *Rules are of the form $L_0 \Leftarrow L_1 \land ... \land L_n$, where $L_i(0 \leq i \leq n)$ are annotated literals. (It is noted that rules containing variables are assumed to represent any ground instances of them.)*

The annotated literals $L_1, ..., L_n$ in the right hand side of a rule is called antecedents and L_0 is called a consequent of the rule. A knowledge base of an agent is a set of rules. A knowledge base Kb consisting of rules with names $r_1, ..., r_n$ is represented by $Kb = \{r_1,\ ...,\ r_n\}$ or $Kb = \{r_1 : L_0^1 \Leftarrow L_1^1 \land ... \land L_m^1., \cdots,\ r_n : L_0^n \Leftarrow L_1^n \land ... \land L_m^n.\}$.

Definition 4 (Formulas). *Formulas are defined inductively as follows.*

1. *Annotated literals are formulas.*
2. *If $F_1, ..., F_n$ are annotated literals, $F_1 \land, ..., \land F_n$ is a conjunctive formula.*
3. *If F_1 is a literal and F_2 a conjunctive formula, $F_1 \Leftarrow F_2$ is a formula.*

Definition 5 (Negation of Annotation [5]). *The negation of an annotation is defined as:* $\neg(\mathbf{t}) = \mathbf{f}, \neg(\mathbf{f}) = \mathbf{t}, \neg(\top) = \top, \neg(\bot) = \bot$.

Definition 6 (Satisfaction [5, 12]). *Let I be a function from the Herbrand base under consideration to $\mathcal{T}$, and F a formula. We write $I \models F$ to say that I satisfies F, and $I \not\models F$ that I does not satisfy F. Then $I \models F$ is defined as follows.*

1. *For an annotated atom* $A : \mu$, $I \models A : \mu$ *iff* $I(A) \succeq \mu$.
2. *For an annotated literal* $\neg L : \mu$, $I \models \neg L : \mu$ *iff* $I \models L : \neg\mu$.
3. *For a conjunctive formula of the form* $F_1 \wedge ... \wedge F_n$, $I \models F_1 \wedge ... \wedge F_n$ *iff for every* i $(i = 1, ..., n)$, $I \models F_i$.
4. *For a formula of the form* $F_1 \Leftarrow F_2$, $I \models F_1 \Leftarrow F_2$ *iff* $I \models F_1$ *or* $I \not\models F_2$.

Definition 6 (2) gurantees that it is not necessary to consider any negated literals since negations can be implicitly present in the form of atoms annotated with **f** [5].

Definition 7 (Model [5, 12]).

 - *An interpretation* I *is a model of a formula* F *iff* $I \models F$.
 - *An interpretation* I *is a model of a knowledge base* Kb, *symbolically,* $I \models Kb$ *iff* I *satisfies evry rule in* Kb.

Definition 8 (Logical consequence [5, 12]). *Let* Kb, I *and* F *be a knowledge base, an interpretation and a formula respectively.* F *is a logical consequence from* Kb, *symbolically,* $Kb \models F$ *iff for every interpretation* I, *if* $I \models Kb$ *then* $I \models F$.

It should be noted that this notion of logical consequence is given along the axis of the amount of knowledge or information, not the axis of the measure of truth [2, 3].

The logicians or computer scientists in the Occident (e. g., Dunn, Belnap, Blair, Subrahmanian, Kifer, Arieli, etc. [10, 2, 5, 12, 1]) have not considered a wide variety of meanings of the four values of the tetralemma from various viewpoints. It seems to be enough for their purposes that the number of truth values is four and the mathematical structure is a lattice. As discussed in the previous Section, we have regarded the tetralemma as epistemic states of propositions, which is typically attendant to the eastern thought and mind. For our purpose, GHC with annotations as the tetralemma will make it possible to build a logic of argumentation with the following advantages:

 - We need not to worry about inconsistency caused by each agent's knowledge base, due to the paraconsistency of GHC,
 - GHC gives us an easy way to represent and build knowledge bases for argumentation,
 - GHC allows us to directly construct arguments under incomplete, vague, partial, indefinite, imprecise, plausible knowledge and information, having four values in mind. In other knowledge representation, the multi-valuedness is, in general, hidden in the interpretation of formulas.
 - The tetralemma suggests a way of handling the inexpressible and inexplicable which are impredicative symbolically. For example, $p : \bot$ and $p : \top$ are their representation. This might lead to another way to grasp without explicit representation and reason.

One weak point of the paraconsistent logic programming language is that it lacks the so-called weak negation (or default negation) the extended logic programming has (ELP). Interested readers should refer to [28] for the extended generalized logic programming language (EGAP) as a knowledge representation and the argumentation framework for it. EGAP includes two negations: the epistemological negation and default one like in ELP. The argumentation model developed in [28], however, differs from the present paper in its philosophy.

4 Paraconsistent Argumentation Framework

Now having various meanings of the tetralemma in Section 2 in mind, we will get down to building a new argumentation model. The argumentation framework AF for the paraconsistent logic programming language is a triple $\langle \Gamma, C, D \rangle$, where $\Gamma = \{Kb_1, ..., Kb_n\}$ is a multiple theory of knowledge bases of agents, C is the conventional wisdom or social standards, and D is the defeat relation based on the notion of 'difference as a momentum of argumentation'.

4.1 Arguments

The rules of GHC are of the form, $L_0 \Leftarrow L_1 \wedge ... \wedge L_n$. Then, we define arguments as follows.

Definition 9 (Arguments). *An argument is a finite non-null sequence $[r_1, ..., r_n]$ of ground instances of rules in a knowledge base such that*

1. *for every i $(2 \leq i \leq n)$ and for every $L_j : \mu_j$ $(1 \leq j \leq m)$ in the antecedent of r_i, there exists a rule $r_k(k < i)$ whose consequent is $L_j : \mu_k(\mu_k \succeq \mu_j)$. Then $L_j : \mu_k$ is called a ground of the antecedent of the rule r_i, and*
2. *no pair of distinct rules in the sequence have the same atomic formula in their consequents.*

The condition (1) above yields the correctness of arguments and the condition (2) is for the uniqueness of arguments. For example, $[p(a) : \mathbf{t}, p(a) : \top]$ is not an argument. We sometimes abuse symbols such as $A = [r_1, ..., r_n]$ or $A = [r_1 : L_0^1 : \mu_0^1, \cdots, r_n : L_0^n : \mu_0^n \Leftarrow L_1^n : \mu_1^n \wedge ... \wedge L_m^n : \mu_m^n.]$ for arguments, where $r_1, ..., r_n$ are rule names.

Definition 10 (Conclusions of arguments). *The consequents of rules in an argument A are called conclusions of the argument A.*

Obviously every conclusion of an argument A is a logical consequence from A. The converse does not hold, for example, $p(a) : \bot$ is a logical consequence from an argument $[p(a) : \top]$, but it is not a conclusion of the argument. For another example, $q : \top$ is a logical consequence from a knowledge base $\{q : \mathbf{t}, q : \mathbf{f}\}$ which is equivalent to a knowledge base $\{q : \top\}$ called a reductant in [12], and hence could have been a logical consequence from an argument $[q : \top]$. For these anomaly, we take a stand that we take into account only arguments constructed by rules provided explicitly. Also we should note that this reflects a view that we do not live with logic, but with argumentation in the daily life, and Easterners' preference for logical vs. dialectical arguments [18]. We would rather welcome the difference between logic and argument to building our argumentation framework. For the reductant above, it should be left as a reorganization problem of knowledge base.

Definition 11 (Subarguments). *An argument A' is a subargument of an argument A iff A' is a subsequence of A satisfying the conditions of arguments.*

4.2   Difference as a Momentum of Argumentation

Identifying two opposites such as A and $\neg A$ is a typical momentum of argumentation or dialogue in general in the previous argumentation models [6] as well as in the western culture. In this paper, we will depart from this fixed idea and introduce a broader and liberal one, that is, "difference as a momentum of argumentation". Otherwise, we might have introduced such a way of defining a conflict between arguments that is induced by the order of the truth values. For example, an annotated literal $p : f$ is entitled to attack an annotated literal $p : \top$ since $\top \succeq$ **f**), and conversely $p : \top$ is not entitled to attack $p : f$ since $p : \top$ contains the information of $p : f$. Put it differently, this would be said to be roughly an attack relation based on the measure of truth in the logical lattice $L4$ [2, 3]. In this paper, however, we give such a formalization that this "difference" should be identified alike or fairly among the four truth values, expecting a more versatile development of argumentation or dialogue. In other words, it would be said to be roughly an attack relation based on the amount of knowledge in the approximation-lattice $A4$ [2, 3].

Definition 12 (Attack). *Let A_1 and A_2 be arguments. Then A_1 attacks A_2 iff $L : \mu$ is a conclusion of A_1 and $L : \mu'(\mu \neq \mu')$ is a conclusion of A_2*

Definition 13 (Coherent). *A knowledge base is coherent iff it does not include any two rules whose consequents have the forms of $L : \mu$ and $L : \mu'(\mu \neq \mu')$ respectively.*

Note that arguments as subsets of a knowledge base are always coherent according to the condition 2 of the argument definition.

Definition 14 (Conflict-free [8]). *A set Args of arguments is conflict-free iff no argument in Args attacks an argument in Args.*

The attack relation is symmetric and thus can not decide which side is superior to. To remedy this, we introduce two superiority criteria to compare and judge conflicting arguments. One is a social criterion aimed at incorporating conventional wisdom or standards. The other is a formal syntactic one. The reason why we introduce such two kinds of criteria is just to avoid biased unfair judgements although they are still preliminary and tentative.

Definition 15 (Conventional wisdom or standards). *The conventional wisdom or standards C is a set of annotated literals satisfying: For any $L_1 : \mu_1$ and $L_2 : \mu_2 \in C$, if $L_1 = L_2$ then $\mu_1 = \mu_2$.*

An argument with a conclusion against the conventional wisdom or standards (in other words, a conclusion with a different truth value from that of the conventional wisdom or standards) may be considered unacceptable for the time being. Of course, we should have thought of the conventional wisdom of a society so that agents constantly challenge and modify it since the emergence and evolution of conventions are highly dynamical phenomena. In this paper, however, we will not deal with this issue since it is beyond the aim of this work, and distinguish two kinds of social attack: indirect (hence weak) and direct (hence strong) as follows.

Definition 16 (Social attacks).

1. *Let A_1 be an argument and A_2 be an argument with a conclusion $L : \mu$, and $L : \mu' \in C$. Then A_1 indirectly and socially attacks A_2 iff A_1 attacks A_2 and $\mu \neq \mu'$.*
2. *Let A_1 be an argument with a conclusion $L : \mu_1$ and A_2 an argument with a conclusion $L : \mu_2 (\mu_1 \neq \mu_2)$. Then A_1 directly and socially attacks A_2 iff $L : \mu_1 \in C$.*

For syntactically determined criteria of arguments, we introduce a comparatively objective one. It should be noted that the following criterion is different from Loui's evidential criterion, which simply compares the number of evidences as the grounds of arguments [15].

Definition 17 (Syntactic attack by the evidential inclusion). *Let A_1 be an argument including a rule r_1 whose consequent is $L : \mu$ and A_2 be an argument including a rule r_2 whose consequent is $L : \mu' (\mu \neq \mu')$. Let S_1 be a set of factual grounds of antecedents of r_1 and S_2 be a set of factual grounds of antecedents of r_2. Then A_1 syntactically attacks A_2 iff S_2 is a proper subset of S_1.*

Definition 18 (Priority order of attacking force). *Attack$\prec$Syntactic attack by the evidential inclusion$\prec$Indirect and social attack$\prec$Direct and social attack.*

Definition 19 (Defeat). *An argument A_1 defeats an argument A_2 iff A_1 attacks A_2 and the priority order of A_1's attack is higher than that of A_2's attack.*

The defeat relation is not necessarily asymmetric and thus we need one-directional defeat relation.

Definition 20 (Strictly defeat). *Let A_1 and A_2 be two arguments. Then A_1 strictly defeats A_2 iff A_1 defeats A_2 and A_2 does not defeat A_1.*

5   Semantics for the Argumentation Framework

We have proposed an argument model which idiosyncratically makes the most of the four-valuedness. In this section, we are interested in characterizing a set of justified arguments which corresponds to a set of valid formulas in the formal logics. We will give a fixpoint semantics for our argumentation framework, following a pioneering work by Dung on the argumentation based semantics of the extended logic programming [8, 9] and the work by Prakken and Sarter on the legal argument models for the extended logic programming language [19], whose theoretical parts derive from the Dung's work. We extend their treatment for the semantics and proof theory of argumentation frameworks to a multiple theory of knowledge bases described in terms of the paraconsistent logic programming language with the four-valued interpretation. In doing so, we will add explanation to the definitions introduced in Section 4, from Eastern and dialogical points of views.

Our argumentation framework assumed each agent has its own knowledge base. We let $Args_{Kb}$ be a set of arguments built from a knowledge base Kb in a multiple theory $\Gamma = \{Kb_1, ..., Kb_n\}$. Then, we define $Args_\Gamma = Args_{Kb_1} \cup ... \cup Args_{Kb_n}$. Γ will be omitted when it is implicitly assumed. In this paper, we will not consider merging knowledge bases of each agent since it is unrealistic at least at first to do so like in other works on arguement models [6]. Of course, each agent could have had knowledge about the knowledge of other agents during the argument process, but we will not take into consideration such dynamism in this paper. It is just noted that $Args_\Gamma \subseteq Args_{Kb_1 \cup ... \cup Kb_n}$.

Definition 21 (Acceptability of arguments [8]). *An argument A is acceptable with respect to a set of arguments, $S \subseteq Args_\Gamma$ iff each argument defeating A is strictly defeated by an argument in S.*

Dung first introduced this definition that plays a key role in the fixpoint theory below. Symbolically, an argument A is acceptable wrt. $S \subseteq Args$ iff $\forall x \exists y.(x \ defeats \ A \rightarrow x \ is \ defeated \ by \ y \in S)$. Here we will digress a little from the subject but touch upon its significance from a different angle. This definition is very dialectical in the sense that in order to define the acceptability of an argument, an antagonist who inhibits the argument from becoming acceptable and a protagonist who supports the argument are assumed, and those opposing two are united in the form of such a relation that the former is strictly defeated by the latter. In other words, the definition by the medium of antagonists and protagonists is said to be founded on the unity of opposites and have a form of the negation of the negation in the Hegelian and Marxist dialectics. This definition would remind us of Cauchy's definitions of limit and convergence in analysis (e.g., $\forall \epsilon \exists N \forall n.(n \geq N \rightarrow |a_n - a| < \epsilon)$.

Definition 22 (Characteristic function [8]). *Let S be any subset of $Args_\Gamma$. The characteristic function F of a multiple theory Γ is defined as follows.*

- $F_\Gamma : Pow(Args_\Gamma) \rightarrow Pow(Args_\Gamma)$
- $F_\Gamma(S) = \{A \in Args_\Gamma \mid A \ is \ acceptable \ wrt. \ S\}$

By the well-known result, F_Γ has a least fixpoint $lfp(F_\Gamma)$ since F_Γ is monotonic w. r. t. the set inclusion [29, 14]. On the basis of this result, the notion of a justified argument is defined as follows.

Definition 23 (Justified, overruled, defensible [19]). *For a multiple theory Γ and an argument A, we say that*

- *A is justified iff A is in the least fixpoint of F_Γ denoted by $JustArgs_\Gamma$),*
- *A is overruled iff A is defeated by a justified argument,*
- *A is defensible iff A is neither justified nor overruled.*

An annotated literal $L : \mu$ is said to be a *justified conclusion* in Γ when it is a conclusion of a justified argument.

Definition 24 (Finitary [8]). *A multiple theory Γ is finitary iff each argument in $Args_\Gamma$ is attacked by at most a finite number of arguments in $Args_\Gamma$*

Then, we have the following propositions whose proofs are basically similar to [8, 19]. Interested readers should refer to [31] for the proofs.

Proposition 1 (Iterative calulation of fixpoint [8, 19]). *For a multiple theory Γ, define the following sequence of subsets of $Args_\Gamma$,*

- $F^0 = \emptyset$
- $F^{i+1} = F_{Args_\Gamma}(F^i)$

1. *Then, $\cup_{i=0}^\infty(F^i) \subseteq JustArgs_\Gamma$.*
2. *If $Args_\Gamma$ is finitary, then $\cup_{i=0}^\infty(F^i) = JustArgs_\Gamma$.*

From here on, we assume $Args_\Gamma$ is finitary.

Proposition 2. *The set of justified arguments is conflict-free.*

Proposition 3. *If an argument is justified, then all its subarguments are justified.*

6   Dialogical Proof Theory for the Argumentation Framework

As in the previous section, we assume we have a multiple theory $\Gamma = \{Kb_1, \ldots, Kb_n\}$ and $Args_\Gamma$. We introduce the dialogical proof theory in which an argument is justified in terms of dialogues put forward by agents. The following dialogue is different from [19] in the points that it is defined for a multiple theory of knowledge bases of each agents, and the dialogue is to be done with a more free protocol among agents than that of [19].

Definition 25 (Dialogue). *A dialogue is a finite nonempty sequence of arguments $[Arg^1, \ldots, Arg^n]$, $Arg^i \in Args_\Gamma$ for any i, such that*

1. *If i $(i \geq 3)$ is odd, Arg^i is a minimal (w.r.t set inclusion) argument strictly defeating Arg^{i-1}.*
2. *If i $(i \geq 2)$ is even, Arg^i defeats Arg^{i-1}.*
3. *If i and j are odd and $i \neq j$, $Arg^i \neq Arg^j$.*
   (n is called the length of a dialogue.)

At first glance, this definition looks unfair in the point that agents at the even stages can put forward the same arguments, but agents at the odd stages are not permitted to do so. This is because in order for the first argument put forward to be justified, it has to overturn all possible attacks during the dialogue whether they are repeated ones or not, and the repetitions at the odd stages may lead to an infinite loop that is no more a dialogue which can determine justified arguments. The dialogue definition is one whose goal is to justify an argument, not a chat talking about nothing. Also note that agents of this dialogue simply do not need to take turns to put forward arguments between proponents and opponents. It allows agents to take both stance of proponents and opponents. So we would say that it is not only a dialogue or polylogue but also a monologue by self-criticism. We think this might be a better setting for argumentative dialogue since our knowledge base lies in a paraconsistent state in general and an inconsistent one in the sense of classical logic. Finally, the minimality condition prohibits arguments from pretending to be different from previous ones, with some redundant and irrelevant rules.

Definition 26 (Dialogue tree). *A dialogue tree is a finite tree of dialogues such that*

1. *Every branch is a dialogue.*
2. *If i is odd, the children at node Arg^i are all arguements defeating Arg^i. The height of a dialogue tree is the length of the longest branch in the dialogue tree.*

Definition 27 (Provably justified). *An argument A is a provably justified argument iff there is a dialogue tree with A as its root, and the length of any branch (dialogue) in the tree is odd. We call such a tree a justified dialogue tree.*

An annotated literal $L : \mu$ is called a provably justified conclusion when $L : \mu$ is a conclusion of a provably justified argument.

The following important propositions can be obtained in the same manner as [8, 19]. So the proofs are omitted here (see [31] for the proofs).

Proposition 4 (Soundness). *If an argument A is provably justified, it is justified.*

Proposition 5 (Completeness). *Let Γ be finitary. If an argument A is justified, it is provably justified.*

Proposition 6. *If an argument A is provably justified, all its subarguments are provably justified.*

7 Illustrative Examples

We have attempted to apply our argument model to a variety of arguments, particularly to issues involved in an Eastern view and mind of thought, such as the difference between knowledge and wisdom [13], dying words of people, significance of pilgrimage [7], ethical issue on animal rights and liberation [26, 21] and so on. Here we describe three argument examples in illustration of the argumentation framework, in which arguments are developed with knowledge bases, beyond simply saying either true or false.

Example 1 (Western and Eastern arguments against Aristotle's belief). Aristotle believed that the heavier a body is, the faster it falls to the ground. We write this as

$$A_{Aristotle} = [aristotle\_hyp : \mathbf{t}].$$

Then an Western agent argues against it as follows (this is actually said to be Galileo's logical and analytic argument [18]):

$A_{Western} = [$
$brake(L, H) : \mathbf{t},$
$faster(L + H, H) : \mathbf{t},$
$slower(L + H, H) : \mathbf{t} \Leftarrow brake(L, H) : \mathbf{t},$
$aristotle\_hyp : \top \Leftarrow faster(L + H, H) : \mathbf{t}, slower(L + H, H) : \mathbf{t}].$

This argument represents, in a sense, a proof by reductio ad absurdum. On the other hand, an Eastern agent puts forward such an Eastern holistic argument as:
$A_{Eastern} = [$
$aristotle\_hyp : \mathbf{f} \Leftarrow distrust\_decontextualization : \mathbf{t},$
$distrust\_decontextualization : \mathbf{t}].$

Obviously, $A_{Aristotle}$ is defeated by $A_{Western}$ and $A_{Eastern}$, and results in being overruled by two culturally different kinds of counter-arguments: an Western analytic argument and an Eastern holistic one.

Example 2 (The death penalty institution). Consider a multiple theory $\Gamma = \{Kb_1, Kb_2, Kb_3\}$ together with
$C = \{decrease(crime) : \mathbf{f}\}$, where
$Kb_1 = \{$
r_1: heal(execution, the_bereaved): $\mathbf{f}$,
r_2: hate(the_bereaved, criminal): $\mathbf{t}$,
r_3: desire(the_bereaved, death_penalty):$\top \Leftarrow$
      heal(execution, the_bereaved): $\mathbf{f} \wedge$ hate(the_bereaved, criminal): $\mathbf{t}$.,
r_4: decrease(crime): $\mathbf{t}$.,
r_5: deterrent(death_penalty, crime): $\mathbf{t} \Leftarrow$ decrease(crime): $\mathbf{t}$.,
r_6: assent(death_penalty):$\top \Leftarrow$
      desire(the_bereaved, death_penalty): $\mathbf{f} \wedge$ deterrent(death_penalty, crime): $\mathbf{t}$. }.

The agent with Kb_1 has both stances of assent and dissent for the death penalty institution. $Args_{Kb_1}$ coinsits of an argument: $A_1 = [r_1, r_2, r_3, r_4, r_5, r_6]$, and its subarguments: $A_2 = [r_1, r_2, r_3]$, $A_3 = [r_4, r_5]$, $A_4 = [r_1]$, $A_5 = [r_2], A_6 = [r_4]$.

$Kb_2 = \{$

r_7: hate(the_bereaved, criminal): **t**,

r_8: desire(the_bereaved, death_penalty):**t**$\Leftarrow$ hate(the_bereaved, criminal): **t**.,

r_9: assent(death_penalty):**t**$\Leftarrow$ desire(the_bereaved, death_penalty): **t**.

r_{10}: atone(death, crime): **t**.,

r_{11}: assent(death_penalty): **t**$\Leftarrow$ atone(death, crime): **t**. $\}$.

The agent with Kb_2 assents the death penalty institution. $Args_{Kb_2}$ consists of 5 arguments $A_7 = [r_7, r_8, r_9]$, $A_8 = [r_7, r_8]$, $A_9 = [r_7]$, $A_{10} = [r_{10}, r_{11}]$, $A_{11} = [r_{10}]$.

$Kb_3 = \{$

r_{12}: regret(the_dead): **f**

r_{13}: atone(death, crime): **f**$\Leftarrow$ regret(the_dead): **f**.,

r_{14}: assent(death_penalty): **f**$\Leftarrow$ atone(death, crime: **f**.

r_{15}: decrease(crime): **t**.,

r_{16}: deterrent(death_penalty, crime): **f**$\Leftarrow$ decrease(crime): **t**. $\}$.

The agent with Kb_3 dissents the death penalty institution. $Args_{Kb_3}$ conists of 5 arguments $A_{12} = [r_{12}, r_{13}, r_{14}]$, $A_{13} = [r_{12}, r_{13}]$, $A_{14} = [r_{12}]$, $A_{15} = [r_{15}, r_{16}]$, $A_{16} = [r_{15}]$.

Then, $F^0 = \emptyset$

$$F^1 = F_{Args_\Gamma}(F^0) = \{A_4, A_5, A_9, A_{14}, A_{16}, A_{15}, A_2, A_{13}\}$$

F^1 is a set of arguments acceptable w. r. t. $\emptyset$. In fact, A_4, A_5, A_9, A_{14} are not defeated by any arguments, A_{16} is attacked by A_1, A_3 and A_6, but it directly and socially attacks them. Thus A_{16} is not defeated by its attackers A_1, A_3 and A_6, or rather it strictly defeats them. Similarly, A_{15} is attacked by A_3 and A_6, but it indirectly and socially attacks A_3, and directly and socially attacks A_6. Thus A_{15} is not defeated by its attackers A_3 and A_6, or rather it strictly defeats them. A_2 and A_{13} strictly defeat their attackers A_8 and A_{11} respectively through syntactc attack by the evidential inclusion.

$$F^2 = F_{Args_\Gamma}(F^1) = \{A_4, A_5, A_9, A_{14}, A_{16}, A_{15}, A_2, A_{13}, A_{12}\}$$

A_{12} is only one argument to be added to F^1 since it is attacked by A_1, A_7 and A_{10}, but it is not defeated by A_1 and A_{10} since it indirectly and socially attacks A_1, and it syntactically attacks A_{10}. A_7 defeats A_{12}, but it is strictly defeated by $A_2 \in F^1$.

$$F^2 = F^3 = ... = JustArgs_\Gamma.$$

A set of justified arguments is thought of as reflecting a present social wind about the death penalty institution. This suggests a promising possibility of applying argument-based agent systems to decision or policy-making in the actual or virtual e-government system.

Next, let us turn our eyes to the dialectical proof theory and see how a dialogical tree of A_{12} is constructed. A_7 is only one argument defeating A_{12} among $Args_\Gamma$. However, it is strictly defeated by A_2 in $Args_\Gamma$. The dialogue stops there since there is no arguments defeating A_2. Therefore we say that

A_{12} is dialogically justified and the consequent $assent(death\_penalty) : \mathbf{f}$ of the argument A_{12} is a dialogically justified conclusion.

Example 3 (A path to enlightenment). There are two agents who have a different idea on how to acquire wisdom. Then we assume some of the well-known religious or moral teachings as an conventional wisdom.

$C = \{emptiness : \mathbf{t}, no\_substance : \mathbf{t}, dependent\_arising : \mathbf{t}, everything\_$
$changing : \mathbf{t}\}$

The following is a knowledge base of an agent who aspires to enlightenment with some of the teachings of Buddhism [17], Daoism [13] and Zen [27]:

$Kb_1 = \{$
r_0: no_substance:$\mathbf{t}$,
r_1: dependent_arising:$\mathbf{t} \Leftarrow$ no_substance:$\mathbf{t}$,
r_2: everything_changing:$\mathbf{t}$,
r_3: emptiness:$\mathbf{t} \Leftarrow$ dependent_arising:$\mathbf{t} \wedge$
        everything_changing:$\mathbf{t}$ (Initial Buddhism),
r_4: spiritual_enlightenment:$\mathbf{t} \Leftarrow$ emptiness:$\mathbf{t}$,
r_5: spiritual_enlightenment:$\mathbf{t} \Leftarrow$ attain_wisdom:$\mathbf{t}$,
r_6: attain_wisdom:$\mathbf{t} \Leftarrow$ remove_knowledge:$\mathbf{t}$ (Daoism),
r_7: remove_knowledge:$\mathbf{t} \Leftarrow$ persist_in_things:$\mathbf{f}$,
r_8: persist_in_things:$\mathbf{f} \Leftarrow$ have(worldly_desire):$\bot$,
r_9: know_enough:$\mathbf{t}$,
r_{10}: everything_connected:$\mathbf{t} \Leftarrow$ dependent_arising:$\mathbf{t}$(Buddhism),
r_{11}: everything_connected:$\mathbf{t}$,
r_{12}: persist_in_things:$\mathbf{f} \Leftarrow$ everything_connected:$\mathbf{t}$,
r_{13}: persist_in_things:$\mathbf{f} \Leftarrow$ know_enough:$\mathbf{t}$,
r_{14}: training:$\mathbf{t}$,
r_{15}: have(worldly_desire):$\bot \Leftarrow$ training:$\mathbf{t}$,
r_{16}: meditation:$\mathbf{t}$,
r_{17}: have(worldly_desire):$\bot \Leftarrow$ meditation:$\mathbf{t}$(Zen Buddhism). $\}$

The next may be a worldly agent's knowledge base.

$Kb_2 = \{$
r_1: remove_things:$\mathbf{f} \Leftarrow$ add_things:$\mathbf{t}$,
r_2: have(worldly_desire):$\mathbf{t}$,
r_3: add_things:$\mathbf{t} \Leftarrow$ have(worldly_desire):$\mathbf{t}$,
r_4: attain_knowledge:$\mathbf{t} \Leftarrow$ add_things:$\mathbf{t}$,
r_5: attain_wisdom:$\mathbf{t} \Leftarrow$ attain_knowledge:$\mathbf{t}$. $\}$

The noble truths from syncretism finally brings a way to spiritual_enlighten_ment:$\mathbf{t}$ through attainning wisdom by means of training and meditation. It is a justified conclusion that defeated a way of attainning wisdom through simply attaining knowledge.

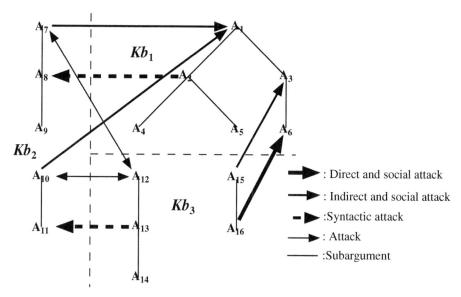

Fig. 2. An example of the attack relation in a multiple theory $\Gamma = \{Kb_1, Kb_2, Kb_3\}$ with C.

8   Incorporation of Dialectics into Argumentation

We have attempted to incorporate some aspects of Hegelian and Marxist dialectics in which the extended logic programming language was employed as the knowledge representation language for argumentation [23, 30, 24, 25]. Among other things, the three laws of the dialectics: (1) the unity of opposites, (2) the transformation of quantity into quality, and (3) the negation of the negation, in particular, are considered most useful for argument-directed computation as well just as they are prominent notions for explaining a social or historical developmental process from contradictions. In this section, we briefly present an idea of introducing dialectical reasoning or thought to our argumentation model. We will embody the dialectical dynamism in relation to argumentation as follows. In the dialectical proof theory of our argumentation framework, the argumentation proceeds with mutually casting arguments and counterarguments, resulting in 'justified' (sort of 'win') or 'overruled' (sort of 'lose') of the either side. However, if an argument has not been settled, it might be better or necessary for the both sides to attain an agreement (consensus) satisfactory to some extent rather than leaving it unsettled, proposing a dialectical consensus. This is obviously a way to reach truth by arguments (dialogue), and are sort of inventive and/or creative social processes in the sense that they cannot be attained by other types of reasoning such as deduction, induction, abduction and analogy.

We will just sketch our tentative suggestion towards dialectical reasoning in a consistent way with our tetralemma-based argumentation. Suppose that the issue is of the form $A : \mathbf{t} \wedge B : \mathbf{f}$, and the first part $A : \mathbf{t}$ is justified by the argument, but the second part $B : \mathbf{f}$ is overruled by the argument. Then if $B : \perp$

is justified by an opponent's argument, the Aufheben process (a sort of oracle) lifts up the conflict and proposes $A : \mathbf{t} \wedge B : \bot$ as a dialectical agreement. This is a realization of one aspect of the dialectics by Hegel, that is, the logical development of thought or reality through thesis and antithesis to a synthesis of these opposites. The Hegelian dialectic accepts the contradiction as a real aspect of the world, which is continually overcome and continually renews itself in the process of change. The above temporal agreement might be challenged by other agents all the time in the future. Then, all the processes may be viewed as the developmental process by the law of the negation of the negation. (Interested readers should refer to [24] for another example in a series of arguments on the pros and cons of gene-altered crops and foods, such as genetically modified corn). As to the law of the transformation of quantity into quality, we will need to interleave it in the processes of applying the dialectical laws of (1) and (3) by paying special attention to the quantity parameter included in knowledge base.

9   Concluding Remark and Future Work

Starting with the quest for the meanings of the tetralemma overlooked so far, we arrived at a logic of argumentation based on the tetralemma. We should note that it is not a simply extended argumentation framework in which arguments can be done with multi-valued knowledge bases, but it allows for Eastern arguments as well as Western arguments. It is aimed at achieving a fusion of Eastern and Western reasoning in argumentation. The main technical contributions of the paper are summarized as follows: (1) the elucidation of the various meanings of the tetralemma, (2) the use of the tetralemma in knowledge representation and argumentation, (3) the introduction of difference as a momentum of argumentation.

We have incorporated many philosophical ideas into the argumentation framework for agents. But theoretically, we would say that if we depicts the research program as 'Argument model = Argumentation framework + Fixpoint semantics × Dialogical proof theory', our theoretical contribution mainly lies in the Argumentation framework, as far as we employ Dung's fixpoint theory for argumentation semantics and Prakken's dialogical system for argumentation proof theory as a stable developmental scheme of argumentation. Here it is noted that we analogize 'Argument model = Argumentation framework + Fixpoint semantics × Dialogical proof theory' with 'Theory = Axiom + Logic (semantics and proof theory)' in the scheme of traditional logic. Natural number theory and group theory, for example, only differ in the axiom part and share the logic part.

We hope that what we have attempted here could lead to bridge the gulf of incommensurability between at least Occidental and Oriental schemata and notations. For our argumentation framework, we have taken a syncretic or eclectic approach to the fusion of Eastern and Western logical argumentation. We think that it makes the best of both worlds. Both the combination of Western and Eastern rationalism would be useful for decision-making in the agent society as well as in the human society. Only either of them will lead to the cul-de-sacs.

In the future, we are going to introduce a more fruitful and versatile rebuttal relation based on bilattices which fuses two axes: the amount of knowledge and the measure of truth in the four-valued lattice *Four*. The tetralemma-based logic of argumentation begins where logos ends just as fuzzy logic begins at the eastern edge where western logic ends. Of course we admit that there is more East in the West than meets the eye.

Acknowledgments

We would like to thank the anonymous reviewers, and the editors and authors of this volume, who contributed to increase the quality of this paper through their both technical and philosophical reviews.

References

1. Arieli, O. and Avron, A.: The Value of the Four Values, Artificial Intelligence, pp. 97-141, 1998.
2. Belnap, D. D.: How a Computer should Think, in Ryle G.(ed.): Contemporary Aspects of Philosophy, Oriel Press, pp. 30-56, 1977.
3. Belnap, D. D.: A Useful Four-Valued Logic, in Dunn, J. M. and Epstein, G.(eds.): Modern Uses of Multiple-Valued Logic, D. Reidel Pub. Comp., pp. 8-37, 1977.
4. Bharadwaja, V.: Form and Validity in Indian Logic, Indian Institute of Advanced Study, 1990.
5. Blair, A. H. and Subrahmanian, V. S.: Paraconsistent Logic Programming, Theoretical Computer Science, Vol. 68, pp. 135-154, 1989.
6. Chesnevar, C. I., Maguitman, A. G. and Loui, R. P.: Logical Models of Argument. ACM Computing Surveys, Vol. 32, No. 4, pp. 337-383, 2000.
7. Cousineau, P.: *The Art of Pilgrimage*, Conari Press, 1998.
8. Dung, P. M.: An Argumentation Semantics for Logic Programming with Explicit Negation, Proc. of 10th Int. Conference on Logic Programming, pp. 616-630, 1993.
9. Dung, P. M.: On the Acceptability of Arguments and its Fundamental Role in Nonmonotonic Reasoning, Logic Programming and N-person Games, Artificial Intelligence, Vol. 77, pp. 321-357,1995.
10. Dunn, J. M.: Intuitive Semantics for First-Degree Entailment and Coupled Trees, Philosophical Studies, Vol. 29, pp. 149-168, 1976.
11. Jayatilleke, K. N.: The Logic of Four Alternatives, Philosophy East and West, Vol. 17, pp. 69-83, 1967.
12. Kifer, M. and Subrahmanian, V .S.: Theory of Generalized Annotated Logic Programming and its Applications, J. of Logic Programming, Vol. 12, pp. 335-397, 1992.
13. Laozi: Dao De Jing, The book of the Way (translation and commentary by Roberts, M.), Univ. California Press, 2001.
14. Lloyd, L.W.: Foundations of Logic Programming, Springer-Verlag, 1984.
15. Loui, R.P.: Defeat Among Arguments: A System of Defeasible Inference, Computational Intelligence, Vol. 3, No. 2, pp. 100-106, 1987.
16. Murti, T. R. V.: The Central Philosophy of Buddhism - A Study of the Madhyamika System -, George Allen and Unwin Ltd., 1960.

17. Nāgārjuna: The Fundamental Wisdom of the Middle Way, Nāgārjuna's Mūlamadhyamakakārikā (translated and commented by Garfield, J. L.), Oxford University Press, 1995.
18. Nisbett, R. E.: The Geography of Thought: How Asians and Westerners Think Differently... and Why, The Free Press, 2003.
19. Prakken, H. and Sartor, G.: Argument-based Extended Logic Programming with Defeasible Priorities, J. of Applied Non-Classical Logics, Vol. 7, No. 1, pp. 25-75, 1997.
20. Raju, P. T.: The Principle of Four-Cornered Negation in Indian Philosophy, Review of Metaphysics, Vol. 7, pp. 694-713, 1954.
21. Regan, T.: Defending Animal Rights, Univ. Of Illinois Press, 2001.
22. Ruegg, D. S.: The Uses of the Four Positions of the Catuṣkoṭi and the Problem of the Description of Reality in Mahayana Buddhism, J. of Indian Philosophy, Vo. 5, pp. 1-71, 1977.
23. Sawamura, H., Umeda, Y. and Meyer, R. K.: Computational Dialectics for Argument-based Agent Systems, Proc. of the Fourth International Conference on MultiAgents Systems (ICMAS'2000), IEEE Computer Society, pp. 271-278, 2000.
24. Sawamura, H.: Computational Realization of Dialectics by Argumentation, Working Notes of the IJCAI'2001 Workshop on Inconsistency in Data and Knowledge, pp. 50-59, 2001.
25. Sawamura, H., Yamashita, M. and Umeda, Y.: Applying Dialectic Agents to Argumentation in E-Commerce, Electronic Commerce Research, Vol. 3, pp. 297-313, 2003, Kluwer Academic Publishers, Netherlands.
26. Singer, P.: Animal Liberation, New York Review of Books, 1975.
27. Suzuki, D. T.: The Zen Doctrine of No-Mind, edited by C. Humphreys, Samuel Weiser, Inc., 1972.
28. Takahashi,T., Umeda, Y. and Sawamura, H.: Formal Argumentation Frameworks for the Extended Generalized Annotated Logic Programs, 7th International Conference on Knowledge-Based Intelligent Information and Engineering Systems (KES'2003), Lecture Notes in Artificial Intelligence, Vol. 2773, Springer-Verlag, pp. 28-38, 2003.
29. Tarski, A.: A Lattice-Theoretical Fixpoint Theorem and its Application, Pacific Journal of Mathematics,Vol. 5, pp. 85-309, 1955.
30. Umeda, Y., Yamashita, M., Inagaki, M. and Sawamura, H.: Argumentation as a Social Computing Paradigm, Proc. of 3rd Pacific RIM Int. Workshop on Multi-Agents (PRIMA'2000), Lecture Notes in AI, Vol. 1881, pp. 46-60, 2000.
31. Umeda, Y., Takahashi, T. and Sawamura, H.: An Argumentation Framework based on Paraconsistent Logic, J. of Artificial Intelligence of Japan, Vol. 19, No. 2, pp. 83-94, 2004. (in Japanese).
32. Yamauchi, T.: Logos and Lemma, Iwanami, 1974. (in Japanese).

Agent-Based Support System
for Project Teaming for Teleworkers

Kenji Sugawara

Department of Information and Network Science, Chiba Institute of Technology
2-17-1, Tsudanuma, Narashino-shi, Chiba-ken 275-0016 Japan

Abstract. Telework is becoming an important aspect of our social life, and it is raising many new problems for us to solve, such as how to match the most appropriate teleworkers to the most appropriate positions of a project, thus dynamically organizing a project team (*Optimal Project Teaming*) in a huge telework community. The objective in this paper is to propose a concept of a web-based and agent-based support system for project teaming carried out in a huge telework community, and develop a prototypical system based on the concept. We defined a model of project teaming in telework community, and pointed out current problems in web-based job matchmaking. Next, we proposed a concept of agent-based support system for project teaming which consists of an agent-based job matchmaking process and an elaborating process of the result by collaborative agents. The domain-specific heuristics used in the agent-based support process are formalized, and each agent in two processes is designed. Finally, a prototypical system based on the design is demonstrated.

1 Introduction

In recent years, IT has become an integral component of every aspect of our social infrastructure. Our lifestyle now includes new activities, such as teleworking [1][2], e-commerce, and even e-government. It also includes new problems for us to solve, such as searching in an exploding infosphere and the need for intelligent information filtering.

The agent technology and other related technologies are increasingly expected to serve as effective solutions to the above problems that are caused by immature IT [3][4]. Agent-based applications, such as matchmaking and web-search applications [5], are continuously developing and maturing through the course of research and experiments.

There have been many researches to aid the matchmaking process among service providers and service requesters using intelligent agents. For example, the Intelligent Software Agent Group at CMU has developed several matchmaking systems [6][7] for an agent to find another who has the desired ability to carry out a task. Also, researchers in the Market-Based Method Group at the University of Pennsylvania are trying to use market-based methods such as auctions to help the service requester find the best service provider[8][9].

M.W. Barley and N. Kasabov (Eds.): PRIMA 2004, LNAI 3371, pp. 279–290, 2005.

The goal of our project is to develop an agent-based system to support teleworking activities. Telework includes the following two categories:

(1) A work style of a virtual enterprise composed either of geographically separated departments within the same company or of departments of different companies.
(2) A work style of a temporary and dynamic organization, which is formed by small companies and individual teleworkers in order to gain and fulfill projects.

Currently, there are almost 4 million teleworkers in Japan and about 28 million teleworkers in the US. It is reported that the number of teleworkers in the world in following years will increase greatly. Telework is becoming an important aspect of our social life and, at the same time, it is raising many new problems for us to solve. One problem related to the second category of telework, which is also the focus of our research, is how to match the most appropriate teleworkers to the most appropriate positions of a project, thus dynamically organizing a project team (*Optimal Project Teaming*). This is an important service to support people in a huge teleworking community.

The objective in this paper is to propose a concept of a web-based and agent-based support system for project teaming carried out by the second category of teleworkers, and develop a prototypical system based on the concept. In section 2, we formalized a model of Project Teaming in Telework Community, and pointed out current problems in web-based job matchmaking in section 3. In section 4, we proposed a concept of agent-based support system for project teaming in a huge telework community, which consists of an agent-based job matchmaking process and a elaborating process of the result by collaborative agents. The heuristics used in the agent-based support process is formalized in section 5. In section 6, each agent in two processes is designed. Prototypical system based on the design is explained in section 7.

2   Project Teaming in Telework Community

In a telework community, teleworkers may cooperate and/or compete with one another for contracts. Every task of a project can be delivered by matchmaking between teleworkers. Thus, a project team can be formed dynamically by distributed teleworkers. For example, when a teleworker becomes a job consignor of a project, who we call a employer in the project team, he can divide the project into many tasks and consigns those jobs he cannot finish individually to other teleworkers by using the matchmaking system. When such action happens in a hierarchy (a teleworker takes a contract as a worker and consigns some of his tasks out as a employer, as shown in Fig. 1), a project team can be formed. The relationships can be seen as a tree. Such a process is called Project Teaming. The team is dynamic because of the short-term relationship between employers and workers. Teams organized in this way can be very distributed. In the above project teaming process, how efficiently the matchmaking agents work affects the efficiency of the process greatly.

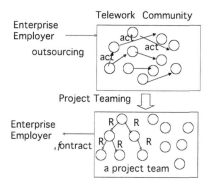

Fig. 1. Project Teaming in Telework Community

3   Current Problems in Web-Based Job Matchmaking

There are many web portals that provide information and simple utilities to help tele-workers find jobs and/or workers. Information provided on web portals is public information. Information not available on web portals which needs to be made clear through contacts and negotiations by teleworkers is non-public information. A common scenario of contract making based on the current information and existing technology provided by web portals might be (as shown in Fig. 2): A teleworker searches the portal and makes a list of contract candidates. He then uses email, telephone, or other means to contact each candidate on the list to obtain non-public information. According to the public and non-public information he obtains, he will make his decisions. In this process, we see the following two kinds of burdens for teleworkers,

(1) There is a great deal of information to check before deciding on a list of appropriate contract candidates.
(2) It is very time-consuming for a teleworker to obtain non-public information.

Our system aims to remove these burdens in the job matchmaking process in project teaming defined in section 2.2 by having intelligent agents maintain non-public information and providing an agent-based matchmaking system.

4   Overview of Agent-Based Support System for Project Teaming

The structure of the proposed support system is shown in Fig. 3. It consists of two layers of agent spaces. The lower layer called Job-Matchmake-Agent Space (**JMAS**) is a set of agents and databases. This agent space JMAS is a place where each agent carries out Job-finding tasks for a worker, which is collaborating with agents which carry out Worker-finding tasks for employers. In order to deal with large number of job-requests and worker-requests in JMAS, the function of the agents and the protocols between agents are designed simply to carry out a job matchmaking process in practically short interval. The upper layer called Elaborating-Agent Space (**EAS**) is a set of agents which act for workers and employers to elaborate job matchmaking

Fig. 2 Web-based Job Matchmaking Support System

information which gained by agent's activities in JMAS using heuristics of workers and employers. We call the job request information on heuristics used in JMAS as **primary information**, and worker request information used in EAS as **secondar information**.

JMAS consists of the following agents;

(1) Job Search Agent (JSA)

When JSA receives a Primary Job Request (**PJR**) from a Worker Agent (**WA**) in EAS, JSA writes Job Request Information (**JRI**) which is included in the PJA into JRI Database (**JRIDB**). Then JSA searchs Worker Request Information (**WRI**) from WRI Database (**WRIDB**) to make a List of Job Candidate (**LJC**) based on the Job Evaluation Criteria (**JEC**) which is also included the PJA. After making a LJC, JSA query the rank of JRI of itself in JRIDB for all Worker Search Agents (**WSA**) included in the LJC. A LJC which includes pairs of a job candidate and self rank of the job candidate is sent back to the WA.

(2)Worker Search Agent (WSA)

When WSA receives a Primary Worker Request (**PWR**) from a Employer Agent (**EA**) in EAS, WSA writes WRI which is included in the PWR into WRIDB. Then WSA searchs JRI in JRIDB to make a list of JRIs ranked by Worker Evaluation Criteria (**WEC**) included in the PWR. When a JSA ask the rank of it self for the WSA, the WSA sends back the rank it has made to the JSA.

Upper layer EAS consists of the following agents;

(3)Worker Agent (WA)

When WA receives Job Request (JR) from a worker via a user interface, WA generates a PJR and Secondary Job Request (**SJR**) from the JR. The generated PJR is sent to the corresponding JSA. SJR includes the worker's heuristics to elaborate a LJC from JSA such as elaboration strategy and criteria. After elaborating the LJC, the results are sent to the worker.

(4)Employer Agent (EA)

When EA receives Worker Request (WR) from an employer via a user interface, EA generates a PWR and Secondary Worker Request (**SWR**) from the WR. The PWR is sent to the corresponding WSA. SWR includes the employer's heuristics to elaborate a LJC collaborating with WAs.

The details of design of the agents and the database will be discussed in the later part.

5   Domain Specific Model of Job Request and Worker Request

5.1   Representation of Job Request

JR is defined by a pair of a primary job request PJR and a secondary job request SJR,

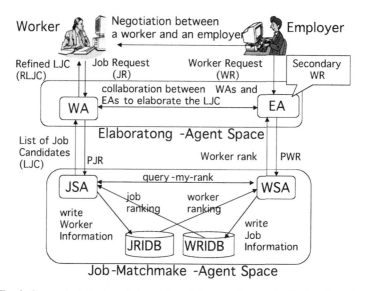

Fig. 3. Conceptual Design of Agent-based Support System for Project Teaming

$$JR = < PJR, SJR >.$$

PJR is defined by a pair of JRI and **JRH** (Job Ranking Heuristics),

$$PJR = <JRI, JRH >.$$

JRI is primary information of worker's request on desirable jobs to contract. JRI is described as a record which is written in a table in the JRIDB as the following form;

$$JRI = < jr\text{-}id, w\text{-}id, expiration, ITEM\text{-}LIST >.$$

Where "jr-id" is the identifier of the JRI, "w-id" is the identifier of the worker, "expiration" is a time when the request is expired, and ITEM-LIST is a list of items such as

$$item = < item\text{-}name, item\text{-}value >$$

The "item-name" will be used as keys for job matchmaking. For example, it includes "work skill"," requested salary ", "desirable work style", "desirable work place", "work carrier", and so on. The "item-value" should be written depending on the "item-name".

JRH defines heuristics of a worker to search candidates of jobs he wants to contract and to rank them into order of preference of the worker. JRH is described as a set of rules which represents heuristics depending on abilities, preference and carrier of each worker for ranking WRI. JRH is a program of domain-specific and worker specific heuristics, which is described a set of rules which represents heuristics depending on abilities, preference, carrier of each worker for ranking WRI, and is interpreted by the JSA to search WRIDB and to make a ranking of the searched list of WRI. The program is described as a set of rules which is interpreted by a production system which is implemented in JSA and executed actions designated by the worker to achieve the task of search and rank. The reason why the RHF is programmed by production model is the followings;

(a) (a)Because it is difficult for the designer of this support system to define the universal evaluation function to rank the set of WRI for every worker, the criteria of searching WRIDB and ranking candidate retrieved from WRIDB should be defined depending on the heuristics of each worker.

(b) (b)Because there are many areas of jobs to support, enormous volume of WRI in each area of job and heterogeneous representation of WRI, mathematical model approach to designing matchmaking mechanism to deal with huge and heterogeneous requests does not seem to be practical to develop this kind of support system.

SJR is a set of secondary job requests to elaborate a LJC in order to reduce burdens of the worker's negotiation with employers who are included in the LJC. The SJR is also a set of rules as well as RHF and consists of several kinds of heuristics such as analysis of LJC which is set back from JSA, decision of items to elaborates, strategy of elaboration with corresponding EA and so on.

5.2 Representation of Worker Request

WR is defined by a pair of a primary worker request PWR and a secondary worker request SWR,

$$WR = <PWR, SWR>.$$

PWR is defined by a pair of WRI and **WRH** (Worker Ranking Heuristics),

$$PWR = <WRI, WRH>.$$

WRI is primary information of employer's request on desirable workers to employ. WRI is described as a record which is written in a table in the WRIDB as the following form;

$$WRI = <wr\text{-}id, e\text{-}id, expiration, item\text{-}list>$$

where "wr-id" is the identifier of the WRI, "e-id" is the identifier of the employer, "expiration" is a time when the request is expired and ITEM-LIST is a list of items such as

$$\text{item} = <\text{item-name, item-value}>$$

The "item-name" includes "necessary work skill", "proposed salary", "work style", "work place", "desirable work carrier", and so on. The "item-value" should be written depending on the "item-name".

WRH defines heuristics of an employer to search and rank workers into order of preference of the employer. WRH is a program of domain-specific amd employer specific heuristics whichh is also described as a set of rules and works like JRH. When WSA receive a message of query-ranking from JSA, WSA sends back the rank of the JRI of the JSA which is ranked in the previous action to the JSA.

SWR is a set of secondary worker requests to collaborate with WA to notify requested information to an EA which ask secondary information to be used for elaborating its LJC. The SWR is not provided for the WSAs in JMAS, because they can not be formalize in the form of table of a database or the employer don't want to open the information in the teleworking community. SWR is described as a set of rules to analyse an request from a WA and decide the content of responding message according to situation of matchmaking.

5.3 Model of Elaboration of LJC

Let p be a name of worker who is supported by WA[p] and JSA[p], and let LJC[p] be a LJC sent by JSA[p]. LJC[p] is an ordered list of pairs of $<$ WRI[q], R[q]$>$ where q is a name of an employer who propose the WRI[q], WRI[q] is a WRI proposed by q and R[q] is a rank of JRI[p] in the ordered list of JRIs which is made by WSA[q]. O(WRI[q]) is a rank of WRI[q] in the ordered list LJC[p]. Let sum[p,q] be a sum O(WRI[q]) + R[q] in LJC[p] and let MinP(LJC[p]) be a pair of $<$ WRI[q], R[q]$>$ of which sum[p,q] is the minimum in the LJC[p]. Let MinN (LJC[p]) be O(WRI[q]) + R[q] of the MinP(LJC[p]).

The criterion of elaboration of LJC[p] which determines the behavior of WA is defined as follows;

[C1] If O(WRI[q]) = 1 & R[q] = 1 then WA[p] reports the LJC[p] to the worker p.

[C2] If MinN(LJC[p])$<=$ D[p] and N= O(WRI[q]) of MinP(LJC[p]) then WA[p] tries to elaborate the pair $<$JRI[p], WRI[q]$>$ collaborating with EA[q] where O(WRI[q])$<=$ N.

[C3] if MinN(LJC[p])$>$ D[p] then WA[p] sends a new PJR generated by JRH to JSA[p] again and reports it to the worker p.

D[p] is called "decision number" to determine the behavior of WA[p] which is stored in SJR. In the [C2], WA[p] modify the original JRI[p] to new JRI[p] depending on the content of $<$ WRI[q], R[q]$>$ by production system interpreting a set of rules in JRH. Receiving the message from WA[p], EA[q] generate a pair of a new rank of the JRI[p] and modified WRI[q]. After finishing this operation for every $<$ WRI[q], R[q]$>$ of which rank is higher than the rank on MinP(LJC[p]), WA[p] send the list of triple of < modified JRI[p], modified WRI[q], modified R[q]> to a worker p. The worker p analyse the elaborated LJC and determine the negotiation strategy to contract better job. Although the protocol for elaboration of the LJC is still simple for reducing the teleworkers proposed in this paper, we believe this support service is more useful for project teaming for teleworkers than the service shown in Fig.2 because they should keep watching, searching and checking the enormous volume of WRIs and JRIs. We are improving this protocol to reduce the burden of teleworkers more intellectually.

6 Design of Job Matchmaking Agents

6.1 Design of JSA and WSA in JMAS

Fig. 4 shows a state transition diagram of a JSA. It has three states: "wait PJR", "search & rank WRIDB" and "ask self rank". When JSA receives a PJR from a WA at a state "wait PJR", JSA writes JRI in the PJA into JRIDB and stored JRH in PJR into a production system of JSA. Then JSA change the state to "search & rank WRIDB". At the state, JSA searchs job candidate from WRIDB based on a search strategy designated by a worker's heuristics stored in the JRH. The set of job searched candidates is ranked in order of preference based on the worker's job evaluation criterion which is stored in JRH. The ordered list of candidates is called a partial LJC. When the partial LJC is completed, JSA changes the state to "ask self rank". At the state, JSA sends a message of "query-my-rank" to WSAs listed in the partial LJC. When the LJC is filled out as a list of pairs of WRI and self rank of WSA, JSA sends the completed LJC to WA and changes the state to "wait PJR".

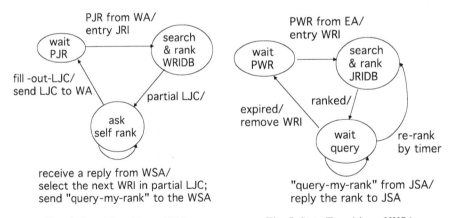

Fig. 4. State Transition of JSA   **Fig. 5.** State Transition of WSA

Fig.5 shows a state transition diagram of a WSA. It also has three states; "wait PWR", "search & rank JRDBI" and "wait query". When WSA receives a PWR from EA at a state "wait PWR", WSA writes WRI into WRIDB and stored WRH into a production system in WSA. Then WSA changes the state to "search & rank JRIDB".

At the state, WSA searchs worker candidates from JRIDB and ranks the searched set of JRIs based on the heuristics stored in the production system. When the ranked list of JRIs is completed, WSA changes the state to "wait query" and waits a message from JSAs. When WSA receives "query-my-rank" message from a JSA, it replies the rank of the JRI of JSA in the ranked list of it to the JSA. When the WRI of the WSA is expired, WSA removes the WRI from WRIDB and changes the state to "wait PWR".

6.2 Design of WA and EA in EAS

Fig.6 shows a transition diagram of WA. When WA receives JR at "wait JR", it sends PJR to JSA and changes the state to "wait LJC". When WA at "wait LJC" receives LJC, it activates JRH[D] to make a decision of the next action based on the criterion and changes the state to "decision". At "decision", when [C1] is decided, WA sends the original LJC to a worker, when [C2], WA activates JRH[E] and changes the state to "elaboration", and when [C3], WA sends a new PJR to JSA modified by a set of rules in JRH[D] and changes the state to "wait LJC". At "elaboration", when a WRI[q] is selected as a objective to elaborate, WA modifies the original JRI to a new JRI based on the JRH[E] and sends a message "elaborate(new JRI)" to the EA[q] and waits the reply message. After finishing the operation, WA sends the elaborated LJC (ELJC) to a worker and changes the sate to "wait JR".

Fig.7 shows a state transition diagram of EA. When EA receives "elaborate (JRI[p])" from WA[p] at the state "wait message", it activates the WRH. When the process of elaboration is finished, EA sends the new rank of modified JRI[p] and a modified WRI[q] to WA[p].

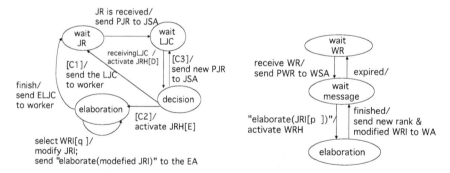

Fig. 6. State Transition of WA   **Fig. 7.** State Transition of EA

7 Prototypical System of Agent-Based Support System for Project Teaming for Teleworkers

Fig.8 shows a prototypical system developed based on the proposed model which consists of an EAS server and a JMAS server working in PCs. Agents in EAS and JMAS are developed using an agent framework named DASH which provides an agent programming language R-DASH and a virtual machine DASHVM to execute multi-agent systems programmed by the language. Architecture of a DASH agent is shown in Fug.8, consisting of Communication Module CM, Knowledge Module KM and Action Module AM. CM sends and receives ACL with other agents and put the data parsed from the ACL to KM. KM is a simple production system which interprets a set of rules programmed using R-DASH. The data from CM is written in a working memory in the production system. AM is a set of procedures programmed using Java, which are invoked by a fired rule in the production system. The procedures are called "action" of an agent in DASH framework. For example, a database can be operated by KM using these interface programs stored in the AM as actions of the agent. A virtual machine DASHVM is developed using Java, and distributed agents working on a DASHVM can communicate with agents working on other DASHVMs distributed in a network.

An employer accesses a web interface program and creates an EA for a WR in EAS and a WSA in JMAS in this prototypical system. A worker also creates a WA and JAS to search a LJC and described his JR using the web interface. The JR and WR are dealt with by WA, JSA, EA and WSA and the search result LJC is informed to the worker. If the worker decide that he should organize a sub-project to carry out the contract as shown in Fig.1, then he create his EA and WSA newly as an employer, and wait contacts on job contract with workers.

In this empirical system, we have not developed an intelligent user interface for workers and employers. So, users should describe their JR and WR using R-DASH and SQL language via web interface as shown in Fig.8. An example of web interface to describe R-DASH is illustrated in Fig.9. It is a very difficult problem to acquire user's heuristics and describe it by a program language. Our next research plan is to develop such intelligent user interface.

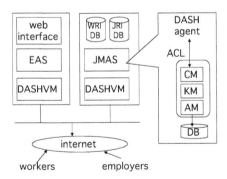

Fig. 8. Prototypical System of Agent-based Support System

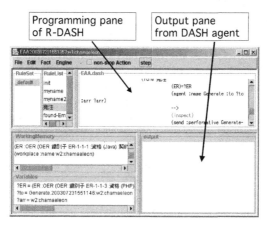

Fig. 9. User Interface provided in DASH framework

8 Conclusion

In this paper, we proposed a conceptual design of agent-based support system for project teaming for teleworkers, and developed a prototypical system based on the conceptual design. A goal of our project is to develop a framework to provide intelligent services for various kinds of and huge telework communities because telework is becoming an important aspect of our social life and the number of teleworkers is going to increase greatly all over the world. Therefore, to provide a better support service for teleworkers is emergent and challenging issues for creating the next generation work style.

For example, searching for work partners or employers using current web services imposes a heavy burden for especially individual telewprkers, because they have to search a very big list for several candidates, and then contact the candidates to obtain non-public information and to negotiate for a better situation. Compared to this, proposed system reduces the burdens of teleworkers partially supported by agents which act for them in the processes of searching job candidates and elaborating the information.

Agent-based matchmaking technologies have been studied in several projects which we should refer to in order to develop our system [7-10]. The studiies are focused on the technology based on the ontology-based matching approach, the game-theory-based matching approach and domain-independent approach to providing common matchmaking function. On the other hand, our design in this paper is domain-specific and worker/employer-specific approach to developing heuristic-based matchmaking based on the domain of teleworking. It may be very effective to integrate this approach to develop the practical support system for job matchmaking.

There are many problems to solve in the proposed design to use this system in the practical situation of teleworking. We should add the functions of user interface and security to EAS and of scalability to JMAS for example.

Acknowledgement

The author would like to thank the members of the Dynamic Networking project funded by the Japanese Society for Promotion of Science, for their contributions and comments on the conceptual design of this system. The DASH framework, which is used to develop the prototypical system, has been developed and improved by professor Shiratori, professor Kinoshita, professor Hara and their graduated students.

References

1. Bailey, D.E. and Kurland, N.B. "A review of telework research: Findings, new directions, and lessons for the study of modern work", Journal of Organizational Behavior, 23(4): 383-400
2. Anne E. Dunning, "Telecommuting Policy: Implementation and Efficacy" http://web.mit.edu/adunning/www/telecom/telecom.htm
3. Kenji Sugawara, "An Agent-Based Framework for Developing Flexible Distributed Systems", Proceedings of First IEEE International Conference on Cognitive Informatics (ICCI), 2002, pp. 101-106
4. Jennings, N.R., "An Agent-based Approach for Building Complex Software System", CACM, Vol.44, No.4, pp.35-41, 2001
5. G. Michael Youngblood, "Web Hunting: Design of a Simple Intelligent Web Search Agent", http://www.acm.org/crossroads/xrds5-4/webhunting.html
6. K. Decker, K.Sycara, and M. Williamson, "Middle-agents for the Internet", Proc. 15th IJCAI, 1997, pp.578-583
7. K.Sycara, J. Lu, M. Klusch, and S. Widoff, "Matchmaking among Heterogeneous Agents on the Internet", Proceedings of the 1999 AAAI Spring Symposium on Intelligent Agents in Cyberspace, March, 1999
8. Harker, P. T. and Ungar, L. H. "A Market-Based Approach to Workflow Automation" , In Proc. NSF Workshop on Workflow and Process Automation in Information Systems, Athens, GA, 1996.
9. Jose, R. A. and Ungar, L. H. "Auction-Driven Coordination for Plantwide Optimization", In Proc. Foundations of Computer-Aided Process Operation FOCAPO, 1998.
10. Sycara K., Widoff S., Klusch M. and Lu J., LARKS: Dynamic Matchmaking among Heterogeneous Software Agents in Cyberspace, Autonomous Agents and Multi-Agent Systems, 5, pp.173-203, 2002

An Interface Agent
for Wrapper-Based Information Extraction

Jaeyoung Yang[1], Tae-Hyung Kim[2], and Joongmin Choi[2]

[1] Openbase Inc., Seoul, Korea
jyyang@openbase.co.kr
[2] Department of Computer Science and Engineering,
Hanyang University,
Ansan, Kyunggi-Do 426-791, Korea
{tkim,jmchoi}@cse.hanyang.ac.kr

Abstract. This paper proposes a new method of building information extraction rules for Web documents by exploiting a user interface agent that combines the manual and automatic approaches of rule generation. We adopt the scheme of supervised learning in which the interface agent is designed to get information from the user regarding what to extract from a document and XML-based wrappers are generated according to these inputs. The interface agent is used not only to generate new extraction rules but also to modify and extend existing ones to enhance the precision and the recall measures of Web information extraction systems. We have done a series of experiments to test the system, and the results are very promising.

1   Introduction

Information extraction is the task of obtaining a particular fragment of a document that is relevant to the user interest. In general, information extraction is difficult mainly due to the heterogeneity inherent in different information sources. For example, Fig. 1 shows two different display styles of conference *CALL FOR PAPERS* pages, one with the list style and the other with the table style.

In order to cope with structural heterogeneity, the information-extraction systems usually rely on extraction rules tailored to a particular information source, often called the *wrappers*. In the previous methods of information extraction for semi-structured Web documents, wrappers are generated manually or automatically. In the manual wrapper generation method, the wrapper is written by a human expert who analyzes documents and builds rules. ARANEUS [1] and TSIMMIS [3] are the example systems that adopt the manual approach. The manual method reveals highly precise performance, but generally it is not scalable and effective.

On the other hand, the automatic method is known as the wrapper induction [4] in which the agent program analyzes a set of example documents and produces a wrapper through learning. Automatic wrapper induction can be based

M.W. Barley and N. Kasabov (Eds.): PRIMA 2004, LNAI 3371, pp. 291–302, 2005.

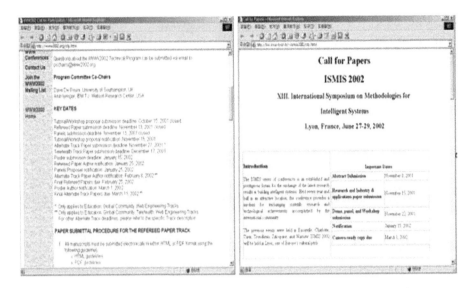

Fig. 1. Example of heterogeneous information sources.

on either heuristics or domain knowledge. Heuristic wrapper induction uses simple heuristics, e.g. *a dollar sign followed by a digit such as $250 denotes the price information*, to recognize the pattern of the target information. This approach has been adopted by most traditional wrapper-based information extraction systems such as SHOPBOT [2], STALKER [5], WHISK [6], and MORPHEUS [8]. Knowledge-based wrapper induction tries to solve the ineffectiveness of naive heuristics by defining and applying the domain knowledge during wrapper generation. Knowledge-based approach is expected to extract more features from the document than the heuristic approach. We have implemented knowledge-based information extraction systems named XTROS [9] and XTROS+ [10]. Overall, the automatic wrapper-generation method is scalable and effective than the manual one, but it also has difficulty in generating correct rules due to the diversity and the heterogeneity of Web information structures. Also, the generated rules are sometimes unreliable.

To take advantage of both the preciseness of manual extraction-rule construction and the scalability of wrapper induction, this paper proposes a new method of building information extraction rules for Web documents through the user interface agent. This method combines manual and automatic approaches of rule generation. We adopt the scheme of supervised learning in which a user interface agent is designed to get information from the user regarding what to extract from a document and XML-based wrappers are generated according to these inputs. The interface agent is used not only to generate new extraction rules but also to modify and extend existing ones to enhance the precision and the recall measures of Web information extraction systems.

This paper is organized as follows. Section 2 presents our approach of information extraction system based on the interface agent. Section 3 defines the format of XML-based extraction rules. The algorithms of rule learner and rule interpreter are described in Section 4. Section 5 assesses the system with some experimental results. Finally, Section 6 concludes with the summary and future direction.

2   Interface Agent

The system architecture of the information extraction system we are proposing is shown in Fig. 2. In this system, the user inputs are obtained and converted into training examples through the interface agent. The rule learner, also called the wrapper generator, analyzes the training data and produces information extraction rules. These rules play the role of the wrapper and stored in the rule repository. The rule interpreter executes the learned rules for real Web documents to extract the target information.

The interface agent acts as a mediator between the user and the rule learner in the task of recognizing the category of each data fragment to be extracted. In order to do this, the interface agent provides an environment in which the user can easily assign a category to a user-selected data item. As a result of a series of interactions via the interface agent, training examples are produced and supplied to the rule learner. The interaction between the user and the interface agent is accomplished by the drag-and-click action of the mouse and the popup menu, which enables the user to select a data item to be extracted and assign a category to it.

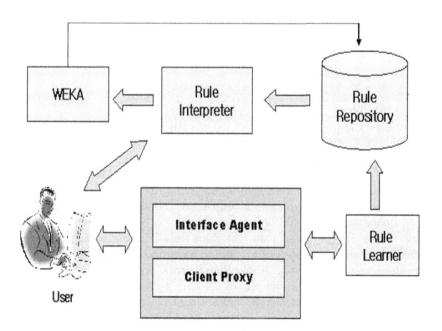

Fig. 2. The architecture of an information extraction system with an interface agent.

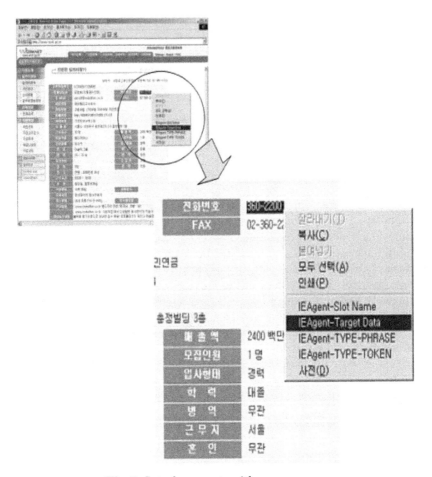

Fig. 3. Interface agents with popup menus.

A running example of the interface agent with the popup menu is shown in Fig. 3. The user first selects a data fragment from a Web document displayed in the interface by dragging it with the mouse. (In our example, a phone number is selected.) Then, the user clicks the right mouse button to bring up a special menu that enables the user to assign a category to the data item by selecting the *Slot-Name* menu and typing in a proper slot name in a dialog box. (In our example, *phone number* would be an appropriate slot name.) Finally, when the user selects the *Target-Data* menu, the data item is automatically associated with the slot name and stored as a training example. The interface agent also delivers the trigger information to the rule learner. A trigger is the symbol or word that helps to recognize the role of the target data item. In this example, the trigger for the *phone number* slot might be *TEL*, *Tel*, or *Telephone*. Triggers and slot names are determined according to specific application domains.

In short, the interface agent is required to have the following capabilities: recognition of mouse events initiated by the user, convenient display of Web

```
⟨Domain_name⟩
  ⟨Slot_name⟩
    ⟨pattern⟩
      ⟨id⟩ String ⟨/id⟩
      ⟨type⟩ TOKEN | PHRASE ⟨/type⟩
      ⟨trigger⟩ String ⟨/trigger⟩
      ⟨format⟩ [TRIG] String* TARG {String}* String* ⟨/format⟩
    ⟨/pattern⟩
        .. other patterns
  ⟨/Slot_name⟩
  .. other slots
⟨/Domain_name⟩
```

Fig. 4. Format of information extraction rules.

documents, and acceptance of user feedback. To facilitate these functions, the interface agent is implemented by extending popup menus of a Web browser(in our paper, the Microsoft Internet Explorer) and by employing a proxy server. Extending popup menus to the browser is realized by adding new events to the context menu of the Internet Explorer in the MS Windows registry. Once extending the popup menus, the user input committed to the interface agent is delivered to the proxy server that relays information to the rule learner. Likewise, all the menu handling events are processed in the proxy server.

3 IE Rule Format

Information extraction rules are written in XML for readability and maintainability. The format of rules used in this paper is shown in Fig. 4.

An extraction rule corresponds to a single domain. A rule consists of a set of slots with different slot names, and each slot consists of a set of information patterns. An information pattern, denoted by the `<pattern>` element, is the smallest unit of a rule, and is obtained from the user input. Patterns are incrementally added to a slot as more user inputs come, and the learning is performed based on this pattern information.

The `<pattern>` element consists of several subelements including `<id>`, `<type>`, `<trigger>`, and `<format>`. Among these, the value for `<trigger>` is obtained from the user input, and other values are determined automatically by analyzing the data. The `<id>` element denotes the identifier of a pattern. The `<type>` element indicates the structural type of the target data, and is defined as either TOKEN or PHRASE. Here, TOKEN means the target data must be separable as a single token in the document sentence, and PHRASE means the target consists of multiple words and the correct data can be extracted by partial matching. The `<trigger>` element plays the role of delimiter to determine whether the current rule should be applied to the target sentences. Only one trigger is assigned for

```
<Job_offer>
  <Company>
    <pattern>
      <id> companyName01 </name>
      <type> TOKEN </type>
      <trigger> (주) </trigger>
      <format> [TRIG] TARG </format>
      <format> TARG [TRIG] </format>
    </pattern>
    ... other patterns
  </Company>
  <From_to>
    <pattern>
      <id> from_to01 </id>
      <type> PHRASE </type>
      <trigger> 접수기간 </trigger>
      <format> [TRIG] : TARG {DATE} </format>
    </pattern>
    ... other patterns
  </From_to>
  ... other slots
</Job_offer>
```

Fig. 5. An example rule for job advertisement.

each pattern, but each slot may be associated with several triggers. This phenomenon handles the situation where particular information can be expressed differently with various terms. The <format> element describes the position of the target data and its structural characteristics. Here, [TRIG] is the reference to a <trigger> element in a pattern, TARG is the target information to be extracted, and {String} is a string that should be included in the target data or in the sentence. <format> is used in analyzing strings in the rule interpreter, and the system is able to extract the right information from a wide range of documents by defining multiple <format> elements.

Figure 5 is an example of information extraction rules generated from a real Web site for job advertisement. In this rule, the first pattern is related to the *company name*, and the second pattern is for the *application submission period*. As you can see in this rule description, the <trigger> element acts not only as the initiator of sentence analysis, but also as a delimiter that indicates the existence of a particular slot data by redescribing it in the <format> element.

4   IE Rule Learner and Rule Interpreter

The rule learner produces patterns of information extraction rules from the user inputs obtained through the interface agent. The information provided by the interface agent includes slot names, target data, and trigger information. By

```
procedure Learner(examples)
  let rule_set = { };
  for each slot:
    for each example in examples:
      patterns = pattern_learner(examples);
      add pattern to rule_set;
  return rule_set;


procedure pattern_learner(examples)
  let patterns = { };
  repeat for each example in examples
    receive input_data from user;
    if input_data is not null
    then find covers
      build pattern
      add pattern to patterns
    remove those examples in examples covered by pattern
  until examples is null
  return patterns
```

Fig. 6. Pattern learning algorithm by using the covering algorithm.

analyzing these data, the rule learner first determines whether the type of target data is TOKEN or PHRASE, and sets the value of the <type> element accordingly. Then, the rule learner finds the trigger and input data, identifies the relationship between the two, and sets the value of the <format> element. For example, in a document sentence *TEL: 031-400-5666*, if the target data is *031-400-5666* and the trigger is *TEL*, the value of <format> should be [TRIG]: TARG.

Basically, the rule learner uses a covering algorithm. In this algorithm, a set of training documents are collected, and every time a new pattern is produced, the learner calculates the covering value of the pattern. Here, the covering value of a pattern is the number of training documents from which the system can extract the target information successfully by using the pattern. According to this covering value, the learner decides whether the new pattern should be accepted or rejected. In our system, the threshold of covering value for accepting a new pattern is set to 2. Figure 6 describes the pseudo-code of pattern learning by using the covering algorithm.

The rule interpreter executes the rules obtained by the rule learner to extract the target information from real documents. The rule interpreter works as follows. First, the test documents are reconstructed as a set of sentences. Next, each sentence is analyzed to determine whether the trigger words occur in the sentence. Only the sentences that contain the triggers are selected, and by applying the value of the <format> element, it is determined if the structural

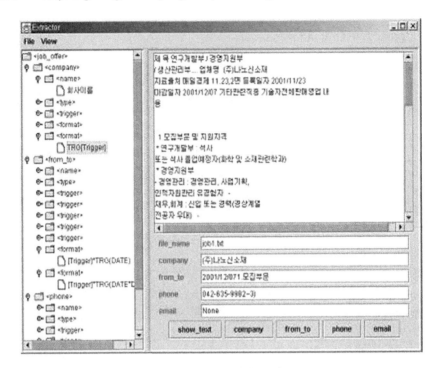

Fig. 7. A running screen of the rule interpreter.

characteristics of the target data is matched with the rule. If the matching is successful, `TARG` part which indicates the correct target data is extracted as a result.

The rule interpreter is implemented by using the XML DOM parser and the Java language. Figure 7 shows a running screen of the rule interpreter. In this figure, the left pane of the window shows the hierarchical structure of the generated XML rule, and the right pane shows the preprocessed document at the top and the result of information extraction at the bottom.

Rules are verified and refined by using the WEKA module [7] that uses the decision tree method. The rules are reconstructed by using the decision tree, and by this way, new rules can be generated. Adding new rules generated from the decision trees to the rule repository enhances the precision and recall measures. Also, the original rules can be verified by re-generating them by decision trees. Furthermore, learned rules can be modified by WEKA if they are not matched with the newly generated rules.

Figure 8 shows the input data including rules and sample data used by the WEKA module to produce decision trees. The attributes are those used in extracting slot values from learned patterns, and the data is produced by the rule interpreter.

```
@relation job.phone

@attribute type {TOKEN, PHRASE}
@attribute trigger {Tel, 문의, 전화}
@attribute format {[TRIG] TARG{PN}, [TRIG]*TARG{PN},
                   [TRIG]*:TARG{PN}}
@attribute rightAccess {yes, no}

@data

phrase,전화,[TRIG]*:TARG{PN},no
token,전화,[TRIG]*TARG{PN},yes
phrase,전화,[TRIG] TARG{PN},yes
....................................
```

Fig. 8. Rules and data used by the WEKA module.

5   Experimental Results

Performance of our system is evaluated for a collection of documents in three domains: online bookstores(Book), job advertisements(Job), and conference call for papers(CFP). For the Book domain, we choose 32 bookstores in the Internet, and collect five search-result pages from each store. Collected documents are divided evenly into training and test sets. For this domain, we extract the author, the publisher, and the price information. A similar document-collecting process is done for the Job domain, and we extract four kinds of target information including the company's name, phone number, and email address, and the job application deadline. For the CFP domain, we select the first 100 documents from the search results of Google for the conference call for papers, and divide them into 50 training documents and 50 test documents. The target information in this domain includes the submission deadline, the date for acceptance notification, and the date for camera-ready version submission.

Figure 9 shows the precision and recall measures for the three domains. For the Job domain described in Fig. 9(a), the precision and recall values are both over 80 percent in average. In particular, the measures are over 90 percent for the email address attribute, since there are only a few number of trigger words and also the format of the target data is limited, which makes the recognition easier. Since a single trigger exists for each pattern, the precision and recall measures get higher as there are more patterns. In the case of the phone number which is mostly represented in digits, the chances are that it can be mistakenly recognized as the submission deadline. In this case, the triggers play crucial role in distinguishing the two kinds of data.

Fig. 9(b) depicts the result for the CFP domain. Here, the measures for the paper submission deadline are good, so are the date for acceptance notification.

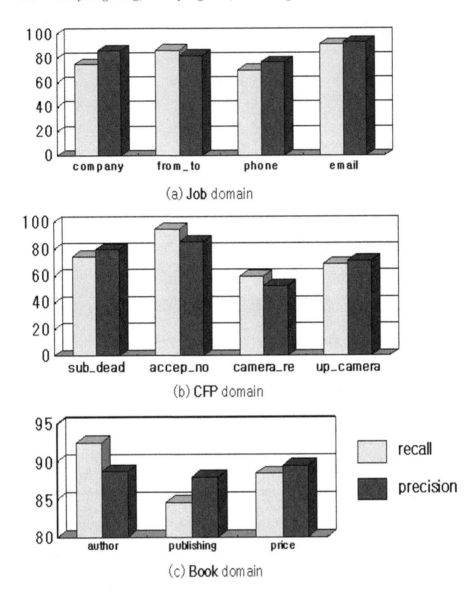

(a) **Job** domain

(b) **CFP** domain

(c) **Book** domain

Fig. 9. Experimental results for three domains.

But, the recognition of the date for camera-ready submission is not done well, since the word *final version* which rarely occurred in the training documents appeared frequently in the test documents. This is the result of overfitting of learning algorithm to the training data. To remedy this, we have used the WEKA module that performs the learning processing again to enhance the extraction performance of the system. In this case, by adding the word *final* as a new trigger in WEKA, the measures for the camera-ready attribute get better while the

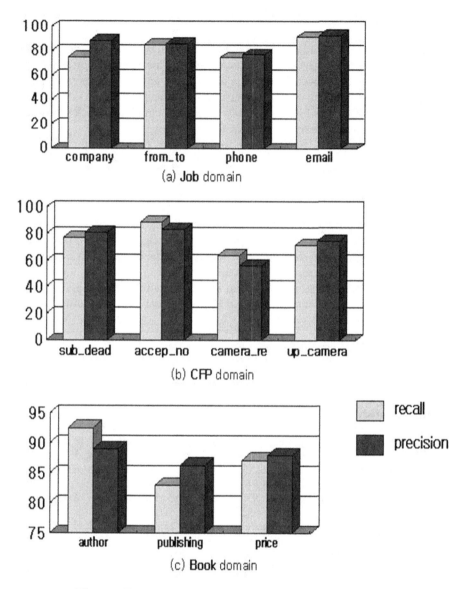

Fig. 10. Experimental results by using the WEKA module.

results for other attributes remain unchanged. This is reflected in the up-camera part of the figure, whereas camera-re indicates the original result.

To evaluate the effect of rule refinement by using the WEKA module more specifically, we test the system by adding new patterns obtained from the decision tree structure of WEKA to the original learned rules. The result is shown in Fig. 10. We found that in average only one or two new patterns are added to the original rule, which are effective enough to contribute to the improvement of 6% in recall and 1% in precision.

6   Conclusion

We have presented a new method of building information extraction rules for Web documents through the user-interface agent. This method combines the manual and automatic approaches of rule generation, and adopts the scheme of supervised learning in which a user interface agent is designed to get information from the user regarding what to extract from a document, and XML-based wrappers are generated according to these inputs.

In a prototype system that we have implemented, the user inputs are obtained and converted into training examples through the interface agent. The rule learner analyzes the training data and produces information extraction rules, and the rule interpreter executes the learned rules for real Web documents in order to extract the target information. Our prototype system shows good performance for a collection of documents in three different domains.

One of the limitations of our approach is that the triggers have to be rigourously handled, which means that the word comprising the trigger must be exactly matched to activate it. To resolve this, we are working on managing a semantic ontology for each domain to facilitate the semantic matching of trigger words. Also, we plan to employ a learning method that uses both positive examples and negative examples to avoid overfitting.

References

1. P. Atzeni, G. Mecca, P. Merialdo: Semi-structured and structured data in the Web: Going back and forth. Proc. ACM SIGMOD Workshop on Management of Semistructured Data (1997) 1–9
2. R. Doorenbos, O. Etzioni, D. Weld: A scalable comparison-shopping agent for the world wide web. Proc. Int. Conf. on Autonomous Agents (1997) 39–48
3. J. Hammer, H. Garcia-Molina, S. Nestorov, R. Yerneni, M. Breunig, V. Vassalos: Template-based wrappers in the TSIMMIS system. Proc. ACM SIGMOD Int. Conf. on Management of Data (1997) 532–535
4. N. Kushmerick: Wrapper induction: Efficiency and expressiveness. Artif. Intell. **118** (2000) 15–68
5. I. Muslea, S. Minton, C. Knoblock: A hierarchical approach to wrapper induction. Proc. Int. Conf. on Autonomous Agents (1999) 190–197
6. S. Soderland: Learning information extraction rules for semi-structured and free text. Machine Learning, **34** (1999) 233–272
7. I. Witten, E. Frank: *Data Mining: Practical Machine Learning Tools and Techniques with Java Implementations*, Morgan Kaufmann (1999)
8. J. Yang, E. Lee, J. Choi: A shopping agent that automatically constructs wrappers for semi-structured online vendors. Lecture Notes in Computer Science. **1983** (2000) 368–373
9. J. Yang, J. Choi: Knowledge-based wrapper induction for intelligent Web information extraction. In: N. Zhong, J. Liu, Y. Yao (eds.), *Web Intelligence*, Springer (2003) 153–172
10. J. Yang, J. Choi: Agents for intelligent information extraction by using domain knowledge and token-based morphological patterns. Lecture Notes in Artif. Intell. **2891** (2003) 74–85

Building Web Navigation Agents Using Domain-Specific Ontologies

Jaeyoung Yang[1], Hyunsub Jung[2], and Joongmin Choi[3]

[1] Openbase Inc., Seoul, Korea
`jyyang@openbase.co.kr`
[2] KT Corp., Daejeon, Korea
`flyhigh@kt.co.kr`
[3] Department of Computer Science and Engineering,
Hanyang University, Ansan, Korea
`jmchoi@cse.hanyang.ac.kr`

Abstract. This paper proposes a method of constructing navigation agents that provide more personalized Web navigation by exploiting domain-specific ontologies. In general, ontology is regarded as the specification of conceptualization that enables formal definitions about things and states by using terms and relationships between them. In our approach, Web pages are converted into concepts by referring to domain-specific ontologies which employ a hierarchical concept structure. This concept mapping makes it easy to handle Web pages, and also provides higher level classification information. The proposed navigation agent eventually recommends the Web documents that are associated with the concept nodes in the upper-levels of the hierarchy by analyzing the current Web page and its outwardly-linked pages.

1 Introduction

With the rapid growth of the Internet, people are facing the information overload that makes the users spend more time and put more efforts to find the information they need. To resolve this problem, the idea of *Web personalization* has been suggested by using the mining technology [8]. The mining methodologies that help the navigation by personalized information can be classified into Web content mining, Web usage mining, and ontology-based mining.

Webwatcher, Syskill&Webert, Letizia, and Webmate use the Web content mining technique. Webwatcher [5] can be considered as a tour guide that takes explicit goals from a user and recommends relevant hyperlinks. Syskill&Webert [10] gets explicit feedbacks from a user, and makes a decision whether a page is an interest based on the rank of page links. Additionally, this system recommends documents by retrieving them from the Lycos with the requesting queries built from a user profile. Letizia [7] is an interface agent system that recommends hyperlinked Web pages based on a user profile built from implicit feedback. Webmate [3] is a system based on a stand-alone proxy server that monitors user's behaviors, builds profiles, computes similarity measures, and recommends Web documents according to these measures.

M.W. Barley and N. Kasabov (Eds.): PRIMA 2004, LNAI 3371, pp. 303–316, 2005.
© Springer-Verlag Berlin Heidelberg 2005

WebPersonalizer [8, 9] combines the Web usage mining with the Web content mining in order to make more sophisticated recommendation. In this system, profiles are produced by the usage mining technique, and document weights are measured by the content mining technique. Another research on the personalization by using Web usage mining can be found in [11].

OBIWAN [2] uses ontologies to help navigation. This system is based on a personal ontology, and each site has an agent that communicates with regional agents which provide and characterize web pages in a local site.

However, most of previous researches about the Web personalization reveal many problems. First, most personalization methods only adopt lexical analysis by using term frequencies to measure the impact of words, without considering their semantic relations to other terms in the document. Second, they assume that user's information needs are fixed, only fail to cope with the frequent changes in user interests. Third, most systems require explicit inputs from the user about whether he or she has interests in the topic. This could be a burden to the user who would not want to interact with the system, and also the results may be subjective. Consequently, the performance of a system adopting this strategy may not get better without explicit inputs. Finally, for the systems using the Web mining techniques, extracting useful information itself is a hard work and the performance is not promising for frequently-changed Web pages.

We try to solve these problems by using an ontology-based recommendation agent. We propose a method of building Web navigation agents that facilitate effective browsing by providing personalized information for the domain of Web news sites in which the semantic structures of Web documents are clearly defined and the changes in contents occur frequently. By these agents, Web pages are classified according to the ontology that describes the semantic structures of pages. This classification leads the agents to identify semantic contents and relations contained in the pages, and grasp users' specific intentions while browsing. For recommendation, Web pages are fetched by a look-ahead search and those matched with user's need are selected as locally optimal pages. We use the selected pages to construct a user profile in order to provide more personalized and high level news articles that satisfy user's interests. The general architecture of our personalized Web navigation system is depicted in Fig. 1.

This paper is organized as follows. Section 2 explains problem domains and our views of optimal pages in Web navigation. Section 3 presents the ontology structure used in this paper. Section 4 describes recommendation and classification procedures using ontology. Section 5 describes the implementation and evaluation of the classification with some experimental results. Finally, Section 6 concludes with summary and future direction.

2   Web Navigation Using Hyperlinks

A model for the Web structure can be represented by a graph $G = \{V, E\}$, where each node in V denotes a Web page and each edge in E denotes a hyperlink between pages. The graph consists of a virtually infinite number of vertices

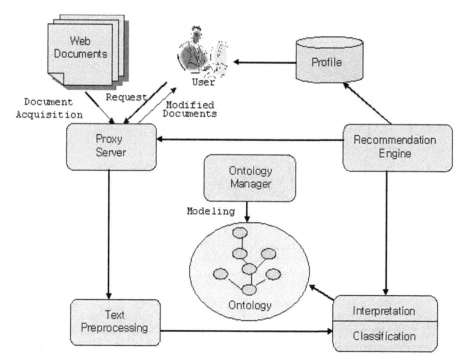

Fig. 1. Architecture for our personalized Web navigation system.

$V = \{v_1, v_2, \cdots\}$ and edges $E = \{e_1, e_2, \cdots\}$, so searching a particular page that satisfies the user's information need is an impractical task. To resolve this problem, we modify the model by redefining the graph as $G = SG_1 \cup SG_2 \cup \cdots$, meaning that the graph consists of an infinite number of subgraphs SG_i, but each subgraph has a finite number of nodes and edges. Each subgraph can be regarded as a local group of pages obtained by considering the point of current browsing. Our efforts are focused on finding a locally optimal page in a subgraph which contains the currently fetched page and has a reasonable number of nodes.

This subgraph model has different characteristics compared to the ordinary graph model, mainly due to the properties of the Web structure. First, while the graph model has a fixed start node, the subgraph model has a dynamic start node depending on the current page. Second, goal nodes are also fixed in the graph model, whereas goals in the subgraph model are changed according to the start node. Finally, the subgraph model does not have a fixed structure as in the graph model, rather its structure is changing according to time and network states.

In this paper, some assumptions are made in the course of finding and recommending the page that is most relevant to user's information need. First, at any point in browsing, the current page node may have hyperlinks to several pages with different weight values, and among these pages, we select the one with the largest weight value as a locally optimal page. We hope that if the

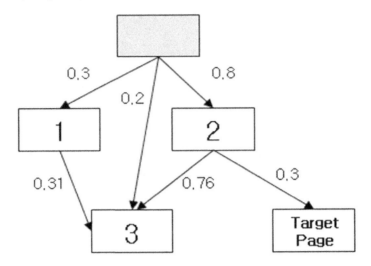

Fig. 2. Local Web structure with weighted links.

agent continues to chase locally optimal pages, we may end up with the globally optimal page. However, in reality, this may not be the case since the agent may be stuck with a local maximum that is not a global maximum. Figure 2 shows this problem graphically.

In this figure, a directed arc indicates that two nodes are connected by a hyperlink in the direction of the arrow. The number on each edge is the similarity value between the connected nodes. Suppose the shaded node in the figure denotes the current page the user is looking at, and the target page is an optimal page that has to be found. The agent searches a locally optimal page from the current page by examining the three hyperlinked pages in the next depth level. Since the link to the page 2 has the highest similarity score, the agent moves to it. At the node of the page 2, the agent will do the same operation, and moves to the page 3. In this case, although the target page is optimal, the agent selects other document in the graph as the optimal page. We will not mention how to solve this problem in detail in this paper, although we solve it by using an optimization strategy such as the hill-climbing search.

The second assumption is that even when the user switches to other pages by explicitly typing in the URL of a Web page during browsing, the agent knows the appropriate ontology used to convert the content of the page into a set of concepts. In other words, our agent is assumed to have a corresponding domain-specific ontology when the domain is changed by the user explicitly.

3   Ontology as a Knowledge Base

An ontology is defined as a *specification of conceptualization*, and is comprised of the *objects* and their *relationships* [4]. Also, an ontology is an axiomatic characterization of the meaning of a logical vocabulary. Hence, an ontology consists

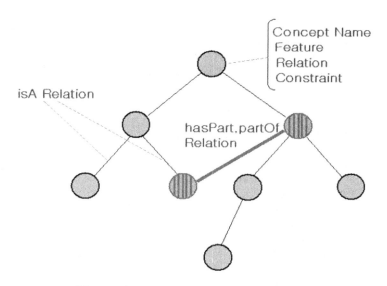

Fig. 3. The general structure of an ontology.

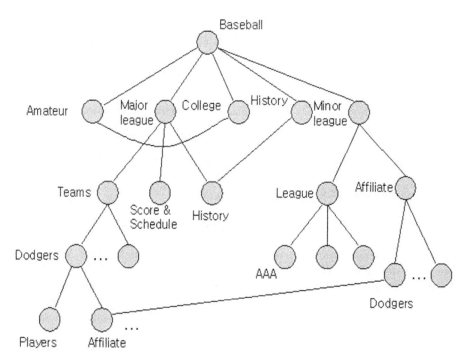

Fig. 4. Concept hierarchy for the *baseball* domain.

```
<Ontology>
<OntoDef>
<OntoName>Baseball</OntoName>
<Features>baseball,MLB,season,American,League,
           National,major,minor,game,score
</Features>
<Relations><Relations />
<Constraints > <Constraints />

   . . .

  <OntoDef>
  <OntoName>history</OntoName>
  <Features>basebal,histori,world,seri,
             award,record,hall,fame,star,post,mvp
  </Features>
  <Relations>hasPart (baseball-major league-history)
  </Relations>
  <Constraints> (all) followedBy (star)
  </Constraints>
  </OntoDef >

   . . .
</Ontology>
```

Fig. 5. Expressing hierarchical ontology by XML.

of a representative vocabulary for objects and relations that define the interrelationships between objects.

In this paper, we use an ontology as a knowledge base. The knowledge base is treated as a vocabulary that consists of logical terms and axioms. Our assistant agent is able to convert the contents in a page into a corresponding set of concepts. An advantage of this concept mapping is that the agent can provide the information about a Web page not by a sequence of frequently-occurring terms but by a hierarchy of concepts so that the agents can recognize what is contained in a page.

We focus on constructing the ontology for the classification of Web documents [6]. In order to facilitate the description and the classification of the hierarchical conceptual structure of Web pages, the ontology is represented by a hierarchy of nodes where each node denotes a *concept*, a *feature*, a *relation*, or a *constraint*. A concept is a name to represent a node. A feature consists of words and phrases (a sequence of words) to describe a concept. A relation describes the interrelationship between concepts by using OOP-like relationships such as *isA*, *partOf*, and *hasPart*. The *isA* relation defines a generalization or specialization connection, and *partOf* and *hasPart* relations define inclusion connections. A constraint has two conditions: *isRelatedTo* and *followedBy*. Closely related features or conditions are used to solve ambiguity in word-based document analysis to improve the accuracy. Figure 3 shows the general structure of an ontology.

Figure 4 shows an example ontology for the *baseball* domain, and Fig. 5 shows its XML representation. Here, *history* is defined as a child concept of *baseball* which is the topmost concept, and at the same time, another *history* is defined in the path of *baseball-major league-history*. This feature is realized in the XML representation by using the nested concept definitions and the constraint descriptions.

4   Navigation Agent as a Classifier

In this paper, the classification of Web pages is a task of mapping a document to a suitable node in the concept hierarchy. Documents are mapped to the most relevant node by navigating the concept hierarchy from the root node, and only those children nodes whose parent node is satisfied with the similarity measure are considered. Otherwise the last traversed node will be the proper node for the document. Clearly, a document is not necessarily mapped to a leaf node in the hierarchy. As a result, we are able to represent a concept hierarchy using a small number of nodes, and do more sophisticated recommendation using hierarchical classification. Our navigation agent can also provide high-level Web document recommendation using this concept hierarchy.

Equation (1) is the similarity measure function for the classification. A node with the highest score will be the relevant concept that is regarded as the class for a document.

$$Sim(Node, d) = \frac{\sum_{i=0}^{N} freq_{i,d}/Max_{l,d}}{N} \cdot \frac{V_d}{V} \tag{1}$$

In this equation, d is the current document, $Node$ is a node in the concept hierarchy, N is the total number of features, $freq_{i,d}$ is the frequency weight of the feature i in d, $Max_{l,d}$ is the maximum of all values of $freq_{i,d}$, V is the total number of constraints, and V_d is the number of satisfied constraints in d. Relations are also used in the course of classifying document in a way that, if a node has relationships with other nodes in terms of *partOf* or *hasPart*, the navigation agent measures the similarity including these relationships. Then, the agent records the last mapped node along with the path from the root to this mapped node in the user profile.

To recommend personalized Web documents, we use a user profile that reflects the user's interests and preferences. In the user profile, each interest is represented by a pair of information <P, R>, where P is the path for a mapped node from the root in the hierarchy after the classification, and R is the number of requests to the corresponding document for the same interest. In this way, the user profile can be regarded as a weighted ontology with the concept hierarchy in which a weight is represented by a number that reflects the degree of fitness to user interests. Figure 6 shows the structure of the user profile in which the paths are represented by bold lines and the number of requests is represented by a number inside a node.

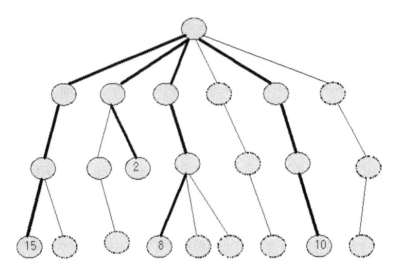

Fig. 6. The structure of the user profile.

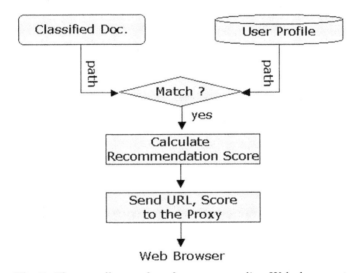

Fig. 7. The overall procedure for recommending Web documents.

Candidate documents are fetched by using the look-ahead search starting from the user-specified document. Recommendations are done based on a measure called the *recommendation score(RS)* that is calculated and assigned to each candidate document. Equation (2) shows how to measure the recommendation score for a document.

$$RS(d) = \sqrt{DD(d) \times PD(d)} \tag{2}$$

Fig. 8. An example page about baseball.

Here, DD denotes the *document distance* and PD denotes the *profile distance*. DD considers the distance between the node in the concept hierarchy that is mapped from the current document and the node mapped from the document obtained from look-ahead search. Equation (3) shows how to measure the document distance for a document. Here, $dist(d, d_i)$ denotes the difference in path length in the hierarchy between the current document d and the document d_i which is a result of the look-ahead search. (N is the collection of documents obtained from the look-ahead search.) Notice that the document distance is the location-based factor that considers only the node position in the concept hierarchy.

$$DD(d) = Max_i \left(\frac{1}{\log_2(dist(d, d_i) + 1) + 1} \right), d_i \in N \qquad (3)$$

The profile distance PD considers the profile information. Equation (4) shows how to measure the profile distance for a document.

$$PD(d) = Max_i \left(\frac{freq_{p,i}}{Max\ freq_{p,l}} \times \frac{1}{\log_2(Cdist(d, p)+1) \times \log_2(Wdist(d, d_i)+1)} \right) \qquad (4)$$

In this equation, $\frac{freq_{p,i}}{Max freq_{p,l}}$ normalizes the number of visits to the node(or the path to the node) which is associated with the document page. Also, $Wdist(d, d_i)$ is a Web distance that denotes the number of hyperlinks from the current doc-

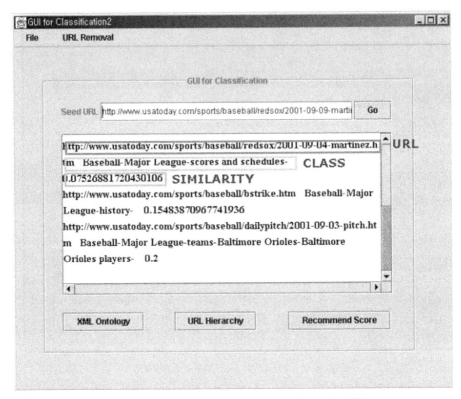

Fig. 9. An interface for extracting hyperlinks from the Web pages.

ument d to a candidate document d_i in the Web space, and $Cdist(d,p)$ is a concept distance that is the distance between the current document d and the node p in the concept hierarchy that reflects user's interest. As in Equation (3), d_i is a member of N.

We assume that the nearest document from the currently visiting node in the concept hierarchy is the most relevant page, so we assign a high RS score to this node. Weights are assigned differently by traversing the path from the current node to the root node. An advantage of using this strategy is that the navigation agent is able to recommend a concept in the upper level of the hierarchy. As the final step, the user gets the Web page that is regarded as relevant by the agent based on RS scores, and this recommended page is augmented with the links to other relevant documents. The overall procedure for recommending Web documents by using user profiles is depicted in Fig 7.

5   Empirical Results

The navigation agent recommends hyperlinks, annotated with a concept hierarchy. An example page about baseball is shown in Fig. 8, from which the system extracts hyperlinks by using the interface as shown in Fig. 9.

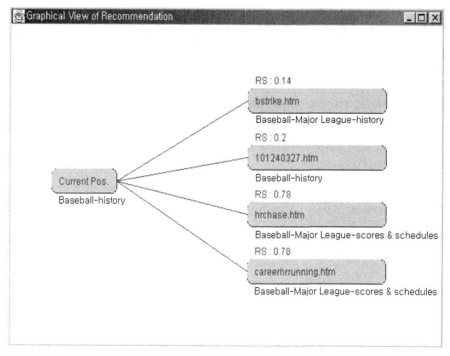

Fig. 10. The result of recommending four high-scored documents.

Figure 10 shows the result of recommending four high-scored documents, along with annotations of mapped concept. The recommendation scores are calculated by considering the user profile and the classified documents. Measuring the performance of recommendation is a subjective task, mainly because the user decides whether the recommended pages are correct. Hence, instead of measuring the performance of recommendation, we have tested the performance of classification using ontology. Actually, the performance of recommendation intensively depends on the accuracy of the classification.

To evaluate the performance of our classification procedure using ontology, we test the system with the wired news about the baseball. The ontology about the baseball is already shown in Fig. 4. We collect documents in the *recreation*, *sports*, and *baseball* categories of the Yahoo search engine [12]. We select those documents that belong to this category in Yahoo and also to a concept in the ontology at the same time. We feed these documents to the classification module to examine whether they are classified into the same category as in Yahoo. We have tested the total of 421 document pages about *baseball*, 56 of which belong to the *history* category, 79 to *amateur*, 122 to *college*, 108 to *minor league*, and 56 to *major league*.

For the purpose of precision comparison, we test two different methods: the one is constructing the ontology solely by a human and the other is constructing it automatically by using the TF-IDF technique [1]. The procedure of automatic

class	Features used to construct the ontology	
	TF-IDF method	Manual method
college	athlet,coach,schedul,univers,field, colleg,ncaa,countri,student,camp	CIBA,ABIC,NAIA,NCAA,summer, leagu,basebal,colleg,confer,univers
amateur	basebal,ponsor,tournament,coach, school,plai,organ,top,champion,lub	school,colleg,AAABA,AABC,league, MSBL,MABL,associ,amateur,club
history	leagu,home,player,histori,game,hit, bat,run,pitcher,mark	basebal,histori,world,seri,award, record,hall,fame,star,mvp
minor	leagu,ticket,minor,fan,box,stadium, club,manag,start,affiliat	A,AA,AAA,rooki,leagu,minor,basebal, independ,affiliat,game
major	league,mlb,major,world,nation, seri,nl,al,top,roster	basebal,MLB,clubhous,roster,season, roundup,american,nation,league,major

Fig. 11. Features used to construct the ontology.

construction of the ontology is as follows. As we already have the ontology frame, we calculate term weights by using TF-IDF for the documents in each category of Yahoo so as to generate the features used in leaf nodes of the ontology. We select 10 low ranked terms as the features and assign these features to each leaf node. Then, we go up one level to a parent node and filter out 10 low ranked features from the child nodes. Figure 11 compares the list of features obtained by the two methods.

Figure 12 shows the precision measures about whether the documents are classified into the *baseball* class, which is the topmost class in the hierarchy. In this experiment, we compare the manual ontology construction method with the automatic one. The average precision for the manually-built ontology is 82.7% and that of automatically-built ontology is 84.2%. From this result, we can notice that the constructing method using TF-IDF shows a little bit better performance than the manual method. It is mainly caused by the TF-IDF characteristics that prefer terms occurred in several documents uniformly.

6   Conclusion

In this paper, we propose a method of building personalized agents that help a user with the navigation on the Web by using ontology. The navigation agents represent the semantic relationship between Web documents by a concept structure, and classify them using the ontology that consists of the concepts. The navigation agents based on the ontology identify user's information need more efficiently and correctly. The agents are able to provide personalized information based on the user profile when the user is browsing the Web.

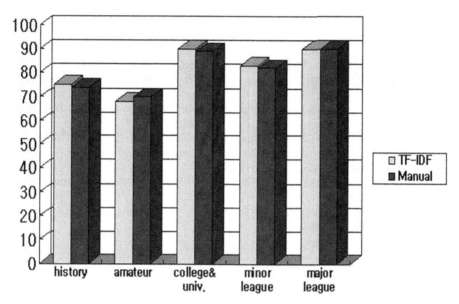

Fig. 12. Percentage of being classified into the *baseball* class.

The tests for classification and recommendation are not done with very large amount of data, but if we use the ontology constructed by combining manual and automatic methods, we could get more accurate classification results.

We have described the navigation agents with domain-specific ontologies. But there are some challenges, which we have to resolve. First, the manual construction of the ontology is time consuming, and we are developing an interface for extracting semantic concepts or relationships to facilitate the automatic or semi-automatic construction. Second, in this paper, we assign a document only to a single class, but a document can be assigned to several classes. We study algorithms on multi-class assignment. Third, we may need to construct a collaborative system for supporting information sharing. Finally, since the look-ahead search takes a fair amount time, a new method that reduces the time to fetch documents in the next hyperlink level should be studied.

References

1. R. Baeza-Yates and B. Ribeiro. *Modern Information Retrieval*, Addision Wesley, 1998.
2. J. Chaffee and S. Gauch. Personal Ontologies for Web Navigation. In *Proc. 9th Intl. Conf. on Information and Knowledge Management (CIKM'00)*, pp.227-234, 2000.
3. L. Chen and K. Sycara. Webmate: A Personal Agent for Browsing and Searching. In *Proc. of 2nd Intl. Conf. on Autonomous Agents,* pp. 132-139, 1998.
4. T. Gruber. Toward Principles for the Design of Ontologies Used for Knowledge Sharing. *International Journal on Human and Computer Studies*, 43(5/6): 907-929, 1995.

5. T. Joachims, D. Freitag, and T. Mitchell. Webwatcher: A Tour Guide for The World Wide Web. In *IJCAI'97,* pp.770-777, 1997.
6. W. Koh and L. Mui. An Information Theoretic Approach to Ontology-based Interest Matching. In *IJCAI'01 Workshop on Ontology Learning,*, 2001.
7. H. Lieberman. Letizia: An Agent that Assists Web Browsing. In *IJCAI'95,* pp.475-480, 1995.
8. B. Mobasher, R. Cooley, and J. Srivastave. Automatic Personalization Based on Web Usage Mining. *Communications of ACM*, 43(8): 144-151, 2000.
9. B. Mobasher, H. Dai, T. Luo, Y. Sung, and J. Zhu. Integrating Web Usage and Content Mining for More Effective Personalization. In *Proc. of First Intl. Conf. on E-Commerce and Web Technologies (ECWeb2000)*, pp.165-176, 2000.
10. M. Pazzani, J. Muramatsu, and D. Billsus. Syskill&Webert: Identifying Interesting Web Sites. In *Proc. of 13th Natl. Conf. on Artificial Intelligence*, pp.54-61, 1996.
11. M. Spiliopoulou. Web Usage Mining for Web Site Evaluation. *Communications of ACM*, 43(8): 127-134, 2000.
12. Yahoo!. http://www.yahoo.com

Agent-Based System for Confirming User Appointment Through SMS Callback URL Push

Jung-Jin Yang

School of Computer Science and Information Engineering
The Catholic University of Korea, Yeouido Post Office, P.O.Box 960,
35-1 Yeouido-dong, Yeongdeungpo-gu, Seoul, Korea (150-010)
Tel: +82-2-2164-4377, Fax: +82-2-2164-4777
jungjin@catholic.ac.kr

Abstract. With the drastic increase of mobile phone usage, infrastructures have been established to better network and connect the users. Consequently, the services through mobile devices, called M-services, are thriving with plausible applications. This work presents building an agent-based system for confirming user appointment through Callback URL, which is using SMS on the mobile phone in order to reduce the rate of failing appointment and the loss from such failures. To avoid the degradation of the system caused by the excessive accesses per try, methods in processing large-scale transactions and preventing obstacles, along with the comparison of the two methods are introduced.

1 Introduction

Nowadays, the mobile phone is a commodity and it is the most common way of directly communicating with others. With the availability of the infrastructure for networking mobile phones, people can obtain additional services apart from the basic voice communication. Mobile services (M-Services) range from Internet to VOD services through IMT2000 and CDMA EVDO. Additionally, the integration of multimedia with contents such as games and leisure instigates users to demand such services on mobile devices even more. This paper presents the building agent-based system used to confirm user appointment through SMS (Short Message Service) Callback URL Push along with examples of actual applications. WAP (Wireless Application Protocol) Push is presented as a way of implementing SMS Callback URL, and the use of SMS-based WAP Push 1.0 is applied for the compatibility and interoperability superior to that of WAP Push 1.2 that does not provide the service necessary. The domestic population of mobile phone users exceeds 30,000,000 people and it is still on the rise. This brings our attention to the servers dealing with large-scale traffic. This paper also focuses on the prevention of failovers, which is getting over failure, and the solution to traffic problems.

Overall, the agent-based system for confirming user appointment is expected to reduce the rate of dishonored appointments. Moreover, the database for the appointments can be used in analyzing the characteristics of a member or a guest who has an appointment. Hence the analyzed data can be utilized in accordance with eCRM(electronic Customer Relationship Management) to help business marketing and other additional services. This paper consists of protocol description in implementing Callback URL Push, architecture of an agent-based system for confirming

M.W. Barley and N. Kasabov (Eds.): PRIMA 2004, LNAI 3371, pp. 317–328, 2005.

user appointments, core network technology and constructing a scheme according to its scope, and components of traffic processing. The empirical result and the plans for future development are presented in Section 5 and 6 respectively.

2 Related Work

The base protocols and services for implementing "Callback URL" is described in this section along with the traffic processing with respect to 2-tier and 3-tier architectures.

2.1 2-Tier and 3-Tier Architecture

In implementing "Callback URL," two network models may be employed. The first is the 2-tier architecture which embodies both the Presentation Logic and Business Logic simultaneously, and the latter is the 3-tier which separates and presents the two in different positions.

2-Tier [1] architecture embodies the Presentation Logic on the client system through the typical client/server model's immense server model. Because it materializes the Business Logic on the server, it carries problems such as errors in data handling, difficulty in maintaining and conserving the application, dependency on the database, and a substantial lack of supportive languages.

3-Tier [1] architecture employs a middleware to disperse transaction loads and to increase the efficiency in managing the transactions. The clients use the middleware to request services from mid-level server modules. These server modules connect and handle database by stably allocating the requests, thus providing trustworthy services. Middleware software agent, like the former singular system computing, can easily embody disperse computing, and is usually placed between the management structure and the applied programs to help as a bridge between the client and the server.

2.2 Infrastructure

1) Protocols

WAP Push [2] is employed in implementing the two-way SMS. WAP Push service sends SMS messages through the WAP Gateway, and this can log on to the Internet via WAP Protocol. Push service provides services even without specific requests from customers, and this helps the user obtain diverse pertinent information, and in the case of WAP Push, WAP Push 1.0 [3] and WAP Push 1.2 [3] versions are being researched upon its foundation. Currently WAP Push 1.0 service is performing as the SMS basis service and WAP Push 1.2 is interacting with it. If WAP Push 1.0 is not linked with SMS, it cannot function as an interactive device. Hence WAP Push 1.2 makes up for this shortcoming by providing an interactive service disregarding its connection to SMS. Figure 1 shows the structure of WAP Push 1.2. WAP Push 1.2 consists of the Push Initiator which is connected to the Internet, Push proxy gateway, and the mobile phone known as the WAP client. Protocols consist of the Push Access Protocol for Internet access, and the POTAP (Push Over-The-Air Protocol) for wireless Internet connection.

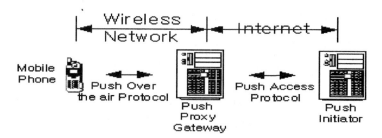

Fig. 1. WAP Push 1.2 Structure

SMS Data formation consists of the following:

- Destination Address : Receiver's number
- Teleservice ID : Service number
- User Data : Data
- Callback Number : Number used to receive the call

Methods in implementing SMS Callback URL Push are different for every mobile phone producer in the Republic of Korea [9][11]. KTF, using 016 and 018 as the first three digits of the cell phone number, and LG Telecom using 019 have opened their telecommunication nets to put the SMS Callback URL into effect, but SK Telecom establishes its own SK Network and use its private net for the SMS Callback URL. In other words, KTF and LG are able to use the Public Network through the Internet, whereas SK Telecom must install a private VPN. SK's reclusive policy leads to budget increase in implementing the mobile solution. The Internet's VPN is an alternative, but since this depends on SK's policy, the possibility of its embodiment is the only issue under consideration.

2) Method of Traffic Processing

If the users that simultaneously log on to the system are few in number, handling the traffic is not a big issue since the web server can sufficiently manage the users. However, if the number exceeds 1000, we observe that some problems occur. In the case of the Apache web server, the system slows down or crashes if more than 1000 people log on at once; IIS (Internet Information Server) is even worse [4]. Moreover, if the environment is based on 2-tier, the traffic load freezes its own system due to the failure of its Business Logic. To allocate the load, network load balancing should be employed or L4 Switch should be installed. This, however, only pertains to the allocation of the Web server connection and not to the Business Logic. For Business Logic, constituting 3-tier architecture is probably the best solution. Business Logic management is possible if a Web Application Server (WAS) agent [5] is set up at the channel that connects to the Web server, and TP Monitoring agent at each telecommunication connecting channels to facilitate the allocation. TP Monitoring agent functions to handle the transactions in a Client/Server environment, here in the C/S environment of the telecommunication companies.

3   System Architecture

This section describes the architecture of the agent-based system for confirming user appointment. Along with the overall architecture, problems and solutions to Multi-

Routing and the analysis of its extent and expense, 3-tier architecture for processing large-scale traffic is discussed.

3.1 SMS Callback URL Push

SMS Callback URL Push is a WAP push service based on the basis of SMS. WAP Push 1.2, which has previously been mentioned, is not in use and there are no cellular phones or services that support this system. Therefore, the WAP Push 1.0 interaction can be implemented through the WAP Push based on SMS by sending the URL address when connecting on the SMS message. The general concept is similar to the SMS Callback Number Push, but in the case of SMS Callback URL Push, the URL address pertains to the Internet URL not the return number. This can be explained by analyzing the services provided by SMS. SMS can be employed by practically applying it to specific purposes, such as sending and receiving short messages, offering broadcasting services and conversation services. Broadcasting services send messages to people within the range of a particular base station, and conversation services send and receive messages between the user's cellular phone and Web server [6]. These practical applications provide methods in implementing the SMS Callback URL [8]. Within the parameter of the SMS, Teleservice parameters can be used, and instead of the Callback Number a Callback URL can be designated. For example, a Teleservice ID can be assigned at the SMS Header and a Callback URL after that.

The flow of sending and receiving messages in implementing the application of WAP Alert [3] is following. The Content Provider (CP) Server agent embodies the application of WAP Alert, and the SMS Server sends the message from the CP Server agent to the cellular phone. The cellular phone, upon receiving the message, connects to the CP Server agent. SMS interaction is activated through such a process, and Teleservice ID is defined by the practical services to specific purposes so that the SMS message inside the User Data may designate a Callback URL to allow the user to connect to the site appointed by the Callback URL.

3.2 Overall Architecture

Figure 2 shows the reservation confirmation agent system's complete system configuration. The user connects to the CP Database System via personal computers, phones, or cellular phones, and makes a reservation. According to the reservation data, the CP Server agent operates the SMS Callback URL Push through the SMSS (Short Message Service Server) before the reserved date, and the user, upon receiving a message, presses [Send] or [OK] button to connect to the pertaining URL.

After logging on, the user may choose options such as [Visit], [Postpone], [Cancel]. After the user chooses one of the options, the CP Server agent saves the information in the CP reservation Database System and accepts reservations again to fill in the vacancies of those cancelled. This shows the workflow of the existing system configuration, and the focus of this work is on the communication process through a two-way transmission. Therefore, in implementing this service, traffic will occur twice as much as the one-way traffic SMS service and controlling the overflow of traffic is crucial.

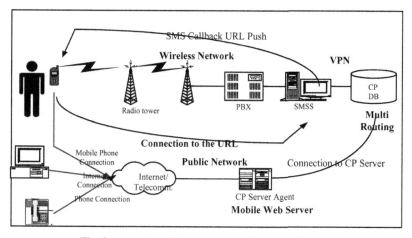

Fig. 2. Agent-based Reservation Confirmation System

3.3 SMSS (Short Message Service Server)

SMSS is a server that is connected to other businesses in order to provide SMS services. SMSS is in charge of transmitting short messages accompanied by SMS Callback URL data. The user, upon receiving the message, logs on to the URL by pressing [OK] or [Send] button on his/her cellular phone. SMSS is an important element in transmitting the Callback URL via short messages. Because SMSS is in the C/S environment of telecommunication companies and is liable to traffic problems, the conversion to 3-tier system is essential.

3.4 Mobile Web Server Agent (CP Server Agent)

Mobile Web Server agent is a CP server agent, so users ultimately perform their tasks through the CP server agent. In the case of the reservation confirmation agent system discussed in this paper, users can access the reservation contents and modify their reservation data. Not only reservations, but services such as Mobile Poll and stock exchange are also available; such applications may be developed with the arrival of new contents. Also, the language used for wireless Internet is based on XML, thus the possibility of integrating XML data with other compound systems is high. The goal of this work is to suggest ways that allow users to choose among [Visit], [Postpone], [Cancel] to automatically update the reservation database from the data saved in the Mobile Web Server, mainly used for reservation confirmation. In the case of [Postpone] and [Cancel], the reservation database's reservation data is deleted to receive new reservations. CP server agent is operated by Business Logic, but the web server cannot accommodate so many simultaneous users and the problems of Business Logic remain. A switch-over to 3-tier architecture is necessary.

3.5 Traffic Processing and Measuring Against Obstacles

Figure 3 is different from the previous CP reservation system in Figure 2 since it established a separate Presentation Logic and a Web Application Server (WAS) agent toward the back to allocate and manage traffic. Business Logic is embodied in place of WAS agent. For a two-way configuration, Fail Over, Session Clustering, and Network Load Balancing are also shown. TP Monitoring agent is situated near the connecting channels to the telecommunication C/S environment. For continual connection, TP Monitoring agent's UCS (Universal Character Set) aids in facilitating the connection with the telecommunication companies. Through this system configuration, WAS agent manages the traffic from the Web, and between the Web server and WAS, Stream Pipe is used instead of TCP/IP therefore doubling the efficacy of internal telecommunication performance. However, to employ the Stream Pipe, the Web server and WAS agent must be placed on the same node. In the case of the TP Monitoring agent, continual connection is possible only through UCS, thus emphasizing the importance of applying the TP Monitoring agent supports the UCS.

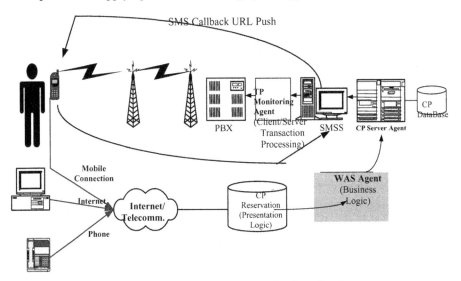

Fig. 3. WAS Agent-based Reservation Confirmation System

3.6 Application of WAS Agent and TP Monitoring Agent

WAS agent manages the connections coming through from the Web server. Because the Stream Pipe method is quicker than that of TCP/IP in telecommunicating between the Web server and WAS agent, it is obviously better to place the Stream Pipe [5] to facilitate the transmission. However, the Web server and WAS agent must be placed on the same node, and at the same time a double configuration is needed to prevent failures.

When the same service is running on multiple servers, data based load can be distributed depending on a custom or specified range of data. System based load balancing: this type of load balancing gives the control of assigning greater load to a more robust server in case users are working with a heterogeneous server environment. If one server has more RAM, CPUs, etc. than other servers, then users can force that server to undertake a greater load. Depending on traffic to a node, if traffic increases, TP-Monitor agent dynamically distributes traffic to other nodes.

There are two ways in configuring session clusters that settle problems occurring between the Web server and WAS agent. In the case of Figure 4 (a), if one part is defective, all requests are channeled to the other side which is still in tact. This seriously deteriorates the performances of the session engines. This method shows the classical example of session clustering, and the session data management is comparatively slow [1]. The remainder in Figure 4 (b) keeps a session management agent so that the session data is equally allocated to each engine. This system distributes the system resources evenly thus preventing an overflow in a single engine.

Two methods are available for overload dispersion and hindrances. One is assigning the task to the adjacent node as soon as the problem occurs. If this freezes the adjacent node, another adjacent node is designated to carry out the task. This can cause a domino effect and crash the whole system. A solution to solve this chain reaction and final crash must be devised – a method in which the concentrated load that is automatically relocated to the adjacent node should be equally allocated to all other nodes. The demerit of the chain reaction can be compensated with a better solution. Seemingly, the necessity of a manager agent emerges to evenly distribute the loads as in Figure 5. An action to automatically restart the system after its crash also needs to be taken.

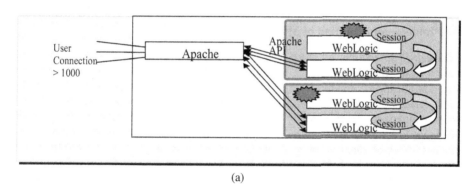

(a)

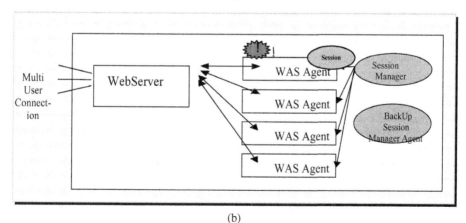

(b)

Fig. 4. Application of WAS Agent

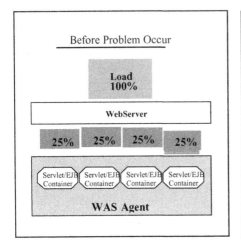
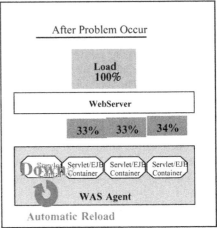

Fig. 5. Load-Balancing based on TP-Monitoring Agent

4   Implementation

4.1   Problems and Solution of Multi-routing in Implementation

As explained in section 2.2, SMSS and the CP Server agent are the key factors in executing the SMS Callback URL Push service, which connect through private nets of telecommunication companies or the VPN. The system configuration for such service can be divided into two different methods, of which one is as follows. SMSS and CP server agent are connected directly by Fast Ethernet Adapter by a Cross Cable. SMSS only needs to set a Gateway address for the telecommunication companies' equipment and the CP Server agent needs to set a Gateway address for the Internet Service Provider. This prevents problems that occur in setting a Multi Route address which cause links between the SMSS and telecommunication companies to become disconnected. This method, however, brings about difficulties in management since a supervisor must manage the CP Server and SMSS by connecting from the CP Server to the SMSS server through the Thin Client [1][12] or control two completely separate servers. The problem can be resolved by integrating the SMSS and CP Server.

4.2   Implementation Scheme

The expense and extent of the implementation must be considered. If many equipment and private line fees for the SMS Callback Push service are considered, by collecting information about the total number of SMS transmissions, first, a self-developed server may be established or secondly a separate business branch that receives the service [7] from the Application Service Provider (ASP) may be created so that it may manage the tasks of other corporations or organizations simultaneously. In establishing a self-developed server, expenses concerning internal supervision and system construction are likely to increase, but it would be adequate to utilize it when sending a large number of SMS transmissions. The latter can provide services to various organizations and can become a profit-making system since it is established as an independent corporation. Corporations using the ASP for SMS transmission are able to economize on their budgets since the system establishment is cheaper and is favorable for small quantity SMS transmissions.

The configuration of the Web server and WAS agent pictured in section 3.4 for the existing two-way SMS system traffic and hindrances is designed that each node has an identical Web server and WAS agent so that in the case of a Fail Over, system clustering or session clustering occurs along with the reallocation of transactions due to its 3-tier formation. Moreover, since the Web server and WAS agent are operated on the same node, the Stream Pipe telecommunication is employed to double the efficiency compared to TCP/IP. The TP monitoring agent manages the transactions for the telecommunication companies composed of the C/S environment. Telebanking and Mobile Banking are additional services that can be provided through SMS transmission.

4.3 Activation Method

When sending the previous reservation data to the user by SMS in Figure 6, in reading the data from the CP Server the transaction of the CP Server database is executed from the telecommunication companies' TP Monitoring agent. When receiving an SMS for the reservation made for his or her medical treatment, the user connects to the pertaining URL by pressing [OK] or [Send] button of the cellular phone. The user may choose among [Visit], [Postpone], and [Cancel] that appear on the URL screen. After selecting, the result is managed by the Business Logic situated within the WAS agent to renew the database and receive new reservations or preserve the reservations made before. If the user chooses [Postpone], it can be set up so that an automatic call is made to the pertaining organization. In this case, the Call Setup must be established for each telecommunication company and transaction management is carried out by the TP monitoring agent.

Fig. 6. SMS on Client Side in Korean

5   Empirical Result and Analysis

In this section, the expected results for the reservation confirmation agent system are reviewed, and the methods for minimizing the losses incurred by the reservations along with its profits are explained based on the cases of actual application.

5.1 Effect of Confirming Appointment Agent System

The following is the expected effects of the SMS Push service only.

- Decrease of unfulfilled reservations
- Decrease of No-Show rate (Increase of customer feedback)
- Decrease in Call center calls (Save on employee salaries and telecommunication expenses)
- Increase in customer appreciation
- Decrease in overall expenses

This paper examined the unfulfilled reservation and the losses it incurred from the initiation of the system to the present. The following charts 1), 2), and 3) show Hospital A's improvement concerning the unfulfilled reservations before December 2001 and after January 2002 until the present.(As a part of the project mentioned in this paper, Hospital A in Kyong-gi Province of our nation has established the reservation confirmation agent system in December 2002 which has taken effect beginning January 2003.)

Separator		Rate of Failure	No Show	Call Center
Effect	Before	15%	5%	
	After	5%	3%	50%

1) Reservations made in Hospital A (Period: January 2001 to December 2003)

# of Patient Reserved per Day	2000 persons/Day
AVG. # of Patient Reserved per Month	40000 persons/Month

2) Unfulfilled reservations for Hospital A

AVG. Rate of Failure before the System introduced (AVG. of last 3 yrs)	30% (432000 persons)
AVG. Rate of Failure after the System (2003-01 to 2003-08)	16% (51200 persons)

3) Unfulfilled reservations after employing the reservation confirmation system

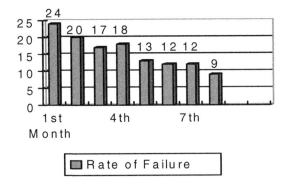

There is another example employing eCRM via reservation confirmation agent system database, where characteristics of a customer are evaluated to provide information that may be applied on marketing information. Frequent users and those who keep their reservation promises may receive special services or benefit from reduced rates, which may strengthen customer service support systems that can, in turn, elevate the status of the organization. Also, by researching customer participation, targeting customers that are trustworthy can give rise to new services and businesses. For example, in the case of the reservation confirmation agent system employed at the airport, those clients who have a low rate of unfulfilled reservations may receive more mileages or a special reduction. The continuous interaction between the corporations and customers could become the basis for customer maintenance. In short, because Repeat Customers can be secured by this method, greater profit can be expected from the additional services that will be provided to such customers in the future.

The test was carried out by dividing the transaction time for the WAS agent and the transaction time for the TP Monitoring agent. Table 1 shows the task execution speed for the existing system's Web server tests.

Table 1. Task Execution Speed in Web server

Action Taken	Checked Item	Synchronous Threads (2Min. Duration)		
		100	200	500
Select	Total Hits	691	708	
	Hit's per Second	5.75	5.89	
	Error Occurrences (Socket Error)	0	0	
	Average Response Time (Unit: Second)	29.695	28.955	
Insert	Total Hits	738	7.34	
	Hit's per Second	6.14	6.16	
	Error Occurrences (Socket Error)	0	0	
	Average Response Time (Unit: Second)	14.011	27.575	
Update	Total Hits	700	688	
	Hit's per Second	5.83	5.73	
	Error Occurrences (Socket Error)	0	0	
	Average Response Time (Unit: Second)	14.840	29.629	

Table 2 presents the results for the WAS agent environment.

Table 2. Task Execution Speed in WAS Agent

Action Taken	Checked Item	SYN. Threads (2Min. Duration)		
		100	200	500
Select	Total Hits	2678	3575	1561
	Hit's per Second	22.28	29.75	12.99
	Error Occurrences (Socket Error)	0	0	0
	Average Response Time (Unit: Second)	3.854	5.596	22.399
Insert	Total Hits	2045	2228	669
	Hit's per Second	17.16	18.54	5.57
	Error Occurrences (Socket Error)	0	0	0
	Average Response Time (Unit: Second)	4.912	8.686	32.970
Update	Total Hits	2181	2277	783
	Hit's per Second	18.15	18.95	6.57
	Error Occurrences (Socket Error)	0	0	0
	Average Response Time (Unit: Second)	4.735	8.565	34.603

As shown in the result, the result for Select is 10 times greater and the results for Insert and Update are 3 times faster. There are no entries for in the Table 1 under column "500" because the Web server is unable to handle more than 500 users simultaneously and has crashed. However, as shown in the Table 2, WAS agent is able to manage more than 500.

The following shows the results for the performance of SMSS connected to telecommunication companies. The results after applying existing TCP/IP socket telecommunication and TP Monitoring agent are shown in Table 3. As is evident in the result, the performance has improved by ten times, and transaction management is far superior than that of the existing socket telecommunication.

Table 3. The Performances of SMSS with TCP/IP Socket and TP Monitoring Agent

Occurrences Separator		10Times		20Times		40Times	
Socket	Node	First	Second	First	Second	First	Second
	1	13.67	15.54	35.07	33.80	61.47	61.83
TP Agent	Node	First	Second	First	Second	First	Second
	1	1.20	2.00	2.43	2.96	4.44	4.52

6 Future Work and Conclusion

The work in this paper discusses the ways to improve service portability through SMS-based WAP Push. The application of an agent-based system for reservation confirmation is presented using Callback URL Push to improve the profit of the businesses where reservations are made frequently. It opens up the possibility of other services through SMS Callback URL Push such as e-Health information. Derivative industries of building and applying intelligent agent systems have a promising future with the extended infrastructure of wireless network. We must look into the agent-based location prediction systems and hope to expand the scope of location-based contextual services for our future profit and convenience.

References

1. Robert orfail, dan harkey, Client/Server Survival Guide(wiley), 2002
2. SMS Callback Push Development Documentataion by MorningTech, 2002
3. http://www.wapforum.org
4. C.U. Kang, "Introduction to Mobile Telecommunication" , YangSeo-Gak, 1999
5. Tmax Soft Incorporation, JEUS White Paper, 2001
6. DigitMate Incorporation, "WAP Push Wireless Internet", 2001
7. Message Wise Medical Documentation by MorningTech, 2000
8. SMS Callback URL Push Service Development Specification (Ver 1.5). : SK Telecom Platform Research Group, 2002
9. Y.H. Kim, Window2K/.NET , HongReung Publisher, 2000
10. http://www.mosca.co.kr/mosca.htm
11. Y.H. Kim and J.J. Yang, " The Study of Preventing Reservation Loss through SMS Callback URL Push", Proceedings of KIISS 2002, Seoul, Korea, pp 457—465, 2002
12. http://www.middleware.com/

Author Index

Lecture Notes in Artificial Intelligence (LNAI)

Vol. 3214: M.G.. Negoita, R.J. Howlett, L.C. Jain (Eds.), Knowledge-Based Intelligent Information and Engineering Systems, Part II. LVIII, 1302 pages. 2004.

Vol. 3213: M.G.. Negoita, R.J. Howlett, L.C. Jain (Eds.), Knowledge-Based Intelligent Information and Engineering Systems, Part I. LVIII, 1280 pages. 2004.

Vol. 3209: B. Berendt, A. Hotho, D. Mladenic, M. van Someren, M. Spiliopoulou, G. Stumme (Eds.), Web Mining: From Web to Semantic Web. IX, 201 pages. 2004.

Vol. 3206: P. Sojka, I. Kopecek, K. Pala (Eds.), Text, Speech and Dialogue. XIII, 667 pages. 2004.

Vol. 3202: J.-F. Boulicaut, F. Esposito, F. Giannotti, D. Pedreschi (Eds.), Knowledge Discovery in Databases: PKDD 2004. XIX, 560 pages. 2004.

Vol. 3201: J.-F. Boulicaut, F. Esposito, F. Giannotti, D. Pedreschi (Eds.), Machine Learning: ECML 2004. XVIII, 580 pages. 2004.

Vol. 3194: R. Camacho, R. King, A. Srinivasan (Eds.), Inductive Logic Programming. XI, 361 pages. 2004.

Vol. 3192: C. Bussler, D. Fensel (Eds.), Artificial Intelligence: Methodology, Systems, and Applications. XIII, 522 pages. 2004.

Vol. 3191: M. Klusch, S. Ossowski, V. Kashyap, R. Unland (Eds.), Cooperative Information Agents VIII. XI, 303 pages. 2004.

Vol. 3187: G. Lindemann, J. Denzinger, I.J. Timm, R. Unland (Eds.), Multiagent System Technologies. XIII, 341 pages. 2004.

Vol. 3176: O. Bousquet, U. von Luxburg, G. Rätsch (Eds.), Advanced Lectures on Machine Learning. IX, 241 pages. 2004.

Vol. 3171: A.L.C. Bazzan, S. Labidi (Eds.), Advances in Artificial Intelligence – SBIA 2004. XVII, 548 pages. 2004.

Vol. 3159: U. Visser, Intelligent Information Integration for the Semantic Web. XIV, 150 pages. 2004.

Vol. 3157: C. Zhang, H. W. Guesgen, W.K. Yeap (Eds.), PRICAI 2004: Trends in Artificial Intelligence. XX, 1023 pages. 2004.

Vol. 3155: P. Funk, P.A. González Calero (Eds.), Advances in Case-Based Reasoning. XIII, 822 pages. 2004.

Vol. 3139: F. Iida, R. Pfeifer, L. Steels, Y. Kuniyoshi (Eds.), Embodied Artificial Intelligence. IX, 331 pages. 2004.

Vol. 3131: V. Torra, Y. Narukawa (Eds.), Modeling Decisions for Artificial Intelligence. XI, 327 pages. 2004.

Vol. 3127: K.E. Wolff, H.D. Pfeiffer, H.S. Delugach (Eds.), Conceptual Structures at Work. XI, 403 pages. 2004.

Vol. 3123: A. Belz, R. Evans, P. Piwek (Eds.), Natural Language Generation. X, 219 pages. 2004.

Vol. 3120: J. Shawe-Taylor, Y. Singer (Eds.), Learning Theory. X, 648 pages. 2004.

Vol. 3097: D. Basin, M. Rusinowitch (Eds.), Automated Reasoning. XII, 493 pages. 2004.

Vol. 3071: A. Omicini, P. Petta, J. Pitt (Eds.), Engineering Societies in the Agents World. XIII, 409 pages. 2004.

Vol. 3070: L. Rutkowski, J. Siekmann, R. Tadeusiewicz, L.A. Zadeh (Eds.), Artificial Intelligence and Soft Computing - ICAISC 2004. XXV, 1208 pages. 2004.

Vol. 3068: E. André, L. Dybkjær, W. Minker, P. Heisterkamp (Eds.), Affective Dialogue Systems. XII, 324 pages. 2004.

Vol. 3067: M. Dastani, J. Dix, A. El Fallah-Seghrouchni (Eds.), Programming Multi-Agent Systems. X, 221 pages. 2004.

Vol. 3066: S. Tsumoto, R. Słowiński, J. Komorowski, J.W. Grzymała-Busse (Eds.), Rough Sets and Current Trends in Computing. XX, 853 pages. 2004.

Vol. 3065: A. Lomuscio, D. Nute (Eds.), Deontic Logic in Computer Science. X, 275 pages. 2004.

Vol. 3060: A.Y. Tawfik, S.D. Goodwin (Eds.), Advances in Artificial Intelligence. XIII, 582 pages. 2004.

Vol. 3056: H. Dai, R. Srikant, C. Zhang (Eds.), Advances in Knowledge Discovery and Data Mining. XIX, 713 pages. 2004.

Vol. 3055: H. Christiansen, M.-S. Hacid, T. Andreasen, H.L. Larsen (Eds.), Flexible Query Answering Systems. X, 500 pages. 2004.

Vol. 3048: P. Faratin, D.C. Parkes, J.A. Rodríguez-Aguilar, W.E. Walsh (Eds.), Agent-Mediated Electronic Commerce V. XI, 155 pages. 2004.

Vol. 3040: R. Conejo, M. Urretavizcaya, J.-L. Pérez-de-la-Cruz (Eds.), Current Topics in Artificial Intelligence. XIV, 689 pages. 2004.

Vol. 3035: M.A. Wimmer (Ed.), Knowledge Management in Electronic Government. XII, 326 pages. 2004.

Vol. 3034: J. Favela, E. Menasalvas, E. Chávez (Eds.), Advances in Web Intelligence. XIII, 227 pages. 2004.

Vol. 3030: P. Giorgini, B. Henderson-Sellers, M. Winikoff (Eds.), Agent-Oriented Information Systems. XIV, 207 pages. 2004.

Vol. 3029: B. Orchard, C. Yang, M. Ali (Eds.), Innovations in Applied Artificial Intelligence. XXI, 1272 pages. 2004.

Vol. 3025: G.A. Vouros, T. Panayiotopoulos (Eds.), Methods and Applications of Artificial Intelligence. XV, 546 pages. 2004.

Vol. 3020: D. Polani, B. Browning, A. Bonarini, K. Yoshida (Eds.), RoboCup 2003: Robot Soccer World Cup VII. XVI, 767 pages. 2004.

Vol. 3012: K. Kurumatani, S.-H. Chen, A. Ohuchi (Eds.), Multi-Agents for Mass User Support. X, 217 pages. 2004.

Vol. 3010: K.R. Apt, F. Fages, F. Rossi, P. Szeredi, J. Váncza (Eds.), Recent Advances in Constraints. VIII, 285 pages. 2004.

Vol. 2990: J. Leite, A. Omicini, L. Sterling, P. Torroni (Eds.), Declarative Agent Languages and Technologies. XII, 281 pages. 2004.

Vol. 2980: A. Blackwell, K. Marriott, A. Shimojima (Eds.), Diagrammatic Representation and Inference. XV, 448 pages. 2004.

Vol. 2977: G. Di Marzo Serugendo, A. Karageorgos, O.F. Rana, F. Zambonelli (Eds.), Engineering Self-Organising Systems. X, 299 pages. 2004.

Vol. 2972: R. Monroy, G. Arroyo-Figueroa, L.E. Sucar, H. Sossa (Eds.), MICAI 2004: Advances in Artificial Intelligence. XVII, 923 pages. 2004.